Advance Praise for *The Technological Revolution in Financial Services*

"The financial crisis of 2008–2009 reshaped global banking regulations. How will changes in technology and consumers' demand affect the finance industry in the post COVID-19 world? This book identifies the most important trends and challenges, and provides invaluable insights for managers, policymakers, and consumer advocates."

Thomas Philippon, Max L. Heine Professor of Finance,
Stern School of Business, New York University

"King and Nesbitt have edited a comprehensive book on how the financial services industry is being disrupted by fintech. This book details new strategies and business models arising from fintech. It does an excellent job laying out the broad forces transforming the financial services industry."

Raghavendra Rau, Sir Evelyn de Rothschild Professor of Finance,
Co-founder and Academic Director, Cambridge Centre for Alternative
Finance, Cambridge Judge Business School, University of Cambridge

"This book reaffirms my assertion that banking is being fundamentally changed by technology, but will survive with some new players and some old players coming together in a new model of providing and distributing value."

Chris Skinner, CEO of The Finanser, Chair of The Financial Services Club,
and Author of *Doing Digital, Digital Bank, ValueWeb,* and *Digital Human*

"King and Nesbitt have put together an excellent collection of articles in this book that sheds valuable light on the dynamics of the future evolution of the financial services industry with the expanding role of fintech and the possible competitive challenges banks and other traditional players will face from information technology firms like Google. This book is an essential read for banking scholars, regulators, and financial service executives seeking insights into future strategies to cope with these seismic changes."

Anjan Thakor, John E. Simon Professor of Finance, and Director
of the WFA Center for Finance and Accounting Research,
Olin School of Business, Washington University in St. Louis

"King and Nesbitt have brought forth a great perspective on the digital transformation happening at every level of the financial services sector. This is a reference book to put into every hand across the industry."

Peggy Van De Plassche, Managing Partner, Roar Growth

"A very timely compendium of informed and insightful analyses and forecasts of the effects of technology on the structure, dynamics and organizational architecture of the financial services industry. I highly recommend this to both technologists eyeing opportunities for change and long-time incumbents of this – overly established – industry."

Mihnea Moldoveanu, Vice Dean, Learning, Innovation and Executive
Programs, Desautels Professor of Integrative Thinking, and Professor of
Economic Analysis, Rotman School of Management, University of Toronto

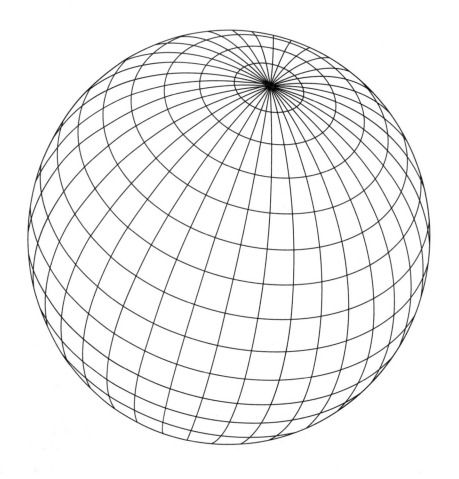

Instructor resources for this book are available on a tab on the book's webpage via the University of Toronto Press website: utorontopress.com

The Technological Revolution in Financial Services

How Banks, Fintechs, and Customers Win Together

Edited by Michael R. King and Richard W. Nesbitt

Foreword by Paul Desmarais III

UNIVERSITY OF TORONTO PRESS
Toronto Buffalo London

ISBN 978-1-4875-0602-5 (cloth)
ISBN 978-1-4875-3313-7 (PDF)
ISBN 978-1-4875-3314-4 (EPUB)

Library and Archives Canada Cataloguing in Publication

Title: The technological revolution in financial services : how banks, fintechs, and customers win together / edited by Michael R. King and Richard W. Nesbitt.
Names: King, Michael R. (Michael Robert), 1967– editor. | Nesbitt, Richard, 1955– editor.
Description: Includes bibliographical references.
Identifiers: Canadiana (print) 20200252631 | Canadiana (ebook) 20200252879 | ISBN 9781487506025 (cloth) | ISBN 9781487533144 (EPUB) | ISBN 9781487533137 (PDF)
Subjects: LCSH: Financial services industry – Technological innovations. | LCSH: Financial Institutions – Technological innovations. | LCSH: Finance – Technological innovations.
Classification: LCC HG173 .T43 2020 | DDC 332.1 – dc23

University of Toronto Press acknowledges the financial assistance to its publishing program of the Canada Council for the Arts and the Ontario Arts Council, an agency of the Government of Ontario.

Canada Council Conseil des Arts
for the Arts   du Canada

ONTARIO ARTS COUNCIL
CONSEIL DES ARTS DE L'ONTARIO
an Ontario government agency
un organisme du gouvernement de l'Ontario

Funded by the   Financé par le
Government   gouvernement
of Canada   du Canada

Canadä

I dedicate this book to my wife, Yanna, and our sons, Robert and Peter, who have supported my academic journey.
– Michael R. King

This book is dedicated to my family: Lucy, who has been a constant supporter and partner; my wonderful daughters, Olivia and Lillian, who have now finished their university degrees and are on to their own great adventures. I would not be anything without them.
– Richard Nesbitt

Contents

Section I: The Structural Forces Transforming Financial Services

Figures and Tables

Figures

Tables

Foreword

As the CEO of Sagard Holdings and a co-founder of Portag3 Ventures and Diagram Ventures, I am excited by the changes taking place in financial services. We are moving from an industry built on geographic proximity, product offering, and efficiency to one that competes on customer service, product suitability, and adaptability.

Historically, the business and service models of many financial institutions revolved around the local branch or regional office. These outposts were spread across the country, serving geographic catchment areas. For customers, the competitive differentiators were branch accessibility and access to a wide range of financial products that met their personal and business needs. For financial institutions, the quest for economies of scale drove a strategy of building highly integrated businesses. The customer experience was poor, featuring complicated onboarding, long wait times, and highly inflexible systems.

Our world is changing rapidly. We are moving from a financial industry that competes on local presence and generic products to one focused on specialized products tailored to each customer's needs. Customers are no longer constrained by physical proximity. They are supporting businesses that differentiate themselves based on convenience, service, specialization, and product suitability. The

Internet, mobile phones, and data networks are enabling customer-segmented businesses that provide entire suites of financial or other services tailored to a specific sector, business, or individual.* This customization was not possible in the geographically constrained world of the past; there were simply not enough clients in a specific industry or targeted demographic within the branch catchment area to justify such an expensive, specialized service.

But end-to-end integration and scale are becoming a handicap more than a competitive advantage as these business models reduce adaptability. Every component of financial services can be outsourced from innovators whose modern technology stacks enable a superior customer service and more efficient operations at a lower cost.

The drive towards specialization and the reorganization of the financial-services industry – into either narrow service providers or vertically integrated incumbents – is opening the door to both specialized new entrants (fintechs, technology companies, etc.) and platform businesses that combine payroll, payments, e-commerce, and other services. These digital utilities – think Amazon, Shopify, Ceridian, Stripe – hold significant customer data and are positioned to provide customers with a simple, highly segmented and focused solution (for example, merchant loans). These new entrants will be powered by specialized business-to-business service providers offering Banking-as-a-Service, Know Your Customer (KYC)-as-a-Service, and other innovations.

To compete, it has never been more important for incumbent financial institutions to gain a deep understanding of their customers' needs and to provide the services in a truly differentiated way.

---

* Companies will think of themselves as more than just financial-services providers. For example, American Express thinks of itself as a travel, dining, and lounging company. Wealthsimple thinks of itself as a lifestyle company.

Financial institutions built to serve everyone will end up serving no one. Incumbents who believe they need to keep all products, services, and processes in-house will not be competitive in any of them.

I believe the most successful financial-services companies of the future will be highly focused on a specific customer segment. They will keep a few proprietary services and functions in-house while partnering with outside providers to compete in what will become a highly segmented and competitive marketplace.

Paul Desmarais III

Acknowledgments

This book began life in early 2017 as a discussion between the co-editors, Michael King and Richard Nesbitt. We were debating how the financial-services industry was changing post-crisis, particularly as a result of the arrival of fintech. We organized a one-day conference in Toronto on 23 June 2017, titled *The Future of Banking and Financial Services*, jointly sponsored by the Scotiabank Digital Banking at Ivey Business School and the Global Risk Institute in Financial Services (GRI). The positive feedback from that event convinced us that we needed to share the insights from our expert speakers with a broader audience, which led to this edited volume. We gratefully acknowledge the financial support for this project from Scotiabank, the Tangerine Chair in Finance at Western University's Ivey Business School, and the Lansdowne Chair in Finance at University of Victoria's Gustavson School of Business.

We wish to thank each of the authors who contributed their considerable knowledge to the chapters of this book. These global experts from Canada, the United States, and the United Kingdom provide us with a rare insight into how the financial services industry will evolve in the decade ahead. While many commentators expect the disruption to pick up pace, few are willing to predict how these changes will impact customers and the financial institutions that serve them. The authors in this book boldly outline how the customer financial experience will be transformed in the future. We also acknowledge the many experts that we consulted in preparing these chapters who are not named as authors. They were invaluable in answering our questions and sharing their views on key developments in their industry. Finally, we thank Jennifer DiDomenico and the team at University of Toronto Press for their guidance and support.

The Technological Revolution in Financial Services

Introduction: The Technological Revolution in Financial Services

Michael R. King and Richard W. Nesbitt

Change is a constant theme in banking and financial services. The industry never stands still, with every decade witnessing innovations that lead to new products, services, and ways of doing business. The financial sector is characterized by waves of expansion and consolidation in response to both short-term shocks and longer-term structural forces.

While the financial industry is continuously evolving, the past decade has seen a breadth and depth of changes that are unprecedented in our lifetimes. These changes are being driven by a combination of structural forces that are transforming this industry: heightened regulation, technological disruption, and changing demographics. These forces are lowering barriers to entry and increasing competition from within and outside the industry.

A diversity of new entrants is challenging the incumbent banks, asset managers, insurance providers, and other industry stakeholders (collectively "incumbents"). The new entrants range from entrepreneurial financial-technology (fintech) start-ups to large, nonfinancial technology-based companies (techfins and bigtech). This increased competition is forcing banks, asset managers, and other incumbents to improve their product offerings and customer service. While some new entrants may be looking to disrupt and replace incumbents, others seek to partner with or sell to them.

Overall, the technological revolution in banking and financial services is a good news story for customers. Individuals and small businesses are benefiting from new innovations that improve the user experience while reducing its cost. They soon will have access to a full suite of financial products and services how and when they like. Underbanked customer segments are also better served, with technology promoting greater financial access, inclusion, and understanding.

Learning Objectives and Key Questions

The goal of this edited volume is to provide insights into the evolution and future landscape of banking and financial services over the coming decades. This book exposes financial practitioners, policymakers, and students pursuing careers in financial services to the views and insights of industry leaders, regulators, and academic researchers. The contributions to this volume address the following questions:

1. What are the primary structural forces transforming banking and financial services?
2. How are these forces changing the competitive landscape and the value proposition for customers?
3. How should incumbents adapt their strategies and business models to respond to these challenges?
4. What actions do senior leaders and executives at financial institutions need to take to be successful in this new environment?

Our working hypothesis is that traditional banks, asset managers, and insurers will continue to dominate financial services. But the most successful incumbents will partner with fintech start-ups to provide a better experience to customers at a lower cost. Fintechs are leveraging technology to provide innovative solutions to address customer pain points and improve the user experience. But only a handful of fintechs will succeed in building scale, with many pivoting to sell their products to incumbents.

Rather than being disrupted by fintechs, banks will be more threatened by large technology companies whose platform ecosystems encompass financial activities including payments, deposits, lending, and investing. The Chinese techfins Alibaba and Tencent are pioneers whose strategies are being copied by bigtech companies like Amazon, Apple, Facebook, and Google. These players will prove to be the real competitors to incumbents on the financial landscape over the next decade.

We highlight how bank business models need to adapt to these challenges and threats in order to be successful. Our goal is to provide the reader with a critical appreciation of the trade-offs facing the financial-services industry and to highlight the strategies bank executives need to adopt to succeed in this changing environment. Successful incumbents will be those who shift from a product-centric perspective to a customer-centric orientation. They need to partner with fintech start-ups in many specialty areas and exploit new technologies and data to provide customers with a better experience at a lower cost. What may be an even larger task – incumbents need to transform their cultures, incentive structures, and governance to be able to meet these challenges.

The book outlines the strategic implications for the financial industry in North America, Europe, and other advanced economies. The dynamic between fintech companies and incumbents in advanced economies with developed financial systems and markets is very different from the path in emerging market economies where these institutions are less developed. While the expert contributors in this volume provide global insights on technological developments affecting financial services, the examples and prescriptions are largely based on advanced rather than developing economies.

The Structural Forces Driving Transformation

The expert contributors provide a roadmap on how this industry will evolve in light of three structural forces that are driving the transformation of financial services globally – changes that will have a profound impact on our economies and societies.

1. Heightened Regulation Post-GFC

The heightened regulation that followed the shock of the 2008–2009 global financial crisis (GFC) continues to affect the direction and profitability of the financial-services industry. The GFC was unlike previous banking and currency crises that have punctuated the financial sector over the past forty years. It was not limited to one set of bad actors, like the 1998 Long-Term Capital Management crisis, but brought down the strong with the weak. It was not confined to one set of financial institutions, like the 1990s U.S. savings and loan (S&L) crisis, but affected all financial actors from banks to insurance companies, from money-market funds to government-sponsored entities. The GFC was not confined to one country or region, like the 1994 Mexican peso crisis or the 1997 Asian financial crisis, but damaged financial systems around the world. Worse still, it was not contained within the financial economy, but spread to the real economy, causing a coordinated global recession, dubbed the Great Recession. The GFC continues to impact the industry a decade later, as can be seen in the continuing struggles of European banks and sovereigns.

The public backlash post-GFC was loud and intense. Angry citizens elected populist politicians who set about re-regulating financial services, ring-fencing banking activities, erecting national borders, and segmenting financial markets. The G20 countries, working through the Financial Stability Board (FSB), introduced comprehensive and far-reaching regulations designed to stabilize the global financial architecture. International efforts overlapped and, in some cases, conflicted with national regulations such as the U.S. Dodd-Frank Act (2010) and the U.K. Banking Reform Act (2013). The result may be a financial sector that is safer and more stable, but it is also less profitable, with lower returns on capital; less liquid; and more fragmented, with greater competition from shadow banking and other non-regulated players.

The GFC had an unexpected benefit – it unleashed a wave of innovation and technological disruption from within and outside the industry. A first source of disruption was industry insiders who left incumbents to launch entrepreneurial start-ups. These former bankers understood where the industry profit pools were located and set about draining them. A second source of disruption was outsiders who drew inspiration from innovations in consumer-product, social-media, design, and e-commerce companies. These entrepreneurs saw an opportunity to disrupt financial services while the incumbents were weak and unhappy customers were willing to try new financial providers. A third source of disruption was incumbent banks that had been bailed out or nationalized during the GFC. These near-death experiences spurred a change of culture and creativity, allowing some banks to reinvent and reposition themselves as digital challengers and leaders in innovation.

2. Innovation Fueled by New Technologies

The opportunity to disrupt incumbents coincided with a wave of technological innovation that provided the tools for disruption. New entrants and incumbents leveraged both existing and emerging technologies such as the Internet, smartphones, peer-to-peer (P2P) networks, application programming interfaces (APIs), and distributed ledgers, among many others. These tools were combined to provide customers with financial products and services through digital channels – a business model known as fintech.

The term "fintech" was used in different contexts during the late 1980s and 1990s.[1] In 1994, the *American Banker* published its inaugural list of the "Top 100 companies in FinTech," featuring the data-processing company Fiserv, the computer manufacturer NCR, and the news agency Reuters in the top three positions. Over the last decade the media have used "fintech" to describe the thousands of entrepreneurial start-ups that are offering financial products directly to retail customers and small businesses online or through mobile applications (apps). Fintech start-ups operate in different lines of business, including personal finance, crowdfunding, P2P lending, robo-advisors, payments, and insuretech, among others. The media also use fintech to describe the electronic money Bitcoin, and the world of cryptocurrencies and distributed ledgers known as blockchain. Box I.1 (at the end of this chapter) provides a description of blockchain and distributed ledger technologies (DLTs,) with examples of use-cases in financial services.

Between 2014 and the first half of 2019, KPMG estimates that fintech start-ups have attracted close to $400 billion of equity funding from angel investors, venture capitalists (VCs), corporate VCs, institutional investors, and strategic partners.[2] By year-end 2019, CB Insights counted sixty-six fintech unicorns with private valuations of $1 billion or more.[3]

While advocates say fintech is new, practitioners counter that technology investments have been a hallmark of the financial services industry for a century or more. In fact, a study for the Chartered Financial Analyst (CFA) Institute describes the current wave as "Fintech 3.0," the third era of technological innovation that followed two earlier periods:[4]

- Fintech 1.0 began in 1866 with the laying of the transatlantic cable and ended in 1966 with the development of the facsimile (fax) machine. This era was characterized by analog technology that transmitted continuous electrical pulses of varying amplitude.
- Fintech 2.0 began in 1967 with the appearance of the automatic teller machine (ATM) and ended in 2008 with the GFC. This era featured the transmission of discreet binary values, allowing data to be shared rapidly over an ever-growing network of computers.
- Fintech 3.0 began in 2009 and is characterized by the use of technology to deliver financial products and services directly to retail customers and businesses. This era is driven by start-ups and new entrants, with distinct variants in developed versus developing countries.

Despite the media's focus on the customer-facing fintechs, many start-ups are building innovative business-to-business (B2B) technologies to increase the efficiency of the back office of incumbents. These applications work behind the scenes to enable front-office customer interactions, to speed the clearing and settlement of securities, or to facilitate payments and other basic banking functions. If the world of fintech is an iceberg, business-to-customer (B2C) applications are the part visible above the water, while B2B applications below the surface are many times greater in number, size, and diversity.

Incumbents have responded by investing to upgrade their legacy information-technology (IT) systems, both to reduce costs through automation and to meet the burdensome reporting and compliance requirements of new regulations. Banks reportedly employ between two and three back-office staff for every front-office employee. One consultancy estimated that automating costly back-office processes could reduce banks' costs by up to $20 billion each year by 2022.[5] With a decade of new regulation and litigation now coming to an end, investment and talent at incumbents can be redirected to new technologies, products, and services. Incumbents that succeed in this technological transformation will retain customer relationships and improve profitability and returns over the coming decade.

3. Demographic Changes Fueling the Transformation

This technological disruption of financial services is linked to demographic trends, specifically the arrival of millennials and the retirement of baby boomers. While fintech adoption has varied across age cohorts, now we all expect a better experience at a lower cost for financial services.

Many fintechs first gained a foothold by appealing to millennials, who are the cohort born between 1981 and 1996 (and in 2019 ranged from twenty-two to thirty-eight years old). Millennials are called digital natives, because they are comfortable with technology and suspicious of or hostile toward traditional financial intermediaries. Older millennials have grown up with social media and the heightened expectations concerning user experience created by technology companies like Apple. Younger millennials have never known a time without smartphones and the Internet. Millennials have been the earliest adopters of fintech applications and put greater trust in consumer brands (like Facebook and Google) than in banks. They value the ability to view their finances online 24/7, putting convenience ahead of security.

The baby boomers, born in the two decades after World War II, are very different. Baby boomers are close to retiring or retired. They put their trust in incumbents and value face-to-face contact when dealing with their finances. Baby boomers may never be fully comfortable with a completely automated banking experience. They are more focused on security and privacy concerns. No surprise here, as they are also the generation with significant financial assets that they seek to preserve, enhance, and ultimately pass on to the next generation. They are slower to adopt fintech products and more likely to visit bank branches and seek personal contact from advisors. Baby boomers are also more cost-sensitive, given the impact of the GFC and Great Recession on their retirement savings. The aging population and declining workforce are also forcing greater use of automation and technology to deliver financial services.

Structure of the Book

This book is divided into three main sections. The first section examines the structural forces and technologies transforming financial services and how these catalysts are changing customer expectations and the competitive landscape. The second section examines the business models and value propositions of new entrants and how incumbents are adapting their strategies and business models to respond to these challenges. The third section focuses on what actions senior financial leaders need to take to be successful in this new digital era.

SECTION I: The Structural Forces Transforming Financial Services

This first section consists of six chapters that set the stage and explain the context for the technological transformation of financial services.

Chapter 1: Financial Technologies and the
Disruption of Financial Services

R. Jesse McWaters was the financial-innovation lead at the World Economic Forum, where he has co-authored five reports with working groups of practitioners on the future of financial services. In "Financial Technologies and the Disruption of Financial Services," McWaters examines the supply-and-demand factors behind the rise of fintech, including the role of regulators who desired to foster competition and lower costs for consumers post-crisis. The strategies of these innovators are deliberate and predictable, targeting the pain points of customers where the profit pools were largest in payments, lending, and wealth management. But he warns that fintechs face an uphill battle to win customers' trust and build scale.

Incumbent financial institutions have spent considerable time and resources reinforcing their defenses against these new entrants. By innovating internally and increasing their efficiency, incumbents can replicate the innovations of fintechs, as seen in the example of asset managers like Vanguard with robo-advisors. In addition to building out new internal capabilities, many incumbent financial institutions have sought to invest in or acquire emerging fintechs, or have partnered with them. Many incumbents, however, are struggling to be fast followers because of a lack of organizational agility and the burden of complying with existing and new regulations.

Looking to the future, McWaters highlights the rise of the Chinese techfins Ant Financial and Tencent, which have built vast financial empires on the back of highly successful digital-payments products. While fintechs in the advanced economies appear to be alleviating the same frustrations for consumers, unlike the techfins, these fintechs have fragmented the customer experience across many applications and platforms. To be successful, incumbents need to move away from a product-centric focus to a customer-centric focus built around digital platforms. He warns that a failure to adapt will leave incumbents as the manufacturers of financial products on platforms owned and operated by bigtech companies like Amazon or consortiums of fintechs.

Chapter 2: The Economic Forces Driving Fintech Adoption across Countries

Jon Frost is a senior economist in the Innovation and the Digital Economy unit of the Bank for International Settlements, where he researches fintech and digital innovation. In "The Economic Forces Driving Fintech Adoption across Countries," Frost highlights the curious geography of fintech adoption across advanced, emerging-market, and developing economies. The pattern of adoption is puzzling, showing little regard for the state of economic development or political boundaries. Frost provides data on the size and breadth of fintech activity globally, showing that it remains tiny by comparison to the global financial system but that it is growing fast and becoming economically relevant in some specific markets.

Frost argues that the pattern of fintech adoption is explained by four factors: unmet customer demand, competition, regulation, and trust. First, fintech innovations are increasing financial inclusion where households do not have a bank account or access to basic financial services. Fintech is also fulfilling unmet demand for credit and payment services (including remittances) to individuals and small businesses globally. Second, fintech is having more success in countries where there is less domestic competition and financial services are relatively more expensive. Academic researchers are documenting this connection using cross-country studies comparing the cost of credit, payments, and other services.

Third, regulators in some jurisdictions are taking steps to increase local competition by easing entry for fintechs. And fintechs may be strategically entering jurisdictions where existing regulations are less strict, or incumbents are facing increased compliance costs. Fourth,

Frost links fintech adoption to two dimensions of trust: the loss of trust in financial incumbents in countries where the financial crisis hit hardest, and the trust placed in new technologies by younger age cohorts. Frost concludes that fintech activities may address specific market failures but remain subject to the same well-known risks present elsewhere in finance. Supervisors and market participants alike need to monitor and adapt to changing players and networks that may increase financial efficiency and economic growth but also pose threats to financial stability.

Chapter 3: Banking and Finance since the Global Financial Crisis

Tiff Macklem is the current dean of the Rotman School of Management at the University of Toronto, and a board member for a large Canadian bank. In "Banking and Finance since the Global Financial Crisis," Macklem gives an insider's account of how policymakers responded following the collapse of Lehman Brothers, and outlines the intended and unintended consequences of the subsequent regulatory reforms. At the systemic level, the G20 leaders wanted to make banks safer and end the moral hazard problem of "too big to fail" banks, while ensuring that core financial markets continued to function effectively, and market-based financing by shadow banks became a source of resilience rather than a vulnerability. Macklem concludes that these reforms have made the financial system safer but have contributed to the fragmentation of the global banking system and a decline in financial-market liquidity.

Macklem argues that the GFC and its aftermath have forced bankers and business schools to broaden the scope of finance, to put a renewed focus on culture and ethics, and to consider "non-financial" risks from employee conduct, technological disruption, and climate change. At the bank level, Macklem views weak cultural foundations and significant ethical failures at global banks as leading causes of the GFC. Compensation schemes that delivered large bonuses for short-term returns encouraged excessive risk taking and led some individuals to commit stunning conduct failures. Bank CEOs, boards of directors, and regulators have come to recognize the importance of culture for creating social norms that influence what people do when nobody is looking. Business schools have a role to play in teaching future business leaders about ethical issues and moral failures. Academic research shows that reminding people of the social and moral considerations of decision making is effective in overcoming the situational effect caused by roles dominated by money and numerical calculations. Universities need to provide more simulation-based experiential learning, while moving the curriculum beyond traditional financial topics to risk management broadly conceived.

Looking forward, Macklem highlights two mega-forces affecting the economy, finance, and society: technological disruption and climate change. While new technologies, from artificial intelligence (AI) to blockchain, are creating new opportunities, Macklem argues for more focus on commercializing innovations and equipping startups with the business judgment to succeed. He points to the success of Rotman's Creative Destruction Lab (CDL) for helping science-based ventures at the seed stage to resolve failures in the market for business judgment, raise capital, and scale their businesses. On climate change, Macklem highlights the need for sustainable finance to move beyond its niche in financial markets to the mainstream. Already, more extreme weather events linked to climate change are generating more frequent extreme-loss events and – even under the best scenarios – this situation is expected to worsen. The financial sector, he argues, has a critical role to play in channeling savings to more sustainable investments and helping households and businesses manage new climate-related risks.

Chapter 4: Data and Privacy in the Next Decade

Brian O'Donnell spent more than two decades in risk management and treasury at a large Canadian bank, including serving as its chief data officer. Today he is co-founder of a data advocacy company that helps individuals and businesses to protect and monetize their data. In "Data and Privacy in the Next Decade," O'Donnell observes that industry experts and global think tanks are focusing on individual privacy rights and methods to protect personal data. Around the globe, regulators are introducing legislation to strengthen consumer privacy rights.

Data are often being sold and resold, and then being analyzed and exploited in ways individuals never contemplated when they accepted the "Terms and Conditions" of mobile applications (apps) and software. O'Donnell describes a lopsided business model, where the benefits and power are held by the app provider and the risk is left with the individual. Significant efforts and progress are needed to help individuals deal with this model and the evolving cyber risk it creates.

Open-banking legislation allows customers to share their financial data held by banks with fintech firms over application programming interfaces (APIs). The goal is to promote innovation and greater competition in the banking industry. But open banking raises concerns, chiefly related to data safety and security. Today banks invest significant resources, time, and focus to ensure that their security levels are among the highest of any industry, and that customers' personal information and transaction data are secure. Will fintech start-ups be able to provide this same level of data security? Will they actively protect client data? Or will they try and monetize the data like so many other technology companies and app developers?

O'Donnell describes a new model of "Personal Data Advocacy" as a logical extension of current trends in technological advancement and regulatory policy. He argues that it is time for the banks to help their clients gather, store, secure, and thereby truly own their personal data, so that the benefits and value flow back to the customer, not to third parties.

Chapter 5: How "Open" Is the Future of Banking?
Dr Markos Zachariadis is a professor in Information Systems and Digital Innovation at the University of Manchester and has given expert testimony to government committees on open banking and application programming interfaces (APIs). In "How 'Open' Is the Future of Banking? Data Sharing and Open Data Frameworks in Financial Services," Zachariadis examines the trend towards legislating open banking across different jurisdictions and its impact on financial services. At its core, the financial-services industry is predominantly an information business. Access to and sharing of data can provide significant advantages to players in the industry and change the shape of competition in financial services.

Data sharing in finance has a long history, with screen scraping and APIs being used in recent years by financial institutions and fintechs to share data and develop new products. An API is a technology or a set of instructions that allows two systems or computers to "talk" to each other over a network using a common data standard. APIs can be internal or external to an organization and built on open standards or closed. Open-banking legislation has generally included a requirement for banks to provide open APIs based on common standards, data formats, and security arrangements to allow customers to share their financial transaction data with third parties. But different countries are pursuing their own individual paths to open banking.

While open access to data provides numerous benefits to the financial ecosystem and end-customers, Zachariadis notes that hoarding data for exclusive use can offer significant competitive advantages to a single organization or a narrow group of organizations, leading to a monopolistic environment. Hoarding data is also an effective barrier to competition that is common in banking markets globally. For this reason, open banking will significantly increase the competitive dynamics in the finance industry. It may lead to changes in incumbent business models, as well as in the financial system's infrastructure.

Zachariadis argues that the legislation for and voluntary adoption of open APIs in finance are laying the foundation for the emergence of multi-sided platforms and the fintech ecosystems around them. The successful incumbents or challenger banks will seek to control these platform ecosystems and intermediate interactions between fintechs and the end customer. This business model would allow banks to sell more innovative services to their customers, keeping customers engaged on their own platforms and allowing the banks to reap the benefits from data monetization. To achieve this position, forward-looking banks should voluntarily invest in and create premium APIs that exceed mandated interfaces and provide increased functionality to third parties, growing their open-banking ecosystem.

Chapter 6: The Impact of Banking Regulation on Technological Innovation

Greg Wilson has been a consultant and author on financial-services policy and regulation for forty years, with a recent focus on U.S. policy and regulatory reforms after the global financial crisis. In "The Impact of Banking Regulation on Technological Innovation," Wilson provides an overview of the U.S. regulatory landscape in the decade following the passage of the Dodd-Frank Act and plots a path forward for banks and fintechs alike. He provides a roadmap to the overlapping agendas of the U.S. agencies responsible for banking regulation and concludes that they lack a coherent and comprehensive strategy on technology and innovation.

While most crisis-related reforms are now in place, banks and regulators are struggling with implementation and oversight at a time when new nonbank competitors are seeking to offer financial services to the public. While innovation and technology are nothing new to incumbents, they remain an important source of competitive advantage on the one hand, and a source of disruption on the other. Wilson illustrates this point by examining the entry of PayPal, Walmart, and Amazon into financial services. He also reviews the U.S. Treasury's 2018 report on these fintechs and nonbank financials. He defines what bank regulators call "responsible innovation," which has three dimensions: competition, consumers, and compliance.

According to Wilson, the two regulatory issues to watch to anticipate how U.S. regulators will proceed on innovation and technology are real-time payments settlements and anti-money laundering (AML). New technologies have undermined the Federal Reserve Board's control of the outdated U.S. payments system and are pushing the board to make improvements to allow real-time settlement. Technology and innovation are also undermining the effectiveness of the AML regime in the United States. The agencies responsible may turn to the innovators themselves to address these emerging gaps, while continuing to require compliance and reporting. Going forward, banks and fintechs need to engage with and educate regulators in how to meet customers' needs responsibly.

SECTION II: New Strategies, Technologies, and Business Models
The second section examines the strategies, technologies, and business models that incumbents need to understand and respond to in order to be successful in the coming decade.

Chapter 7: The Competitive Threat from Techfins and Bigtech in Financial Services

Professor Michael R. King has been leading outreach to start-ups, incumbents, and policymakers since co-founding a university fintech research center in 2016. In "The Competitive Threat from Techfins and Bigtech in Financial Services," King examines the threat from technology companies that are moving into financial services. He illustrates this trend through a case study of Ant Financial, the Chinese techfin that grew out of the payments business of Alibaba's e-commerce platform. Ant Financial now offers deposits, loans, investments, bank accounts, and insurance to more than 640 million users. Chinese rival Tencent offers the same financial services bundled through its WeChat app to 1.1 billion users.

The North American equivalents to the techfins are known as "bigtech," highlighting that their main competitive strength comes from massive datasets on customer transactions and behavior in their platform ecosystems. King argues that Amazon, Apple, Facebook, and Google all pose a threat to incumbents, as they possess massive customer bases, well-recognized brands, a focus on customer experience and design, and expertise in the technologies driving fintech. He illustrates the bigtech strategy using a case study of Amazon in financial services, showing how Amazon's experimentation in payments that began more than a decade ago has built a foundation for offering loans, methods of payment, and other financial services today. He points to Facebook's proposed launch of a digital currency to facilitate low-cost money transfers and payments globally as a signal of its future plan to take a leading position in retail financial services.

Chapter 8: Creating Strategic Value by Partnering with or Acquiring Fintechs

Jay D. Wilson is a senior member of Mercer Capital's Depository Institutions practice and leads their fintech industry team. He is also the author of the 2017 book *Creating Strategic Value through Financial Technology*, published by Wiley Finance. In "Creating Strategic Value by Partnering with or Acquiring Fintechs," Wilson assesses the different options for banks and other incumbents who are looking to engage with fintech start-ups. In particular, he contrasts the dominant position of the largest banks against the weaker position of many small community banks spread around the country that collectively represent the largest number of U.S. banks. Community banks are under threat from heightened competition, higher regulatory and compliance costs, a challenging interest-rate environment, and demographic changes in rural America.

Larger U.S. banks have the budgets and the expertise to develop digital solutions in-house. Smaller banks are in a more difficult position, caught between well-funded competitors on the one hand and low-cost innovators on the other. Wilson argues that the solution is to form partnerships with fintech companies in order to leverage innovation and new technologies to offer customers enhanced services while remaining competitive with the larger banks. Fintech can boost revenues from fees and commissions while reducing expenses related to branch operating costs.

Wilson outlines a framework for fintech partnerships consisting of four steps: determine how fintech might complement or enhance the bank's existing strategic plan; identify attractive fintech niches and companies within those niches; develop a business case for each of the available options; and compare the costs and execute on the best strategy. Wilson provides three case studies of successful and failed bank-fintech partnerships. He then outlines a strategy for identifying, valuing, and acquiring a fintech start-up.

Chapter 9: A Fintech Founder's Perspective on the Future of Financial Services

Andrew Graham is the co-founder and CEO of Borrowell, an online lender and Canada's largest fintech when measured by number of users. In "A Fintech Founder's Perspective on the Future of Financial Services," Graham describes how he got the idea for his start-up by identifying a pain point facing a specific customer segment, namely credit-card holders with strong credit histories who rolled over balances but could borrow for less. Borrowell partnered at an early stage with two Canadian banks – Equitable Bank, which purchased loans originated on the platform, and Canadian Imperial Bank of Commerce (CIBC), which licensed the software for offering loans online. Graham notes that a key selling point for CIBC was the user experience, as Borrowell's software made it very easy for borrowers to get through the process of applying for a loan.

Graham describes how Borrowell solved the number one problem facing a fintech business – acquiring customers. Borrowell was having a difficult time connecting with customers who would qualify for their loans and had to turn down many who applied because of poor credit history. The founders realized that most borrowers did not know their credit scores, which led them to their "give and get" business model. Borrowell began giving customers their credit score for free, a viral promotion that attracted thousands of customers but did not lead to enough loans to justify the expense. Borrowell then evolved their business model to partner with more than forty financial institutions to build a marketplace offering credit cards, auto loans, mortgages, savings accounts, checking accounts, and insurance. This model is now growing and has attracted $90 million Canadian in equity funding from angels, venture capitalists, and strategic partners.

Graham concludes by describing the management problems of scaling a business, illustrating how growth may be harder for a start-up than finding product market fit. He also discusses the difficulties of partnering with much larger institutions. Graham dismisses the view that most fintechs pose a threat to incumbents and makes the case instead for banks of all sizes to partner with fintechs. He concludes by discussing the importance of the fintech ecosystem and government support to encourage start-ups and promote innovation.

Chapter 10: How the Global Asset-Management Industry Will Change

In "How the Global Asset-Management Industry Will Change," Richard Nesbitt and Satwik Sharma summarize the views of this industry based on in-depth interviews and collaboration with global leaders in the asset-management business. Successful incumbents are being confronted with many strategic challenges, only one of which is managing technological change. These senior leaders agreed that technological innovation is having a profound effect on the asset-management business in many ways – some of which are more subtle or less visible than in other sectors. The chapter identifies what are viewed to be the key drivers of the asset-management industry in the next decade. The economy and its ultimate direction will continue to have a dominant effect on the industry. Demographic change, global changes in wealth patterns, and regulation will all have a material effect on the industry. The chapter re-examines the rise of exchange-traded funds (ETFs) and passive investing strategies, which are now matched with APIs and algorithms to provide digital wealth management via robo-advisors. The authors explain how technology-enabled advisors can provide a higher level of customer service at a lower cost. Investments in technology will have a material impact on the competitive position of asset managers, making the choice of where to invest critical to the success of the business.

Chapter 11: Next-Generation Financial Advice: Reimagining Wealth Management in the Age of Technology

In "Next-Generation Financial Advice: Reimagining Wealth Management in the Age of Technology," Chuck Grace and Andrew Sarta summarize their research and interviews with key players about the future of the wealth-management industry. While robo-advisors have grabbed most of the media attention, the authors broaden the discussion to examine what they call "Next-Generation Financial Advice." They view the future as a hybrid model of a human financial advisor partnered with technologies such as data analytics and machine learning. This combination increases the value of financial advice and enhances the client experience.

They outline seven broad opportunities or themes that guide next-generation financial advice. Integrating digital technology into wealth management can lead to cheaper, more efficient, and more accessible service for clients. Human advisors remain uniquely skilled at subjective and behavioral tasks, while machines are better at evaluating large quantities of data. Technology will free the advisor from having to perform a growing number of routine tasks, like rebalancing a portfolio or optimizing the asset mix. The technologies to provide superior digital advice are already available and include generic technologies such as cloud computing, social media, machine learning, and online portals with more specialized tools such as digital customer onboarding, psychographic profiling, account aggregation, and lean digital manufacturing tools.

The authors argue that successful organizations will collaborate around the client experience. Incumbents are burdened with siloed, product-centric IT systems with little connectivity, making it impossible to get a holistic picture of the client's financial situation. In contrast, new wealth-management platforms developed by fintech entrants (including robo-advisors) are typically more flexible and modular, leveraging application programming interfaces (APIs) and open architectures. This situation points to mutually beneficial opportunities for incumbents and fintechs to collaborate. Control of customer data is a pivotal issue that is being addressed by open-banking regulations, which will accelerate innovation. The authors identify the main external and internal barriers to change for organizations of different sizes. A common problem is a lack of understanding of how to manage intelligence-based innovation, as the existing strategy literature focuses on manufacturing-based innovations.

Chapter 12: Treasury and Technology

Peter Levitt is executive vice-president and treasurer at CIBC, and Tom McGuire is executive vice-president and group treasurer at Scotiabank. In "Treasury and Technology," Levitt and McGuire explain the role of treasurer at a global bank and how technology is changing the Treasury function. The Treasury department essentially provides the circulatory system of the bank or can be viewed as its engine room. Treasury manages balance-sheet resources (capital, funding, and liquid assets) and balance-sheet risks (liquidity, interest-rate, and foreign-exchange risks) to enable the bank to achieve its overall strategy. Treasury's responsibilities entail a host of low-end and high-end technological capabilities.

Over many years, each bank has developed proprietary and customized IT systems to deliver on the mandate described above, including producing risk metrics and generating reports for management and regulators. These IT systems are used for current resource and risk-position reporting, scenario analysis, forecasting, and stress-testing exercises. Three key factors influence the use of technology in a Treasury function:

- Massive data accumulation creates the need for unique technology investments for the Treasury function. Banks require powerful and stable computer systems to collect, store, process, and secure tremendous volumes of data.
- A bank is subject to significant regulatory requirements. Treasury must manage a multitude of laws and regulations,

including solvency/capital requirements and liquidity requirements (LCR and NSFR). These regulations are complex and involve significant use of technology and modeling capabilities for things such as determining risk-weighted assets (RWAs) for capital adequacy, and economic value of equity (EVE) or earnings at risk (EAR) for structural interest-rate risk management.

- Certain complex Treasury functions related to balance-sheet risk management require technology to support modeling and management. In particular, valuations and hedging are complex activities. Bank balance sheets are made up of financial instruments that need to be valued in order to measure and manage risk. This valuation must reflect both changes in exogenous variables and hedge exposures.

Chapter 13: Technology and Reimagining the Future of Housing

Evan Siddall is CEO of Canada Mortgage and Housing Corporation (CMHC) and Vicki Martin is a senior specialist in CMHC's Housing Finance Policy group. In "Technology and Reimagining the Future of Housing," Siddall and Martin examine the importance of technological change in the largest single product area within most lenders from the perspective of the national provider of mortgage insurance. CMHC is exploring new approaches to underwriting and mortgage-insurance adjudication, using technology, analytics, and artificial intelligence. Lenders are under increased pressure in many lines of business from start-ups and new non-financial entrants. However, the lessons from other industries – hotels, taxis, recorded music – show that "asset light" business models can attack incumbents – and quickly. Notably, the opportunity to make use of data using technology may shift the competitive balance even further.

The authors propose five factors that are influencing the technological future of mortgage lending:

1. Automated Mortgage Processing: Mortgage originators were early adopters of fintech in Canada.
2. Distributed Ledgers and Funding: CMHC is co-investing with Accenture in a blockchain proof of concept involving mortgage funding.
3. Artificial Intelligence Underwriting: AI applications make quality lending decisions based on data and logic.
4. Peer-to-Peer Lending: Just as individuals increasingly own distributed energy systems and entertainment companies have been disintermediated by YouTube stars and social media influencers, financial institutions similarly face an increasingly decentralized future.
5. Changes in Property Tenure: Fintech will enable new models and radically reduce transaction costs to accelerate these changes. These will appeal to the millennial "sharing generation" while reaping the benefits of increased asset utilization.

The authors foresee a much different mortgage market within just a few years. Where value exists in digital fractionalization, the nearly costless use of technology will create new economic opportunities.

SECTION III: Succeeding in the Fintech Era
The final section outlines what actions senior leaders in the financial sector need to take to succeed in the fintech era.

Chapter 14: The Business Case for Gender Diversity in Financial Services
Brenda Trenowden has worked in the global financial services industry for close to thirty years. As the global chair of the 30% Club since

2016, she has also been leading a global organization that campaigns for better gender balance on company boards and in senior management of organizations. In "The Business Case for Gender Diversity in Financial Services," Trenowden outlines the business case for gender balance, which is a performance issue and not just a social issue. She summarizes a large body of research connecting increased gender diversity with improved financial performance measured using accounting metrics and market returns. In addition to financial benefits, she explains the benefits for talent attraction and retention, innovation and productivity, and customer engagement.

Trenowden outlines the successful strategy pursued by the 30% Club in the United Kingdom, a strategy that has been exported to fourteen countries and regions globally. When the 30% Club campaign was launched in 2010, the largest 100 publicly listed companies in the United Kingdom had only 12.5 percent female representation on boards, including twenty-one all-male boards. Knowing that "what gets measured gets done," the 30% Club set a realistic target of 30 percent female representation on company boards of directors by 2015. By recruiting board chairs at supportive companies to go out and lobby their peers and getting government support, the 30% Club created a competitive dynamic among laggards and attracted media attention that generated rapid results. By the end of the 30% Club's first campaign in 2015, female representation in the United Kingdom's 100 largest listed companies had increased from 12.5 percent to 26 percent (and there were no all-male boards). By 2019, this figure had reached 31 percent female representation overall with 63 of the 100 companies having at least 30 percent women on their boards. Since 2016 the 30% Club has focused on executive management recruiting and the talent pipeline, and engaging investors who can see the benefits to long-term shareholders returns.

Trenowden acknowledges that many companies do not know where to start when it comes to addressing gender diversity. She therefore outlines six concrete actions senior leaders can take: recognize and address hidden biases; diagnose the problem and set measurable targets; provide gender-neutral job descriptions; change hiring practices; match women with senior sponsors; and provide female role models.

Chapter 15: Bank Strategy and Innovation
Utilizing Technology

As CEO of the TMX Group, Richard Nesbitt orchestrated the merger of Canada's two largest exchanges and then secured a competitive advantage by adopting new, high-speed trading infrastructure. He left to become CEO of CIBC World Markets at the height of the GFC, then joined the Global Risk Institute for Financial Services as CEO in 2014. In "Bank Strategy and Innovation Utilizing Technology," Nesbitt summarizes the views from senior banking executives on how to develop a strategic framework for implementing technology. Strategy is about where the organization is today, where it wants to go in the future, and how it plans to get there. Nesbitt argues that technological innovation itself is not a strategy but a tool for achieving strategy. Both incumbents and fintech new entrants need to understand that the key drivers of success in financial services are risk management and managing the customer-competition nexus.

Banks are risk-taking entities that are highly leveraged, highly cyclical, and therefore highly regulated. Banking is basically a commodity business offering undifferentiated goods with many substitutes, leading to high competition with low margins. By applying leverage, banks generate high returns for shareholders, with risk taking limited by regulation. But the cyclicality of the industry means that loan losses materialize at the same time as growth slows, pointing to the important role of both risk management and regulation to ensure viability.

Technological innovation can help banks to succeed by establishing a competitive advantage over their peers. This competitive advantage comes from improved risk-management tools and improved cost efficiencies. Technology also makes possible new channels for distribution at lower cost, new products and services, expanded data collection, and a better understanding of customers' needs. Nesbitt stresses that the goal of technological innovation is to benefit the customer by providing a better experience. He highlights that when technology is mismanaged, it can also seriously damage a bank's franchise, as illustrated by TSB Bank's flawed upgrade of its IT systems.

Technological innovation is an important part of a successful bank's product offering for its customers. Nesbitt points to two primary threats for banks: (i) the disruptive potential of technology, which enables nonfinancial firms to compete for financial products; and (ii) the changing expectations and needs of customers, which can leave behind banks who fail to adapt. The outlook on these two issues is unclear. Conditions could arise where banks prosper in this technological age by incorporating emerging technologies and adapting to customer needs. Banks will succeed by building these twin objectives into their business strategy while continuing to manage leverage, cyclicality, and regulation in their business.

Conclusion: Putting the Customer First

In this final chapter, "Conclusion: Putting the Customer First," co-editors Michael King and Richard Nesbitt summarize the key takeaways from this edited volume. They outline six themes to guide both incumbents and new entrants in the coming decade.

The first message is that technology will change financial services, just not in the way or the time horizon stakeholders expect. The authors debunk two myths around disruption. First, while some fintechs will challenge the banks directly in the B2C space, most fintechs will seek to partner with incumbents in the B2B space. Second, technologies like blockchain and artificial intelligence have been overhyped, leading to disappointing results in the short run, but will ultimately transform financial services in the long run.

The second message concerns business strategy. Various contributions highlight the importance of promoting innovation and leveraging technology. It is worth stressing, however, that technology is not a strategy but a tool to achieve strategy. Technology and applications are widely available or can be imitated rapidly by fast followers. They do not provide a sustained competitive advantage. Done right, technology can support a business strategy that provides a unique and sustainable value proposition to customers. But done wrong, a failed roll-out of technology can lose customers' trust and damage a financial incumbent's franchise.

The third message is that trust in banking remains paramount. The loss of the public's trust in banks due to the GFC created an opening for new entrants. But trust has to be safeguarded and built over time. In financial services, trust is intertwined with data security and privacy. While open banking will create opportunities to develop new products and services for customers, it must be matched by protection of data, restrictions on its use, and investments in cybersecurity.

The fourth message is that regulation and risk management remain pillars of financial services. Regulations exist to protect consumers and businesses, forcing banks to address risks and behaviors that are costly or detrimental to their customers and shareholders. Regulations promote a level playing field and financial stability, lowering bank borrowing costs and making high leverage possible. Risk management is vital for protecting the franchise and delivering a competitive advantage in an industry characterized by cycles and disruptions.

The fifth message is that not all fintechs will survive, but a few will have an over-sized impact. As with the 1999 dot-com bubble, a day of reckoning is approaching for many fintechs. After a period of failures and consolidation, a few fintech champions will have a transformative impact on financial services. And the winners may include Chinese techfins like Ant Financial, or North American big-tech companies like Amazon and Facebook.

And, finally, the longest-lasting impact of the technological revolution in banking will not be the disruption of incumbents or the leveraging of new technologies. It will be the improved customer experience. The successful financial intermediaries of the next decade will be focused on the needs of the customer, recognizing that this industry exists to serve them.

Box I.1 Blockchain and Distributed Ledger Technology (DLT)

A blockchain is an electronic distributed ledger that records ownership of an asset with multiple identical copies held on different computers connected over a network. This ledger is protected using encryption, such that no one can modify it without getting permission from the majority of users. All relevant parties need to agree that the information contained in the ledger is true. The process of reaching consensus, or consensus mechanism, must be based upon a set of rules that are agreed to by all parties. The computer software and protocols for recording, sharing, and synchronizing distributed ledgers is referred to generically as distributed ledger technology (DLT).

When the term "blockchain" first appeared around 2009, it referred exclusively to the distributed ledger for the electronic currency Bitcoin. But "blockchain" has now become an umbrella term describing distributed ledgers with many different features. Blockchains may be public or private, permissionless or permissioned, and use different mechanisms to reach consensus. But all blockchains provide an electronic record of ownership that is shared, secure, tamper-proof, and therefore trusted.

Electronic ledgers, encryption, and peer-to-peer (P2P) networks have been around for decades. The financial-services industry has many examples of private, centralized ledgers that record commercially sensitive information. One example is a corporation's record of share ownership, which is used to determine voting rights on corporate actions and to distribute dividends. The identities of shareholders and their holdings are recorded on a ledger that is private and held by a trusted third party. Transactions are only disclosed to trading counterparties, with this information sent to a depositary institution that has authority to modify the ledger.

A blockchain can provide benefits in this setting and similar use-cases involving clearing, settlement, and record keeping. The clearing and settlement process is expensive and time-consuming when trading financial securities. Because financial counterparties do not trust each other, they need to agree on the terms of each trade, sign documentation, and complete delivery versus payment on an agreed settlement date. Some trades may be agreed verbally and processed manually, leading to human error and failures to settle.

Many similar financial transactions rely on multiple financial intermediaries who verify or audit data and transactions. These intermediaries have market power and charge high fees for their specialized services. By providing a trusted, single electronic ledger, blockchain can eliminate these financial intermediaries and their associated costs. Santander InnoVentures estimates that the application of DLT could reduce such back-office costs by up to $20 billion per year by 2022.[6]

Advanced blockchain platforms support the coding of smart contracts, which are computer programs that execute a series of transactions after some pre-specified event occurs. For example, a smart contract may be programmed to transfer money to a seller after receiving confirmation of delivery of a security. By removing human decision making, smart contracts can shorten settlement, minimize mistakes, increase transparency, and generate cost savings.

One example is the blockchain company R3, which assembled a consortium of banks and other partners to develop an enterprise distributed ledger for the financial services industry known as Corda. Corda was built to meet the security, privacy, scalability, reliability, and throughput requirements of the regulated financial-services industry. Corda is flexible and interoperable and can be used to record ownership of any asset. It is a private blockchain, so only the counterparties to a transaction can see the details. There is no broadcasting or global sharing of data. Transactions are validated and confirmed one at a time, not batched and processed in blocks. Consensus is reached using third parties, called notary nodes, who verify and confirm transactions, with no wasteful mining or proof-of-work consensus mechanisms. Corda also features smart contracts and includes regulatory and supervisory observer nodes to meet compliance needs.

Blockchain and DLTs have many valuable use cases, but this technology is not the solution for everything. There are use-cases where a blockchain makes sense and others where the benefits do not exceed the costs. Blockchain can improve any business activity that involves a network of stakeholders who need to share valuable information without its being compromised or altered. In the financial services industry, blockchains have been built for the following use-cases:

Syndicated Loans: The syndicated loan market relies on manual processes and multiple, hard-to-audit communications that are inefficient, costly, and operationally risky, particularly for lenders. Fusion LenderComm offers a distributed ledger to provide banks with accurate information on demand. This central portal records all communications between an agent and the banks in a syndicate, and provides immediate transaction information for all parties on a deal.

Securities Lending and Repo Markets: Banks and institutional investors hold large amounts of high-quality liquid assets that are posted as collateral or held on the balance sheet to meet regulatory requirements. Existing settlement practices are inefficient and create expensive intra-day exposures to counterparties. HQLAx has developed a distributed ledger to provide cost-effective liquidity management and collateral transfers in the global securities lending and repo markets.

Letter of Credit: Banks use letters of credit (LOCs) to finance cross-border trade. An LOC may require up to twenty-seven individual documents to be exchanged and signed by counterparty banks. A blockchain would combine individual LOCs and add electronic verification at each point, reducing execution times, costs, and risks for all stakeholders in cross-border trade.

Clearing and Settlement of Derivatives: In 2018, the Depository Trust & Clearing Corporation (DTCC) advanced to the testing phase of its project to re-platform its credit derivatives Trade Information Warehouse (TIW) on a distributed ledger technology. The solution will enable DTCC and its clients to streamline and automate derivatives processing across the industry, increasing speed and eliminating redundant processing capabilities and associated reconciliation costs.

NOTES

1 According to the search engine Factiva, the term "fintech" first appeared in the mid-1980s in the title of an industry newsletter, the *FinTech Electronic Office*, edited by Peter Knight. See: Knight, P. (1985, 10 July). Technology: Machines leap the language barrier / electronic translating. *The Financial Times*.

2 KPMG. (2019, 31 July). The pulse of fintech H1 2019. https://assets.kpmg /content/dam/kpmg/xx/pdf/2019/07/pulse-of-fintech-h1-2019.pdf.

3 CB Insights. (2019). The state of fintech: Investments and sector trends to watch. https://www.cbinsights.com/research/report/fintech-trends -q4-2019/.

4 Arner, D.W., Barberis, J., & Buckley, R.P. (2017). Fintech and regtech in a nutshell, and the future in a sandbox. CFA Institute Research Foundation.

5 Santander InnoVentures. (2015, 15 June). The fintech 2.0 paper: Rebooting financial services. http://santanderinnoventures.com/wp-content/uploads /2015/06/The-Fintech-2-0-Paper.pdf.

6 Ibid.

SECTION I

THE STRUCTURAL FORCES
TRANSFORMING FINANCIAL SERVICES

CHAPTER ONE

Financial Technologies and the Disruption of Financial Services

R. Jesse McWaters

In January 2014, at the Annual Meeting of the World Economic Forum in Davos, Switzerland, a group of nearly fifty C-suite executives from some of the world's largest banks, insurers, and asset managers gathered for a closed-door meeting to consider a troubling development. In the wake of the global financial crisis a strange new breed of start-up had begun to emerge. Unlike past assailants, who had largely matched the appearance and the demeanor of the financial establishment, these new "fintechs" wore hoodies and preached the Silicon Valley gospel of disruption. The order of the day would be to consider the new approaches to lending, payments, and wealth management being advanced by these upstarts to determine if they represented a true competitive threat.

As the meeting drew to its appointed close two hours later, the consensus was clear (though not universal). While some of the innovations being explored by these "fintech" new entrants were interesting, they simply could not compete with the scale of incumbent firms – nor would it be possible for them to rapidly establish the customer trust that financial institutions had built, in some cases over a span of centuries. Even ignoring these factors, it was broadly agreed that no new entrant could hope to achieve success within the unforgiving regulatory environment of financial services – particularly given the exceptionally watchful eye of regulatory and supervisory authorities following the global financial crisis of 2008.

And yet – despite all of the experience and confidence in that room – we find ourselves five years later in a world where thirty-nine fintechs have attained the coveted title of "unicorn" for their valuations in excess of $1 billion USD, boasting an aggregate valuation of more than $147 billion USD.[1] While incumbent financial institutions remain the dominant players in almost every market where they operate, the contours of the competitive landscape have radically shifted. Fintechs have seized the initiative and now drive the pace and direction of innovation in the financial sector.

How did this happen? And more importantly where does the financial ecosystem go from here? Are fintechs asteroids to the incumbent "dinosaurs"? Will incumbents crush the fintech revolution in due time? Or is the answer something else entirely – perhaps involving the large technology firms whose insatiable appetite for data has left them ever more interested in the minutiae of financial products and services?

This chapter will explore these questions in three sections. The first will examine the forces that have enabled the emergence of fintechs and the key characteristics of their business models, before considering the most significant obstacles they face to continued growth. The second section will consider the key strategies that incumbent financial institutions have deployed in their response to the fintech threat – as well as the impediments they face to delivering on these strategies. The third and final section will consider the forces shaping the evolutionary path of the financial ecosystem – looking beyond the dualist narrative of fintech versus incumbent to consider how emerging business models that draw on the lessons of digital platforms in other sectors might fundamentally remake the financial ecosystem.

Section 1 – The Rise of Fintech

With the benefit of hindsight, it is easy to criticize the financial incumbents for a lack of vision in foreseeing the fintech revolution of the last five years. But, standing in their shoes in 2014, the case for skepticism was strong. After all, the foundational business models of banks, insurers, and asset managers had been largely unchanged for decades, and where technological disruption had occurred – such as with the advent of the automated teller or the electronification of capital markets – these innovations had been led by and were to the benefit of these largest firms. Given this history, how had so many small firms so quickly made inroads into the financial sector?

The Rise of Fintech – Why Now?

Both supply and demand forces supported the rapid proliferation of fintech start-ups. On the demand side, several factors appear to have increased consumers' openness to trying an alternative provider of financial services. In the wake of the financial crisis, many consumers lost trust in their financial institutions and felt a general antipathy towards them. A 2012 survey by *The Guardian* newspaper announced that trust in banking had hit a five-year low, with 71 percent of Britons surveyed indicating that they "did not think banks have learnt their lesson from the financial crisis."[2] These same customers had seen technology companies drive enormous improvements in the quality of both digital and physical services, making the clunky and often paper-based processes of financial institutions look increasingly out of date. Indeed, customers might reasonably ask themselves why, if Amazon could facilitate free two-day shipping on a growing range of products, international wire transfers could take up to five days to complete[3] and cost upwards of $45 USD?[4]

On the supply side, the advent of cloud service providers played an important role in reducing the fixed cost of launching any digital business. While the Internet start-ups of the early 2000s were often forced to make massive capital outlays on server capacity, today's new businesses are able to access storage and computing capabilities on an "as a service" basis from providers like Amazon Web Services and Google Cloud, enabling them to scale their technology costs dynamically as their businesses grow.[5]

At the same time, the unique macroeconomic conditions following the global financial crisis supported a capital-rich environment, as ultra-low interest rates triggered a "quest for yield" that drove enormous sums of money into alternative asset classes like venture capital. In the United States, annual venture-capital investment rose rapidly from $27.2 billion USD in 2009 to an astonishing $130.9 billion USD in 2018, exceeding the previous high set in the year 2000.[6] At the same time, fintech's share of that growing pie rapidly expanded – with global venture-capital investments in fintech rising from $8.3 billion USD in 2014 to $25.6 billion USD in 2018 (a compound annual growth rate or CAGR of close to 25 percent).[7]

But the most important shift that enabled the emergence of fintechs across the Western world came from the regulatory establishment – the very place that incumbents viewed as their strongest defense against disruption. While scrutiny of incumbent financial institutions increased dramatically in the post-2008 period, many regulators also began to seek opportunities to foster increased competition in financial markets. The most notable case was in the United Kingdom, where an overhaul of the financial regulatory infrastructure in 2013 led the newly created Financial Conduct Authority (FCA) to have the promotion of "effective competition in the interests of consumers" as one of its three core operational objectives.[8]

Many regulators saw fintech as a promising opportunity to foster competition that would lower costs and improve both the quality and accessibility of financial products. To facilitate the growth of these firms, many regulatory authorities built out programs specifically designed to encourage and enable the proliferation of fintech innovators. A 2019 report by the Cambridge Centre for Alternative Finance found that at least thirty-three jurisdictions had established "innovation offices" whose goal is to "engage with, and provide regulatory clarification to, financial services providers that seek to offer innovative products and services," while a further thirty-one had established "regulatory sandboxes" designed to "allow market participants to test new financial services or business models with live customers."[9]

The Rise of Fintech – Predictable and Deliberate

Together these supply-and-demand forces created an ideal environment for an explosion of agile high-tech start-ups with the goal of reshaping the financial sector on their own terms. Indeed, the sheer breadth of fintech innovation – extending across the domains of payments, lending, wealth management, and even insurance – could be overwhelming. In interviews with early observers, many noted that new entrants seemed to be appearing almost at random, making it challenging to determine which innovations would have a meaningful impact.[10]

On closer examination, a common theme unites these innovators, revealing their actions to be deliberate and predictable. Fintechs have attacked – and continue to attack – incumbent players where the greatest sources of customer friction meet the largest profit pools.[11] Viewed through this lens, the common DNA connecting fintechs across various sub-sectors of financial services becomes clear. In the sections that follow we will explore the evolution of some of the most important fintech business models in payments, lending, and wealth management to consider how they conform to this thesis.

Fintechs in Payments

Perhaps the best example of this highly focused approach to disruption can be seen in the payments sector. In many ways, this sector was less primed for disruption because of ongoing innovation by the major card networks (e.g., NFC "tap and go" payments) and the success of earlier payments innovators from the 2000s, most notably PayPal. Rather than attempting to disrupt established payments infrastructure, successful fintechs made judicious use of existing payment rails, while developing products that targeted several areas where both margins and customer frustration remained high.

For example, U.K.-based TransferWise sought to streamline the process of currency exchange and transfer, giving consumers a user-friendly method of making cross-border payments quickly with a flat, transparent fee structure.[12] U.S.-based Square sought to simplify the process and fee structure of accepting credit-card payments for small merchants. While both firms are often perceived by users as having disrupted the underlying payments infrastructure, they in fact sit on top of incumbent rails (domestic bank transfer systems in the case of TransferWise and major card networks in the case of Square), having found opportunities to simplify and reduce the cost to end users.

The impact of this strategy has been significant. TransferWise now reports that their user base collectively transfers over £2 billion every month between sixty-nine countries in forty-seven currencies,[13] helping them become Europe's most valuable fintech, with a 2019 valuation of $3.5 billion USD.[14] At the same time, Square's gross payments volume has grown at a CAGR of 44 percent since its launch, and in 2018 it facilitated over $84 billion USD in transactions.[15]

Fintechs in Lending

A similar narrative can be seen among fintechs in the consumer and small-business lending space. Widespread attention has been given to so called "peer-to-peer" lending models that sought to disintermediate banks from the role of matchmaker between those in need of a loan and those with excess funds to lend. Theoretically, such a model allows both parties to enjoy better rates (lower interest payments in the case of the borrower and higher interest rates in the case of the lender). In practice, this business model proved challenging, however, with banks able to secure much lower costs of funding and much more stable sources of funds (in the form of deposits) for their loans than competing peer-to-peer platforms.[16] As a result, few true peer-to-peer lenders have scaled successfully.

Instead, successful fintech lenders, particularly those in the United States, shifted away from individuals as a source of capital in favor of more traditional sources such as hedge funds and the sale of securitized loans to institutional investors.[17] Rather than differentiating themselves based on sources of funds, these fintechs have focused on opportunities to reduce customer frustration by offering more streamlined and digital loan-origination processes that could reduce the time between application and fulfillment from weeks to minutes.[18] New entrants have also actively explored novel adjudication metrics that draw on nontraditional data such as bill payments or social media network graphs, to lend to individuals previously excluded from most incumbent offerings, such as "thin file" borrowers with limited credit history.

This use of alternative data has allowed fintech lenders to significantly lower the cost of underwriting loans to small and mid-sized businesses by directly ingesting data from their payment flows and sales in online marketplaces.[19] For example, in 2014, payments fintech Square announced the launch of Square Capital, a new arm of their business that would offer loans to finance working capital to their small business users based on data gleaned from the businesses' payment flows.

Like their peers in payments, fintechs focused on lending have seen impressive growth. S&P Global Market Intelligence estimates that U.S. loan originations by these actors have seen a 106.6 percent CAGR from 2013 to 2018, with a combined $140 billion USD in loans issued over that period.[20]

Fintechs in Wealth Management

In the wealth management space, fintechs have largely focused on closing the "advice gap" faced by a growing number of individual investors. In past decades, many workers could rely on a defined-benefit pension that provided certainty that they would receive some percentage of their salary for the remainder of their life post-retirement. More recently, though, employers have shifted away from these offerings in favor of defined-contribution schemes such as 401Ks in the United States, Individual Savings Accounts (ISAs) in Great Britain, or Registered Retirement Savings Plans (RRSPs) in Canada. From 1968 to 2007, the percentage of U.S. workers with defined-contribution plans increased from 45 percent to 53 percent, while the percentage with defined-benefit plans declined from 63 percent to 32 percent.[21] This shift has forced individuals to take greater responsibility for managing their retirement savings, while at the same time subjecting them to the risk that they will outlive their retirement savings.

Unfortunately, few individuals have the financial literacy to meet this challenge themselves. The average American respondent answered fewer than three out of five basic financial-literacy questions correctly.[22] For most of them, the cost of receiving impartial advice from a fiduciary remains out of reach, with even a basic financial plan typically costing from between $1,000 to $3,000 USD per annum.[23] Fintech innovators in wealth management have therefore sought to identify and offer financial advice to these individuals at a significantly lower cost via "robo-advisors."

Robo-advisors essentially seek to automate the basic activities of a human advisor, such as evaluating the client's financial needs and identifying financial products to meet those needs (often low-fee exchange-traded funds built by large incumbent asset managers). They also typically manage the ongoing rebalancing of that user's portfolio as her age, risk tolerance, and financial goals change over time. They may even automate more sophisticated activities such as tax reporting or tax-optimization strategies. Interestingly, most of these features are not new innovations but rather established tools of professional wealth managers, who provide them to high-net-worth clients. Robo-advisors have made these services available to all individuals at a low cost.

The compelling value proposition of robo-advisors has supported a rapid growth in customer awareness of these platforms and the accumulation of assets by a number of early movers. In the United States, for example, Betterment and Wealthfront managed $17.6 billion USD and $15.0 billion USD respectively as of Q2 2019.[24] While that remains a small fraction of the more than $37 trillion USD in total U.S. assets under management,[25] it shows a strong willingness of consumers to explore this alternative wealth-management structure.

The Rise of Fintech – Obstacles along the Road

While fintechs have made real progress, it would be a mistake to conclude that the road ahead is clear. Indeed, the obstacles that fintechs face bear out the expectations of incumbent leaders who surmised that fintechs would face difficulties in navigating the regulatory complexity of the financial sector, building customer trust, and competing with the massive scale of established financial institutions.

While regulators have significantly increased their openness to new entrants, this does not mean that complying with the regulatory landscape is easy or inexpensive. For example, nonbank lenders who want to operate in the United States must be licensed by each state in which they operate, adding significantly to the cost, managerial complexity, and lead time of launching a new offering. Moreover, while many regulators have opened innovation centers, this should not be taken to mean that they look kindly upon the free-wheeling approaches to compliance that have served "disruptive" start-ups in other sectors. An excellent illustration of this is U.S. bro-kerage fintech Robinhood, whose ambitious roll-out of high-interest checking and savings account products in December 2018 needed to be abandoned only a day later under intense regulatory scrutiny.[26]

Such headlines do not help fintechs in their already uphill battle to build customer trust. It is true that customers' trust in financial incumbents has been eroded and that customers are now more will-ing to *consider* doing business with fintechs. Surveys suggest, how-ever, that customers still view incumbent financial institutions as a safer destination for their money, even compared to fintechs that have secured all the necessary regulatory approvals.[27]

But the most serious challenge that fintechs face is scaling their busi-ness to profitability. The billions of dollars of loans and transactions that fintechs have facilitated are certainly indicators of their impres-sive progress over the past five years. But financial services is a low-margin business where massive levels of volume – that few fintechs have attained – are required for sustainable profitability. Achieving that scale can be an extraordinarily expensive prospect – particularly with customers who are hesitant to try a new service provider. Aggres-sive guerrilla marketing tactics have been a cornerstone of Trans-ferWise's success but also mean that in 2016 the marketing budget represented the organization's single largest cost.[28] This is equally true for lending, where marketplace lenders like Prosper and Lending Club are reported to spend $350 to $400 USD per customer acquired.[29] The market data provider Morningstar estimates that the cost of acquiring a new client can be as high as $1,000 USD for robo-advisors.[30]

Fintechs show enormous promise in identifying and rapidly deploying innovative offerings that address incumbent inefficiency and customer frustration. But what remains uncertain is whether they will be able to gain enough momentum to establish a dominant market position, particularly given that incumbents have not been idle in the face of the fintech incursion.

Section 2 – The Incumbent Response

Despite incumbents' initial skepticism towards the disruptive potential of fintechs, the past five years have seen incumbents invest significant time and capital into reinforcing their defenses against these would-be entrants. In so doing, many financial institutions have realized that fintechs are more than just a competitive threat; they also represent an opportunity. The rapid growth of the fintech ecosystem has the potential to let smart incumbents externalize aspects of their research and innovation functions – allowing them to wait and see which new offerings gain traction before acting as a "fast-follower."[31] Properly executed, such a strategy provides financial institutions with a supermarket for capabilities, allowing them to use a mix of replication, investment, and partnerships to rapidly deploy new offerings that capitalize on winning fintech ideas.[32] In the section that follows we will consider the inroads that financial incumbents have made in deploying these strategies, as well as the serious practical challenges that they face to establish themselves as successful fast-followers.

The Incumbent Response – Innovating Internally and Replicating Fintechs

The most impactful strategies deployed by fintechs tend to revolve around innovative improvements to customer experience and process efficiency. Entrenching the advantages of these innovations is a challenge for fintechs, as they are usually not patentable and cannot be kept secret. As a result, incumbent financial institutions are often in a strong position to replicate fintech innovations and deploy them directly to their customers. Incumbents are therefore able to use fintech innovators to gather data on which new business models and customer engagement strategies are the most effective before investing significant capital into building out those capabilities.

The most successful example of this can be seen in the response of incumbent asset managers in the United States to the threat from robo-advisors. In 2015, Charles Schwab, a large San Francisco-based bank and brokerage firm launched its own robo-advisor, called Intelligent Portfolios, which it made available at no cost to its customers.[33] Shortly thereafter, Vanguard, the world's second-largest asset manager, announced a similar offering called Vanguard Personal Advisor Services.[34] Unlike fintechs, these incumbents were able to take advantage of their established sales channels and automatically enroll existing customers in these services. This enabled them to grow their assets under management at a significantly faster pace than their fintech competitors, despite not having been first to market. As of the second quarter of 2019, Vanguard Personal Advisor Services had an impressive $140 billion USD in assets under management and Schwab Intelligent Portfolios had $41 billion USD, significantly more than Betterment's $17.6 billion USD and Wealthfront's $15.0 billion USD.[35] Because of this impressive incumbent performance, many fintech robo-advisors have found their valuations under considerable pressure, with some reportedly reduced by more than 60 percent.[36]

Attempts to replicate fintech offerings extend well beyond wealth management, and in some cases the fintech threat has even driven impressive levels of cooperation between incumbent firms. For example, in response to the success of U.S. peer-to-peer payment app Venmo, more than ninety incumbent banks (including

JPMorgan Chase, Capital One, Wells Fargo, and Bank of America) have partnered to offer a competing service called Zelle.[37] Early signs suggest this effort has been a success, given that Zelle's 2018 payment volume of $122 billion USD was almost double Venmo's $62 billion USD.[38]

In some cases, incumbents have even sought to mimic fintech innovators in their build-out of entirely new lines of business. In 2016, investment banking titan Goldman Sachs announced its intention to enter the retail banking space, providing deposit accounts and loans to everyday customers via an online-only digital bank called Marcus. The new offering brought together the brand and experience of an incumbent financial institution with a digital-first approach. Marcus has since attracted 1.5 million customers and $22 billion USD in deposits as well as having issued more than $3 billion USD of loans.[39]

The Incumbent Response – Investing in Fintechs

In addition to building out new internal capabilities, many incumbent financial institutions have sought to invest in or acquire emerging fintechs. For example, in 2015, rather than building its own robo-advisor, as Vanguard and Charles Schwab had done, Black-Rock (the world's largest asset manager) acquired FutureAdvisor, then the third largest robo-advisor in the United States.[40] They also made a subsequent direct investment in European robo-advisor Scalable in 2017[41] and in U.S. robo-advisor Acorns in 2018.[42]

To facilitate these kinds of investments a growing number of incumbent financial institutions have chosen to establish corporate venture-capital funds. In fact, CB Insights reports that one third of fintech investment rounds in 2018 included contributions from at least one corporate venture-capital fund.[43] In the United States, Citibank's Citi Ventures arm has been particularly aggressive, making thirty-seven investments between 2013 and 2017, followed by Goldman Sachs with twenty-five investments over the same period, including Square and small-business lender OnDeck. European bank Santander has also actively pursued this strategy through their Santander Innoventures arm, whose portfolio of nineteen fin-techs[44] includes marketplace lending unicorn Kabbage[45]

The Incumbent Response – Partnering with Fintechs

The third, and broadest, means by which incumbents are seeking to respond to fintech innovation is through partnership with fintechs that possess complementary capabilities. Perhaps the best and most frequently cited example of this strategy is the partnership between JP Morgan Chase and small and medium enterprise (SME) lender OnDeck Capital, announced in 2016. This arrangement sought to combine OnDeck's ability to quickly and efficiently adjudicate small and mid-sized business loans of less than $250,000 USD with the massive scale of JP Morgan's U.S. operations. High overhead costs had traditionally limited JP Morgan's ability to profitably serve customers seeking these smaller loans. In the words of JP Morgan CEO Jamie Dimon, the partnership with OnDeck would help JP Morgan succeed at "the kind of stuff we don't want to do or can't do."[46] Santander signed a similar agreement with SME lender Kabbage with the goal of providing small and mid-sized businesses in the United Kingdom with "a premiere lending platform that provides access to capital within a matter of minutes."[47]

JP Morgan is far from alone in their desire to pursue fintech partnerships. The PwC 2017 Global FinTech Report revealed that 82 percent of incumbent financial institutions expect to increase fintech partnerships in the next three to five years.[48] Even members of the conservative world of reinsurance have sought out partnerships, such as Munich Re, who have signed agreements with several insuretechs, providing them with the capital necessary to backstop their offerings and the expertise in both pricing and operating across borders.[49]

The Incumbent Response – Barriers to Fast-Following

While the narrative of replicating, investing in, and partnering with fintechs is strong on paper, successfully deploying these strategies is no simple matter for incumbent financial institutions. That's because a successful fast-follower strategy requires more than just the ability to leverage existing scale and customer relationships; it also demands a strategic focus on reinvention and the organizational agility to deliver on the "fast" part of "fast-following." Unfortunately, these are two qualities that many incumbent financial institutions have struggled to cultivate.

Part of the reason that a sustained focus on business-model reinvention has been difficult to maintain is that regulatory and supervisory authorities have demanded that incumbents focus their attention elsewhere. The decade since the global financial crisis has seen the roll-out of expansive new regulations and the creation of new regulatory authorities. The U.S. Dodd-Frank Act alone is more than 2,300 pages long,[50] while Europe's Markets in Financial Instruments Directive (better known as MIFID II) is a stunning 30,000 pages, containing 1.5 million paragraphs.[51]

Adjusting to these regulations has been a full-time job for incumbents, consuming vast amounts of human capital and funds that might otherwise have been invested in new and innovative product offerings. In the years following the global financial crisis, JP Morgan announced 13,000 new hires in their compliance and control functions.[52] Citi reported that their compliance department had reached 30,000 employees.[53] As a result, the cost of compliance for even the most scale-efficient financial institutions averages as much as 14 percent of noninterest income,[54] placing serious pressures on profitability.

Moreover, a lack of organizational agility is a key reason that these regulatory changes have consumed so much of incumbents' time and capital. A lack of agility is the most serious impediment to incumbents' ability to be fast-followers. Most incumbents are "supertankers" that require enormous time and energy to change course. This means that adjusting to new regulatory requirements – to say nothing of reinventing their business strategy – can take months, if not years. Ironically, a key reason for this lack of agility is that incumbents were arguably *the* first movers in the use of computers by the private sector. Since as early as 1954, financial institutions have been using computers to conduct complex computations and maintain customer records.[55] Unfortunately, as these investments in mainframe systems became central to the organization, incumbents found themselves increasingly saddled with an outdated and inflexible technical architecture that limited their agility by imposing significant costs and lead-time requirements on any modifications to the "legacy" core systems.[56]

Together, the hobbled agility of incumbent financial institutions and their divided focus on innovation have limited the potential impact of the three strategies discussed in this section. Securing the necessary talent and capital to quickly replicate a fintech offering is an obvious challenge when we consider that as much as two-thirds of the total information technology (IT) spending of most large Western financial institutions is dedicated to the maintenance of outdated legacy systems and that much of what remains is consumed by "must-do" regulatory and compliance projects.[57]

Partnerships between incumbents and fintechs also face significant barriers, in no small part due to the challenges of integrating fintechs' modern, cloud-based technology with incumbents' legacy IT systems. Even when technical integration is not required, however, fintechs often find themselves frustrated by the slow internal processes and more complex regulatory requirements of incumbent institutions.

Finally, even investing in fintech innovation can be challenging for incumbents. With so many dedicated venture-capital funds able to leverage their established reputations and deal-flow networks to identify the next fintech unicorn, corporate venture-capital funds are at risk of adverse selection. Moreover, even when incumbents are able to acquire stakes in a high-performing fintech, it is not always obvious how that ownership position can be parleyed into an impactful partnership or other actionable business strategy.

Section 3 – The Future of Financial Services

The rise of fintechs has driven a process of competitive digitization that has reduced costs, increased the speed of delivery, and improved the accessibility of financial products and services; but it has not fundamentally transformed the financial experience of most individuals or small businesses – at least not in the Western world. In China, on the other hand, the impact of fintech innovators has been much more profound. To see what the future of financial services could look like in Europe and North America, it is useful to consider the rise of the "techfin" in China.

The Future of Financial Services – China and the Rise of the "Techfin"

Ant Financial (a subsidiary of Chinese e-commerce giant Alibaba) and Tencent (creator of WeChat, China's most successful messaging app) have led a revolution in the structure of the Chinese financial system. Both companies are now sitting in the center of vast financial empires built on the back of highly successful digital payments products. More than 800 million individuals use Tencent's WeChat Pay service, while 620 million use Ant Financial's Alipay service,[58] giving the two technology giants a combined 90 percent[59] market share of the 58.8 trillion yuan (approximately $8.5 trillion USD) that Chinese consumers spent via their phones in 2016.[60] From this dominance in payments, both firms have built out extensive digital banking operations. And Ant Financial has established a money market fund, Yu'ebao ("spare treasure"), whose $168 billion USD in assets under management make it the largest in the world.[61]

More important than the success of these technology firms in the domain of financial services is the way in which they have defined a new structure for China's financial ecosystem. Chinese customers' financial lives are much more tightly integrated with other aspects of their digital experiences than are those of most Western consumers. WeChat, in particular, has developed a tightly integrated ecosystem where users can order a taxi, send gifts to family members, book hotels, and pay bills all from a single app. Looking forward, could the structure of the financial ecosystem in North America and Europe find itself fundamentally reshaped to the same degree that the Chinese ecosystem has been? Several shifts in the strategic context of financial services are under way that point in just this direction.

The rise of fintech has alleviated a great many frustrations related to specific products and services, but it has also further fragmented the customer experience of its users, making it more difficult for them to have a clear vision of their financial self. This frustrates the appetite of both retail customers and small businesses to improve their financial health – an all-too-common need that neither fintechs nor banks have made significant inroads into addressing over the past five years. (The partial exception is the impact of robo-advisors on long-term retirement planning.)

This customer frustration exists against a backdrop of rapid improvements in the capabilities of artificial intelligence that open opportunities for digital service providers to give customers the kind of personalized advice they are looking for in their day-to-day financial lives. At the same time, the data that would be necessary to "train" such systems are being unlocked by a series of regulatory changes, often called "open banking," that give customers the right to share their detailed financial data with almost any reputable third party they wish. Together, these changes are driving a growing number of executives and analysts to consider a financial future whose fundamental building blocks look very different from those that make up the current system.

The Future of Financial Services – from Products to Platforms

Today's financial system is fundamentally product-centric. Products, and groupings of products, define the organizational structure of most incumbent financial institutions, which tend to be vertically integrated with the "manufacturing" of the underlying product, the front-office management of customers, and any back-office infrastructure. These products, however, exist in siloed lines of business with limited data sharing taking place between product groupings (partially because of the challenges of integrating each product's respective legacy IT systems). This architecture means that a customer who holds multiple products with a single institution might struggle to get a clear view of their consolidated holdings from that institution – to say nothing of across multiple institutions. It also almost certainly means that an individual's products will not be customized in order to accommodate their specific needs.

But what if financial services were to be reshaped in the same way as other vertically integrated and product-centric industries that have been disrupted by platform-based digital ecosystems? Imagine a digital platform that draws together all the relevant information about a customer – their existing financial product holdings, their behavior traits, and their plans for the future. This customer-centric platform could automate tedious financial tasks, optimize product selection, and provide customized financial advice. A 2018 report by the World Economic Forum called such a service "self-driving" finance.[62]

Such a platform would be particularly well positioned to focus its attention on providing the customer with advice if few – or perhaps none – of the products offered by the platform were produced in-house. Rather than a traditional financial institution, selling only its own in-house products, our hypothetical customer-centric platform would behave more like Amazon, providing customers with the recommendations and fulfillment services necessary to navigate a universe of competing financial product "manufacturers."

Such an environment would be radically different for those "manufacturers." Where these organizations once relied on captive customers who faced significant frictions if they wished to change financial institutions, a customer-centric platform would make it easy for users to compare the costs and characteristics of products from multiple providers. In other sectors where digital platforms have gained prominence, such as the retail and music industries, the shift has radically altered competitive dynamics, creating a "superstars and long tails" market structure, where a small number of scale players dominate the market for commoditized products, while many small and highly agile players exploit profitable niches.[63]

To summarize this narrative – the customer-centric platform imagined here would completely transform the structure of the financial ecosystem. It would cause a shift away from today's product-centric world to a customer-centric one where customer experience is curated by digital platforms, and product manufacturers compete for the attention of platform users and to be recommended by the platform's algorithms. This notion might sound fantastical, but a growing number of experts believe the combination of open-data regulation and technological pressures will push the sector in this direction. A 2018 report by consultancy EY is particularly blunt, calling "the traditional operating model [of incumbents] unsustainable" and arguing that players in the financial ecosystem "will have to embrace the platform-based business model, either as an active participant on others' platforms, or on platforms of their own."[64]

The Future of Financial Services – Who Will Own the Future?

All of this raises the obvious question – if the structure of the financial ecosystem stands to be reshaped in the coming years, who will play what roles in this future structure? There is no way of being sure, but several interesting scenarios exist.

One of the most frequently discussed scenarios foresees large Western technology firms known as bigtechs – Google, Facebook, and Amazon – entering financial services as platforms for customer experience. These tech firms have extensive experience curating digital experiences – often supported by cutting-edge artificial intelligence – and enormous scale in their existing user base. More importantly, they have deep troves of personal data about the individuals who use their services, data that could be combined with those individuals' financial data (made accessible thanks to open-banking legislation) to support product personalization and detailed financial advice. Perhaps most compelling of all, such a strategy would not require technology firms to "become banks," but rather would enable them to provide financial advice and product brokerage while leaving incumbent financial institutions and fintechs to conduct the more capital- and regulatory-intensive work of product manufacturing.

Such a scenario would see financial services in the Western world take a similar path to recent developments in China, where techfins like Ant Financial and Tencent have become the primary owners of an individual's customer experience. It is difficult to determine the level of interest that the North American technology firms have in pursuing such a strategy. But if the notion seems far-fetched, it is worth considering that Facebook recently announced plans to launch a new payments mechanism on several of its platforms, including WhatsApp.[65] This move bears a strong resemblance to WeChat's initial push into payments. At the same time, many incumbent financial institutions may be actively conditioning their customers to ask Amazon for help in managing their financial lives by developing "skill-packs" that enable customers to use voice commands to perform bank transactions via Amazon's digital assistant, Alexa.[66]

Fintechs are also actively thinking about the shift of the financial services ecosystem towards a platform model. Many new digital banks (sometimes called "challenger banks" or "neo-banks") aspire to use a platform model to accelerate their growth. For example, rather than building out its own international money-transfer offerings, German digital bank N26 chose to directly integrate with TransferWise.[67] N26 also partnered with Allianz to provide their credit card customers with travel insurance.[68] A platform approach allows digital banks like N26 to more rapidly expand their suite of product offerings, providing direct integration to best-in-breed products offered by a mix of fintechs and incumbents, while freeing themselves to focus on offering an agile and customer-centric digital experience to their clients.

Finally, it would be wrong to overlook the potential of incumbents, a growing number of which have publicly expressed interest in transforming themselves into platforms. One of the most vocal advocates has been Ralph Hamers, CEO of the Dutch Bank ING, who in 2018 declared at Europe's largest fintech conference that "if you truly want to empower customers, you have to provide them with the most relevant offering – even if some of the products and services are not your own."[69] Such a shift would be an enormous transition for incumbent financial institutions, requiring a massive technological transformation as well as a cultural and operational shift away from their existing product-centric silos. But, while these impediments are large, we must be careful not to overlook the strength of incumbents' position as the current "owners" of customers' financial experiences, particularly given that these relationships have proved exceptionally "sticky" even in the face of deep customer frustration. After all, the average eleven-year tenure of a marriage in the United Kingdom is significantly outstripped by the average seventeen-year relationship between a Briton and their primary financial institution![70]

Of course, none of these scenarios are mutually exclusive. It is possible that large technology companies, fintechs, and incumbents could all succeed at establishing themselves as a platform for the distribution of financial products and advice. Moreover, any shift towards a platform model of financial services would likely be to the advantage of product-focused fintechs, giving them the opportunity to scale more rapidly by using their operational agility to optimize their product offerings for niche segments on a given platform.[71] But that is not to say that we should carelessly adopt an "everyone can win" narrative for the future of financial services.

As we have already discussed, the shift to a platform ecosystem will exert intense competitive pressure on manufacturers of financial products, supporting the growth of the largest and most agile firms. It will also undercut "mid-market" players who might previously have succeeded based on a number of "pretty good" products that have neither the scale to succeed as low-cost commoditized offerings nor the focus to build out defensible niches.

Even more important, it is unlikely that the many players currently seeking to establish themselves as platforms can all be successful. Experiences from the transition of other industries to a platform model suggest that there are strong oligopolistic, and in some cases even monopolistic, tendencies in platform ecosystems that help early movers consolidate their success in ways that make them extremely difficult to dislodge.[72] While today a given jurisdiction might feature dozens to thousands of financial institutions – each managing the relationships with their customers – a platform model of financial services is likely to have only a handful of players who succeed in establishing themselves as winners.

Conclusion

The financial ecosystem in the Western world has found itself at something of an impasse. A wave of fintech innovators has injected new energy into the financial sector with their dream of upending established business models and finding new ways to meet customers' needs; yet their path to scale is by no means assured. On the other hand, incumbent financial institutions with established scale and experience are now awakened to their need to innovate but struggle to do so under the weight of their legacy technical infrastructure and divided focus.

As we look toward the future of financial services, it may well be that the incumbents who met in Davos five years ago and the fintechs seeking to disrupt them were both correct. The state of financial offerings was – and remains today – out of touch with consumers' expectations for digital services. Fintechs are right that technology will play a central role in delivering efficient, customer-centric, and advice-oriented offerings – disrupting the established architecture of the financial ecosystem in the process. But at the same time, incumbents are also correct that operational scale and deep customer trust will remain critical aspects of succeeding in financial services for years to come. Moreover, this rapidly changing financial landscape will make regulatory supervision even more important – demanding that regulatory authorities develop the agility necessary to balance the opportunities of financial innovation with emerging threats to customer protection and financial stability. If they can succeed in doing this, the real winners from the ongoing disruption of the financial ecosystem won't be fintechs, incumbents, or even the large technology firms – it will be their customers.

NOTES

1 CB Insights. (nd). Fintech trends to watch in 2019. *CB Insights,* Research Report. https://www.cbinsights.com/research/report/FinTech-trends-2019/.
2 *The Guardian.* (2012, 9 August). Financial crisis five years on: Trust in banking hits new low. https://www.theguardian.com/business/2012/aug/09/financial-crisis-anniversary-trust-in-banks.
3 TD Canada Trust. (nd). How do I send a wire transfer? https://td.intelliresponse.com/accounts/index.jsp?requestType=NormalRequest&id=231&question=How.
4 Tierney, S. (2019, 11 October). Wire transfers: What banks charge. https://www.nerdwallet.com/blog/banking/wire-transfers-what-banks-charge/.
5 Palmer, M. (2012, 29 February). Cloud computing cuts start-up costs. *Financial Times.* https://www.ft.com/content/fc871bca-58e1-11e1-b9c6-00144feabdc0.
6 Pitchbook, News and Analysis. (2019, 9 January). Pitchbook – NVCA venture monitor. https://pitchbook.com/news/reports/4Q-2018-pitchbook-nvca-venture-monitor.
7 CB Insights. (nd). Fintech trends to watch in 2019. *CB Insights,* Research Report. https://www.cbinsights.com/research/report/FinTech-trends-2019/. This 2018 figure excludes an outlier $14 billion USD investment into Ant Financial in Q2 of 2018 that accounted for 35 percent of 2018 investment in fintech.

8 Financial Conduct Authority (FCA). (2016, 21 April). About the FCA. https://www.fca.org.uk/about/the-fca. Last updated 30 July 2019.
9 UNSGSA FinTech Working Group and CCAF. (2019). Early lessons on regulatory innovations to enable inclusive fintech: Innovation offices, regulatory sandboxes, and regtech. Office of the UNSGSA and CCAF: New York and Cambridge, U.K. https://www.unsgsa.org/files/2915/5016/4448/Early_Lessons_on_Regulatory_Innovations_to_Enable_Inclusive_FinTech.pdf.
10 World Economic Forum. (2015, June). The future of financial services: How disruptive innovations are reshaping the way financial services are structured, provisioned and consumed. http://www3.weforum.org/docs/WEF_The_future__of_financial_services.pdf.
11 Ibid.
12 TransferWise Content Team. (2018, 14 March). How TransferWise works: Your step-by-step guide. TransferWise. https://transferwise.com/gb/blog/how-does-transferwise-work.
13 TransferWise. (2018, 24 April). TransferWise mission report Q1 2018. https://transferwise.com/gb/blog/transferwise-mission-report-q1-2018.
14 Browne, R. (2019, 22 May). TransferWise is now Europe's most valuable fintech start-up, with a 43.5 billion valuation. https://www.cnbc.com/2019/05/22/transferwise-valued-at-3point5-billion-after-292-million-secondary-sale.html?yptr=yahoo.
15 Clement, J. (2019, 12 March). Square annual gross payment volume 2012–2018. Statista. https://www.statista.com/statistics/575437/square-annual-payment-volume/.
16 Shubber, K. (2016, 17 November). Peer-to-peer may have changed banking, but banking still won. *Financial Times*. https://ftalphaville.ft.com/2016/11/16/2179884/peer-to-peer-may-have-changed-banking-but-banking-still-won/.
17 Vallee, B., & Zeng, Y. (2019). Marketplace lending: A new banking paradigm? *Review of Financial Studies* 32(5): 1939–82.
18 World Economic Forum. (2017, August). Beyond fintech: A pragmatic assessment of disruptive potential in financial services. http://www3.weforum.org/docs/Beyond_FinTech__A_Pragmatic_Assessment_of_Disruptive_Potential_in_Financial_Services.pdf.
19 Armstrong, R. (2019, 29 January). How online platforms shook small-business lending in America. https://www.ft.com/content/5c68d948-1efb-11e9-b126-46fc3ad87c65.

20 S&P Global Market Intelligence. (2018). 2018 US digital lending market report. http://marketplacelendingassociation.org/wp-content /uploads/2018/11/SP-2018-US-Digital-Lending-Mkt-Report.pdf.

21 Greenbush Financial Group, LLC. (nd). The shift from defined benefit to defined contribution plans. https://www.greenbushfinancial.com/the -shift-in-retirement-and-importance-of-education/. Accessed 30 January 2019.

22 Board of Governors of the Federal Reserve System. (2018, 19 June). Report on the economic well-being of U.S. households in 2017 – May 2018. https://www.federalreserve.gov/publications/2018-economic-well-being -of-us-households-in-2017-preface.htm. Accessed 5 January 2019.

23 Coombes, A., & O'Shea, A. (2018, 7 December). How much does a financial advisor cost? *Nerd Wallet*. https://www.nerdwallet.com/blog/investing /how-much-does-a-financial-advisor-cost/.

24 Barron's. (2019, 29 July). https://webreprints.djreprints.com/4642511400002 .pdf.

25 Fages. R., Beardsley, B., Brömstrop, I., et al. (2018, 19 July). Global asset management 2018: The digital metamorphosis. BCG (Boston Consulting Group). https://www.bcg.com/en-ch/publications/2018/global-asset -management-2018-digital-metamorphosis.aspx. Accessed 5 January 2019.

26 Rooney, K. (2018, 17 December). What fintech can learn from Robinhood's "epic fail" of launching checking accounts. CNBC. https://www.cnbc .com/2018/12/17/what-fintech-can-learn-from-robinhoods-epic-fail.html.

27 Wilson, K. (2017, 8 June). RFi Group Opinion – Technology companies gaining on banks in battle to win consumer trust. RFi Group. https:// www.rfigroup.com/rfi-group/news/rfi-group-opinion-technology -companies-gaining-banks-battle-win-consumer-trust.

28 Williams-Grut, O. (2016, 7 September). TransferWise spent £12.3 million on advertising last year – its biggest expense. *Business Insider*. https://www .businessinsider.com/ transferwises-2016-accounts-marketing-revenue-loss-profit-2016-9.

29 Harris, A. (2018, 8 March). SoFi is paying top dollar to acquire its prime customers. *Fast Company*. https://www.fastcompany.com/40539348 /sofi-pays-premium-prices-to-acquire-its-prime-customers.

30 Wadhwa, T. (2016, 14 July). One of the hottest investment styles might be "financially unviable." *Business Insider*. https://www.businessinsider .com/robo-advisors-may-be-financially-unviable-2016-7?IR=T.

31 World Economic Forum. (2017, August). Beyond fintech: A pragmatic assessment of disruptive potential in financial services. http://www3

.weforum.org/docs/Beyond_FinTech_-_A_Pragmatic_Assessment_of
_Disruptive_Potential_in_Financial_Services.pdf.

32 Ibid.

33 Schwab, C. (nd). Our robo-adviser does the work, so you don't have
to. Schwab Intelligent Portfolios®. *Charles Schwab Intelligent Portfolios.*
https://intelligent.schwab.com/. Accessed 5 January 2019.

34 Vanguard. (2015, 5 May). Vanguard introduces personal advisor services,
lowers minimum to investors with $50,000. *Vanguard.* https://pressroom
.vanguard.com/news/Vanguard_Introduces_Personal_Advisor_Services
_Lowers_Minimum.html.

35 Barron's. (2019, 29 July). Robos look beyond investing. https://webreprints
.djreprints.com/4642511400002.pdf.

36 Verhage, J. (2018, 24 March). Wealthfront valuation said to drop about a
third in new funding. *Bloomberg.* https://www.bloomberg.com/news
/articles/2018-03-23/wealthfront-valuation-said-to-drop-about-a
-third-in-new-funding.

37 Zelle. (2019). Get started. https://www.zellepay.com/get-started.

38 Shevlin, R. (2019, 11 February). Venmo versus Zelle: Who's winning
the P2P payments war? *Forbes.* https://www.forbes.com/sites
/ronshevlin/2019/02/11/venmo-versus-zelle/#349934c93c62.

39 Mathis, W. (2018, 1 June). Goldman Sachs expects Marcus to get
"very big, very profitable." *Bloomberg.* https://www.bloomberg.com
/news/articles/2018-05-31/goldman-sachs-expects-marcus-to-get
-very-big-very-profitable.

40 Loizos, C. (2015, 26 August). BlackRock acquires Sequoia-backed
future advisor. *TechCrunch.* https://techcrunch.com/2015/08/26
/blackrock-acquires-sequoia-backed-futureadvisor/.

41 Jessop, S., & Hunnicutt, T. (2017, 19 June). BlackRock takes Scalable Capital
stake in Europe "robo-advisor" push. *Reuters.* https://www.reuters.com
/article/us-blackrock-scalablecapital/blackrock-takes-scalable-capital
-stake-in-europe-robo-advisor-push-idUSKBN19A322.

42 BlackRock. (2018, 9 May). BlackRock and Acorns partner to expand
financial participation among the next generation of investors. https://
www.blackrock.com/corporate/newsroom/press-releases/article
/corporate-one/press-releases/acorns-pressrelease-newsroom-final.

43 CB Insights. (nd). Fintech trends to watch in 2019. *CB Insights.* Research
Report. https://www.cbinsights.com/research/report/FinTech-trends-2019/.

44 CB Insights. (2018, 12 April). Where top European banks are investing
in fintech in one graphic. *CB Insights.* https://www.cbinsights.com
/research/europe-bank-FinTech-startup-investments/.

45 Santander Innoventures. (nd). Portfolio companies. http://santan derinnoventures.com/portfolio-companies/. Accessed 6 January 2019.

46 *The Economist.* (2015, 5 December). Love and war – Banking and fintech. https://www.economist.com/finance-and-economics/2015/12/05 /love-and-war.

47 Kabbage. (2016, 3 April). Kabbage and Santander UK partner to accelerate SMB growth. https://www.kabbage.com/blog/kabbage-santander-uk -partner-accelerate-smb-growth/.

48 PwC. (2017). Redrawing the lines: Fintech's growing influence on financial services. https://www.pwc.com/jg/en/publications/pwc-global-fintech -report-17.3.17-final.pdf.

49 Munich RE. (2017, 16 January). Reinventing insurance for the digital generation. https://www.munichre.com/topics-online/en/digitalisation /reinventing-insurance-digital-generation.html.

50 Holmes, F. (2017, May). These are the 5 costliest financial regulations of the past 20 years. *Business Insider.* https://www.businessinsider.com/these -are-the-5-costliest-financial-regulations-of-the-past-20-years-2017 -5?IR=T#march-2010-foreign-account-tax-compliance-act-fatca-3.

51 Groenfeldt, T. (2018, 4 April). Understanding Mi FID II's 30,000 pages of regulation requires regtech. *Forbes.* https://www.forbes.com/sites /tomgroenfeldt/2018/04/04/understanding-mifid-iis-30000-pages -of-regulation-requires-regtech/#2be03ae52919.

52 Henry, D. (2014, 9 April). JPMorgan's Dimon calls settling legal issues "nerve-wracking." *Reuters.* https://www.reuters.com/article/us -jpmorganchase-dimon-idUSBREA3822W20140409.

53 Patel, S.S. (2014, 14 July). Citi will have almost 30,000 employees in compliance by year-end. *MarketWatch.* http://blogs.marketwatch .com/thetell/2014/07/14/citi-will-have-almost-30000-employees -in-compliance-by-year-end/.

54 Thomson Reuters. (2018). Cost of compliance. Special report. https://legal .thomsonreuters.com/content/dam/ewp-m/documents/legal/en/pdf /reports/cost-of-compliance-special-report-2018.pdf.

55 Bank of America. (2014, 12 August). Bank of America revolutionizes banking industry. https://about.bankofamerica.com/en-us/our-story /bank-of-america-revolutionizes-industry.html.

56 World Economic Forum. (2018, August). The new physics of financial services, p. 73. http://www3.weforum.org/docs/WEF_New_Physics_of _Financial_Services.pdf.

57 Citi GPS: Global Perspectives & Solutions. (2018, March). The bank of the future – The ABCs of digital disruption in finance. *Citibank.* https://

www.citibank.com/commercialbank/insights/assets/docs/2018
/The-Bank-of-the-Future/124/.

58 Yifan Xie, S. (2018, 29 July). Jack Ma's giant financial startup is shaking the
Chinese banking system. *WSJ Online.* https://www.wsj.com/articles/jack
-mas-giant-financial-startup-is-shaking-the-chinese-banking-system
-1532885367.

59 Chandler, C. (2017, 13 May). Tencent and Alibaba are engaged in a massive
battle in China play video. *Fortune.* http://fortune.com/2017/05/13
/tencent-alibaba-china/.

60 Pengying. (2018, 19 February). China's mobile payment volume tops 81
trln yuan. *Xinhua.* http://www.xinhuanet.com/english/2018-02/19
/c_136985149.htm.

61 Wildau, G., & Jia, Y. (2019, 28 January). Ant Financial's money market fund
shrinks to 2-year low. *Financial Times.* https://www.ft.com/content
/35bbbef6-20a8-11e9-b126-46fc3ad87c65.

62 World Economic Forum. (2018, August). The new physics of financial
services. http://www3.weforum.org/docs/WEF_New_Physics_of
_Financial_Services.pdf. Accessed 6 June 2019.

63 Brynjolfsson, E., Yu, H., & Smith, M.D. (2010, September). Long tails versus
superstars: The effect of IT on product variety and sales concentration
patterns. MIT Center for Digital Business. http://ebusiness.mit.edu/erik
/Long%20Tails%20Versus%20Superstars.pdf.

64 EY (Ernst & Young). (2018). A vision for platform-based banking. https://
assets.ey.com/content/dam/ey-sites/ey-com/en_us/topics/financial
-services/ey-a-vision-for-platform-based-banking.pdf. Accessed 6 June 2019.

65 Morris, S. (2019, 28 May). Banks and regulators cast wary eye over Facebook's
crypto plans. *Financial Times.* https://www.ft.com/content/2713a6b6
-816a-11e9-b592-5fe435b57a3b.

66 Capital One. (nd). "Alexa, ask Capital One, what's my balance?" https://
www.capitalone.com/applications/alexa/.

67 N26. (nd). Seamless international money transfers with TransferWise.
https://n26.com/en-eu/transferwise. Accessed 5 January 2019.

68 N26. (nd). N26 black. https://n26.com/en-de/black. Accessed 5 January
2019.

69 Hamers, R. (2018, 7 June). "Being open is the way" – Ralph Hamers. ING.
https://www.ing.com/Newsroom/All-news/Being-open-is-the-way
-Ralph-Hamers.htm.

70 Collinson, P. (2013, 7 September). Switching banks: Why are we more loyal
to our bank than to a partner? *The Guardian,* sec. Money. https://www
.theguardian.com/money/2013/sep/07/switching-banks-seven-day.

71 World Economic Forum. (2018, August). The new physics of financial services. http://www3.weforum.org/docs/WEF_New_Physics_of _Financial_Services.pdf.

72 Choudary, S.P. (2017, 8 May). The dangers of platform monopolies. https:// knowledge.insead.edu/blog/insead-blog/the-dangers-of-platform -monopolies-6031.

CHAPTER TWO

The Economic Forces Driving Fintech Adoption across Countries

Jon Frost[1]

Fintech is being adopted across markets worldwide – but not evenly. Why not? This chapter reviews the evidence. In some economies, especially in the developing world, adoption is being driven by an unmet demand for financial services. Fintech promises to deliver greater financial inclusion. In other economies, adoption can be related to the high cost of traditional finance, a supportive regulatory environment, and other macroeconomic factors. Finally, demographics play an important role, as younger cohorts are more likely to trust and adopt fintech services. Where fintech helps to make the financial system more inclusive and efficient, this could benefit economic growth. Yet the market failures traditionally present in finance remain relevant, and may manifest themselves in new guises.

The Curious Geography of Fintech Adoption

In the past few years, financial technologies (fintechs) have *emerged* in every major region of the world – in both advanced economies and emerging-market and developing economies (EMDEs).[2] But the rate of fintech *adoption* differs considerably. Adoption is used here to refer to the widespread use of a new application, product, or process. While fintech activities are generally small compared to the overall financial system, there are some economies where fintech is growing to an economically important scale. And while fintech is a niche activity confined to certain business lines in some countries, in others it is moving into the main-stream of financial services. This pattern of fintech adoption is puzzling, as it does not reflect either economic development or political boundar-ies. This chapter addresses the question "*What explains the wider adoption of fintech innovations in some economies and markets, but not in others?*"

Cross-country evidence on fintech adoption is patchy, but the data available are improving. They show that new fintech providers have established a strong foothold in mobile payments, especially for retail customers. As one category of fintech, techfin and bigtech players are increasingly important as payments providers in some countries but not in others. For instance, bigtech mobile payments made up 16 percent of GDP in China, according to the most recent data, but less than 1 percent in the United States, India, and Brazil (figure 2.1, left panel).[3] Especially in EMDEs, mobile payments are benefiting from the high number of consumers with mobile phones, which often exceeds those with bank

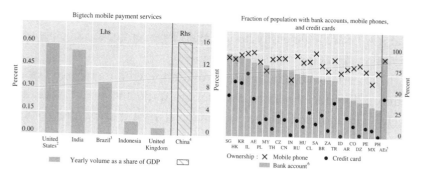

Figure 2.1 Mobile payments and bank accounts[1]

Sources: World Bank; Forrester Research; GlobalData; iResearch; Mercado Libre; Nikkei; Worldpay; national data; BIS calculations.

[1] 2017 data. [2] 2016 data. [3] Estimate based on the public data for Mercado Libre. [4] Only mobile payments for consumption data (i.e., excluding mobile payments for money transfer, credit card payments, and mobile finance). [5] Advanced economy average. [6] Respondents who report having an account at a bank or another type of financial institution or report personally using a mobile money service in the past 12 months.

accounts or credit cards (figure 2.1, right panel). In many African countries, and in Chile, Bangladesh, and Iran, over 20 percent of the population had a mobile money account in the latest World Bank survey.[4]

Meanwhile, peer-to-peer (P2P) lending, marketplace lending,
and other fintech credit platforms are now economically sizeable in
some segments. For instance, fintech lenders made up 8 percent of
new mortgage lending in the United States in 2016, and 38 percent
of unsecured personal lending in 2018.[5] These platforms are economically relevant in the financing of small and medium enterprises
(SMEs) in China, the United States, and the United Kingdom. In the
United States and the United Kingdom, such platforms extended
15.1 percent and 6.3 percent of equivalent bank credit to SMEs,
respectively.[6] Within the United Kingdom, the Cambridge Centre
for Alternative Finance (2017) finds that most credit is provided in
and from London and the southeast, but that other regions (e.g.,
the northeast) received more in funding than they provided. Fintech credit, including credit extended by bigtech platforms, has also
achieved scale in Korea and Kenya (figure 2.2). Yet such credit is
quite small in much of continental Europe, the Middle East, and
Latin America – generally far less than 1 percent of the stock of outstanding credit by banks and other lenders.[7]

In asset management, fintech providers, including robo-advisors,
offer an interface for retail investors to trade and invest ("wealthtech"), either directly or through financial institution partners. There
is increasing fintech activity in insurance markets ("insuretech"),
and even in some wholesale applications like trade finance. Yet in
wholesale markets – like syndicated lending, derivatives markets, or
clearing and settlement – fintech penetration remains low, notwith-
standing potential applications of distributed ledger technology.[8]

Overall, when compared with an incumbent financial system
with assets of USD $382 trillion globally in 2017, fintech activity is
tiny. Fintech credit extended in 2017, at USD $545 billion, is about

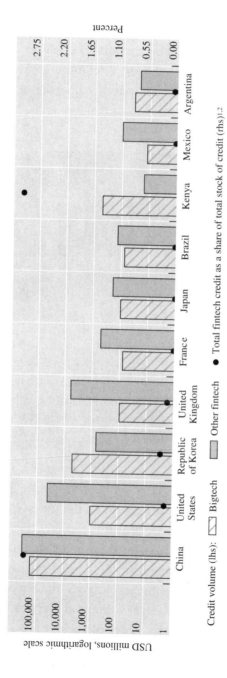

Figure 2.2 Total fintech credit volume by jurisdiction in 2017

Figure includes estimates. Bars are sorted by total fintech credit volume.

Sources: Cambridge Centre for Alternative Finance; IMF WEO; World Bank; national data.

[1] Fintech credit (including bigtech credit) divided by the sum of credit to the private nonfinancial sector (including fintech credit). [2] Calculated on a selected set of countries.

0.14 percent of the stock of global financial system assets (figure 2.3). Similarly, even at the height of the speculative bubble in crypto-assets in January 2018, when the price of Bitcoin surged to USD $20,000, this market was minuscule compared with existing financial assets.

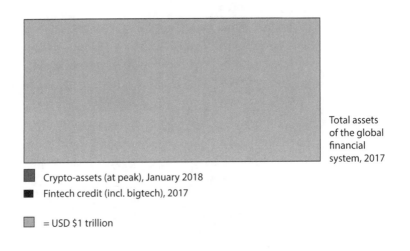

Total assets of the global financial system, 2017

■ Crypto-assets (at peak), January 2018
■ Fintech credit (incl. bigtech), 2017

▢ = USD $1 trillion

Figure 2.3 Global fintech activity relative to the global financial system. The value of financial assets is represented by the area of the respective field.

Sources: FSB (2019d); Cambridge Centre for Alternative Finance; coinmarketcap.com; author's calculations.

Nonetheless, the cross-country differences in the scale of fintech adoption are notable. Even within countries, certain cities – like Hangzhou, Seattle, and Tel Aviv – have become unexpected hotbeds of fintech activity. Meanwhile, some traditional financial centers – like Tokyo and Milan – have less fintech activity than would be expected by their position in other areas of financial services.[9]

To explain the curious geography of fintech adoption, I collect evidence from different areas of financial services, sorting these into the key forces behind adoption. Aside from technological advances, the key forces are unmet demand, the competitive environment, regulation, and changing demographics. Understanding these economic drivers helps us not only to understand current developments but also to look ahead at where fintech may continue growing, and whether this is desirable. Where fintech helps to provide services to those traditionally excluded from the financial system, or to overcome specific market failures (information asymmetry, reducing transaction costs, etc.), it may enhance economic efficiency and growth. Some of these effects are already visible. Where adoption is driven by regulatory arbitrage or rent-seeking, activities are less beneficial.

Widening the Tent: Fintech for Financial Inclusion

Around the world, about 1.7 billion adults lack access to a bank account.[10] Especially in EMDEs, many households rely primarily on cash for day-to-day transactions, and this is closely linked with the large size of unregistered economic transactions (often called "the informal economy"; see Hart, 1973). Among those with a bank account, services like credit, insurance, and wealth management may not be accessible at all – or not at an affordable price for consumers. Even in advanced economies, certain groups lack access to basic financial services, including ethnic and religious minorities, migrant workers, and refugees.

In a number of cases, there is evidence that unmet demand has been a driver of fintech adoption. This adoption has helped to expand the reach of financial services. Perhaps the most famous example is M-Pesa, the mobile money transfer system introduced by Kenya's telecom provider Safaricom in 2008. M-Pesa now operates in multiple countries across East Africa, North Africa, and South

Asia, and counted 32 million users in 2018. Unmet demand for basic banking, means of payment, and money transfer services is likely the key factor behind the rapid growth of mobile payments offerings in countries like India, southeast Asia, and Latin America.[11]

Various studies provide evidence that unmet demand is also a driver for fintech credit. In China, Hau and colleagues (2018) show that fintech credit mitigates supply frictions (such as a large geographic distance between borrowers and the nearest bank branch) and allows firms with a lower credit score to access credit. In the United States, Tang (2019) finds that fintech credit complements bank lending for small-scale loans. Jagtiani and Lemieux (2018) find that Lending Club has penetrated areas that are underserved by traditional banks. In Germany, De Roure and colleagues (2016) find that fintech credit serves a slice of the consumer credit market neglected by German banks. In Argentina, Frost and colleagues (2019) show that 35 percent of the small borrowers from Mercado Libre, an e-commerce platform, would not be eligible for bank credit based on their credit bureau score. Looking across countries, these authors find that bigtech credit is more prevalent when there is a low density of bank branches relative to the population.

Another example of this trend is in remittances services. As anyone who has lived abroad will attest, cross-border transfers of cash are often slow and expensive, and this problem is even more acute for money sent by workers to their families in EMDEs – often in small amounts and to geographically remote locations. The World Bank finds that the average cost to send US $200 to EMDEs is 6.84 percent, or $13.68.[12] The decline in correspondent banking relationships in recent years has heightened these concerns, as this raises the costs to send money to certain jurisdictions, particularly EMDEs.[13] Not surprisingly, remittances (and cross-border payments more generally) are one area where fintech providers have gained a relatively stronger foothold.

Overall, the evidence suggests that fintech is growing where the current financial system is not meeting demand for financial services. In many cases, fintech innovations may require a higher upfront investment but a lower cost per new customer relationship.[14] While fintech activities are still larger in absolute terms in richer countries, this may be a factor behind their higher *relative* importance in some EMDEs, as a share of economic activity.

The World Outside: Macroeconomics and the Cost of Finance

Fintech adoption has been greater in countries where financial services are relatively more expensive, or there is less competition among providers. Philippon (2016) discusses the relatively high and stable "unit cost" of finance in the United States over time, and the potential of fintech to provide greater efficiency. Financial services have been quite expensive throughout the past decades – despite the advent of computers, electronic trading in financial markets, and other innovations. Since 2002, we are seeing that the costs have started to decline (figure 2.4). Recent survey evidence suggests that competition from fintech and bigtech companies is leading incumbents to introduce new products.[15] Whether and how this competition will influence the aggregate figures on the cost of finance is an open question.

Cross-country data from Bazot (2018) show that financial services remain stubbornly expensive in a number of economies, though they have converged and declined since the 1970s and 1980s. In the most recent available year, fintech credit seems to be somewhat more prevalent in those economies with a higher cost of finance (figure 2.5). Claessens and colleagues (2018) find fintech credit to be higher in countries with a higher average income (reflecting

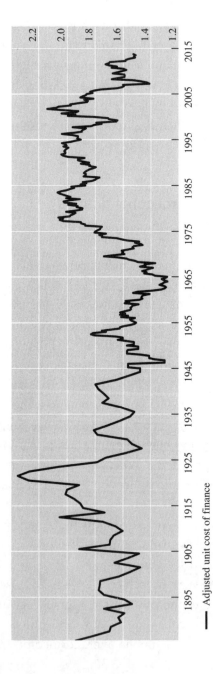

— Adjusted unit cost of finance

Figure 2.4 The cost of financial intermediation in the United States

In percent
Ratio of finance income to intermediated assets, with quality adjustment to take account of firms' and households' characteristics.

Source: Philippon (2016).

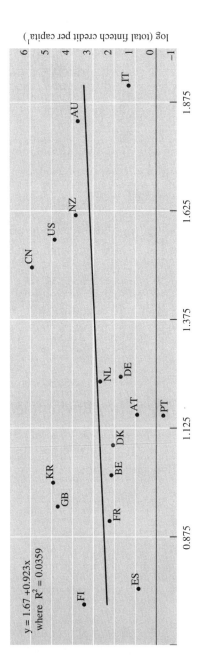

Figure 2.5 Total fintech credit volume in 2017 versus the cost of finance, 2013–2015

1 Sum of fintech credit, divided by population

Sources: Cambridge Centre for Alternative Finance; Bazot (2018).

economic development), and where the banking sector has higher mark-ups (a measure of market power, often reflecting limited competition). In a number of cases, network effects may support greater concentration in the provision of services by platforms over time.[16] Yet some studies find little evidence of these network effects to date.[17]

It is an open question whether the unconventional monetary policies of central banks since the global financial crisis have supported fintech adoption. A study by the IMF (2014) shows that the growth of shadow banking across countries is associated with low interest rates after 2008 and tighter capital regulation, among other factors. As yet, there is no known cross-country evidence connecting low interest rates with fintech credit volumes.

In summary, there may be greater incentives for fintech adoption where banking sectors are relatively uncompetitive. Hence more profitable and fintech new entrants can increase efficiency and lower the costs of financial services.

Rules of the Road: The Regulatory Environment

A number of studies show how the regulatory environment can aid or hinder fintech adoption. Rau (2018) shows that countries with a stronger rule of law, quality of regulation, control of corruption, ease of entry, and higher profitability of extant intermediaries have higher volumes of alternative finance (including fintech credit). Navaretti and colleagues (2017) find that countries with less stringent bank regulation, as measured by a World Bank index, have higher investment in fintech. These countries may also be more permissive toward new entrants. Claessens and colleagues (2018) also find higher fintech credit volumes for these countries. The Cambridge Centre for Alternative Finance (2019) shows that countries where regulation was judged in surveys to be more adequate (rather than excessive or inadequate) had higher alternative finance volumes. The evidence from these studies would *not* tend to support the idea that fintech adoption is driven primarily by regulatory arbitrage, at least at an aggregate level.

Of course, the evidence is necessarily high-level and partial, and it does not account for individual types of regulation. Certain fintech activities could still be driven by regulatory arbitrage. Braggion and colleagues (2018) find that P2P lending in China rose in cities that tightened loan-to-value ratios, consistent with borrowers' tapping P2P credit to circumvent these regulations. Buchak and colleagues (2017) estimate that in the U.S. mortgage market, the higher regulatory burden on traditional banks can explain up to 55 percent of the recent growth of nonbanks, including fintech lenders. Cizel and colleagues (2019) show that bank credit contracts and nonbank credit grows after macroprudential policies are introduced. Studies by Reinhardt and Sowerbutts (2015) and Duijm and colleagues (2019) show that foreign banks and insurers, respectively, expand lending in countries where regulations constrain domestic bank lending. While these results are suggestive, more conclusive evidence will have to wait until researchers have an adequate panel of fintech credit volumes across countries and over time.

A Child of Its Times: Demographic Forces and Trust

At a workshop with senior public-sector officials in 2017, a fintech company executive remarked that "FinTech, like millennials, has been shaped by two major factors: technology, and the global financial crisis." This executive is certainly not the only observer to have noticed these parallels.[18] Indeed, the "genesis block" of the Bitcoin blockchain – the initial piece of code underlying Bitcoin – references the bailouts of banks by the British government in 2009. A neater confluence of technology and the global financial crisis would be hard to come up with. It is perhaps no surprise that millennials, or "digital natives," are also avid users of fintech.[19]

A survey from EY (2017) confirms that younger cohorts are driving adoption of fintech applications. Indeed, in a global sample of digitally active users, fintech usage is 48 percent among those aged twenty-five to thirty-four years, compared with only 9 percent for those seventy-five years and above. Fintech use is also higher in countries with a younger population, such as India, South Africa, and Colombia.[20] Conversely, Bech and colleagues (2018) find that the use of cash is more common in countries with older populations.

Trust in technology by different age cohorts may be a key factor. Bain & Company (2017) find in a survey that 91 percent of Indian respondents, 86 percent of Chinese respondents, and 60 percent of U.S. respondents would consider financial products from technology firms they already use, and that this interest is even higher among younger consumers (ages eighteen to thirty-four). In the past year or two, this trust in technology firms may have declined as a result of a series of high-profile data breaches and scandals ("techlash").[21] Similarly, business practices by fintech firms that are damaging to consumer welfare could in the future undermine trust in these providers.[22] Comprehensive data on the impact of these events on trust in technology or fintech are not yet available.

Once again, there may be exceptions to the trend of greater adoption by the younger generation. For instance, U.S. credit-bureau data show that a majority of online marketplace borrowers were actually from older cohorts ("Generation X" and "baby boomers"). Similarly, Baeck and colleagues (2014) find that over 55 percent of the lenders for U.K. business and consumer lending were age fifty-five and older, while over 60 percent of those receiving funding were in the age bracket thirty-five to fifty-four. Moreover, CB Insights (2018) identifies niche fintech firms that focus specifically on services for seniors, such as in personal financial management, estate planning, and home sharing. Especially in countries with an aging population, there may yet be further innovations targeting an older demographic.

Implications: Financial Inclusion, Competition, and Risk

While technological advances such as smartphones, cloud computing, and big data analytics are present in many economies around the world, greater *adoption* of these fintech innovations is concentrated in markets with several common characteristics. There are several implications for financial services.

First, where fintech helps to enhance financial inclusion – for example, for basic payments services in EMDEs – this is likely to be positive for economic growth and development. There is a large literature on the link between finance and economic growth.[23] There is also cross-country evidence that most indicators of financial inclusion are associated with higher growth.[24] Credit services are the only area where the picture may be more mixed. Fintech credit in particular may help to expand access to finance for SMEs. But if it results in excessive lending or overly high debt burdens for certain borrowers, this could be more problematic.[25]

Second, fintech activity could increase cross-border competition in financial services over time. While many fintech firms start by focusing on one country, there have been a number of examples of cross-border expansion, and of the imitation of successful fintech business models in different markets. Such cross-border financial integration could support greater diversification and risk-sharing across economies. It could also help to reverse some of the decline in cross-border financial activity seen since the global financial crisis.

Given differences in regulation across different markets and the potential for regulatory arbitrage, it is crucial that this cross-border expansion is accompanied by adequate cooperation between global regulators.

Third, while fintech innovations can sometimes overcome specific market failures (e.g., by reducing information asymmetries, transaction costs, etc.), fintech activities will remain subject to the same well-known risks traditionally present in finance. For instance, deposit-like activities remain subject to liquidity mismatch and the potential for bank runs, even when they are offered by nonbanks. New financial assets can still be subject to speculative bubbles, as was the case with Bitcoin in 2017–18.[26] If specific fintech or bigtech firms achieve a large enough scale, there is the potential for them to become systemically important ("too-big-to-fail"), resulting in moral hazard and excessive risk taking.[27] Finally, new forms of interconnectedness, including operational dependencies (such as reliance on third-party services such as cloud computing) could transmit shocks across institutions and markets. Managing these risks will remain the remit of public-sector authorities. Supervisors must continue to adapt regulatory frameworks and crisis-management tools accordingly.

Quite a bit of work still needs to be done to assess these findings. In particular, the quality of data across different economies, while improving, is still not sufficient to draw hard conclusions in many cases. More data are needed to test causality between economic drivers and fintech adoption.

Conclusion

Fintech activity is driven by a range of demand-side and supply-side factors. The available evidence shows that unmet demand (i.e., financial inclusion) is a strong driver in EMDEs and in underserved market segments. The high cost of finance and high banking-sector mark-ups are also important. Regulatory factors can play a role, but in general, regulatory arbitrage does not seem to be a primary driver of fintech adoption to date, at least at an aggregate level. There may be specific activities for which regulatory arbitrage is a factor. Finally, younger cohorts may be driving adoption in many economies, but population aging and changes in societal trust may have more ambiguous effects, shaping not just the extent but the future direction of fintech adoption.

Tentatively, the available evidence supports the idea that fintech adoption – where it enhances financial inclusion – may support economic growth in some jurisdictions, particularly EMDEs. It may also enhance cross-border financial integration. Yet fintech activities will remain subject to the same well-known market failures present in other areas of finance. As such, there is the same need for public policy intervention in the form of adequate and proportionate regulation and supervision.

NOTES

1 The views expressed here are those of the author and do not necessarily reflect those of the FSB, BIS, or DNB. All errors are my own. I would like to thank Michael King, Richard Nesbitt, Leonardo Gambacorta, and Raghu Rau for comments. I also thank Raghu Rau, Tania Ziegler, Thomas Philippon, and Guillaume Bazot for sharing data from their research. I thank Giulio Cornelli for support with data and figures.

2 FSB (2017) defines fintech as technology-enabled innovation in financial services that could result in new business models, applications, processes, or products with an associated material effect on the provision of financial services. Notably, this can include innovation by new firms, existing technology firms, and incumbent financial institutions.

3 Frost et al. (2019); BIS (2019).
4 World Bank (2018).
5 TransUnion (2019); see also U.S. Department of the Treasury (2018).
6 FSB (2019b).
7 Claessens et al. (2018).
8 FSB (2019a).
9 See Ben et al. (2018). The factors explaining city-level differences, including the role of existing industries, could be a very fruitful area of further analysis, drawing on the literature on regional economics. See Chinitz (1961).
10 World Bank (2018).
11 Ibid. At the same time, cash use remains quite high in economies around the world. See Bech et al. (2018).
12 World Bank (2019).
13 FSB (2019c).
14 Philippon (2016).
15 Petralia et al. (2019)
16 Evans and Schmalensee (2016).
17 Tucker (2019).
18 See also Kolodny (2016).
19 "Millennials" are generally defined as the generational cohort born between the early 1980s and late 1990s, following "Generation X" (born between the mid-1960s and early 1980s) and the "baby boomers" (born between the 1940s and 1960s). "Digital natives" refers to those consumers who grew up with digital technologies. See CGFS and FSB (2017).
20 EY (2019).
21 See Nair (2019).
22 For a discussion of consumer protection risks, see Saunders (2019). As she notes, "companies can also be innovative in how they increase their profits, deceive or abuse consumers, or avoid consumer protections" (p. 21).
23 For an overview, see Levine (2005).
24 Sahay et al. (2015).
25 CGFS and FSB (2017).
26 On the history of financial crises and asset and credit bubbles, see Kindleberger and Aliber (2011).
27 FSB (2017) notes that as a result of fintech innovations, "systemic importance and procyclicality could emerge from a number of sources, including from greater concentration in some market segments."

REFERENCES

Baeck, P., Collins, L., & Zhang, B. (2014, November). Understanding alternative finance: The UK alternative finance report 2014. University of Cambridge and Nesta.

Bain & Company. (2017). Evolving the customer experience in banking. https://www.bain.com/contentassets/ff8cd79182eb4cf197f3e47663bebe13/bain_report_evolving_the_customer_experience_in_banking.pdf.

Bazot, G. (2018). Financial intermediation cost, rents, and productivity: An international comparison. Working Papers 0141, European Historical Economics Society (EHES).

Bech, M., Faruqui, U., Ougaard, F., & Picillo, C. (2018, March). Payments are a-changin' but cash still rules. BIS Quarterly Review, 67–80.

Ben, S., Lv, J., Qian, X., Hu, K., Luo, D., Xu, Z., et al. (2018). 2018 global fintech hub report. Cambridge Centre for Alternative Finance and Zhejiang University Academy of Internet Finance.

BIS (Bank for International Settlements). (2019, 23 June). Big tech in finance: Opportunities and risks. BIS Annual Economic Report.

Braggion, F., Manconi, A., & Zhu, H. (2018, January). Can technology undermine macroprudential regulation? Evidence from peer-to-peer credit in China. https://www.bis.org/events/confresearchnetwork1909/braggion.pdf.

Buchak, G., Matvos, G., Piskorski, T., & Seru, A. (2017, March). Fintech, regulatory arbitrage, and the rise of shadow banks. NBER Working Papers, no. 23288.

CB Insights. (2018, December). 20+ fintech startups focused on seniors.

Cambridge Centre for Alternative Finance. (2017, December). Entrenching innovation: The 4th UK alternative finance industry report.

Cambridge Centre for Alternative Finance. (2019, April). Shifting paradigms: The 4th European alternative finance benchmarking report.

CGFS and FSB. (2017, May). Fintech credit: Market structure, business models and financial stability implications.

Chinitz, B. (1961). Contrasts in agglomeration: New York and Pittsburgh. The American Economic Review, 51(2): 279–89.

Cizel, J., Frost, J., Houben, A., & Wierts, P. (2019). Effective macroprudential policy: Cross-sector substitution from price and quantity measures. Journal of Money, Credit and Banking 51(5): 1209–35.

Claessens, S., Frost, J., Turner, G., & Zhu, F. (2018, September). Fintech credit markets around the world: Size, drivers and policy issues. BIS Quarterly Review.

de Roure, C., Pelizzon, L., & Tasca, P. (2016, 20 April). How does P2P lending fit into the consumer credit market? Working paper. http://dx.doi.org /10.2139/ssrn.2756191.

Duijm, P., Frost, J., de Haan, J., Bonner, C., & de Haan, L. (2019, July). International lending of Dutch insurers and pension funds: The impact of ECB monetary policy and prudential policies in the host country. *Open Economies Review 30*(3): 445–56. https://doi.org/10.1007/s11079-019 -09531-z.

Evans, D.S., & Schmalensee, R. (2016). *Matchmakers – The new economics of multisided platforms*. Cambridge, MA: Harvard Business Review Press.

EY. (2017, June). Global fintech adoption index 2017.

EY. (2019, June). Global fintech adoption index 2019.

Frost, J., Gambacorta, L., Huang, Y., Shin, H., & Zbinden, P. (2019). Bigtech and the changing structure of financial intermediation. *Economic Policy*, in press. https://doi.org/10.1093/epolic/eiaa003.

FSB (Financial Stability Board). (2017, May). Financial stability implications from fintech: Regulatory and supervisory issues that merit authorities' attention.

FSB (Financial Stability Board). (2019a, June). Decentralised financial technologies: Report on financial stability, regulatory and governance implications.

FSB (Financial Stability Board). (2019b, June). Evaluation of the effects of financial regulatory reforms on small and medium-sized enterprise (SME) financing: Consultation report.

FSB (Financial Stability Board). (2019c, May). FSB action plan to assess and address the decline in correspondent banking: Progress report.

FSB (Financial Stability Board). (2019d, February). Global monitoring report on non-bank financial intermediation 2018.

Hart, K. (1973). Informal income opportunities and urban employment in Ghana. *The Journal of Modern African Studies 11*(1): 61–89.

Hau, H., Huang, Y., Shan, H., & Sheng, Z. (2018). Fintech credit, financial inclusion and entrepreneurial growth. Working paper.

IMF. (2014). Global financial stability report, October 2014: Risk taking, liquidity, and shadow banking: Curbing excess while promoting growth.

Jagtiani, J., & Lemieux, C. (2018). Do fintech lenders penetrate areas that are underserved by banks? *Journal of Economics and Business, 100*, 43–54.

Kindleberger, C., & Aliber, R. (2011). *Manias, panics and crashes: A history of financial crises*. 6th ed. New York: Palgrave Macmillan.

Kolodny, L. (2016, July). Coming of age in the great recession: A millennial financial perspective. CB Insights Research Brief.

Levine, R. (2005). Finance and growth: Theory and evidence. In P. Aghion & S. Durlauf (Eds.), *Handbook of economic growth*, vol. 1, ch. 12: 865–934. Amsterdam: Elsevier.

Nair, S. (2019, April). Trust in tech is wavering and companies must act. Edelman Research.

Navaretti, G., Calzolari, G., & Pozzolo, A. (2017, 23 December). Fintech and banks: Friends or foes? European economy: Banks, regulation, and the real sector.

Petralia, K., Philippon, T., Rice, T., & Veron, N. (2019). The future of banking: Challenges and opportunities in an era of transformational technology. The Geneva Report.

Philippon, T. (2016, August). The fintech opportunity. NBER Working Paper No. 22476.

Rau, P.R. (2018, August). Law, trust, and the development of crowdfunding. http://www.fmaconferences.org/SanDiego/Papers/Rau_Law_Crowdfunding.pdf.

Reinhardt, D., & Sowerbutts, R. (2015, September). Regulatory arbitrage in action: Evidence from banking flows and macroprudential policy. Bank of England Working Paper No. 546.

Sahay, R., Čihák, M., N'Diaye, P., Barajas, A., Mitra, S., Kyobe, A., et al. (2015). Financial inclusion: Can it meet multiple macroeconomic goals? IMF Staff Discussion Note 15/17.

Saunders, L. (2019, March). Fintech and consumer protection: A snapshot. National Consumer Law Center.

Tang, H. (2019). Peer-to-peer lenders versus banks: Substitutes or complements? *Review of Financial Studies* 32(5): 1900–38.

TransUnion. (2019, 21 February). Fintechs continue to drive personal loan growth. Press release.

Tucker, C. (2019). Digital data, platforms and the usual [antitrust] suspects: Network effects, switching costs, essential facility. *Review of Industrial Organization* 54(4): 683–94. https://doi.org/10.1007/s11151-019-09693-7.

U.S. Department of the Treasury. (2018, July). A financial system that creates economic opportunities: Nonbank financials, fintech, and innovation. Report to President Donald J. Trump.

World Bank. (2018, April). The Global Findex database 2017.

World Bank. (2019, June). Remittance prices worldwide.

CHAPTER THREE

Banking and Finance since the Global Financial Crisis

Tiff Macklem[1]

Overview

Over the past dozen years, I have witnessed the transformation of the global financial system up close, first as Canada's G7/G20 finance deputy, then as the senior deputy governor at the Bank of Canada, and most recently as dean of the Rotman School of Management at the University of Toronto and chair of the Government of Canada's Expert Panel on Sustainable Finance. This chapter provides my perspective on the transformation of banking and financial services from these multiple perches. It starts by focusing on the extraordinary events of the 2008–2009 global financial crisis (GFC), the sweeping regulatory reforms that followed, and the importance of ethics and culture. It then considers the impact of new disruptive technologies and financial technology (fintech) start-ups on the industry. Finally, it examines the emerging role of financial services in addressing climate change.

The first driver of transformation was the crisis. The GFC toppled storied financial institutions and caused a Great Recession that destroyed millions of jobs and trillions of savings around the world. As a tenuous stability was re-established in 2009, thanks to extraordinary government guarantees, policymakers and supervisors from the G20 countries negotiated a far-reaching package of regulatory reforms designed to foster enduring stability and buttress the underlying financial infrastructure. These regulatory efforts have increased the safety and soundness of banks and have altered the competitive landscape. While most of these effects were intentional, the reforms may also be having some unexpected consequences, such as increasing the fragmentation and reducing the liquidity of global financial markets. The lessons from the crisis and the impact on the financial system are being reflected in business schools, affecting what we teach, how we teach, and the programs we are developing.

The GFC damaged the public's trust in leading financial institutions, whose failures of governance and risk management were at the heart of the crisis. Trust was further eroded in the following years as a series of ethical failures by employees at a growing list of global banks came to the fore, including price fixing, mis-selling, and facilitating money laundering. The resulting regulatory fines have been a major operating cost for the industry and even a prudential issue for some banks. The imperative to restore trust and avoid regulatory fines has led bank boards and CEOs to put an increased focus on culture. Compensation schemes need to be designed to discourage excess risk taking. And for everything that cannot be measured, there is culture. Culture and social norms influence what people do when nobody is looking. Business schools are putting increased emphasis on culture and ethics, while researchers in workplace psychology and organizational behavior are examining why people cheat and how to influence employees to take morally sound decisions.

The second driver has been technology. For anyone in banking, 2007 will forever be the start of the GFC. For anyone in technology, 2007 was the year Apple launched the iPhone, Google introduced its Android operating system, and IBM built the artificial-intelligence

(AI) computer Watson. Then two years later, the Bitcoin network was born, introducing blockchain technology. As banks grappled with the fallout of the GFC, thousands of new fintech ventures emerged, harnessing AI, blockchain, and other technologies to provide a better customer experience at a lower cost. Facing a new frontier of competition, banks woke up to the transformative potential of technology and began investing heavily to delight their customers and increase efficiency. This wave of fintech disruption is also having a profound impact on what and how we teach at business schools, with much greater emphasis on technology, entrepreneurship, and experiential learning. Rotman School of Management (Rotman) introduced and rapidly scaled our Creative Destruction Lab (CDL) program – a seed-stage program for massively scalable, science-based ventures – to accelerate the commercialization of science and educate a new generation of tech-informed business leaders.

The third driver is climate change. Banking and finance have been slower to embrace the challenges and opportunities of climate change than those of new disruptive technologies, but this issue is beginning to garner more attention. Climate change is already front and center in the property and casualty insurance business, which has been facing escalating damage claims as a result of the increased frequency of extreme weather events. For pension funds and other long-term investors, the possibility of stranded assets and the potentially pervasive long-term effects of climate change on the economy are increasingly being integrated into investment strategies. In banking, the response to date has generally been more tactical than strategic, but this too is beginning to change. As we look forward to the next dozen years, sustainable finance looks poised to become mainstream and integral to everyday financial decision making. Business schools have a responsibility to prepare the next generation of finance professionals to address new climate-related risks and seize opportunities to be a bigger part of the solution.

The U.S. Subprime Crisis Goes Global

Despite being more than a decade ago, 9 August 2007 remains a vivid memory for me. I was hiking on Gros Morne mountain on the west coast of Newfoundland with my wife and twelve-year-old daughter. It was a magical eight-hour hike, with hardly another soul to be seen, spectacular subarctic tundra underfoot, and stunning views of Western Brook Pond – the landlocked fjord off the back of Gros Morne. We arrived back at our car around 7:00 p.m. exhausted but inspired by the beauty and vastness of nature, and glowing in the aftermath of a fabulous shared family experience. Little did I know, it would be my last real holiday for the next two years.

As we drove into the nearby village of Rocky Harbour, my Blackberry came within range of a cell phone tower. A series of frenzied messages flooded into my inbox. Far away in New York, two hedge funds belonging to BNP Paribas that were overloaded with U.S. subprime mortgages had failed, and the U.S. financial markets were in turmoil.

By most accounts, 9 August 2007 is now seen as the first day of the global financial crisis. This fact only became clear with the benefit of hindsight, because the trouble initially appeared to be confined to the U.S. mortgage market and, more specifically, the smaller subprime mortgage segment. Table 3.1 provides a timeline of the GFC.

Through the fall of 2007, structured financial products, including mortgage-backed securities (MBSs), asset-backed securities (ABSs), and their related derivatives, became illiquid, and parts of the financial system froze. Faced with what looked like a liquidity crisis, central banks, led by the European Central Bank, the U.S. Federal Reserve (the "Fed"), and the Bank of Japan, sprang into action, flooding the financial system with liquidity. While this robust collective response had an immediate calming effect, volatility soon returned.

Table 3.1. Timeline of the global financial crisis, June 2007 to October 2008

DATE	EVENT
14–22 Jun 2007	Rumors surface that two Bear Stearns hedge funds invested in securities backed by subprime mortgages had incurred heavy losses.
10–12 Jul 2007	Two credit-rating agencies – Standard & Poor's and Moody's – downgrade large numbers of mortgage-backed securities (MBSs) and collateralized debt obligations (CDOs).
30 Jul 207	Germany's IKB is rescued by a group of public and private German banks following losses on U.S. subprime mortgages.
9 Aug 2007	BNP Paribas freezes redemptions for three investment funds. The European Central Bank provides unlimited overnight liquidity at its policy rate.
13–17 Sept 2007	U.K. mortgage lender Northern Rock is nationalized following a bank run.
11–23 Oct 2007	Moody's downgrades 2,500 subprime bonds issued in 2006, followed by a series of Standard & Poor's subprime downgrades in the following days.
12 Dec 2007	The U.S. Federal Reserve ("Fed") sets up U.S. dollar swap lines with four central banks and announces the Term Auction Facility to provide term discount window loans to banks.
15–31 Jan 2008	Citigroup announces $18 billion of write-downs on mortgage-related exposures. The rating agencies downgrade monoline insurers. The Fed delivers a 75-basis-point inter-meeting rate cut, followed by another 50-basis-point cut the next week. The ECB, the Fed, and Swiss National Bank carry out long-term funding operations in U.S. dollars.
11–16 Mar 2008	The Fed announces the Term Securities Lending Facility and the Primary Dealer Credit Facility. Faced with an acute liquidity shortage, Bear Stearns is acquired by JPMorgan.
13 Jul 2008	U.S. authorities announce measures to support Fannie Mae and Freddie Mac.
7 Sept 2008	Fannie Mae and Freddie Mac are taken into government conservatorship.
15 Sept 2008	Lehman Brothers Holdings Inc. files for Chapter 11 bankruptcy protection.
16 Sept 2008	The U.S. Reserve Primary money market fund "breaks the buck," triggering large fund redemptions. The U.S. government takes control of insurance company AIG.
19 Sept 2007	The U.S. Treasury announces a temporary guarantee of money market funds and releases details of a $700 billion Troubled Asset Relief Program (TARP).

DATE	EVENT
25 Sept 2008	U.S. authorities take control of Washington Mutual, the largest U.S. thrift institution.
29 Sept 2008	The U.K. nationalizes mortgage lender Bradford & Bingley. Fortis receives a capital injection from the Netherlands, Belgium, and Luxembourg. The initial TARP proposal is rejected by the U.S. Congress. U.S. authorities force the sale of Wachovia's banking operations.
30 Sept 3008	Financial group Dexia receives a government capital injection. Ireland announces a blanket guarantee on all deposits and the bonds of six Irish banks.
3 Oct 2008	The U.S. Congress approves the revised TARP. Fortis is nationalized. Wells Fargo announces a merger with Wachovia.
6 Oct 2008	German property lender Hypo Real Estate receives a government credit line.
7 Oct 2008	The US Treasury announces the Commercial Paper Funding Facility (CPFF).
8 Oct 2008	Six central banks announce a coordinated round of policy cuts. The U.K. government announces a comprehensive support package for U.K. banks.
9 Oct 2008	The Netherlands announces a capital injection for ING Bank and support for its banks and insurance companies. France announces debt guarantees for Dexia.
13 Oct 2008	France and Germany announce comprehensive support packages for their banks. The U.K. announces capital injections for HBOS, Lloyds TSB, and Royal Bank of Scotland.
14 Oct 2008	The U.S. Treasury announces $250 billion of TARP funds are to be used to recapitalize banks, and discloses capital injections for the nine largest U.S. banks.
16 Oct 2008	Switzerland announces a recapitalization and asset purchase scheme for UBS.
20 Oct 2008	The Netherlands announces a capital injection for ING Bank.
27 Oct 2008	The U.S. Treasury announces capital injections for seven U.S. regional banks.

Source: Factiva; company websites.

By early to mid-2008, what had at first looked like a *liquidity crisis* confined to the U.S. subprime mortgage market had morphed into a *solvency crisis* for a small number of global banks that had gorged themselves on U.S. subprime mortgages. Again, central banks and regulators moved quickly to rescue or resolve troubled institutions, including brokering the sale of Bear Stearns to JPMorgan in March 2008.

By the fall of 2008, the crisis had morphed again into a global *systemic financial crisis*. As the summer came to a close, the government-sponsored mortgage behemoths Fanny Mae and Freddie Mac were nationalized on 7 September 2008. A week later, on 15 September, the U.S. investment bank Lehman Brothers & Co. filed for bankruptcy after weekend negotiations coordinated by U.S. authorities failed to find a buyer. The crisis immediately went viral, taking down global banks on both sides of the Atlantic. Wholesale funding markets closed, precipitating a violent credit crunch and the worst recession since the Great Depression, later called the Great Recession.[2]

Faced with a global systemic financial crisis, governments of major countries did the unimaginable – they guaranteed all systemically important financial institutions (SIFIs). This extraordinary government support restored confidence in the financial system, and by the beginning of 2009, the focus of policymakers began to shift from *emergency response* to *reform*.

The Impact of Regulatory Reforms

By wide acknowledgment, Canada came through the financial crisis better than any other Group of Seven (G7) country. It was perhaps for this reason that I was asked – as Canada's finance deputy at the G7 forum and the Group of Twenty (G20) forum – to co-chair the working group charged with forging a consensus on recommendations to strengthen the regulation and supervision of the financial system.[3] At the April 2009 summit in London, England, G20 leaders agreed to a sweeping plan of action designed to:

- make banks safer;
- end the moral hazard problem of "too big to fail";
- ensure continuously functioning core financial markets; and
- transform shadow banking into a resilient source of market-based finance.

The G20 leaders called on the newly established Financial Stability Board (FSB) to rewrite the rules of global finance and oversee their consistent implementation.

A decade later, it is time to reflect on what has really changed in banking and finance. I tackle this question from a new vantage point now, as dean of Rotman. My perspective is part senior government official, part professor, and part someone who now has to "eat his own cooking" as a board member of an international bank.

The short answer is that the fundamentals of banking and finance and how we teach them have not changed. But sweeping regulatory and policy changes have significantly altered the competitive land-scape for banking. The system is safer as a result.

To make banks safer, regulators agreed to stronger capital, leverage, and liquidity requirements, collectively known as Basel III. This triumvirate introduces three potentially binding constraints, where there was really only one before the crisis – minimum capital requirements. The newly harmonized bank capital requirements have dramatically increased both the quantity and quality of capital. Banks in the United States and Europe have increased their common equity by more than $1.1 trillion from the lows at year-end 2008 to year-end 2016.[4] A Canadian-style leverage limit has been introduced, and new liquidity standards are in place, putting a new focus on high-quality liquid assets.

To end the problem of "too big to fail," the largest global banks are now subject to additional capital requirements and more intense supervision. Governments have new resolution powers, and banks are required to prepare living wills that enable the recovery or resolution of a bank over a weekend. Regulators have agreed to cross-border protocols to better manage the failure of a global bank. To protect taxpayers, new requirements for bail-in capital have been developed to allow a bank to be recapitalized by its creditors, without recourse to money from taxpayers.

To ensure continuously functioning core financial markets, many over-the-counter derivatives have been pushed onto exchanges, and new central counterparties are in place, with margin requirements to ensure finality of settlement. These changes provide an essential firewall to limit contagion when a counterparty comes under stress.

The shadow-banking fault lines that most contributed to the severity of the crisis have been addressed. New disclosure and skin-in-the-game requirements improve transparency and align incentives for securitized products. And potential spillovers from shadow banking into the core of the financial system have been reduced.

Taken together, these sweeping regulatory changes have made the system considerably safer. By historical standards, the reform has moved at light speed and benefited from nearly unprecedented international cooperation. The result today is a financial system that is more stable, with banks that are more focused on core banking. The fundamentals of banking may not have changed, but the business of banking has been substantially affected.

The following additional crisis-related regulatory standards have also recently come into force or have been slated for implementation:

- the International Financial Reporting Standards accounting standard, which changes the treatment of expected losses (IFRS9);

- the EU's second Markets in Financial Instruments Directive (MiFID II), which introduces new standards for pre- and post-trade transparency in the European Union;
- the Basel III Net Stable Funding Ratio; and
- the Fundamental Review of the Trading Book.

Regulators have imposed vastly higher expectations on banks to combat money laundering and terrorist financing, requiring banks to invest heavily in know-your-client (KYC) processes, analytic systems to monitor transactions and flag suspicious activity, and enhanced due-diligence and anti-money-laundering (AML) controls. These developments continue to absorb bank management and board attention, and require investments in people, technology, and processes.

In addition, new post-crisis issues are increasingly attracting supervisory attention. These include sales practices, cybersecurity, data privacy, and third-party risk management. Not surprisingly, many of the jobs created in banking in recent years have been in compliance, IT systems, and risk management.

Unintended Consequences on Financial Markets

The sweeping reforms may have had some unintended consequences. While many of the impacts have been intended, others have not. In my mind, two unintended consequences stand out: the fragmentation of banking and markets, and the potential for a decline in market liquidity.

After years of becoming more integrated across borders, the banking system and financial markets have become fragmented as national regulators seek to protect their citizens.[5] As a consequence, the ability of international banks to manage capital across their global platform has been reduced at the same time as capital buffers have been increased. Requirements by host regulators for more local capital have reduced the efficiency of capital allocation, imposing additional costs. Increasingly, host regulators also require more local people, systems, and governance. While this ring-fencing may make host regulators feel more secure, the resulting fragmentation not only reduces the efficiency of the financial system, it also undermines its systemic stability by mitigating the risk reduction that comes from diversifying across different geographies and economies.

Liquidity is more complicated still. While the evidence is mixed, it suggests that structural changes in the market may lead to reduced liquidity in times of stress.[6] A growing proportion of traded securities are held by large institutional investors and other large asset managers, for whom market making is neither a core business nor a core competency. This situation is compounded by the rapid growth of high-frequency traders (HFTs). HFTs have done much to narrow bid-ask spreads in normal market conditions, but they typically pull back as soon as markets begin to behave erratically. As a result, liquidity can go from abundant to scarce very quickly.

The impact of these structural forces is being amplified by their interaction with new regulatory requirements. New higher capital rules on the trading book have substantially increased the capital costs of market making at the same time as the entry of new players is reducing its profitability. Not surprisingly, global banks are pulling back from this activity.

The Volker Rule is a restriction on proprietary trading by banks operating in the United States, introduced as part of the 2010 Dodd-Frank Wall Street Reform and Consumer Protection Act. This rule came into effect in the summer of 2015 and has further discouraged market making. While the Volker Rule is a U.S. law, the strong extraterritoriality of this legislation and the U.S. penchant for large fines have effectively made it a global standard. And while there is an exemption for market making in U.S. government bonds, the complexity of the rule, the fact that the onus is on banks to prove a trade is in support of a customer, and the uncertainty around the interpretation and enforcement of the rule are all having a chilling effect.

The combined effect of these structural and regulatory changes is that market reactions to news are being exaggerated. This reduces the efficiency of the financial system and, in stressed situations, risks undermining market confidence affecting stability. My own view is that both the home-host balance and the Volker Rule deserve some refinement.

While the U.S. administration under President Trump has threatened to repeal the Volker Rule, the restrictions remain in place as of 2019, and repeal looks unlikely. Instead the U.S. Treasury has taken steps to exempt smaller institutions and to reduce the complexity of compliance. On the home-host balance, U.S. regulators during the Obama administration substantially increased expectations for foreign banks operating in the United States. This trend is showing no signs of being reversed.

Banks Discover That "Culture Matters"

For most people working in financial services, the moral failures of the industry are a painful topic. The evidence is compelling that weak culture and significant ethical failures were a key cause of the global financial crisis. Related to this, compensation schemes that delivered large bonuses for short-term returns encouraged excessively risky positions. They created incentives that led some individuals to commit stunning conduct failures. The actions by a small number of individuals have eroded public trust in banks and directed public anger at bankers.

Authorities responded with new regulations and stepped-up enforcement. The FSB developed and agreed new rules for sound compensation practices that align payouts with the horizon of risk. Banks have been investigated and prosecuted for conduct failures.[7] As shown in figure 3.1, the cumulative fines paid by North American and European banks from 2009 to 2016 exceeded $300 billion (G30, 2015; BCG, 2017). Of this amount, the fines paid to agencies of the U.S. government have totaled $150 billion, with the biggest payouts by Bank of America Merrill Lynch, JPMorgan Chase, and Citigroup – three of the largest U.S. bank holding companies.[8]

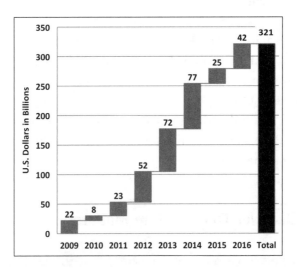

Figure 3.1 Penalties and fines paid by North American and European banks, 2009–2016

Source: G30 (2015), BCG (2017).

For some banks, the scale of fines and settlements has become a prudential issue. They have not been allowed to pay dividends until they restore their capital. For the entire banking sector, conduct-related fines and client litigation and redress have been a major operating cost and a key driver of weak performance. Not surprisingly, for bank executives, board members, and supervisors, *culture* and *conduct* have become big issues.

Culture creates social norms that influence what people do when nobody is looking. Few bank CEOs have survived revelations of significant conduct failures in their institutions, and for good reason. Culture starts at the top with the selection of the CEO, and it cascades down through the institution, supported by effective processes and reinforced by social norms. People respond to incentives. But compensation can only be designed with what you can measure. For everything else, there is culture. For bank management, boards, and supervisors, culture is increasingly seen as a valuable intangible asset that requires investment.

In business schools, the financial crisis and moral failures in financial institutions have attracted new attention to ethical issues. Courses in ethics have taken on new prominence. And researchers in workplace psychology and organizational behavior are studying what people do in banks, why people cheat, and how to influence employees to take morally correct decisions. Some of the results of this research are surprising. It turns out that there may be something special about banks.

Researchers have known for some time that people are more likely to act selfishly and lie when an interaction involves money than when it is strictly social. More recently, research by Rotman's Chen Bo Zhong and co-authors suggests that – independent of whether money is involved – people act more selfishly and are more likely to cheat when problems are reduced to numerical comparison (Wang et al., 2014). In other words, a "crunch the numbers approach" tends to reduce people's attention to the moral content of their decisions. Moreover, this appears to be related to how our brains work. Different parts of the brain specialize in different activities, and when people are working with the calculative part of their brain, they are less attentive to social and moral considerations.

These findings present a challenge for banks. Obviously, financial decisions involve money and extensive, deliberate calculations. As a result, employees working in banks are regularly put in situations where they are more likely to cheat. For anyone on the board of a bank, this finding is sobering, if not downright depressing.

But perhaps equally surprising, the research shows that reminding people of the social and moral considerations of decision making is effective in overcoming the situational effect caused by money and numerical calculations. So, for example, introducing a step in the process that reminds an employee that the customer is a real person – with a partner, children, parents, and friends – is enough to invoke the social part of the brain.

More generally, the research highlights the effectiveness of increasing people's attention to standards of honesty and integrity. Again, this result seems surprising. Don't people know what is honest and what is not? Of course they do; but humans are masters at rationalization. Common rationalizations include the following:

- Everybody is doing it.
- I am underpaid – after all the CEO is making 350 times my salary.
- This really isn't hurting anybody.

Rationalization reduces the psychological pain caused by cheating, making it more likely that the individual will commit an unethical act.

Fortunately, academic research also suggests that by making the ethical dimensions of a decision more explicit, companies can increase the likelihood that their employees will make the morally correct decision (Mazar and Aggarwal, 2011; Mazar and Hawkins 2015; Sharma et al., 2014; Shu et al., 2012 Wang et al., 2014).

This research is already having an impact. CEOs and leaders in financial institutions are spending more time talking about their values. Financial institutions are investing heavily in employee awareness and training, as well as processes to reinforce a culture of integrity and reduce conduct failures.

Teaching Future Finance Professionals

For anyone who invested heavily to learn finance at a leading business school, rest assured that all has not changed. The crisis and the ensuing reforms have not changed the fundamentals of modern finance, nor have they had a meaningful impact on what we teach in our foundational courses. But there has been a significant change in other aspects of what we teach and how we teach.

I cannot speak for all schools, but I suspect Rotman is representative of leading finance programs. The foundational courses continue to cover the enduring fundamentals of finance. But the more advanced courses have evolved considerably to cover financial crises, banking and regulation, and fintech. Courses in derivatives explain how to structure securitized products *and* how powerful incentives and market imperfections can generate large distortions. Understanding theory remains important – but with a greater emphasis on when it applies and when it doesn't.

The GFC has also led to the introduction of entirely new programs. The crisis underlined the catastrophic consequences of failed financial structures and systemic weaknesses in risk management. In response, Rotman launched a "Masters in Financial Risk Management" program that covers traditional financial risks – credit, liquidity, and markets – in depth, while also considering new regulatory, operational, and technology risks. Now that financial institutions are putting greater emphasis on risk management and compliance across all of their functions, the response to this new program has been strong.

The crisis is also having an impact on how we teach. Rotman is a leader in the development and use of interactive, market-simulation-based learning, in which students gain experience in trading and designing financial products on a simulated trading floor. Airline pilots practice flying on simulators before they are entrusted with the lives of passengers. Shouldn't we do the same in finance? Our students now test themselves in a range of situations, including rare events and the realization of unknowable or unforecastable risks. Simulation-based experiential learning provides students with the opportunity to gain valuable practice in taking decisions under uncertainty before they are entrusted with managing the savings of others.

Disruptive Technologies, Innovation, and Business Judgment

As large banks were grappling with the fallout of the GFC, a new frontier of fintech competitors emerged that was unencumbered by legacy assets or IT systems. Combined with their more entrepreneurial spirit, this new generation of fintech companies have innovated rapidly, applying AI, blockchain, and other new technologies to create new digital financial services that offer greater convenience at a lower cost. With lofty ambitions to disintermediate incumbent banks, fintech ventures proliferated rapidly into payments, trading, lending, asset management, insurance, risk management, and more.

But a decade into this fintech wave, a more cooperative landscape has emerged, with many fintechs partnering with large banks that are eager to catch up with new technologies. This is not the first wave of technological innovation banks have faced. And fintechs have discovered that customer acquisition is difficult. Even if people complain about their banks, they can be reluctant to trust their financial affairs to unproven new entrants. This situation has created a coincidence of wants: banks have customers, financial and regulatory expertise, and deep pockets, while fintech ventures bring new business models, new technologies, and a more agile, customer-centric approach to product development. The result has been a welcome acceleration of innovation in banking and finance, together with improved customer service at reduced cost.

The fintech revolution and, indeed, disruptive technologies more broadly are having a profound impact on what and how we teach in business schools. With a new generation of students who are increasingly interested in entrepreneurship, business schools everywhere are leaning into innovation. In finance, this is manifest in new courses and even new programs in financial innovation, including applications of AI and blockchain. But it is also being reflected in more experiential learning opportunities that immerse students in entrepreneurial experiences.

In Canada, many reports blame our long-standing innovation underperformance on the difficulty of accessing venture capital and the scarcity of specialized talent needed to scale new companies. Canada has leading scientists and inventors, but we have been less successful at commercializing and growing businesses based on their intellectual property. Too often, Canadian inventions are commercialized in the United States, with the economic benefits captured south of the border.

At Rotman our approach to innovation has been guided by a fundamental insight. Canada's serial innovation underperformance

reflects more than a paucity of risk capital or experienced entrepreneurs – fundamentally it reflects a failure in the market for
business judgment.

Most of what lies between an invention and a successful company
is business judgment. But buying business judgment can be difficult because the market is thin and new ventures lack the resources
to pay for it. The market for business judgment functions better
in Silicon Valley than anywhere else in the world. The concentration of technology experts, experienced entrepreneurs, global tech
behemoths, and venture capitalists maximizes the opportunities
for matches between demand (first-time entrepreneurs) and supply
(talent and investment).

To address this failure in the market for business judgment, Rotman launched the Creative Destruction Lab (CDL, the Lab) in 2012
to curate matches between promising science-based ventures and
highly successful entrepreneurs. The CDL is a seed-stage program
to develop and scale science-based ventures into global companies.
It focuses on providing the most promising scientists and technologists with access to the very best entrepreneurial business judgment.
CDL start-ups are mentored by highly successful entrepreneurs
through a structured, objectives-based program with a very clear
success metric: equity-value creation. The mentors' efforts are supplemented with support from Rotman's students, who provide the
founders with much-needed business and management capacity.
Students provide financial modeling, assess which market to enter,
help find pilot customers, and support the founders to grow and
scale their business. By working with these founders, the students
gain an incredible entrepreneurial experience at the cutting edge of
technology.

When the Lab was launched in 2012, the goal was to create start-
ups worth $50 million within five years. At 2019, the notional equity

value created by participating start-ups was $4.2 billion.⁹ The Lab has expanded from one Toronto-based cohort taking twenty-five technology-based ventures each year, to seven cohorts of twenty-five ventures each, spanning specialized streams, including AI, blockchain, smart cities, health, quantum computing, and space. The CDL has expanded to four major cities across Canada, and more recently to Oxford, England. We believe that increasing the supply of the scarcest input – business judgment – to the most promising technology-based ventures is critical to reaping the economic benefits of science and technology.

Sustainable Finance and Climate Change

As financial services companies enter a new decade, they face new expectations from shareholders, customers, employees, partners, governments, and regulators on their role in addressing climate change.

The effects of climate change are all around us. Higher average global temperatures and shifting weather patterns are amplifying floods, storms, heat, drought, and forest fires, leading to more frequent and extreme loss events. Even if the Paris Agreement to hold the increase in average global temperature to less than two degrees Celsius is achieved, severe weather events can be expected to become both more intense and more frequent. This outcome will put a premium on investments to adapt to climate change, as well as insurance to help manage new climate risks. Even larger investments will be required to decouple economic growth from greenhouse gas (GHG) emissions and achieve the Paris Agreement scenario.

Finance is not going to solve climate change, but it has a critical role to play in supporting the real economy in the transition to climate-smart growth. The emerging field of sustainable finance is

focused on channeling investment, financial-sector expertise, ingenuity, and influence toward the challenges and opportunities posed
by climate change.

The potential for sustainable finance to accelerate the transition
to low-carbon growth and help households and businesses manage
new climate risks is increasingly being recognized in a number of
jurisdictions, including the European Union, the United Kingdom,
and China. Major financial centers in these countries are beginning
to bring sustainable finance into the mainstream and have ambitions
to become global hubs in this market.

Canada's Expert Panel on Sustainable Finance, which I chaired,
delivered its final report in June 2019: *Mobilizing Finance for Sustainable Growth.*[10] The four-member panel's mandate was to engage with
a wide range of Canadian stakeholders on sustainable finance, to
articulate key challenges and opportunities, and to provide next-
step recommendations to the Government of Canada. Over fourteen
months we consulted widely in Canada, with hundreds of bilateral
meetings abroad, held eleven roundtables across the country, and
received fifty-seven written submissions.

The Final Report provides fifteen recommendations organized
around three pillars.

- The first pillar, *Opportunity*, focuses on identifying more clearly
  the size, scope, and horizon of the climate-smart savings and
  investment opportunities for Canadian households and businesses. It recommends that governments work with the private
  sector to develop a climate-smart vision, an associated capital
  plan for key sectors of the economy, and new tax incentives
  to make climate change part of Canadians' everyday savings
  decisions.
- The second pillar, *Foundations for Market Scale*, provides recommendations for growing and scaling the market in sustainable

finance and bringing it into the mainstream. These include providing:

- an authoritative source of decision-useful climate information;
- a mechanism for effective climate-related financial disclosures from businesses and asset managers;
- legal clarity around the climate-related obligations of investment fiduciaries;
- financial regulations that incorporate climate risks; and
- a climate-knowledgeable ecosystem of professional services providers.

- The third pillar, *Financial Products and Markets for Sustainable Growth*, focuses on the financing needs of sectors of the Canadian economy that are critical to the transition to low-carbon growth, including clean technology innovation, the oil and gas sector, infrastructure, buildings, and electricity generation and transmission.

For the financial services sector, the main message is that sustainable finance needs to go mainstream. Climate-conscious investment and risk management need to become business-as-usual in financial services and embedded in everyday financial processes, decisions, products, and services. This is not going to happen overnight, and in many respects the challenge to fund the transition to low-carbon growth and climate resilience is shared around the world. I expect climate change will be a defining challenge for at least the next two decades.

Business schools are seeing a growing demand from students for courses and programs in sustainable finance and sustainable business. Executives are also looking for education on the roles and responsibilities of directors with respect to climate change. We are only at the beginning in business school research and education at the intersection of climate change and finance.

Conclusion

Hiking in Newfoundland on 9 August 2007, I had no inkling of the enormity of the financial crisis that was little more than a year away. Artificial intelligence was something computer science professors were researching, and its widespread application looked far off. And I had never heard of blockchain. Needless to say, we need to be humble about our ability to predict the future. Nevertheless, let me conclude by looking ahead.

With the regulatory reforms following the crisis largely complete, supervisors are broadening their purview to cover a host of new risks, from anti-money laundering, to privacy breaches, to unethical sales practices and conduct. Without diminishing these new threats, they risk deflecting attention from the fundamental risks in banking. While history is littered with financial crises and each one is different, most share three common features: too little capital, excessive leverage, and heroic assumptions about liquidity. There will be another financial crisis. The longer it is in coming, the greater the risk that we will be forced to relearn the lessons of history.

Expect technology to reshape banking. Banks are already as much technology companies as they are financial intermediaries, and we are only at the beginning in applying new technologies such as AI and blockchain. While fintechs are emerging more as a vital part of the banking ecosystem than a competitive threat, large tech companies – Amazon, Facebook, or Tencent – are potentially much more daunting competitors. Unlike fintechs, they have billions of customers and deep pockets. Whether bigtech will successfully expand into banking will depend as much on banks as on these technology companies themselves. What is more certain is that banking has long been a scale business, and big data combined with AI and blockchain are rapidly increasing the returns to scale. As with many markets, expect to see more of a "winner-take-most" model in financial services.

The imperatives of climate change and the very large investments required to transition to low-carbon growth can be expected to bring sustainable finance into the mainstream. Indeed, within a decade, sustainable finance is likely to become simply finance. The sooner this happens, the better.

Looking ahead, the next decade in banking and finance looks to be no less transformational than the last. The global financial crisis, the stunning conduct failures, the impact of new disruptive technologies, and new climate challenges are a reminder that banking is just as much about people, culture, technology, and innovation as it is about finance. Banks have tremendous intellectual property and expertise in finance, and these resources will remain a core competitive advantage. But one thing looks certain: the future success of banks will demand a broader set of talents, skills, and behaviors.

NOTES

1 This chapter was completed in November 2019. I am grateful to my colleagues at Rotman for input and suggestions, particularly Alexander Dyck, Tom McCurdy, Alan White, and Chen-Bo Zhong. Special thanks to Michael King and Richard Nesbitt for their encouragement and support in writing this chapter. These views are my own.
2 For two comprehensive accounts of the global financial crisis, see: Sorkin (2009), and Geithner (2014).
3 G20 (2009).
4 Based on publicly listed U.S. and European banks reporting data in S&P Compustat. The figure compares the common equity of banks that existed at year-end 2016 with their levels at year-end 2008.
5 FSB (2019).
6 For a summary of research, see: U.S. Securities and Exchange Commission (2017).
7 FSB (2018). Accessed 31 July 2019.

8 Scannell (2017).
9 Alumni companies from the Creative Destruction Lab include: Thalmic Labs (Waterloo), Atomwise (San Francisco), Deep Genomics (Toronto), Nymi (Toronto), Automat (Montreal), Kyndi (Palo Alto), and Heuritech (Paris).
10 The Expert Panel's membership, Terms of Reference, the Interim Report and the Final Report can all be found at https://www.canada.ca/en /environment-climate-change/services/climate-change/expert-panel -sustainable-finance.html.

REFERENCES

BCG (Boston Consulting Group). (2017, March). Global risk 2017 – Staying the course in banking. http://image-src.bcg.com/BCG_COM/BCG-Staying -the-Course-in-Banking-Mar-2017_tcm9-146794.pdf.
FSB (Financial Stability Board). (2018, 23 November). Recommendations for national supervisors: Reporting on the use of compensation tools to address potential misconduct risk. http://www.fsb.org/what-we-do/policy -development/building-resilience-of-financial-institutions/compensation/. Accessed 31 July 2019.
FSB (Financial Stability Board). (2019, 4 June). FSB report on market fragmentation. https://www.fsb.org/wp-content/uploads/P040619-2.pdf.
Geithner, T.F. (2014), *Stress test: Reflections on financial crises*. New York: Crown Publishing.
G20 (Group of 20). (2009, 6 April). Reserve Bank of India. Report of G20 working group on enhancing sound regulation and strengthening transparency. https:// www.rbi.org.in/Scripts/PublicationReportDetails.aspx?UrlPage=&ID=549.
G30 (Group of Thirty). (2015, July). Banking conduct and culture: A call for sustained and comprehensive reform. https://group30.org/publications /detail/166.
Mazar, N., & Aggarwal, P. (2011). Greasing the palm: Can collectivism promote bribery? *Psychological Science, 22*(7): 843–8. https://doi.org/10.1177/09567 97611412389. Medline:21685379.
Mazar, N., & Hawkins, S.A. (2015, July). Choice architecture in conflicts of interest: Defaults as physical and psychological barriers to (dis)honesty. *Journal of Experimental Social Psychology, 59*, 113–17. https://doi.org/10.1016 /j.jesp.2015.04.004.
Scannell, K. (2017, 6 August). US haul from credit crisis bank fines hits $150bn. *The Financial Times*.

Sharma, E., Mazar, N., Alter, A.L., & Ariely, D. (2014). Financial deprivation selectively shifts moral standards and compromises moral decisions. *Organizational Behavior and Human Decision Processes, 123*(2): 90–100. https://doi.org/10.1016/j.obhdp.2013.09.001.

Shu, L.L., Mazar, N., Gino, F., Ariely, D., & Bazerman, M.H. (2012). Signing at the beginning makes ethics salient and decreases dishonest self-reports in comparison to signing at the end. *Proceedings of the National Academy of Sciences, 109* (38): 15197–200. https://doi.org/10.1073/pnas.1209746109. Medline:22927408.

Sorkin, A.R. (2009). *Too big to fail: The inside story of how Wall Street and Washington fought to save the financial system from crisis – and themselves.* New York: Viking.

U.S. Securities and Exchange Commission. (2017, August). Access to capital and market liquidity. https://www.sec.gov/files/access-to-capital-and-market-liquidity-study-dera-2017.pdf.

Wang, L., Zhong, C.-B., & Murnighan, J.K. (2014). The social and ethical consequences of a calculative mindset. *Organizational Behavior and Human Decision Processes, 125*(1): 39–49. https://doi.org/10.1016/j.obhdp.2014.05.004.

 CHAPTER FOUR

Data and Privacy in the Next Decade

Brian O'Donnell

Banks and other financial institutions continue to digitize their services, while finance technology (fintech) companies bring new applications to the digital marketplace. Both trends are growing the volume of personal financial data at an exponential rate. Digitized services drive greater effectiveness and efficiencies for customers (offering lower prices and faster and more convenient services). But they also expose clients to a higher risk of identity theft and fraud. The statistics paint a grim picture:

- In 2017, nearly 17 million Americans were victims of identity fraud.
- Nearly 7 percent of consumers become victims of identity fraud.
- Over 1 million children in the United States were victims of identity theft in 2017.
- It takes most victims at least three months to figure out that they were hacked, and about 16 percent don't find out for three years.

At the same time, individuals have digitized other aspects of their lives by utilizing mobile applications for everything from online shopping to ride hailing to entertainment. While such services improve efficiency in many aspects of our lives, they also expose us to ever-increasing forms of hacking and identity theft. And as we look forward to what World Economic Forum CEO Klaus Schwab terms "the Fourth Industrial Revolution,"[1] we can expect to witness a further acceleration of technology innovation in the coming years. Schwab foresees ever more connected devices and ever more advanced applications, all powered by and generating massive amounts of personal data.

Increasingly, industry experts and global think tanks are focusing on individual privacy rights and methods to protect our treasure trove of personal data. As a result, regulators around the globe are introducing new regulations to strengthen our privacy rights. In 2018, the European Parliament passed the General Data Protection Regulation (GDPR), a European Union law to safeguard individuals and enhance their rights to control their personal data. Back in 2000, Canada passed the Personal Information Protection and Electronic Documents Act (PIPEDA), which continues to be reviewed and strengthened periodically, in keeping with the continuing evolution of technology and personal data. The most recent set of proposals includes public consultations on a new Digital Charter for Canadians.

This chapter explores the ever-changing nature of cyber risks and digital applications. We examine how both regulators and industry participants are responding to these risks, as the speed of technological development makes this an evolving and difficult task. Further, we consider how the data marketplace has developed in a somewhat lopsided manner. Application developers capture most of the upside, and individuals are left with a higher risk of being hacked. We outline why the market for customer data will require significant change going forward. Finally, we consider new opportunities for the financial services industry in general, and retail banks in particular, as individuals come to realize the value and importance of their personal data.

Ever-Increasing Cyber Risks

Incidents of personal hacking and identity theft are growing at exponential rates. The nature of attacks has changed, and they are becoming increasingly sophisticated, ranging from credit-card take-overs to ransomware and botnet attacks. Virtually every citizen should assume they have been successfully hacked at one time or another, whether they realize it or not. As Margot Gilman of *Consumer Reports* says,[2] "[You] pretty much have to accept that criminals can get their hands on your personal information no matter what you do." Consider the following examples:

- the 2016 Dyn cyberattack, where hundreds of thousands of smart devices in private homes were unsuspectingly hijacked and used in a Distributed Denial of Service (DDoS) attack to bring down the Internet across most of the eastern United States;[3]
- the 2016 Yahoo report of two large hacks from previous years – in 2013 a shocking 3 billion accounts, and in 2014 more than 500 million additional accounts;[4]
- the 2017 Equifax hack, where personal information on 143 million Americans was stolen; and[5]
- the 2019 Desjardins Insurance theft, where an employee provided personal information on nearly 3 million Canadians to a third party.[6]

These examples are just a few of the numerous attacks that have penetrated large companies' security defenses in the past five years. It is little wonder that both companies and individuals are feeling increasingly vulnerable to cyber risks.

Recently, ransomware attacks have been on the rise. In a ransomware attack, hackers breach a computer or smartphone and threaten to release personal data unless the individual pays a ransom. Hackers are launching more sophisticated ransomware attacks against banks, companies, and government agencies to obtain private client data, either to hold for ransom or to enable direct personal attacks on citizens. The Facebook-Cambridge Analytica scandal demonstrated that even reputable companies may be selling customer data to third parties. These data are being analyzed and exploited in ways never contemplated by the users when they quickly scrolled through and accepted the "Terms and Conditions" of the application. This is a lopsided business model: all the benefits and power are held by the application provider, and individuals are left with most of the risk.

How Are Regulators Addressing These Risks?

Significant efforts and progress have been made to help individuals deal with this lopsided business model and evolving cyber risks. Lawmakers and regulators have introduced new laws and regulations to protect individuals. The most recent and highest-profile effort culminated in the European Parliament's passing of the General Data Protection Regulation (GDPR) in 2018. With GDPR, Europe has taken a lead position in codifying an individual's personal data and privacy rights, including the following:

- the right to clearly know and understand what data are being gathered from them and what those data will be used for;
- the right to be notified on a timely basis of any data breach (with the right to be compensated to rectify any damages);
- the right to be forgotten, which requires companies to delete an individual's data and cyber profiles upon request.

These regulations are backed by significant enforcement standards along with significant financial fines for noncompliance. While it is not clear that GDPR goes far enough in asserting individuals' ownership rights over their data, GDPR is a significant step in the right direction.

In Canada, cyber and personal privacy regulations continue to evolve. The Personal Information Protection and Electronic Documents Act (PIPEDA) was first enacted in 2000. PIPEDA regulates how private companies gather, use, and protect personal information. It requires the individual's explicit consent. It requires companies to have clear policies and standards to enforce these regulations. And it requires an individual within the company to be responsible for the protection of personal information. The PIPEDA regulations are updated at least every five years, with the May 2019 proposed updates focusing on "Strengthening Privacy for the Digital Age"[7] and establishing a "Digital Charter for Canadians."[8] The new proposals strengthen individual control, enable responsible innovation, and enhance oversight and enforcement rules.

While these proposals are a step in the right direction, it is not clear that government regulations are positioned to deal with the accelerating change that is ongoing in the digital marketplace.

What Is Industry Doing about These Risks?

As computers, smartphones, and other connected devices became widely used over the past forty years, cyber protection software has also been developed, often bundled into Internet and online banking services. Cybersecurity software has evolved over the years. It started with anti-virus software, which protected against computer viruses' being loaded via software and program disks in the old days, or via the Internet as e-mail or text message attachments more recently. A variety of viruses, largely developed to cripple a computer's operating system (such as the ILOVEYOU and Storm Worm viruses), were designed to take advantage of zero-day and other known security vulnerabilities, triggering a cyber race between the patchers and the hackers.

Just as computing capacity and capability have evolved, so viruses have become more powerful. Hackers have developed new types of attacks, including malware (malicious software) and ransomware. These viruses are designed for multiple purposes: to cripple a computer system, to steal passwords (for account takeovers), or to steal personal data and threaten its widespread release unless a ransom is paid. The use of ransomware has grown to be one of the most popular attacks by hackers over the past few years, driven primarily by the opportunity for financial gain. In response, cyber-defense software has expanded its capabilities to detect and delete known malicious software. Traditional firms such as Norton, McAfee, and Avast have all broadened their threat-detection software to deal with more sophisticated malware. Specialty firms such as Malware Bytes have developed strong protection against such advanced attacks. Each of these firms bundles its protection into services that optimize a computer and devices (for example, memory and storage capacities) and manage software and application updates.

Still, cybercrimes continue to proliferate. They range from simple credit-card-account takeovers to broader identity theft (say, to remortgage one's home). They have escalated to sophisticated botnet attacks (or a coordinated distributed denial-of-service attack). More sophisticated attacks result in breaches of companies, financial institutions, and government agencies. In such attacks, large swaths of personal information and data have been stolen and then used to attack individuals.

The financial services industry has seen many examples. In November 2015,[9] JP Morgan Chase suffered a breach that exposed the personal information of 83 million clients. In May 2018, both

Bank of Montreal and a CIBC subsidiary,[10] Simplii, suffered breaches affecting approximately 50,000 clients.

As a result of such breaches, individuals and companies feel increasingly vulnerable to cyberattacks and personal identity theft. Cybersecurity firms and insurance companies now offer a broad range of personal-identity-protection services and insurance as well. Such products offer a range of protection, from case management and legal support in dealing with identity theft, to covering financial losses (often with coverage of up to $1–2 million) in the event that one's identity is stolen and used for larger fraudulent transactions (say mortgaging or remortgaging of a property).

As an example of these broadening protection services, in 2018 the anti-virus software firm Norton bought LifeLock, a new personal-identity-protection and insurance firm. Norton now offers a fully bundled anti-virus, anti-malware, personal-identity-monitoring-and-remediation service, along with personal-identification insurance. The sad reality remains that most individuals are lacking the technical know-how to evaluate these ever-changing threats and protection services. Individuals may believe they are covered by their Internet service provider, or maybe their bank. They may buy this service for their home computer, but not their cell phone, their tablet, or the devices used by their spouse and other family members.

Some innovative technology companies are focused on cybersecurity. Apple, for example, has taken significant steps to enhance their client security features, building the iOS platform that has long been recognized for its strong security features. New companies, such as Canada's SecureKey, have applied new technology solutions, including blockchain, to enhance personal security. SecureKey is an interesting example, as they have partnered with financial institutions and the Canadian government to allow bank clients to use their account login and security features to access public services in Canada such as filing and paying taxes. SecureKey does this without holding customer information or sharing it across partners. Government agencies do not see a customer's financial information, and banks do not see what government services are being accessed. SecureKey is a great example of a new application development company that is advocating for individual privacy and utilizing the "Privacy by Design"[11] principles. Privacy by Design, an approach to systems and app development developed by Dr Ann Cavoukian of Ryerson University, embeds privacy principles into every stage of design and development.

The Arrival of Open Banking

The cyber world does not stand still. Network capacities are growing. New data-intensive applications are expanding (as can be seen with autonomous vehicles, the Internet of Things, sophisticated robotics, advanced health and well-being apps, etc.). These market developments will ensure that an individual's data footprint is growing for years to come.

Laws and regulations are adapting to this new reality. Open banking is a leading example of data regulation. It requires banks to provide application programming interfaces (APIs) to allow customers to share their financial transaction data with fintech companies or other third parties. The objective is to promote innovation and competition in the banking and payment-services industries, while also increasing data safety and security. The U.K.'s Open Banking Act and the European Union's Payment Services Directive II (PSD2) legislated open banking in 2018. This regulation is being studied in Canada and many jurisdictions around the world.

Today it is very difficult for an individual client, or a fintech firm offering a new service, to access the client's historical transaction data. Customers wishing to share their financial data have a choice between painstaking manual processes (such as screen scraping) or providing their bank user name, password, and security protocol answers to a data aggregation service (such as Quicken or Mint), which aggregates the data for them. Both arrangements breach cybersecurity best practices, and may violate the client's terms and conditions agreement with their bank, resulting in the potential for that bank to no longer backstop fraud and account-takeover losses.

Consider this example. Mary has two personal bank accounts, three credit cards from different institutions, a wealth-management account with a money manager, and a small-business account at another bank. Each month, Mary struggles to manually consolidate her financial position and transfer funds between accounts to minimize her bank service fees and interest expense. Year end is an even bigger nightmare, as she tries to consolidate her information for her accountant, on a timely basis, and rebalance accounts to optimize her interest expense and taxes going forward. From time to time Mary sets out to evaluate different offers from different banks. She considers consolidating her accounts but eventually loses enthusiasm for the task, as drudging through her statements causes even more confusion.

With open banking, Mary would likely be offered a much better service. A new fintech firm, perhaps called "FinCon," would offer Mary an automated financial consolidation and analysis service securely via an API to her different bank accounts. This service might work as follows:

- Mary signs up on the FinCon platform, providing permission for FinCon to access her bank, credit-card, wealth-management, and small-business data.
- Using a secure API connection, FinCon accesses three years of Mary's historical data, consolidates her accounts by month, and

provides easy-to-understand reports and recommendations to optimize her accounts.

- At year end, FinCon provides a standard template of critical data to her accountant, again including recommendations to optimize her finances.
- At any time, FinCon may also compare Mary's various accounts to competing services available to her, with a recommendation on how best to move and manage her accounts in order to optimize her service charges and interest expense.
- With millions of small-business customers, FinCon would be able to provide significant insights for Mary to optimize her business operations, including management of suppliers, inventory levels, and customer terms.

FinCon would provide these services by accessing Mary's accounts via open API programs with Mary's permission. This consent would allow FinCon to aggregate all of Mary's transaction records from these firms (along with competing banking offers from across the industry). It is expected that, in response to open banking regulations, financial incumbents would broaden and improve their services and customer offerings and reduce their fees in the face of heightened competition.

Of course, open banking raises safety and security risks, among other concerns. Today banks invest significant resources, time, and focus to ensure that their technology security levels are amongst the highest of any industry, and that a customer's personal information and transaction data are secure. Will fintech start-ups be in a position to provide this same level of data security? Will they actively protect client data? Or will they try and monetize it, as so many other application providers do? And will clients like Mary fully understand the risk that their data might be breached as they are transmitted and stored with new service providers?

In response to these questions, open banking proponents are focusing on user safeguards and remediation processes. In certain jurisdictions, open banking is seen as just a beginning. Australia,[12] for example, has legislated open data for the banking, telecommunications, and energy sectors, with future plans to provide access to health care data.

Personal Data Advocacy – A Retail Banking Opportunity

This chapter has examined two opposing forces. On the one hand, technological innovation is promoting a continued growth and proliferation of personal data. On the other hand, hackers, organized crime, and even some foreign governments are constantly innovating to find ways to steal our data and personal information for financial gain or political motives. These opposing forces present an opportunity for retail banks and other financial institutions. New legislation protecting data privacy (GDPR) and ensuring open banking (PSD2) creates an opportunity for banks to treat their client's personal data as a valuable resource, like money and financial securities.

Bank clients require a means to gather, "deposit," and secure their data assets. They need to provide a secure means for their fintech providers to "withdraw" these data assets for various uses – for example, to organize and optimize their financial affairs, to sell their data to third parties, to analyze their data for valuable insights, or perhaps to donate their data assets to a charity or social cause.

We call this new banking service *Personal Data Advocacy*. This service allows customers to gather all their financial and nonfinancial data in one safe and secure "personal data vault." The data are protected using bank-level security protocols such as multi-faceted authentication and encryption in transit and at rest. The bank helps the customers to view and treat their personal data as an asset, similar to cash and other investments entrusted to the bank for safekeeping. Using secure APIs and advanced data analytics, the bank could develop monetization, cybersecurity, and advisory use-cases for their clients. Further, we think this type of service would correct the current lopsided data business model, which creates billions of dollars of profits for application providers but increases cyber risks for individuals. *Personal Data Advocacy* is a logical extension of current trends in technological advancement and regulatory policy. It is time for banks to help their clients gather, store, secure, and thereby truly own their personal data, so that the benefits and value of the data flow back to the rightful owner.

Conclusion

Advances in information technology and mobile applications in the coming years present both risks and opportunities. While regulators are correctly focused on cybersecurity and individual privacy rights, they are also encouraging innovation and competition through open banking. It appears that the technology evolution will continue to outpace their efforts to protect consumers. This situation creates an opportunity for trusted intermediaries, including banks and insurance companies, to step into this void and support individuals as their lives increasingly migrate to data-intensive smart applications. A *Personal Data Advocacy* service would support individuals and their families by securing their data assets and asserting their ownership over their personal data. It would represent not only a great opportunity to enhance relationships with their clients but also a great business opportunity.

NOTES

1 Klaus Schwab. (2016). The fourth industrial revolution. Geneva: World Economic Forum, New York. https://www.weforum.org/about/the -fourth-industrial-revolution-by-klaus-schwab.

2 Hyshka, A., & McLaughlin, R. (2019, 28 August). Identity theft prevention insurance: Is it worth your money? CTV News, Vancouver. https:// bc.ctvnews.ca/identity-theft-prevention-insurance-is-it-worth-your-money -1.4559956.

3 Menn, J. (2016, 21 October). Cyber attacks disrupt PayPal, Twitter, other sites. Reuters. https://www.reuters.com/article/us-usa-cyber-idUSKCN12L1ME.

4 Perlroth, N. (2017, 3 October). All 3 billion Yahoo accounts were affected by 2013 attack. *New York Times.* https://www.nytimes.com/2017/10/03 /technology/yahoo-hack-3-billion-users.html?0p19G=2870.

5 Bernard, T.S. (2017, 7 September). Equifax says cyberattack may have affected 143 million in the U.S. *New York Times.*https://www.nytimes .com/2017/09/07/business/equifax-cyberattack.html?0p19G=2870.

6 Tomesco, F. (2019, 15 July). Desjardins expands protection plan for members after data breach. *Montreal Gazette.* https://montrealgazette.com /news/local-news/ desjardins-expands-protection-plan-for-members-after-data-breach.

7 Government of Canada. (2018). Strengthening privacy for the digital age. Innovation, Science and Economic Development Canada. https://www .ic.gc.ca/eic/site/062.nsf/eng/h_00107.html.

8 Government of Canada. (2019, 21 May). Minister Bains announces Canada's Digital Charter. Innovation, Science and Economic Development Canada. https://www.canada.ca/en/innovation-science-economic-development /news/2019/05/minister-bains-announces-canadas-digital-charter.html.

9 Crowe, P. (2015, 10 November). JPMorgan fell victim to the largest theft of customer data from a financial institution in US history. *Business Insider.* https://www.businessinsider.com/jpmorgan-hacked-bank-breach-2015-11.

10 Ligaya, A. (2018, 28 May). CIBC, BMO: Hackers may have accessed data of thousands of clients. CTV News. https://toronto.ctvnews.ca/cibc-bmo -hackers-may-have-accessed-data-of-thousands-of-clients-1.3948116.

11 Cavoukian, A. (2020, March). Privacy by Design: The 7 foundational principles. Ryerson University. https://www.ipc.on.ca/wp-content /uploads/Resources/7foundationalprinciples.pdf.

12 ACCC (Australia Competition & Consumer Commission). (2019). Consumer Data Right (CDR). https://www.accc.gov.au/focus-areas /consumer-data-right-cdr-0.

 CHAPTER FIVE

How "Open" Is the Future of Banking? Data Sharing and Open Data Frameworks in Financial Services

Markos Zachariadis

Data Sharing and Open Data in Finance

At its core, the financial-services industry is predominantly an information business. This is mainly because *data* are increasingly becoming the key ingredients and the basis for many of the products and services offered in finance. Data and information are often seen as a fundamental "asset" to stimulate competition and boost growth in the sector. From consumer and business banking, to payments, trading, wealth management, investment banking, and insurance, data are being used not only to maintain financial ledgers and facilitate effective communication of trade and payment instructions but also to assess risk, manage finances, forecast market movements, and optimize portfolio management. As a result, access to and sharing of data can provide significant advantages to players in the industry and change the shape of competition in financial services.

This realization – around the significance of access to data and information – has led many institutions in the various subsectors of the finance industry to invest heavily in information and communication technologies (ICTs) with the hope that they will gain a competitive edge through utilizing data for better money management, cost-effective operations, new product development, and customer acquisition. However, this hasn't always been the main focus. Traditionally, investments in financial technologies have been seen as ways to increase operational efficiencies and cut costs. For example, during the 1950s and into the 1980s, banks sought to deploy mainframe computers to mechanize record keeping and facilitate more efficiently a multitude of transactions (Bátiz-Lazo et al., 2011).

At about the same time, globalization gained momentum and international trade flourished, leading to the emergence of financial telecommunication infrastructures and the creation of messaging standards that allowed corresponding banks to automate data processing (i.e., straight-through processing), reduce manual interventions, and speed up their operations (Scott & Zachariadis, 2012, 2014). In the 1990s, as technology was becoming cheaper and personal computers were deemed more accessible, banks increasingly digitized their processes, aiming to minimize paper-based tasks. The penetration of the Internet also allowed for the development of digital networks and the creation of new communication channels internally and with customers.

While the above efforts were necessary steps in order to achieve better results and provide the pillars for future financial services, the recent revolution in financial technology (fintech)[1] has forced conventional players to reconsider their technology (or digital) strategy and focus more on redesigning processes, rethinking value creation, and monetizing data assets. It's a bit ironic to think that these investments in information technologies (IT) – now called "legacy" infrastructures and old-generation IT – are considered a barrier to digital transformation and one of the reasons incumbent financial institutions find it difficult to adapt to the new technological regime in finance – especially when it comes to the implementation of modern data-access technologies.

In the context of this new wave of "digitalization,"[2] the finance industry has witnessed an increase of data sharing within and across financial institutions, aiming to accommodate solutions that demand a combination of data points residing at different systems. While data sharing in finance can be traced back to the use of inter-organizational financial systems and electronic data interchange (EDI) networks[3] that enabled bilateral data feeds, more recent technologies such as *screen-scraping* (to be discussed later) and *application programming interfaces* (APIs) are being used systematically by financial institutions and fintechs to enhance data-sharing opportunities and explore new possibilities in service development.

The Role of Application Programming Interfaces

An application programming interface (API) is a technology or a set of instructions that allows two systems or computers to "talk" to each other over a network (most usually the World Wide Web or the Internet) using a common data standard. APIs published by a provider are usually accompanied by documentation that specifies their functionality, business use, uptime, constraints, legal implications, etcetera. For that reason, they can also be understood as a contract to engage in a particular relationship or consume a service.[4] APIs have gained significant momentum over the last couple of decades in the technology sector, but also beyond it. They have become the de facto standard for sharing data and enabling communication between colleagues, partners, or third parties. This is largely because they are scalable, secure, and standardized and for that reason can be reused in different settings with very little cost of development (Jacobson et al., 2012).

Initially, the use of APIs in banking was limited to private APIs that were exclusively available to internal staff and "clients" within the boundaries of financial institutions. Such "closed" APIs are often used to unlock the data resources of the organization and try to break data silos, utilizing data in new applications and systems while helping the business run better.

APIs are not restricted to internal or closed. They can also be conceptualized as "boundary resources" that establish simplified and standardized connections beyond the organization and with selected partners or groups of authorized third parties (Ghazawneh & Henfridsson, 2013). This approach offers the possibility for open innovation and the development of an ecosystem of third-party providers (TPPs) who can design and deliver new products.

In payments, such "open" or "external" APIs, have been used by card networks like VISA and MasterCard to integrate their infrastructure with selected e-commerce partners (e.g., VISA Checkout), providing a better customer experience online, or to offer more functionalities in mobile applications such as in-app purchasing (e.g., Masterpass API). Paypal and Amazon Payments have both been running a program for developers who are keen to implement their services.

Banking institutions have also used external APIs to extend their reach to other platforms and increase their sales by enabling authorized third-party access to some of their services (e.g., money transfers, credit functionality, etc.). Several such examples exist in Europe, North America, Africa, and the Asia Pacific, ranging widely based on the level of access and control they provide to their infrastructure and on which third-party providers they allow to use it. For instance, challenger banks, such as Starling Bank in the United Kingdom and Fidor in Germany, have used external APIs aggressively to open up a very wide range of functionality to third parties and are engaging with independent developers to enrich their API platform. BBVA, an incumbent bank in Spain, was also one of the "first-movers" to provide a developer's portal and authorize third-party providers to access its money transfer and other services.

As a general rule, the Euro Banking Association (EBA) distinguishes between "closed" and "open" APIs in banking and provides a spectrum of *open APIs* based on their level of *openness* to third parties (EBA, 2016). This spectrum ranges from "partner" APIs accessible only to banks' preferred partners and developers, through to "public" APIs that are available to anyone (typically after some form of basic registration) (see figure 5.1).

Open Data versus Open Standards

The United Kingdom's Open Data Institute (ODI) provides a similar categorization around data accessibility in the banking sector, ranging between closed, shared, and open data. Based on their interpretation of *open data* as "data that anyone can access, use or share" (ODI, 2016), they highlight that an *open API* does not imply access to open data but rather can be used in closed environments (to facilitate access to sensitive data internally within an organization) or shared infrastructures (to give access to particular group members following authentication or larger populations subject to license that limits use). Using this definition of open APIs, it implies that "open" here refers mostly to the *open standards* of the API technology, data formats, and even security arrangements used to design APIs (and regulate access) rather than the measure of accessibility of these APIs (the two of them often correlate, and this frequently is a source of confusion). As we discuss below, open-standard APIs can be a key enabler for data sharing in the industry, as they are commonly accepted and easily reused.

Nevertheless, the characterization of *openness* and classification of interfaces shouldn't be limited to the accessibility point of view (i.e., who has access to APIs) or to the open-standards classification. One can also measure openness and classify APIs in regard to the number and modes of interactions they can offer. For example, the type

Figure 5.1 From private to public – spectrum of API openness based on accessibility

Source: EBA (2016)

and range of data a third party can access through an API would also signify how open an organization is to the "outside world." In that sense, a "rich" API would incorporate much more data (both in terms of number of variables and period of time) and potentially offer more opportunities for new functionalities.

Another useful distinction is between *read-only* APIs that only allow read access to data, and *read/write* APIs that permit users to also make amendments and edit records at the location where the data reside. The latter characteristic can make a significant difference in the way third-party developers can use these to facilitate new products and services. A typical example in banking that utilizes read/write APIs is that of the "payment initiation," as this requires a new entry on the original database to update the ledger containing the account information of the customer (e.g., the customer's balance, list of transactions, etc.). Table 5.1 provides a comprehensive list with the various dimensions of API openness that should be considered when drafting a data-sharing framework in banking.

Table 5.1. Dimensions of API openness in open-banking frameworks

API accessibility	How accessible are the data being shared? Who can access the APIs (e.g., private customer, partners, members, acquaintances, public)?
API functionality	What categories of data are being shared and what is the level of granularity? How open are these data and how widely can they be shared?
	How many APIs are there and what functionalities/services do they offer (e.g., read-only APIs for Account Information, read/write APIs for Payment Initiation, etc.)?
API usage	How much data can the APIs communicate and how quickly (e.g., bandwidth of the infrastructure and how resilient it is)?
Open APIs	Are open standards used for data sharing (this includes API, data, and security standards)?
Alternative APIs	Are diversified data and technologies (e.g., social media and private data, sensor and mobile technologies, etc.) leveraged to provide better access to financially excluded populations?

The Move to Open Banking

While open access to data provides numerous benefits to the surrounding ecosystem and creates value for end customers, hoarding data for exclusive use can offer significant competitive advantages to a single organization, or a narrow group of organizations, leading to a monopolistic environment.[5] This setting is very common in several banking markets globally. These information asymmetries due to poor availability of meaningful information more often lead to poor market outcomes and are an effective barrier to competition. Ultimately, end customers may be missing out on opportunities to access new and innovative services, as there is less of an incentive to innovate in the sector and create meaningful product differentiations.

In principle, information asymmetries may also lead to a lack of transparency for both prices and quality of services, as there is little prospect for consumers to compare across different providers. An independent study commissioned by the U.K. government seemed to confirm the above negative outcomes for both competition and consumers in the banking sector, a finding that opened the discussion for regulating further data sharing (ODI & Fingleton Associates, 2014).

Data Screen Scraping

At the same time, there has been a strong demand for data access from alternative financial-services providers such as payment-services providers, alternative lenders, financial-advisory and comparison services, accounting-software firms, and even technology companies (fintechs and large tech firms alike). These providers aim to gain advantage and extract considerable value from financial data. To satisfy their demand for data and because of the lack of banking

APIs issued by banks, many third parties started utilizing alternative methods to access information directly from banks through digital interfaces and electronic channels such as online banking websites and mobile applications. This practice, known previously as *data scraping*, became quite popular, leading to an entire market of *screen-scraping* providers (e.g., companies like Yodlee) that offered data-extraction services through "automated, programmatic use of a website, impersonating a web browser."[6]

This screen-scraping approach can be quite effective in allowing third-party providers to mediate activity on behalf of end users, enabling them to perform actions, including accessing information, that they would normally do manually on the online banking website. Screen scraping has been criticized severely by incumbent banks, as it requires customers to give up their log-in credentials (e.g., usernames, passwords, piece of memorable data, etc.) and trust them to the third party. Whereas it is obvious that sharing and storing users' credentials may pose risks (mainly for users but also for the data-scraping service providers), fintechs, third-party providers, and data platforms that benefit from this practice continue to defend their position by showcasing the use of encryption and other security measures while also blaming banks for delaying or refusing to share data through APIs. The extensive application of screen scaping as well as the discussions around its legitimate use in banking have generated one of the most heated debates in finance and effectively brought the case of data sharing forward and to the attention of many stakeholders in finance – *open banking* had already begun!

The Push for Systematic Data Sharing

Considering all of the above, a number of economies around the world set out to explore opportunities around greater, more methodical, and more secure sharing of data in the banking sector and other areas in finance. It was soon acknowledged that a well-formed and effective data-sharing framework would help to achieve many positive outcomes in the sector, such as:

a) the enhancement of competition and lowering of barriers to entry for new entrants;
b) access to better and cheaper products and services for consumers;
c) access to more innovative services; and
d) improved financial inclusion for end users, especially those who struggle to get access to the current financial system (both people from less privileged backgrounds and SMEs that have little or problematic history and that do not satisfy the existing banking access criteria).

Some regulators have also stressed that the customer data held by banks are inherently the customers' data, and thus there must be a systematic way to access and share with third parties they consider beneficial.

Even though there is a general consensus in different parts of the world about the need to carry out the above mandates, these have been dealt with differently by an assortment of public- and private-sector data-sharing initiatives – each with their own approach to consumer access and control over data and digital identity. At a basic level, a data-sharing model should provide for a way to collect and/or create individuals' personal data and give them the opportunity to decide whether and how these data will be shared to third parties safely (Mazer, 2018).

One barrier to this data-sharing effort is the absence of a commonly shared definition of open banking. One can define an open banking framework as follows:

> A secure and standardized technology that, when coupled with rules and procedures, allows consumers to safely create, share, or amend their

financial digital records (e.g., transaction data, payment initiation, identification data, etc.) with authorized third parties offering products and
services.

The above working definition, while not complete by any means,
highlights some of the fundamental characteristics of open banking. One of its key features, based on the explanation above, is that
it creates the platform or infrastructure upon which other participants can build valuable products and services that will make
consumers' lives better. In that regard it resembles the Internet,
upon which valuable software applications sit. In addition, it provides a standardized interface (most commonly an API) that facilitates the connections between various actors participating in the
licensed consortium of firms. Such an interface would normally
sit on top of a common rulebook and technology stack used by
the entire market and would include important components such
as the following:

- a security protocol so that it can be ensured that consumers'
  data are protected;
- an identification framework in order to establish the identity
  and legitimacy of the party on the other end of the interface;
  and
- a consent mechanism and permissions dashboard to verify consumers' agreement to the data-sharing activities and allow them
  to withdraw if agreement is not forthcoming.

The complexity of all the above often creates confusion and mis-
understandings around how an open-banking framework would
function and treat consumers' data. For that reason it is useful to
include a list of what open banking isn't and dispel some common
myths.

The Top Five Open Banking Myths Busted

Myth 1: "Open banking means everyone
will have access to my data!"
Open banking is a consensus-based and opt-in system that can only be triggered if a consumer agrees to give access to their data to certain authorized entities. Consumers can revoke their consent at any time if they choose, and the third party accessing the data will need to delete all the customer information held.

Myth 2: "In order to use open banking I will
need to share my username and password."
No customer will need to share log-in credentials with any of the third parties that seek access to their data. This is the key strength of open banking, making it safe and secure for consumers, unlike other methods such as screen scraping.

Myth 3: "Open banking is a product that
consumers can use."
Open banking is only an enabling technology, not a product or service. It does not deliver propositions to consumers, which come from third-party providers.

Myth 4: "Open banking is new."
Data sharing in banking has been evolving for at least twenty years. One of the reasons regulators have started thinking about it in a more systematic way is that the business models established around open banking and the value for customers by enabling better data sharing were deemed quite significant.

Myth 5: "Open banking is all about APIs."
Certain regulatory frameworks such as the European Union's Payment Services Directive II (PSD2) do not even mention APIs. An API

can never be a business strategy but is only an enabler. One needs to be thinking clearly with a business opportunity in mind centered on the customer – it is entirely customer-centric.

Open Banking Paradigms

U.K. Open Banking

The United Kingdom has been one of the proponents of open banking globally and the first country in the world to consider such a regulatory move in 2011.[7] As such, open banking has been hotly debated between the various stakeholders, consuming a massive amount of political capital in the discussion of its merits, risks, and impact. As early as 2014, the U.K. government commissioned a report that concluded that "greater access to data has the potential to help improve competition in UK banking" (ODI & Fingleton Associates, 2014). The report recommended standardizing bank APIs to allow third parties such as fintechs, developers, and corporates to connect to and access customer data.

An official market investigation by the U.K. Competition and Markets Authority (CMA) confirmed that certain features in the U.K. banking market distorted competition and left banks with "unilateral market power over their existing customer base," leading to a lack of innovation as well as expensive and poor-quality services (CMA, 2016). To remedy this situation, the CMA instructed the creation of an implementation entity – the Open Banking Implementation Entity – to drive the development and delivery of the "open and common banking standards for APIs" in close collaboration with the industry (CMA, 2017).

Given the desire to promote innovation and competition, the CMA order focused initially on the nine largest U.K. banks, which were also called to cover the costs for the development and deployment of the infrastructure. Open banking was also supported by pressure around consumers' rights to their data and around the security and data-privacy risks inherent in data-sharing processes such as screen scraping and card-on-file transactions.

In general terms, the United Kingdom's Open Banking mirrors the European Union's directive on payment services (PSD2)[8] and thus borrows the same kind of regulatory definitions. Having said that, U.K. Open Banking has a few unique characteristics that make it stand out from open banking in other jurisdictions. Firstly, it sets out a single open standard for APIs that provides the specifications that "inform the design, development, and maintenance of an open API" (Payments Forum UK, 2015). Secondly, it provides a governance structure that oversees the standards, ensures that the requests of all stakeholders are addressed, and establishes trust and confidence in the ecosystem. Finally, it owns and maintains a directory of all open banking participants (the "whitelist"), which uses digital certificates to authenticate third parties. Open banking regulation in the United Kingdom went into force in January 2018, triggering a "managed roll out" that had to be met until September of 2019.

European Union Payment Services Directive II

In October 2015, the European Parliament passed new rules to create more innovative payments in the European Union, known as Payment Services Directive II (PSD2). This regulation went "live" in January 2018. The PSD2 is a role-based framework aiming to promote the emergence of new payment-service providers, such as fintechs, and encourage innovative Internet and mobile payments across the European Union. PSD2 uses a licensing structure to enable account-servicing payment-service providers (ASPSPs), such as banks and building societies, to allow their customers to share their data securely with their authorized TPPs without the need of contractual relationships. Third-party providers are generally either account information service providers (AISPs) providing consolidated information on a user's payment accounts, or payment initiation service providers (PISPs) offering an online service to initiate a payment order as requested by the user.[9] PSD2 allows actors to fulfill more than one role. A bank can send out the payments data and can also switch sides and become a third-party service provider that requests access to outside customer data.

As mentioned above, PSD2 does not explicitly require banks to use APIs in order to fulfill their obligations to share customer data. Nevertheless, read/write APIs are deemed the best way forward to access account-information and payment-information services. To facilitate a safe and secure "access to account," the European Banking Authority (EBA) developed a set of Regulatory Technical Standards designed to reduce payment fraud and data bridges. This so-called Strong Customer Authentication mechanism is a form of two-factor authentication designed to prove that end users are who they say they are. PSD2 and the EBA's Regulatory Technical Standards apply to all banks and other ASPSPs across the European Union.

Australian Consumer Data Right

In November 2017, the Australian Government announced the introduction of a Consumer Data Right (CDR) in Australia, heralding the phased-in introduction of open banking from July 2019 onwards.[10] The Australian approach to open banking is different from that of its precursors in Europe. While U.K. Open Banking and EU PSD2 are focused more on competition, Australia's starting point was increasing consumer choice by giving consumers the right to access and share their data seamlessly with third parties. This permitted Australia to take a broader view of data sharing and expand it beyond banking into the telecommunications and energy industries.

While Australian open banking shares quite a few basic principles with other data-sharing movements in banking – such as consumer-centricity; promoting competition; creating opportunities for more, better, and cheaper services; and introducing a safe and fair environment – its major differentiation is that it only allows for read access to data. This means effectively that the regulation does not support payment initiation. In addition, the Australian model handles liability and data-sharing obligations differently. For example, it imposes reciprocal obligations to share data, and liability is more straightforward.

Similar to the other schemes, the Consumer Data Right bill mandates that it "is a right for consumers to choose to safely share their data with accredited, trusted recipients [and] it is not a right for businesses to share consumers' data without their consent" (Australian Government, 2018). In Australia, all authorized deposit-taking institutions (ADIs) are mandated to comply with these data-sharing rules. The framework was scheduled to go into force in the finance sector in July 2019, with consumer data for mortgage accounts, credit and debit cards, and deposit and transaction accounts to be made available by 1 February 2020. The Consumer Data Right is implemented by the Australian Competition and Consumer Commission, which also administers accreditation for participants. Other regulatory bodies are also involved in overseeing different parts of the regulation.

Key Issues for Developing an Open Banking Framework

Nature of the Mandate

One of the most critical decisions that needs to be made around the design and implementation of an open banking framework is how it is introduced. Will it be a legal requirement mandated by the regulator or a voluntary scheme led by the private sector? Evidently, this choice is going to affect the speed and extent to which data openness will happen in the sector. A mandated framework combined with a convincing public-relations campaign advertising the potential benefits for consumers can go a long way in making open banking a reality. Having said that, a government-mandated policy can be slow to draft, introduce, and enforce, especially if the mandate is broad and involves several industries. A private-sector-led initiative can be more flexible and adopt novel approaches to standards and data sharing that are harder to draft. In the latter scenario, the incentives to adopt would be triggered by competitive forces rather than regulatory compliance. In either case, it is important to figure out the level of involvement from the industry and/or the public sector in designing and running the infrastructure and maintaining standards as well as covering the costs.

How Open?

The level of API openness is arguably one of the most significant concerns or debates regulators may have when drafting a regulatory framework for open banking (see table 5.1 above, showing the different dimensions of openness for open banking). As expected, openness may be impacted based on the nature of the mandate. This question is less of a concern in the case of private-sector-led, voluntary data-sharing models.

The Liability Issue

One of the main reasons governments and regulators may choose a mandatory data-sharing rulebook is related to issues around the legal obligations between the different entities that handle customer data. In an open data-sharing environment, one should be able to answer questions such as, "How do we compensate the customer in case something goes wrong?"; "How do we know the customer consented to having their data shared?"; "How do we know which entity lost the data?," and so on.

According to PSD2, in the payments use-case it is always the bank that will make the customer whole in the first instance. The bank will then have the opportunity to turn to the fintech and challenge them for the wrong practice (e.g., a false payment or a mistake). For this reason, PSD2 requires fintech and third-party providers to have liability insurance in place in order to be able to pick up the costs of fraudulent payment initiations. The insurance companies under contract will not pay out unless liability can be established. Taking this into account, any regulator who is keen to put forward a framework of a workable open banking regulation will need to start from that position.

A solid directive will need to be able to assess and trace who the "bad actor" was in the chain, as there may be multiple actors holding the customer's data. For example, in the PSD2's "Account Information Services" space, the liability model is reversed. When the data have been transferred to a regulated actor and now reside in their system, it is the regulated actor, not the bank, who has to make the customer whole if the data are breached and something goes wrong. The bank's obligations are satisfied as long as they have fulfilled two key conditions: firstly, the data must be communicated with a regulated actor, and secondly, they have to make sure that the end customer consented to the data move.

Identification of Third-Party Providers

Unavoidably, the issues around liability discussed above raise questions around the identification of actors in this open-data ecosystem. Providing data access only to regulated parties requires the establishment of a company registry (or central directory) to identify legitimate actors and hold information on their credentials and status. Being on that regulated list will allow parties to claim access to the customer data. If, for any reason, any company on the registry is in violation of data-sharing rules and requirements, they can simply be "unplugged" from the market by having their directory permission removed until they fix the problem.

In the United Kingdom, the central directory is handled and maintained by the Open Banking Implementation Entity. Account providers such as banks, building societies, and payment companies are then enabled to verify the identity of regulated third-party providers. Unfortunately, this approach has not been implemented systematically across the European Union. Some private fintech companies are currently trying to fill this gap. Building identification infrastructures can be quite challenging, especially for maintaining data quality, but it is a pivotal step in the proper functioning of the framework and risk management (Millo, Panourgias, & Zachariadis, 2019).

Digital Identity

Similar to third-party-provider identification, an integrated digital identity for consumers is also important to enable open banking to successfully identify customers and get their consent. Consolidating the digital profiles of an entity (either a consumer or a corporate client) can allow for a secure and unified authentication experience. While a complete digital identity solution (i.e., a reference data standard, unique identifier, or address, etc.) may not be directly provided by the open banking system, this capability should be made available through a "ubiquitous authentication mechanism that consumers can use to access their digital identity regardless of where it is stored" (ODI & Fingleton Associates, 2019).

Existing Data-Privacy Regulations

As open-banking frameworks have customers' data at their heart, it is important to ensure that data-privacy regulations exist in parallel to safeguard consumers' rights. Where this requirement is not in place, there needs to be a program of bold regulatory transformation in data-privacy laws to make sure that consumers are not left "at a higher risk of harm"[11] when implementing data openness in the sector. In the case of Australia, this data-privacy concern was the main reason open banking was delayed until 2020.

The General Data Protection Regulation (GDPR) Directive is designed to harmonize data-privacy laws across the European Union and protect citizens' data privacy. Characterized as "the most important change in data privacy regulation in 20 years,"[12] GDPR obliges entities that store and process consumer data for commercial purposes to acknowledge that the data belong to the user and awards the user the right to choose how these data will be used. GDPR is complementary to PSD2, as it forces third-party providers and banks to handle customer data responsibly, keeping customer transparency and customer data control at the center.

API Standards and Implementation

Perhaps one of the most important elements for an open banking framework is the design and development of API standards. Open and common API standards will allow ecosystem participants (ASPSPs and third-party providers, etc.) to share customer data (e.g., bank account information, transactional and historical account data, payment instructions, etc.) in a similar way that is understood by all parties. API standards provide the specifications – the "recipe" (e.g., architecture, format, documentation, versioning, etc.) – that inform the design, development, and maintenance of APIs. In that context, open API standards can either be private-sector led and created by a consortium of industry organizations, or public-sector led and mandated by an independent entity (such as the U.K.'s Open Banking Implementation Entity).

Having a standardized API makes economic sense. It allows third-party providers to connect seamlessly with deposit-taking institutions without making a huge effort to develop new interfaces each time. This kind of connectedness is a key driver for the development of innovation ecosystems. It can play an important role in the development of new business models in banking and finance more generally, as the industry becomes more "modular" as a result of the openness of data and the connectivity of actors.

Security Standards

Without a doubt, APIs are deemed to be one of the most secure and simplified ways to share data between IT systems and applications. In addition to API standards, security standards that provide a systematic mechanism for accessing the underlying data will create trust and reduce friction. These security standards involve authorization and authentication as well as standardized permission frameworks.

A key debate surrounding security in the open banking debate has been whether alternative data-sharing technologies such as screen scraping and "older" practices should be allowed in modern open-banking systems. The big difference between APIs and screen scraping is that the latter is not permission-based and thus does not let the customer control the degree and duration of the access granted to third parties (be they data aggregators or fintechs that provide account aggregation). This unlimited access potentially creates problems, as it can compromise protection of the account (e.g., may result in leaked credentials or fraudulent use by a rogue agent within the third-party provider). It can also be a violation of the terms and conditions of the account use asserted by the bank. Screen scraping can be costly for developers and unstable for users, as it is not standardized and requires constant attention to changes made to online banking webpages, leading to errors when using outdated data-scraping software.

Data Standards

As open banking and data sharing in finance are gaining momentum across the globe, industry participants and regulators realize the importance of having commonly accepted data standards. Data standards provide the rules and specifications according to which data are represented, formatted, defined, and structured. They allow for a consistent way to describe and record information so that the data can be communicated and processed automatically. Data standards in finance are not new. In the past half-century, there have been numerous standardization efforts to provide rules and formats for the exchange of messages between financial institutions for payments, banking, and other financial-markets businesses. These standards include financial messaging standards for customer payments and checks; financial institution transfers; collection and cash letters;

credits and guarantees; and pre-trade, trade, and post-trade instructions, among many others. Proprietary standards from individual banks or collective (but often exclusive) efforts such as SWIFT message types and the FIX protocol have gradually given way to open-data standards and the creation of ISO-led unified durable standard schemes.

For example, ISO 20022 was created to provide interoperability across the entire finance supply chain and to service many industry subsectors[13] (Scott and Zachariadis, 2014). The EBA's Regulatory Technical Standards require that APIs "shall use ISO 20022 elements, components or approved message definitions."[14] To conform with this direction, all "API payloads" are designed and structured around the ISO 20022 message elements and components where possible. Overall, ISO 20022 promotes interoperability between parties during the payments process and allows users and corresponding systems to communicate using consistent language and formatting.

Payment Systems

Many countries are modernizing their payment systems, an initiative that is complementary to open banking efforts. In countries such as the United Kingdom and Australia, this modernization is happening in parallel to offer banking and nonbanking institutions better access to economy-wide payment infrastructures. In Australia, this need was explicitly articulated in the findings from the public consultation on open banking that concluded in December 2017; these described the importance of New Payment Platform's (NPP) plans to "enable real time person-to-person payments in addition to more data being able to be included in payment information," especially in view of the lack of write-access for payment initiation (Australian Government, 2017).

Concluding Remarks on the Future of Banking

How will open banking affect competition in the financial sector? And what will it do to existing business models? There is no doubt that open banking will have a significant impact on the competitive dynamics in the finance industry. It may also lead to changes in the business models of incumbent banks and other well-established financial intermediaries, as well as the infrastructure of the financial system. Zachariadis & Ozcan (2017) provide an in-depth discussion on how an open API economy in finance can lay the foundation for the emergence of multisided platforms and the fintech ecosystems around them.

Multi-sided platforms can be conceived as networks that reduce transaction costs and create network externalities, facilitating profitable interactions among users when market or hierarchy alternatives are more expensive – often because of the high costs of contracting or customer acquisition (Zachariadis et al., 2018). In the era of open data in banking, this could be a useful business model for incumbents or challenger banks to explore – namely to become mediators of economic activity and sit in the middle of interactions between fintechs and the end customer. Under this multi-sided platform model, bank profits in the future could come from selling technology or access to third-party providers through an electronic marketplace (where the bank can also sell products to their customers) rather than selling traditional banking services to their clients. This business model would allow banks to (re)sell more innovative services to their customers (even though they did not "produce" them) and keep customers engaged on their own platform, reaping the benefits from data monetization. While the above scenario sounds quite attractive and could potentially provide an opportunity for the banks to lead the way in terms of new business models, research shows that banks are facing multiple issues related to their legacy

IT systems, institutional logics, organizational culture, and collaborative appetite (Ozcan, Zachariadis, & Dinckol, 2019).

Alternative business models have been documented in the practitioners' literature. For example, certain banks may choose to function more as "pipelines," leaving the distribution of their products to fintechs and other third parties that provide a better user experience via a digital or mobile channel (e.g., account aggregators and personal-finance-management apps). This partnership is a legitimate business model that, under certain circumstances and market conditions, can be very profitable. Such a business model, often referred to as "banking as a service," would require investment to enhance the bank's core infrastructure, making it cheaper to run but also building good connectivity to services and systems. Depending on the level of service distribution and product creation, a bank can improvise different business models and make strategic choices about how they wish to compete in the industry as it becomes more digitized and digitalized (EBA, 2016).

Looking forward to the API economy in finance, another strategic step when pursuing this new business model (especially in the context of multi-sided platforms) is to voluntarily invest in and create premium APIs that exceed mandated interfaces and provide increased functionality to third parties. These premium APIs offer a profit-making incentive for banks to grow their open-banking ecosystem. This business model is subject to the banks' changing their mindsets and striking successful collaborations with third-party providers, viewing them more as clients and less as competitors.

NOTES

1 While "fintech" is an abbreviation of "financial technology," it is most
  often used to refer to the emergence of an ecosystem of technology
  start-ups that innovate at the heart or on the fringes of financial services

and provide solutions that can help consumers and financial institutions to better handle money and their finances. As explained above, the key difference between "traditional" financial technologies and "new" ways of introducing technology in finance is that older technology implementations focused more on creating more cost-effective operations and achieving efficiencies through automation, while new fintech is geared more towards reconsidering entire business processes and introducing new business models in finance. Popular commentators in this space, such as Chris Skinner, have described fintech as the "R&D function of financial services in the digital world" (see full blog here: https://thefinanser .com/2015/01/ghgh.html/). Another key characteristic of the recent fintech wave has been the interest entrepreneurs and investors – outside financial services and mostly from the tech world – have shown in the finance industry in order to take advantage of existing inefficiencies and "disrupt" the status quo.

2 The difference between "digitization" and "digitalization" is that the former focuses more on the effort to digitize existing processes and tasks (i.e., the move from analog to digital or from a paper-based system to a digital representation of the same data or tasks), while the latter signifies predominantly "a sociotechnical process" and move to a digitally native way of engaging in economic activity that suggests new ways of creating revenue and the adoption of novel business models (Tilson et al., 2010). Digitalization often implies a more customer-oriented inclination to problem solving and engaging with people to address particular needs.

3 EDI systems, which flourished during the 1980s and 1990s, allowed trading partners to exchange structured financial information electronically between separate computer applications (Bátiz-Lazo & Wood, 2002; Iacovou et al., 1995). These were mostly proprietary and less standardized, which meant partners would need to make an investment in order to establish such relationships.

4 For a detailed discussion on the various approaches to and definitions of APIs, as well as their use in open banking, see section "Deconstructing APIs" in Zachariadis & Ozcan (2017).

5 Empirical data have shown that prior regulatory reforms aiming to enhance competition in industries such as transport, telecommunications, and energy have been associated with larger R&D investments, increased outputs, and productivity gains for organizations, as well as lower price levels, better quality services, and more choice for consumers.

6 See Rogers (2017).

7 The first attempt to create a data-sharing model in U.K. banking was the midata initiative launched in 2011 by the Department for Business, Energy and Industrial Strategy (BEIS). The scheme was designed to allow consumers to compare current accounts and increase switching by providing better access to their transaction data in a portable electronic format. See: Gov.UK (2011).

8 The Payment Services Directive II (PSD2) and the EBA's Regulatory Technical Standards were transposed to U.K. law through the United Kingdom's Payment Services Regulations 2017.

9 For detailed definitions see: https://www.openbanking.org.uk/about-us /glossary/.

10 Australian Competition & Consumer Commission (nd.)

11 Prior to the launch of the Australian open banking framework, the Australian Privacy Foundation (APF) claimed that the Consumer Data Rights Bill privacy safeguards were not adequate, and that "risks have been severely underestimated by the Government" (see http://www .privacy.org.au for APF's submission in response to the CDR bill).

12 See the official GDPR webpage for more information: https://gdpr-info.eu/.

13 ISO 20022, also known as UNIversal Financial Industry (UNIFI) message scheme, is a "standard for standards" that defines the guidelines for the development of individual financial messages. It pulls together three distinctive layers necessary for the creation of standards: the *business process and concepts* that provide all the definitions for the processes and roles of actors; the *logical message* layer, which includes all the information needed for the execution of a particular function; and the *syntax* layer that decides on the "physical representation" of the message itself using XML as the principal language. For a detailed discussion of financial messaging standards, see chapter 3 in Scott & Zachariadis (2014).

14 See the following link for a detailed set of API specifications as part of the PSD2 and UK Open Banking regimes: https://openbanking.atlassian.net /wiki/spaces/DZ/pages/1077805207/Read+Write+Data+API+Specificat ion+-+v3.1.2.

REFERENCES

Australian Government. (2017). Review into open banking: Giving customers choice, convenience, and confidence. Australian Government, The Treasury.

Australian Government. (2018). Consumer data right. Australian Government, The Treasury.

Australian Competition & Consumer Commission. (nd). Consumer data right (CDR). https://www.accc.gov.au/focus-areas/consumer-data-right-cdr-0. Accessed 20 July 2019.

Bátiz-Lazo, B., Maixé-Altés, J.C., & Thomes, P. (2011). *Technological innovation in retail finance: International historical perspectives.* New York: Routledge.

Bátiz-Lazo, B., & Wood, D. (2002). An historical appraisal of information technology in commercial banking. *Electronic Markets, 12,* 192–205. https://doi.org/10.1080/101967802320245965.

CMA. (2016). Retail banking market investigation – Final report. Competition and Markets Authority.

CMA. (2017). The retail banking market investigation order 2017. Competition and Markets Authority.

EBA (Euro Banking Association). (2016). Understanding the business relevance of open APIs and open banking for banks. Euro Banking Association Working Group on Electronic Alternative Payments, Information Paper, Version 1.0.

Ghazawneh, A., & Henfridsson, O. (2013). Balancing platform control and external contribution in third-party development: The boundary resources model. *Information Systems Journal, 23*(2), 173–92. https://doi.org/10.1111/j.1365-2575.2012.00406.x.

Gov.UK. (2011, 3 November). The midata vision of consumer empowerment. https://www.gov.uk/government/news/the-midata-vision-of-consumer-empowerment.

Iacovou, C., Benbasat, I., & Dexter, A. (1995). Electronic data interchange and small organizations: Adoption and impact of technology. *MIS Quarterly, 19*(4), 465–85. https://doi.org/10.2307/249629.

Jacobson, D., Brail, G., & Woods, D. (2012). APIs: A strategy guide. Sebastopol, CA: O'Reilly Media Inc.

Mazer, R. (2018). Emerging data sharing models to promote financial service innovation: Global trends and their implications for emerging markets. Independent report supported by The Bill & Melinda Gates Foundation.

Millo, Y., Panourgias, N.S., & Zachariadis, M. (2019). Capitalization by certification: Creating information-based assets through the establishment of an identification infrastructure. In M. Kornberger, G. Bowker, N. Pollock, P. Miller, A. Mennicken, & J. Elyacha (Eds.), *Thinking infrastructures.* Bingley, West Yorkshire: Emerald Publishing.

ODI (Open Data Institute). (2016). Introducing the open banking standard. Open Data Institute, ODI-WP-2016-001.

ODI (Open Data Institute) & Fingleton Associates. (2014, December). Data sharing and open data for banks. Report for HM Treasury. https://www .gov.uk/government/publications/data-sharing-and-open-data-for-banks.

ODI (Open Data Institute) & Fingleton Associates. (2019, June). Open banking, preparing for lift off. https://www.openbanking.org.uk/wp-content /uploads/open-banking-report-150719.pdf.

Ozcan, P., Zachariadis, M., & Dinckol, D. (2019, August). Platformification of banking: Strategy and challenges of challenger versus incumbent banks in UK. Proceedings of the 79th Annual Meeting of the Academy of Management, 9–13. Boston, MA.

Payments Forum UK. (2015). The Open Banking Standard – Unlocking the potential of open banking to improve competition, efficiency and stimulate innovation.

Rogers, T. (2017, 19 July). Screen scraping 101: Who, what, where, when? GoCardless in The Open Banking Hub. https://openbankinghub.com /screen-scraping-101-who-what-where-when-f83c7bd96712.

Scott, S.V., & Zachariadis, M. (2012). Origins and development of SWIFT, 1973–2009. Business History, 54(3), 462–82. https://doi.org/10.1080/00076791 .2011.638502.

Scott, S.V., & Zachariadis, M. (2014). The Society for Worldwide Interbank Financial Telecommunication (SWIFT): Cooperative governance for network innovation, standards, and community. London: Routledge (Global Institutions Series). ISBN-10: 0415631645 | ISBN-13: 978-0415631648.

Tilson, D., Lyytinen, K., & Sørensen, C. (2010). Research commentary – Digital infrastructures: The missing IS research agenda. Information Systems Research, 21(4), 748–59. https://doi.org/10.1287/isre.1100.0318.

Zachariadis, M., & Ozcan, P. (2017). The API economy and digital transformation in financial services: The case of open banking. SWIFT Institute Working Paper No. 2016-001.

Zachariadis, M., Ozcan, P., & Dinckol, D. (2018). The economics and strategy of platforms: Competing in the era of open banking. In E. Maslaveckas (Ed.), The book on open banking: A series of essays on the next evolution of money. Bud Financial Limited.

CHAPTER SIX

The Impact of Banking Regulation on Technological Innovation

Gregory P. Wilson

Introduction

By 2019, the U.S. Dodd-Frank Wall Street Reform and Consumer Protection Act (Dodd-Frank Act) had been almost fully implemented.[1] The combined forces of dynamic innovation, disruptive technology, and aggressive nonbank competitors have been forcing banks and their regulators to react and respond to a new set of challenges. While bank regulators have been doing all that they can to restore the lost consumer trust that resulted from the greatest financial crisis in modern times,[2] they also must address these relentless challenges to the banking and broader financial sectors of the economy.

Going forward, the challenge for U.S. regulators – as for all regulators globally – is twofold: allow innovation and technology to flourish so banks can compete, serve their customers, and fulfill their role in the real economy; and supervise the related risks, especially operational, compliance, and reputational risks. The challenge for banks and their technology partners (and competitors) is to manage technology and innovation in ways that are customer-friendly, responsible, and prudent, while continually engaging the regulators who oversee them.

By the tenth anniversary year of the Dodd-Frank Act (2019), most crisis-related reforms were in place. Enhanced prudential standards for the largest banks – capital, liquidity, stress tests, and greatly increased supervision – are well established, creating a more resilient banking system, according to the financial regulators who are responsible for overseeing the U.S. banking system.[3] New systemic risk protections – living wills, orderly liquidation authority (OLA), the Financial Stability Oversight Council (FSOC), and the Office of Financial Research (OFR) – that did not exist before the crisis are in place and functioning, even if some components like OLA are yet to be tested. Finally, the new Consumer Financial Protection Bureau (CFPB) created by the Dodd-Frank Act has the authority to oversee all aspects of consumer protection that were previously within the purview of the prudential bank regulators, not only for all banks but also for any firm that provides payments or data-processing products and services, as well as any technology company that provides critical services to traditional banks.[4]

There are some signs that the regulatory burden on banks may be easing. In 2018, the U.S. Congress passed the Economic Growth, Regulatory Relief, and Consumer Protection Act,[5] in part as a reaction to the Dodd-Frank Act by a new Republican administration and Congress. While not the deregulation of banks, as some observers claim, this law retains the core principles of the Dodd-Frank Act while tailoring certain provisions to ease the regulatory compliance and reporting burden on banks with less than $250 billion in total consolidated assets. The largest U.S. banks remain subject to significant systemic risk regulation by the Board of Governors of the Federal Reserve System, the Office of the Comptroller of the Currency (OCC), and the Federal Deposit Insurance Corporation (FDIC). As they finalize the remaining Dodd-Frank Act rules, bank regulators also are starting to implement the tailoring requirements in the new law.

Meanwhile, as both banks and their regulators struggle with the implementation and oversight of the nearly 400 post-crisis rules and new tailoring regulations, competition within the banking industry and across the financial services sector remains intense. While individual banks are stronger and the financial system is more resilient than before the crisis, new competitors and new technologies have emerged since then.

New nonbank competitors seek to enter the highly regulated business of banking – buying money from customers (depositors) at one price and selling money to other customers (borrowers) at a higher price, with additional fee-based services provided along the way. Square Financial Services, Inc., for example, filed an application for a *de novo* Utah industrial company (ILC) banking charter in 2017, which finally was approved in March 2020.[6] Starting before the crisis, Walmart tried the Utah ILC approach to enter banking but abandoned that strategy as a result of both intense pressure from traditional bank competitors, especially small community banks, and regulatory delay that included a moratorium on FDIC insurance imposed in the Dodd-Frank Act.[7] In wholesale markets, as banks have tightened lending standards under regulatory pressure in commercial real estate (CRE), for example, new entrants have emerged in the form of debt funds and real estate companies engaged in mezzanine finance to take advantage of the low interest rates and lower standards they offer.

More recently, the OCC, which regulates all national banks in the United States, announced in 2018 that it would begin accepting national bank charter applications from financial technology ("fintech") companies. Other near-banks such as PayPal and retailers such as Amazon and Walmart already offer a broad suite of financial products and services through their partnerships and alliances with bank providers. These new competitors, discussed in more detail in the next section, use innovation and technology to target consumer and corporate users of financial services – especially small businesses – thereby forcing traditional banks to respond in kind to defend, retain, and grow their customer base, especially for deposits. Some of these new entrants will remain competitors of traditional banks, while others will find it more advantageous strategically to partner with banks as innovation and technology continue to evolve.

This chapter examines the regulatory hurdles for banks operating in the United States and how they are adapting to the challenge from fintech new entrants. First, the current use of innovation and new technologies to compete for customers, which is nothing new, is reviewed briefly. Second, the shift from regulators' focusing exclusively on repairing the fallout from the financial crisis to overseeing technological innovation to protect customers and manage risks is explored. Third, two key regulators the U.S. financial agencies are monitoring closely are discussed. Finally, Appendix A provides a detailed overview of U.S. financial regulatory actions as of early 2019.

Leveraging Innovation and Technology to Compete for Customers

The use of innovation, technology, and old-fashioned ingenuity to compete in financial services is nothing new – it just evolves over time. Drive-through teller windows and automated teller machines (ATM) from the last century have given way to mobile banking and digital, real-time payments in this century. Competition within the banking industry remains fierce, while competition from non-bank entrants like retailers and niche product providers continues unabated. As Jamie Dimon, chairman and CEO of JPMorgan Chase & Company, stated in his 2018 letter to shareholders, "technology always creates opportunities for disruption," acknowledging that his competitors like Square and PayPal did things that traditional banks could have done to serve their customers but chose not to do.[8] In fact, technology is helping to disintermediate the historical role of banks as intermediaries in an economy, the bridge between savers and borrowers and facilitator of financial transactions such as payments.

Within the U.S. banking industry, larger banks that can afford to invest in innovation and technology have a distinct competitive advantage over smaller banks that have more limited resources. For example, JPMorgan's Dimon views innovation as integral to the long-term value of his bank. In his 2019 investor-day presentation, he cited two critical factors: continuously investing in the future with expense discipline; and focusing on the customer experience and innovation.[9] Yet, even several years ago, he was looking ahead to focus on innovation and what he defined then as aggressive optimization to best position his bank's operating model for the future while simultaneously adhering to high standards of compliance and safety and soundness.[10] Dimon's statement captures the tension that exists between the use of technological innovation to serve customers and build a strong bank while simultaneously doing so in a way that bank regulators consider to be prudent and responsible. As one of his rising, young digital experts explained during a 2019 interview, "we continually bring our regulators along on our innovation journey."[11]

In his 2017 shareholder letter, Dimon acknowledged the advantages the largest banks have with respect to investing in innovation and technology in ways that smaller banks cannot. Writing that his employees drive innovation and technology, and that in turn technology drives everything the bank does, he revealed that JPMorgan Chase spent roughly $9.5 billion for technology firmwide (approximately 17 percent of noninterest expense), and that about one-third of that was spent on new initiatives. As much as $600 million was spent on emerging fintech solutions across digital, mobile, and part-nering with over 100 fintechs.[12] Dimon understands that large retail-ers like Amazon are as likely to be his future competitors as are other banks or fintechs. "This [investment in technology] is an effort with no finish line," he wrote. "Through continuous innovation, we will seek better ways to serve our clients and extend our competitive advantage."[13]

Capital One, by comparison, considers itself the "original fin-tech." Chairman, CEO, and president Richard D. Fairbank describes his bank's journey for the past twenty-five years as a public com-pany as one that "rethinks how banking works" from the ground up "to build a technology company that does banking," with a goal of empowering the customer digital experience. To that end, 85 percent of Capital One's technology workforce are engineers. Capital One's 2018 agreement to partner with Walmart to be the exclusive issuer of co-branded and private-label credit cards is just one telling example of how a bank joins forces with a major retailer while that retailer concurrently competes directly against banks in other product and geographic areas.[14]

JPMorgan Chase and Capital One are just two leading examples of what the largest U.S. commercial banks are doing with innovation and technology compared to smaller banks. Historically, smaller community banks have found ways to compete against their larger brethren, but now competition from others outside the highly reg-ulated banking industry only complicates their competitive envi-ronment. Nonbanks such as PayPal, Walmart MoneyCenter, and Amazon Web Services (AWS) – all of which partner with banks in some manner – also are major competitive threats to other banks.

For example, PayPal is a licensed money transmitter in all fifty states, but it is not a U.S. bank with its own accounts insured by the FDIC. It offers payments services, debit services, and credit cards. As of 2018, it operated in more than 200 countries; had 254 million active registered accounts; and sent, received, and held funds in twenty-five currencies. It offers its PayPal debit card through Bancorp Bank, an FDIC-insured bank based in Wilmington, Delaware (NASDAQ: TBBK),[15] and PayPal credit through Comenity Capital Bank,[16] a Utah ILC and subsidiary of Alliance Data Systems, a Utah registered holding company (NYSE: ADS). Its "paypal.me" is a peer-to-peer business. It does, however, own a bank in Luxembourg to conduct business throughout the European Union (EU). As a payments company, PayPal also is regulated and subject to enforcement by the CFPB; it is subject to both the consumer protections in Regulation E (Electronic Funds Transfer Act) and the anti-money-laundering provisions of the 2001 USA PATRIOT Act to prevent terrorism.[17]

The Walmart MoneyCenter – the "one stop shop for financial services" – offers a wide suite of products and services to its customers, including money services, gift cards, prepaid debit cards, credit cards, check printing, money transfer (domestically and internationally), check cashing, bill paying, Coinstar (converting coins into cash), money orders, and tax services.[18] Many of these products and services are offered through GoBank, a brand of Green Dot Bank, another Utah-registered holding company.[19] In partnership with American Express, Walmart offers its Bluebird account, which features, among other things, direct deposit, free ATM access, bill pay, money transfer, the Walmart credit card, money management services, membership benefits, and savings accounts ("set-aside").[20]

To date, Amazon is more of a partner to the financial services industry in the wholesale space than a direct competitor, but given its expertise and online footprint, it also could be a formidable retail competitor in the future as well.[21] Amazon's cloud-computing arm AWS currently serves financial services segments – banking and payments, capital markets, and insurance – with technology solutions that include grid computing, security and compliance, disaster recovery and business continuity, data analytics and management, and contact center optimization.

Shift from Financial Crisis Response to Overseeing Technological Innovation

As the 2008 Global Financial Crisis fades and regulators finish writing rules, the band-width of both policymakers and regulators has increased, allowing them more time and resources to consider the impact of technology and innovation on financial-services competition, customers, and compliance (including broader risk management). Moreover, this evolution in regulatory thinking is bipartisan, starting in the Obama administration when it was initiated by the efforts of the former comptroller of the currency, Thomas J. Curry. It continues in the Trump administration and can be expected to evolve for the foreseeable future, given the actions already set in motion. The specific initiatives of the individual bank regulatory agencies will be outlined below. But first, the financial-services principles of the Trump administration and subsequent U.S. Treasury Department reports will be reviewed, to help set the context for further legislative and regulatory efforts to understand and embrace technology and innovation.

Just two weeks into his administration, President Donald J. Trump issued Executive Order 13772 (3 February 2017), which included a set of seven "Core Principles for Regulating the U.S. Financial System" to guide the Treasury Department's review, as well as further recommendations for reform of the financial-services sector to enhance economic growth and serve customers better. While nonbinding, this order is persuasive and has been embraced in spirit by the various financial regulators, including those that are independent agencies. It also formed the predicate for subsequent reports by the U.S. Treasury Department, helping to set the stage for future legislative and regulatory reforms.

The Executive Order's sixth principle is to "make regulation efficient, effective, and appropriately tailored."[22] While the words "innovation" and "technology" do not appear anywhere in the order, they nevertheless form a critical part of the underpinnings for how the Treasury Department and, by extension, the financial regulators, aspire to make regulations more efficient, effective, and tailored going forward to accomplish the same basic goals. Precisely how each separate federal and state financial regulator ultimately decides to meet these principles to achieve its goals in the future will be the subject of ongoing debate on the best means to achieve better regulatory outcomes that benefit consumers and the U.S. economy.

During 2017 and 2018, the Treasury Department produced four separate reports detailing its findings and recommendations for further review and reforms. The first report focused on the banking system, while the fourth and last report focused on the role of nonbank financials, fintech companies, and the role of innovation. It is beyond the scope of this chapter to review all the pertinent aspects of the U.S. Treasury reports, but several items are worth noting to set the stage for the discussion below.

The Treasury's last report published in 2018 acknowledges three current trends, fueled in part by the outcome of the financial crisis: "(1) rapid advances in technology; (2) increased efficiencies from the rapid digitization of the economy; and (3) the abundance of capital available to propel innovation."[23] After reviewing the impact of these trends, Treasury concluded that there was a significant opportunity to enhance innovation in ways that were consistent with the Core Principles for both nonbanks and fintech firms.

Arguably, the same innovation can be utilized by banks and their fintech and retail partners as well. Consistent with the Core

Principles, the Treasury report made a series of more than eighty recommendations designed to enhance economic growth while maintaining critical consumer and investor protections as well as systemic safeguards. Treasury supported the ability of both new business models and traditional banks to leverage technology and innovation to achieve better regulatory outcomes and bolster the prospects for the economy.

The Treasury recommendations for both short-term regulatory and longer-term legislative changes spanned four broad categories, requiring further work by all stakeholders. These four categories are as follows:

- adapting regulatory approaches to changes in the aggregation, sharing, and use of consumer financial data, and to support the development of key competitive technologies;
- aligning the regulatory framework to combat unnecessary regulatory fragmentation, and to account for new business models enabled by financial technologies;
- updating activity-specific regulations across a range of products and services offered by nonbank financial institutions, many of which have become outdated as a result of technological advances; and
- advocating an approach to regulation that enables responsible experimentation in the financial sector, improves regulatory agility, and advances American interests abroad.

Among other recommendations, the Treasury report supported efforts by state bank regulators to enhance the unification and harmonizing of the licensing system across state lines. The U.S. Treasury Department also supported the OCC's efforts (discussed below) to develop a special-purpose national bank charter for fintechs and others that would not be able to gather traditional bank deposits but could offer other bank and bank-like products from innovative new platforms. The report also made recommendations for small-dollar lending, mortgage lending and servicing, the use and protection of consumer data, IRS income verification, and credit bureaus, among other things.[24]

While the U.S. Treasury's report generally was well received by all stakeholders, it is just a report, regardless of how persuasive it is. The United States still has no comprehensive and overarching financial-sector strategy to guide its policymaking. Likewise, unlike some other developed countries, it has no comprehensive and coordinated approach to govern the use of innovation and technology to support the provision and delivery of financial services. Since the U.S. Treasury Department has no formal powers to implement its own report's recommendations by executive fiat, it is up to the Congress and the individual bank regulators, working with all affected stakeholders, to make the necessary statutory and regulatory changes, respectively.

With the four Treasury reports as a starting point, the action now shifts to Congress and the financial regulatory agencies. This section focuses on the most immediate regulatory changes already underway at the individual agencies, but readers also will need to monitor developing legislative changes that address innovation and technology.

In addition to lacking a coherent and comprehensive strategy on technology and innovation, the United States also has a complicated regulatory architecture in which technology and innovation are forced to adapt and respond in overlapping and at times disparate ways. There is no single, unifying statute enacted by Congress to guide the development and use of technology and innovation across the financial services sector. In the United States, three prudential bank regulators, two consumer regulators, two capital market regulators, and one inter-agency committee (FSOC) all have a claim from their unique vantage points on having a say on the policy issues engulfing technology and innovation. Another complication is the federal-state regulatory dynamic and the lack of uniformity and harmonization across state lines on policy issues related to innovation and technology.

A further complication is the lack of a common framework among the United States, Canada, the United Kingdom, the European Union, other Group of Twenty (G20) countries, and the rest of the world regarding innovation across the financial services landscape and the many facets of technology (e.g., the ownership, use, privacy, and security of customer data; architecture (open banking or not); and the application of technology to serve consumers, facilitate compliance, mitigate risks, and enhance financial stability).

Consequently, how U.S. and foreign bank regulators respond and react to – and ultimately regulate and supervise – innovation and technology by the financial institutions they oversee is and will continue to be a critical factor in the provision and delivery of banking services to both retail and corporate customers. As discussed at the end of this chapter, those banks and their fintech partners that take the time and invest the resources to continually engage with and educate their regulators about the way in which they use innovation and technology to serve their customers and manage their risks will have distinct advantages over those banks that do not.

Within the confines of existing law, U.S. regulators are responding to the dynamic structural changes in banking – especially technological innovation – that are reshaping the competitive landscape and affecting how banks serve the financial and related needs of their customers. However, many U.S. laws are outdated and could be modernized to account for technological change and remove any legal ambiguities or unnecessary impediments. For example, the National Bank Act of 1863 gives the comptroller of the currency flexibility to define the business of banking, but that may not be enough to support the granting of a fintech charter to a nonbank that does not take deposits. Money service bureaus (MSBs) are subject to fifty separate state laws, which are not necessarily uniform, and a new national law may be required to allow money to be transmitted more efficiently across state lines, as the Treasury report indicated.

Since the financial crisis, technological innovation has brought U.S. bank regulation once again to another critical inflection point. As former Comptroller Curry stated, "responsible innovation" has "the potential for fintech to improve the lives of ordinary Americans and improve businesses' bottom lines."[25] Exactly how each individual regulator defines "responsible innovation," promulgates rules or guidance to implement it, and then examines for potential supervisory or even enforcement actions remains to be seen and will need to be monitored closely by banks, nonbanks, and other stakeholders.

For the purposes of this chapter, responsible innovation can be considered along three primary dimensions:

- Competition
  - Banks embracing new technologies to innovate and serve their customers better face growing supervisory concerns, potential regulatory approvals, and even disciplinary actions in the future if they get ahead of their regulators without their knowledge and consent; and
  - Nonbanks have been intruding into the business of banking for years, filing new applications and seeking approvals for new charters at both the national and state levels.
- Consumers
  - Protection from fraud, deceptive practices, and abuse;
  - Protection and use of consumer data (ownership, privacy, security);
  - Customer trust;

- Financial inclusion;
- Meeting community needs.
- Compliance
  - Examinations (onsite and offsite inspections and reports);
  - New technologies for better regulatory compliance with the terms of anti-money laundering regulations and the Bank Secrecy Act.[26]

Current U.S. bank regulators embrace technological innovation, but they expect it to be responsible, to be well-managed from a risk perspective, and to have demonstrated benefits for consumers. Bank supervisors will review technological change and innovation as part of their ongoing examination of banks, in some cases requiring formal regulatory approvals and in other cases, for safety and soundness reasons, requiring either changes in, or even cessation of, the use of new technologies to serve bank customers. The three federal prudential regulators and the CFPB, all of which are taking overlapping but slightly different approaches to innovation and the use of technology, are examined next.

Appendix A provides a detailed overview of the activities and focus of U.S. regulatory agencies as of early 2019.

Two Key Regulatory Issues to Watch

While there are numerous innovation issues to watch going forward, ranging from the evolution of online banking and lending to the continuing development of crypto-assets, two issues are immediate priorities for both policymakers and regulators, and therefore are worth monitoring closely in the years ahead. These issues are:

1) achieving real-time payments settlement in the United States to catch up with other developed countries; and

2) leveraging innovation and new technologies to combat money laundering and terrorism financing.

Achieving Real-Time Payments Settlement

Historically, the Federal Reserve has been at the epicenter of the U.S. payment system as both an operator and a regulator, as noted above. Increasingly, however, human ingenuity and innovative technologies have eroded the Federal Reserve's pre-eminence in payments, as both banks and nonbanks employ new technologies and digital operating platforms to meet the payments needs of both consumers and companies and move to real-time payments settlement.

Starting in 2015, the Federal Reserve announced the creation of a new Faster Payments Task Force to facilitate a more strategic effort to "support a broader effort to improve the speed, safety, and efficiency of payments," without formally endorsing a goal of real-time settlement. At announcement, the Faster Payments Task Force consisted of 331 members and was supported by the international consulting firm McKinsey & Company.[27]

The Faster Payments Task Force concluded its work in 2017[28] and issued a final report entitled "The U.S. Path to Faster Payments: A Call to Action."[29] The task force report identified sixteen solutions and ten recommendations, including one that supports fostering continuing innovation using new technology for more efficient and secure payments. But the task force did not mandate real-time settlement.

Even with efforts such as these, the United States still lags behind other countries such as the United Kingdom, Japan, Mexico, and soon the entire European Union with respect to payments in general and real-time payments settlement in particular. Moreover, this lag raises real public policy concerns in the broader economy, such as the impact of payments – and all the direct and indirect fees associated with payment services and the lack of real-time settlement – on income inequality.

On this point, Aaron Klein, director of the Center on Regulation and Markets at the Brookings Institution, asserts that "America's outdated payment system exacerbates income inequality at a scale far larger than commonly understood."[30] Noting that bank products such as Zelle offer real-time payments and that the largest U.S. banks already use a single real-time payment system (RTP), Klein estimates that if just 10 percent of overdraft, payday loans, and check cashing fees could be eliminated with real-time settlement, then roughly $3.5 billion could be saved by those who are most in need of such savings – individuals and working families at the lower end of the economic spectrum. Make other realistic assumptions, and this number could multiply. Using innovation and existing technology, Klein concludes that "Adopting a real-time payment system is one way to make it less expensive to be poor."[31]

Combatting Money Laundering and Terrorist Financing

Since the 1970s, banks have assumed an enforcement role to combat money laundering and, later, terrorist financing under the Bank Secrecy Act and subsequently the USA PATRIOT Act. The primary goal of this mandate is to ensure the integrity, security, and ultimately the continued competitiveness of U.S. financial markets.

In recent years, there has been a growing concern among banks and other stakeholders about the efficacy and usefulness of the current legal regime in the face of changing technology and innovative ways to move money around the globe. For example, many observers question the value and impact of filing tens of thousands of suspicious activity reports (SARs) in terms of achieving the ultimate objective of keeping our financial system safe from bad actors domestically and internationally.

To bring attention to the ongoing role of innovation and technology as a means to address some of these threats, a group of U.S. agencies concerned with anti-money laundering (AML) took the first step in December 2018 by issuing a joint statement on the use of innovation to combat money laundering and terrorism financing.[32] This advisory statement is nonbinding, but it does clarify the current state of thinking by financial regulators and law enforcement on how banks and credit unions can use technology to thwart bad actors in the banking system.

Among other things, the agencies accomplished several things in the context of this informative statement. First, they acknowledged the positive role of private-sector innovation in furthering the effectiveness and efficiency of AML and the Bank Secrecy Act (BSA) compliance programs. Second, the agencies promised to continue an ongoing dialogue and engagement with banks and other stakeholders (e.g., fintech companies) on this issue. Third, the agencies effectively endorsed the concept of being "technology neutral" in achieving their goals, even though they did not use that precise term.

The agencies recognized the value to banks of using innovative technology to enhance risk identification, transaction monitoring, and the reporting of suspicious activity. They applauded banks that were building internal financial intelligence units and leveraging artificial intelligence (AI), digital identity technologies, and machine learning to fight illicit finance.

While stopping short of endorsing the concept of a full "safe haven" for banks that experiment with innovation and technology to fight financial crimes, the agencies did recognize the importance of banks' pilot programs. They went so far as to declare that banks conducting pilot programs should not be subject to supervisory criticisms during examinations and subsequent supervisory actions, even if the pilots fail. The example cited by the agencies was the use of AI to identify suspicious activity in transaction reporting; in this case, the agencies would not automatically assume a deficiency in the bank's normal reporting and compliance system simply because of what AI discovered.

At the same time, the agencies expect banks to maintain their current level of AML/BSA compliance, regardless of whether they utilize technological innovation to assist their compliance program. Stated another way, for the time being, banks will not be able to use AI or machine learning as a substitute for expected compliance. Consequently, banks' investments in pilot programs, new technology, and supporting resources related to AML/BSA compliance will be in addition to – not a substitute for – the current compliance costs and burden. The agencies do acknowledge that, at some point, banks may be able to demonstrate that new technology may reach a state of development and utility that could be considered to be a replacement for, or an enhancement of, existing compliance processes. But before doing so, bank management teams will have to build a credible case to show to their regulators that this approach is justified. Among other things, banks will need to demonstrate how they manage information-security issues, third-party risk management, and continuing compliance, including consumer disclosure and privacy. In this case, early and ongoing engagement with a bank's primary regulator is critical.

Finally, the agencies' joint statement declared that the Financial Crimes Enforcement Network (FinCEN) would consider requests for exemptive relief under current law to facilitate testing of new technologies and pilot programs, if banks can demonstrate that their actions in no way diminish the effectiveness of their current compliance program. As part of this effort, FinCEN announced that it was launching an innovation initiative to better understand the opportunities and risk of new technologies. The other agencies also promised that individually they would create office or internal

projects devoted to responsible innovation and the use of new technologies, entities that in turn would be central points of contact to
facilitate an ongoing dialogue and engagement between banks and
their regulators.[33]

What Banks and Fintech Companies Need to Do Going Forward

To compete and provide value to their customers going forward,
banks and their fintech partners will need to have the full support
of their bank supervisors and engage with them continually as
they deploy new technologies and innovate products and services
responsibly while actively managing any potential new risks.

The use of technology and innovation to compete for customers
across the banking and broader financial services landscape will
continue and likely intensify unabated for the foreseeable future.
Large banks and nonbanks will likely set the pace for innovation
and ingenuity, supported by their own internal resources and
technology investments as well as by alliances with nimble fintech and other third-party providers. While the development of
new fintech charters is relatively new, it is a phenomenon that will
need to be monitored and evaluated closely in the years ahead,
as nonbanks continue to encroach on the historic and once exclusive bank franchise. Even if nonbank competitors do not go all
the way and secure a national or state bank charter, many pre-
sumably will be competitors without a formal license. Moreover,
smaller banks and other providers will be challenged to compete
against not only their larger bank competitors but also these new
nonbank competitors. If history is any indicator, however, smaller
banks and nonbanks, including de novo banks and new technology start-ups, will continue to find ways to meet the needs of

their customers through their unique value propositions and geographic/niche strategies.

A key success factor in the competition for a share of the consumer and corporate wallet will be how financial institutions educate and engage their regulators on their use of innovation and technology to meet the needs of all their customers responsibly. From a competitive perspective, the once relatively clear lines between traditional banks and other financial services providers will continue to blur and largely will be indistinguishable to most end users.

As technology and innovation affect competition and change and intensify over time, regulators will be forced to constantly educate themselves and then react to the impact of market forces. Given the nature of innovation and the dynamic use of technology to meet the twin goals of serving customers and managing attendant risks, financial regulators will find it difficult to lead with respect to the use of technology and innovation. They can and will, however, set the guardrails for how these twin goals are met. To date, U.S. financial regulators, as well as others, have taken the position that innovation and the use of technology must be done responsibly, and in a consumer-friendly way, as a general starting point. Regulators also expect that risk controls used to manage technology and innovation are also prudent and consistent with basic safety and soundness standards that have governed bank supervision historically.

If traditional banks want to compete and create value based on the ways they innovate and use technology, then they will need to excel at several things. First, they will need to have a good story to tell all stakeholders – starting with their customers, but including their investors, employees, and regulators – about how they innovate and use technology in ways that are credible, value enhancing, efficient, secure, and ultimately responsible. Is the value proposition clear, credible, and easily understood? Does it apply equally to all customers in ways that are fair and transparent? Is it responsible in meeting the needs of customers and the communities served?

Next, they will need a compelling innovation and technology sub-strategy that is supportive and seamless with the larger business strategy. To be successful, these sub-strategies will need to be resourced adequately and implemented efficiently, with clear lines of accountability.

From a regulatory perspective, banks will need to ensure that they have a mitigating and resilient risk-management framework for innovation and technology in place across the enterprise. Given the pace of change in innovation and technology, banks also will need to ensure that they engage with and educate their regulators on an ongoing basis on the ways they use innovation and technology to serve their customers and manage the attendant risks. Part of this regulatory risk management will also entail full adherence with the constantly changing compliance requirements at both the national and state levels. How does the use of innovation and technology fit within a bank's existing risk culture? Are the right incentives in place to adequately manage the risks inherent with innovation and technology, especially the reputational and operational risks associated with third-party providers? How are these unique risks identified, measured, managed, and ultimately syndicated with regulators when necessary?

Even if banks have these component parts in place, they also will need to continually rethink and reassess these critical elements for all stakeholders, but especially for the regulatory agencies and individual supervisors who oversee their business from a government and taxpayer's perspective. Engaging proactively with individual bank supervisors to keep them fully educated and continuously informed – "no surprises" – about a bank's use of innovation and technology to serve customers and manage risks is essential to being both competitive and successful in the long-run.

Conclusion

Technological innovation continues to be a driving force affecting the disruption, development, delivery, and competitiveness of financial services in the United States. Unfortunately, there currently is no comprehensive and unifying U.S. policy or single set of regulatory guidelines for its use. Absent new legislation, bank regulators are forced to use their existing statutes to react to technological innovation and reinterpret them as best they can to accommodate increasingly tech-savvy consumers in a dynamic marketplace that is rapidly evolving. The numerous prudential bank regulators at both the federal and state levels as well as the CFPB will continue to react and respond as best they can through their regulation, supervision, and enforcement to balance the competing interests of meeting consumer needs with prudent risk management.

The OCC now accepts applications from fintech firms for national banking licenses, an initiative that will be challenged in the courts by state banking regulators or others as soon as the first application is approved. The Federal Reserve has pledged to move to faster payments, while a significant portion of the banking industry by assets already has moved to a welcomed advancement of real-time payments settlement for their customers. The CFPB, which is not known for issuing broad policy guidance, instead has opted to proceed on an ad hoc, case-by-case basis by issuing no objection letters for innovative new technologies. Meanwhile, the FSOC, which has no direct regulatory power over financial services, acknowledges the potential benefits of technological innovation while cautioning about how the attendant risks are managed from its primary responsibility for financial stability.

In short, both bank and nonbank providers of banking services using technological innovation as part of their strategy and operations will continue to face a fragmented U.S. framework for technological innovation because of a complicated and costly legacy regulatory architecture. Consequently, the United States will likely lag behind more forward-looking approaches in other countries for the foreseeable future. Banks, banks' fintech partners, nonbank competitors, and regulators will need to understand this regulatory reality and then manage it proactively to meet the dynamic and rapidly evolving financial needs of consumers and the economy.

APPENDIX A:
ACTIVITIES OF U.S. BANK REGULATORS AS OF SPRING 2019

Office of the Comptroller of the Currency

The Office of the Comptroller of the Currency (OCC), under both the Obama and Trump administrations, has played a leading role in advocating for the responsible use of innovation and technology to serve all consumers of financial services while simultaneously strengthening banks' profitability. Former Comptroller Curry is credited with first coining the phrase "responsible innovation," starting in 2015: "Our task, as a regulator, is to be sure we have a robust process in place to understand and evaluate new approaches to permit and encourage responsible innovation," Curry stated, "that has benefits for consumers and businesses, while ensuring appropriate risk management and compliance with laws and regulations."[34]

The following year, the OCC issued a set of eight guiding principles, which officially launched its journey into advocating for responsible innovation by the national banks it oversees. The OCC defined the term "responsible innovation" to mean, "The use of new or improved financial products, services, and processes to meet the evolving needs of consumers, businesses, and communities in a manner that is consistent with sound risk management and is aligned with the bank's overall business strategy." Continuing, the OCC explained that:

> This definition recognizes the importance of banks' receptivity to new ideas, products, and operational approaches to succeed in meeting the needs of consumers, businesses, and communities in the rapidly changing financial environment. The definition also emphasizes effective risk management and corporate governance. As we learned in the financial crisis, not all innovation is positive. The financial crisis was fueled in part by innovations such as option adjustable rate mortgages, structured investment vehicles, and a variety of complex securities that ultimately resulted in significant losses for financial institutions and their customers and threatened the entire financial system. The OCC will support innovation that is consistent with safety and soundness, compliant with applicable laws and regulations, and protective of consumers' rights.[35]

Seven months later, the OCC issued its comprehensive framework for responsible innovation and made recommendations in six major areas to guide its future activities. These six areas are: 1) create an Office of Innovation to implement the framework; 2) establish an Outreach and Technical Assistance Program; 3) conduct awareness and training activities; 4) encourage coordination and facilitation; 5) establish an innovation research function; and 6) promote interagency collaboration.[36]

In December 2016, the OCC issued a white paper – "Exploring Special Purpose National Bank Charters for FinTech Companies" – as a means of soliciting public comments and feedback from stakeholders about how innovation and technology can be used and should be regulated.[37] Nine months later, the comptroller issued its licensing manual for evaluating charter applications for fintech companies.[38]

One month after that, Curry elaborated on some of his earlier statements: "Innovation can change everything, but it must fit within the company's business plan, the risks must be understood and managed, and consumers must be treated fairly," he said. "That's what I mean by responsible innovation and that's what innovation must achieve for it to live up to its potential."[39] So, going forward, "responsible innovation" – at least for national banks, but arguably for all U.S. banks – must be considered in the context of treating all consumers fairly, being a good strategic fit that supports a company's business plans, and managing risks, including compliance risk.

The OCC also created an Office of Innovation, launched in January 2017, to act as a clearinghouse and central point of contact to enable banks and nonbanks to better understand bank regulation and supervision related to technological innovation. Its primary purpose is to make certain that national banks and federal savings associations have a regulatory framework that is receptive to responsible innovation and the required supervision to support it. Not surprisingly, the new office focused on three priority areas: 1) safe and sound bank operations; 2) fair access to bank services; and 3) treating bank customers fairly.[40]

Acting Comptroller Keith Noreika, appointed by President Trump when Comptroller Curry departed, also championed the OCC's work related to innovation. "With the lessons of the financial crisis in mind, let me say that the OCC's approach to innovation has the virtue of bringing technology oriented financial companies that provide banking services out of the shadows and into a well-established supervisory and regulatory regime that will promote their safety and soundness and allow the federal banking system and its customers to benefit from their inclusion," he remarked. "It is progress when our agency's consideration of its options spurs actions by others to explore ways innovation and fintech can make banking better and improve services to customers."[41]

When he assumed office, the current comptroller of the currency, Joseph M. Otting, picked up where his two predecessors left off.

Building on the foundation he inherited, Comptroller Otting made the proposal for a national bank license for fintech firms a reality, starting in July 2018. Noting that his actions were consistent with bipartisan efforts at the federal and state levels to strengthen the banking system and enhance the prospects for economic growth, Otting announced that the OCC would begin accepting applications for national bank charters from fintech companies. "The federal banking system must continue to evolve and embrace innovation to meet the changing customer needs and serve as a source of strength for the nation's economy," he stated. "The decision to consider applications for special purpose national bank charters from innovative companies helps provide more choices to consumers and businesses, and creates greater opportunity for companies that want to provide banking services in America. Companies that provide banking services in innovative ways deserve the opportunity to pursue that business on a national scale as a federally chartered, regulated bank."[42]

Comptroller Otting has even carried his message about the value of these special charters overseas to extoll its virtue. "The option to apply for a national bank charter allows these companies to choose the best business model and regulatory structure for their business and strategic goals," he declared in a 2018 speech to international bankers in Tokyo. "Providing a path for fintech companies to become national banks can make the federal banking system stronger by promoting economic growth and opportunity, modernization and innovation, and competition."[43]

As of this writing (March 2020), however, the OCC had not yet approved any fintech application for a nationwide banking license, although there were several applications pending. Moreover, the OCC is likely to be sued by state bank supervisors for granting a national license, so any application ultimately approved by the OCC could trigger a delay in its use by a fintech company until the precise legal status of this new charter is reconciled under current law, which could take years to resolve in U.S. courts.

Federal Reserve

The Board of Governors of the Federal Reserve System, the U.S. central bank, has not been quite as outspoken as the OCC with respect to the need to innovate and use technology, adopting a more cautious and conservative approach in the wake of the financial crisis. Still, the board obviously understands the important role that innovation and technology play in financial services. It does so as both a regulator and an operator of a critical part of the nation's payments system, a position that some observers note presents conflicts of interest for the Federal Reserve to manage.

Nearly ten years after the financial crisis, the Federal Reserve acknowledged in 2017 that it was time to assess the effectiveness and efficiency of its reforms under both the Dodd-Frank Act and its broader regulatory authority over capital and liquidity requirements (i.e., Basel reforms). Without any reference to technology or innovation in his prepared Congressional testimony, then Governor Jerome H. Powell did establish the context and announce the principles by which the Federal Reserve would conduct its fresh regulatory review. By comparison, his testimony came at a time when the OCC was well in the lead in advocating for the use of innovation and technology to better serve customers and mitigate risks.

In his testimony, Governor Powell declared four basic principles that the Federal Reserve would use to guide its regulatory review, principles that continue to be used as of this writing (March 2020). First, the Federal Reserve would preserve and protect what it defined as the "core elements" of its reforms, especially for the largest banks (capital regulation, stress testing, liquidity regulation, and resolvability). Second, the board would tailor its regulatory requirements to the size, risk, and complexity of the companies it regulates and supervises, while noting that community banks face higher costs to meet complex requirements that need to be better calibrated. Third, the board would explore "common-sense ways" to simplify rules and reduce unnecessary regulatory burdens without in any way jeopardizing prudent safety and soundness standards. Finally, the board promised to provide more appropriate transparency about its expectations across multiple dimensions (e.g., stress testing, corporate governance, examination requirements, mergers and acquisitions) to supervised firms as well as the public.[44]

Not long after his testimony, Governor Powell gave an entire speech, at a central banking seminar, on the role of innovation in financial regulation. In the context of exploring ways to improve both the efficiency and the effectiveness of financial regulation, he highlighted the delicate balancing act required by central banks as financial regulators: "for policymakers as well as the private sector, the challenge is to embrace technology as a means of improving convenience and speed in the delivery of financial services, while also assuring the security and privacy necessary to sustain the public's trust."[45]

Other Federal Reserve governors, such as Lael Brainard, have been interested in innovation from another policy perspective – namely, how innovation can foster financial access and inclusion for consumers, families, and small businesses who are underserved today by regulated banks. "The combination of smartphone apps, big data, artificial intelligence, and cloud technology holds out intriguing possibilities in financial services," Governor Brainard stated. "But no single app is likely to be a silver bullet for the complex challenges faced by underserved households and small businesses." In her view, achieving a higher level of financial inclusion will require a more holistic understanding of the many challenges faced by underserved groups to develop the solutions required to meet their unique needs.[46] Technology and innovation can play a critical role. Governor Brainard also has been outspoken on cryptocurrencies and digital assets[47] as well as urging caution in the use of artificial intelligence (AI) and machine learning.[48] Many bankers, in contrast, are actively pursuing AI and machine learning in areas where they believe they can revolutionize financial services and provide better products and services for their customers with appropriate risk mitigation.

The Federal Reserve's first vice-chair for supervision, Randal Quarles, echoed Chairman Powell's concerns about balancing the benefits and potential pitfalls of innovation. This is especially true in the payments system, where many banks have moved to real-time settlement for their customers, while the Federal Reserve still struggles with real-time settlement for the part of the payments system that it operates. In a speech devoted to fintech, payments, and digital currencies, Vice-chair Quarles defined the delicate balancing act facing the central bank: "it is appropriate not only to evaluate the potential of innovations to improve on existing services, but also to judge their ramifications for the safety and soundness of the institutions we supervise and for financial stability." Continuing, he affirmed that, "Although many ... technologies are still nascent, it is important to have an eye on the potential financial stability implications both in the short- and long-run ... Without that resilience, [payments] could face a sudden loss of public confidence and the seizing up of systems and critical activities."[49] Vice-chair Quarles also noted that, with respect to private digital currencies and the distributive ledger technology standing behind them, the board actively monitors current marketplace developments.

Finally, in his new role as chair of the international Financial Stability Board (FSB), Quarles recently outlined his work plan for the FSB in 2019 and beyond. Fintech – "technology-enabled financial innovation that results in material changes to the provision of financial services" – is a key part of that agenda. Quarles acknowledged the claims about the potential promise of fintech to, among other things, reduce economic inequality, increase inclusion, bolster growth, and even reduce volatility and other financial vulnerabilities. Yet, he also addressed the need for a more measured approach: global regulators "must ensure that as we maximize the potential benefits in the development of Fin-Tech we minimize the potential risks and costs" to consumers and financial stability. Continuing, he stated that the FSB's two primary workstreams on this issue will assess: "1) the impact of especially large FinTech firms into the financial services sector; and 2) the potential effects of decentralized financial technolo-gies."[50] Consequently, all stakeholders will need to monitor the FSB's work and actions, just as they do for individual domestic regulators.

Federal Deposit Insurance Corporation

The Federal Deposit Insurance Corporation (FDIC), as both a bank regulator and a deposit insurer, recently has started to explore the impact of innovation and technology more than it had historically done. For example, FDIC Chair Jelena McWil-liams has spoken several times since she took office in 2018 about the impact of technology and innovation on access to banking services and the delivery of those services to bank cus-tomers. In November 2018, following the OCC's example, she announced that the FDIC would also open an Office of Innova-tion for insured banks, which, as of this writing, was not yet operational. In her first speech on fintech and its application in banking, Chair McWilliams listed four key fundamental ques-tions for this new office to explore:

1. How can the FDIC provide a safe regulatory environment to promote the technological innovation that is already occurring?

2. How can the FDIC promote technological development at our community banks with limited research and development funding to support independent efforts?
3. What changes in policy – particularly in the areas of identity management, data quality and integrity, and data usage or analysis – must occur to support innovation while promoting safe and secure financial services and institutions?
4. How can the FDIC transform – in terms of our technology, examination processes, and culture – to enhance the stability of the financial system, protect consumers, and reduce the compliance burden on our regulated institutions?[51]

Consumer Financial Protection Bureau

The final U.S. regulator to consider is the new Consumer Financial Protection Bureau (CFPB), created by the Dodd-Frank Act as a means of centralizing all consumer-protection regulation and supervision in a single agency. In additional to regulating and supervising consumer protection for the largest banks in particular, the CFPB has the basic authority to regulate and supervise fintech firms as well – specifically: 1) to oversee any firm that is "providing payments or other financial data processing products or servicing to a consumer by any technological means," and 2) to "examine technology companies that provide material services to traditional banks, including processing services."[52]

Starting as early as 2014, the CFPB signaled its willingness to consider new and innovative ways to serve consumers through new policy guidance and the use of no-action letters. At that time, it also launched Project Catalyst, which has since been formalized into a separate Office of Innovation.[53] In 2017, the CFPB issued its first no-action letter to Upstart, a company that uses nontraditional or alternative data and modeling techniques in its lending decision making.[54]

Where the OCC and some state bank regulators favor the adjective "responsible" innovation, the CFPB uses the term "consumer-friendly" innovation. To this end, the CFPB's Office of Innovation was established with three specific mandates: 1) updating policies and creating sandboxes through which the bureau can provide regulatory relief; 2) engaging with entrepreneurs and the innovation community; and 3) collaborating with other regulators. To fulfill this new mandate, the CFPB has created five separate but related workstreams that are still a work in progress: 1) utilizing "no-action" letters more readily; 2) establishing its own regulatory sandbox to provide regulatory relief for new products and services while sharing data with the bureau; 3) creating a specific disclosure sandbox; 4) accepting pilot pitches from companies or groups on new ways to innovate; and 5) participating in the Global Financial Innovation Network (GFIN).[55] The GFIN, an eclectic group of twenty-nine regulators, was launched in January 2019 and has an ambitious two-part mission: 1) to provide a more efficient way for innovators to interact with regulators as they look to scale new ideas; and 2) to create a new framework of cooperation among financial services regulators around the world.[56] The CFPB is the only U.S. regulator that currently participates in GFIN.[57]

FINANCIAL STABILITY OVERSIGHT COUNCIL

As noted above, the Financial Stability Oversight Council (FSOC) has no real regulatory powers to guide U.S. financial services policy, including the use of innovation and technology, and therefore relies exclusively on its hortatory powers. In its most recent annual report, the FSOC affirmed that financial innovation can be a good thing for consumers and companies by potentially lowering costs, increasing the speed of payments, and expanding access to, and the availability of, credit. However, it also noted the potential downside risks that could offset the benefits and even increase financial instability. Consequently, the FSOC admonished the financial regulators to do several things going forward to mitigate any potential harm to the U.S. financial system, as follows:

> Accordingly, the Council encourages financial regulators to continue to be vigilant in identifying new products and services, in order to evaluate how they are used and can be misused; monitor how they affect consumers, regulated entities, and financial markets; and coordinate regulatory approaches, as appropriate. Relevant authorities should also evaluate the potential effects of new financial products and services on financial stability, including operational risk. Because financial innovations are new, they may not be identified by agencies' existing monitoring and data collection systems. To ensure comprehensive visibility into innovations across the financial system, regulators should share relevant information on financial innovations with the Council and appropriate agencies. The Council also encourages regulators to consider appropriate approaches to regulation to reduce regulatory fragmentation while supporting the benefits of innovation.[58]

State Banking Regulators

As noted above, the U.S. financial regulatory system is a product of its legacy development in response to numerous crises as well as the federal system of government. In addition to the national authorities, state banking authorities also play a critical role in the regulation and supervision of technological innovation by the financial institutions they oversee, a role that can either facilitate or complicate the approval and subsequent impact of new products, new technologies, and new competitors, particularly nonbank competitors. For example, Square Financial Services' application to the Utah Department of Financial Institutions to charter an industrial bank, which was received by the department in 2017, was approved in March 2020.[59] Simultaneously, Square also received approval from the FDIC to offer deposit insurance to its merchant customers.[60]

The New York Department of Financial Services (DFS) has also been an outspoken advocate for state-licensed fintech firms, as has its trade association, the Conference of State Bank Supervisors (CSBS). As another example, at the beginning of 2019, DFS granted Robinhood Crypto, LLC, a money transmitter and virtual currency, license to buy, sell, and store seven virtual currencies, including Bitcoin and Ether.[61] In late 2018, DFS Superintendent Maria Vullo publicly opposed the OCC's efforts to authorize new national fintech charters as an unlawful national pre-emption of state law: "The OCC's decision to begin accepting applications for special purpose charters is not about consumer choice but is instead a lawless, ill-conceived scheme to destabilize financial markets that are properly and most effectively regulated by the states. Rather than bring about consumer choice, the OCC's attempted action to preempt existing state regulation creates serious threats to the well-being of consumers, especially the most vulnerable ones, who will be at great risk of exploitation by federally-chartered 'too big to fail' entities improperly insulated from New York law."[62] The DFS filed a lawsuit against the OCC to block the granting of a national banking license to fintech firms,[63] and subsequently joined a similar CSBS lawsuit again the Office of the Comptroller of the Currency.[64] These lawsuits were still pending as of March 2020. They likely will take years to resolve, based on other similar precedents, and ultimately may reach the Supreme Court in order to settle the jurisdictional issue regarding whether the national bank regulator can charter a nonbank fintech company.

NOTES

1 Public Law 111–203, H.R. 4173, 21 July 2010.
2 Sivon, J., & Klein, A. (2013, June). The coming clash between financial technology and financial regulators. *Our Perspectives*: Barnett, Sivon, & Natter newsletter. 1.

3 Powell, J.H. (2017, 22 June). Relationship between regulation and economic growth. Committee on Banking, Housing, and Urban Affairs, U.S. Senate, Washington, D.C. https://www.federalreserve.gov/newsevents/testimony/powell20170622a.htm.
4 Wilson, G.P. (2011). *Managing to the new regulatory reality: Doing business under the Dodd-Frank Act*. New York: Wiley Finance.
5 Public Law 115–74, S. 2155. 24 May 2018.
6 Square Financial Services, Inc., Industrial Bank New Charter Application. http://dfi.utah.gov/general-information/application-status.
7 *New York Times*. (2014, 27 September). Finding a door into banking, Walmart prepares to offer checking accounts. B3; Adler, J. (2017, 23 August). Flashback: When Walmart wanted a bank. *American Banker*. www.americanbanker.com/opinion/when-walmart-wanted-a-bank.
8 JPMorgan Chase & Co. (2018). *Annual Report*, 16. https://www.jpmorganchase.com/corporate/investor-relations/document/annualreport-2018.pdf.
9 JPMorgan Chase & Co. (2019, 26 February). Firm overview/Investor Day Presentation. https://www.jpmorganchase.com/corporate/investor-relations/document/2019_firm_overview_ba56d0e8.pdf.
10 JPMorgan Chase & Co. (2016). *Annual Report*, 11. https://www.jpmorganchase.com/corporate/investor-relations/document/2016-annualreport.pdf.
11 Anonymous source, JPMorgan Chase & Co. (2019, 28 March). Telephone interview.
12 JPMorgan Chase & Co. (2017). *Annual Report*, 2017, 54. https://www.jpmorganchase.com/corporate/investor-relations/document/annualreport-2017.pdf.
13 Ibid., 11; Kandell, J. (2018, 21 May). Jamie Dimon is not messing around. *Institutional Investor*. https://institutionalinvestor.com/article/b189czlk410ggh/jamie-dimon-in-not-messing-around.
14 Capital One. (2018). *Annual Report, 2018: Welcome to Banking Reimagined*, 4. http://phx.corporate-ir.net/phoenix.zhtml?c=70667&p=irol-reportsannual.
15 The Bancorp. (nd). http://investors.thebancorp.com/CorporateProfile.
16 Comenity Bank. (nd). https://comenity.com/about.
17 The U.S. Patriot Act was passed by Congress as a response to the terrorist attacks of 11 September 2001. The act allows federal officials greater authority in tracking and intercepting communications, both for purposes of law enforcement and foreign intelligence gathering. See: https://www.paypal.com/us/home; https://en.wikipedia.org/wiki/paypal.

18 Walmart MoneyCenter. (nd). https://www.walmart.com/cp/walmart -money-center/5433.
19 GoBank. (nd). https://www.gobank.com/; https://www.greendot.com/.
20 Walmart MoneyCenter/Bluebird. (nd). https://www.walmart.com/cp /bluebird/1099170.
21 AWS (Amazon Web Services). (nd). https://aws.amazon.com/financial -services/?nc=sn&loc=1.
22 The "Core Principles" are: A. Empower Americans to make independent financial decisions and informed choices in the marketplace, save for retirement, and build individual wealth; B. Prevent taxpayer-funded bailouts; C. Foster economic growth and vibrant financial markets through more rigorous regulatory impact analysis that addresses systemic risk and market failures, such as moral hazard and information asymmetry; D. Enable American companies to be competitive with foreign firms in domestic and foreign markets; E. Advance American interests in international financial regulatory negotiations and meetings; F. Make regulation efficient, effective, and appropriately tailored; and G. Restore public accountability within federal financial regulatory agencies and rationalize the federal financial regulatory framework. See U.S. Treasury Department (2018). *A financial system that creates economic opportunities: Nonbank financials, fintech, and innovation*. Washington, D.C.: U.S. Treasury Department, 3. https://treasury.gov/press-center/press-releases /Documents/A%20Financial%20System.pdf.
23 Ibid., 6.
24 Ibid., 197–211.
25 Curry, T.J. (2017, 28 April). Remarks at FinTech and the Future of Finance Conference. Kellogg School of Management, Northwestern University, Evanston, IL, 1. https://www.occ.treas.gov/news-issuances/speeches/2017 /pub-speech-2017-48.pdf; hereafter: Curry, "Remarks at FinTech."
26 The Bank Secrecy Act (BSA), also known as the Currency and Foreign Transactions Reporting Act, is legislation passed by the United States Congress in 1970 that requires U.S. financial institutions to collaborate with the U.S. government in cases of suspected money laundering and fraud.
27 Board of Governors, Federal Reserve System. (2016, 29 March). Federal Reserve engages in effort to assess faster payments solutions. Press release. https://www.federalreserve.gov/newsevents/pressreleases /other20160329a.htm.
28 Board of Governors, Federal Reserve System. (2017, 24 July). Federal Reserve commends efforts as Faster Payments Task Force concludes. Press

release. https://www.federalreserve.gov/newsevents/pressreleases /other20170724a.htm.

29 Faster Payments Task Force, Board of Governors, Federal Reserve System. (2017, July). The U.S. path to faster payments: A call to action. http:// fasterpaymentstaskforce.org/wp-content/uploads/faster-payments-task -force-final-report-part-two.pdf.

30 Klein, A. (2019, 5 March). Real-time payments can help combat inequality. *Spotlight on Poverty & Opportunity.* https://spotlightonpoverty.org /spotlight-exclusives/real-time-payments-can-help-combat-inequality/.

31 Ibid. See also, Klein, A. (2016, 28 September). Why don't checks clear instantly? Ask the Fed. Thanks to a big force holding back the U.S. payment system, banks could get leapfrogged. https://www.politico.com/agenda /story/2016/09/financial-technology-payment-transactions-federal -reserve-000209; and Humphries, C. (2019, 28 September). 5 signs you, personally, are disrupting the banking system. https://www.politico.com /agenda/story/2016/09/how-does-financial-technology-affect-you-000212.

32 The relevant U.S. agencies are the three federal bank regulators, the National Credit Union Administration (which regulates and supervises federal credit unions), and the Financial Crimes Enforcement Network (FinCEN) at the U.S. Treasury Department. See: Board of Governors of the Federal Reserve System, Federal Deposit Insurance Corporation, Financial Crimes Enforcement Network, National Credit Union Administration, Office of the Comptroller of the Currency. (2018, 3 December). Joint Statement on Innovative Efforts to Combat Money Laundering and Terrorist Financing. https://www.fincen.gov/news/news-releases /joint-statement-innovative-efforts-combat-money-laundering.

33 Ibid.

34 Curry, T.J. (2015, 7 August). Remarks by Thomas J. Curry, Comptroller of the Currency, before the Federal Home Loan Bank of Chicago, 7. https://www.occ.gov/news-issuances/speeches/2015/pub-speech -2015-111.pdf.

35 Office of the Comptroller of the Currency. (2016, March). *Supporting responsible innovation in the federal banking system: An OCC perspective.* Washington, D.C.: Office of the Comptroller of the Currency, 8. https:// www.occ.gov/publications/publications-by-type/other-publications -reports/pub-responsible-innovation-banking-system-occ-perspective .pdf. The OCC's eight principles are: "1. Support responsible innovation; 2. Foster an internal culture receptive to responsible innovation; 3. Leverage agency experience and expertise; 4. Encourage responsible innovation that

provides fair access to financial services and fair treatment of consumers; 5. Further safe and sound operations through effective risk management; 6. Encourage banks of all sizes to integrate responsible innovation into their strategic planning; 7. Promote ongoing dialogue through formal outreach; and 8. Collaborate with other regulators."

36 Office of the Comptroller of the Currency. (2016, October). *Recommendations and decisions for implementing a responsible innovation framework.* Washington, D.C.: Office of the Comptroller of the Currency, 2. https://www.occ.gov /topics/responsible-innovation/comments/recommendations-decisions -for-implementing-a-responsible-innovation-framework.pdf.
37 Curry, T.J. (2016, 2 December). Remarks regarding national bank charters for fintech companies. Georgetown University Law Center, Washington, D.C. https://www.occ.treas.gov/news-issuances/speeches/2016/pub -speech-2016-152.pdf.
38 Office of the Comptroller of the Currency. (2017, March). *Comptroller licensing manual draft supplement evaluating charter applications for financial technology companies.* Washington, D.C. https://www.occ.gov/publications /publications-by-type/licensing-manuals/file-pub-lm-fintech-licensing -manual-supplement.pdf.
39 Curry, T.J. (2016, 2 December). Remarks regarding national bank charters for fintech companies. See note 36.
40 Office of the Comptroller of the Currency, Office of Innovation. (2016, October). Recommendations and decisions for implementing a responsible innovation framework. https://www.occ.gov/topics/responsible-innovation /index-innovation.html.
41 Noreika, K.A. (2017, 19 July). Remarks before the Exchequer Club. Washington, D.C., 3, 6. https://www.occ.gov/news-issuances/speeches /2017/pub-speech-2017-82.pdf.
42 Office of the Comptroller of the Currency. (2018, 31 July). OCC begins accepting national bank charter applications from financial technology companies., NR 2018-74. https://www.occ.gov/news-issuances/news-releases/2018/nr-occ -2018-74.html.
43 Otting, J.M. (2018, 14 November). Remarks to the Special Symposium on International Finance (Tokyo), 9. https://www.occ.gov/news-issuances /speeches/2018/pub-speech-2018-120.pdf.
44 Powell, J.H. (2017, 22 June). Relationship between regulation and economic growth. Statement before the Committee on Banking, Housing, and Urban Affairs, U.S. Senate, Washington, D.C., 4–5; https://www.federalreserve .gov/newsevents/testimony/powell20170622a.htm.

45 Powell, J.H. (2017, 18 October). Financial innovation: A world in transition. Speech to the 41st Annual Central Bank Seminar, Federal Reserve Bank of New York (New York). https://www.federalreserve.gov/newsevents /speech/powell20171018a.htm.
46 Brainard, L. (2018, 17 October). Fintech and the search for full stack financial inclusion. Speech at the FinTech, Financial Inclusion – and the Potential to Transform Financial Services Conference (Boston, MA). https://www .federalreserve.gov/newsevents/speech/brainard20181017a.htm.
47 Brainard, L. (2018, 15 May). Cryptocurrencies, digital currencies, and distributive ledger technologies: What are we learning? Speech at the Decoding Digital Currency Conference Sponsored by the Federal Reserve Bank of San Francisco, 2. https://www.federalreserve.gov/newsevents /speech/brainard20180515a.htm.
48 Brainard, L. (2018, 13 November). What are we learning about artificial intelligence in financial services? Speech at Fintech and the New Financial Landscape (Philadelphia, PA). https://www.federalreserve.gov/newsevents /speech/brainard20181113a.htm.
49 Quarles, R.K. (2017, 30 November). Thoughts on prudent innovation in the payment system. Speech at the 2017 Financial Stability and Fintech Conference (Washington, D.C.). https://www.federalreserve.gov /newsevents/speech/quarles20171130a.htm.
50 Quarles, R.K. (2019, 28 March). The Financial Stability Board in 2019. Speech at the Joint Conference of the European Central Bank and the *Journal of Money, Credit, and Banking* (Frankfurt, Germany), 8; https:// www.federalreserve.gov/newsevents/speech/quarles20190328a.htm.
51 McWilliams, J. (2018, 13 November). Remarks at the Federal Reserve Bank of Philadelphia Fintech and the New Financial Landscape Conference. (Philadelphia, PA); and McWilliams, J. (2018, 15 November). Remarks, Fourth Annual Financial Stability Conference (Washington, D.C.). https:// www.fdic.gov/news/news/speeches/spnov1318.html.
52 Sivon, J. & Klein, A. (2013, June). The coming clash between financial technology and financial regulators. *Our Perspectives*. Barnett, Sivon, & Natter newsletter, 1.
53 Quan, D. (2014, 10 October). We're open to innovative approaches to benefit consumers. Consumer Finance Protection Bureau (CFPB). https://www.consumerfinance.gov/about-us/blog/were-open-to -innovative-approaches-to-benefit-consumers/.
54 Consumer Financial Protection Bureau (CFPB). (2017, 14 September). Upstart "no-action" letter. https://files.consumerfinance.gov /f/documents/201709_cfpb_upstart-no-action-letter.pdf.

55 Consumer Financial Protection Bureau (CFPB). (nd). Mission statement.
    https://www.consumerfinance.gov/about-us/innovation/.
56 Consumer Financial Protection Bureau (CFPB). (nd). The Consumer
    Financial Protection Bureau and the Global Financial Innovation Network
    (GFIN). https://www.consumerfinance.gov/about-us/innovation
    /global-financial-innovation-network/.
57 Canadian members of GFIN include: Autorité des marchés financiers
    (AMF); Alberta Securities Commission (ASC); British Columbia Securities
    Commission (BCSC); and Ontario Securities Commission (OSC).
58 Financial Stability Oversight Council. (2018). *Annual Report, 2018.*
    Washington, D.C.: U.S. Treasury Department, 10. https://home.treasury
    .gov/system/files/261/FSOC2018AnnualReport.pdf.
59 Utah Department of Financial Institutions. (2020, 19 March). Square
    Financial Services, Inc., Industrial Bank New Charter Application. https://
    dfi.utah.gov/general-information/application-status/.
60 Federal Deposit Insurance Corporation. (2020, 18 March). FDIC approves the
    deposit insurance application for Square Financial Services, Inc., Salt Lake
    City, Utah. https://www.fdic.gov/news/news/press/2020/pr20033.html.
61 New York Department of Financial Services. (2019, 24 January). DFS
    continues to advance responsible innovation in New York fintech industry.
    Press release. https://www.dfs.ny.gov/reports_and_publications/press
    _releases/pr1901241.
62 New York Department of Financial Services. (2018, 18 September).
    Statement by Financial Services superintendent Maria T. Vullo regarding
    the OCC's decision to accept fintech charters. Press release. https://www
    .dfs.ny.gov/about/statements/st1809181.htm.
63 Vullo, M.T. (2018, 14 September). New York Department of Financial
    Services, vs. The Office of the Comptroller of the Currency and Joseph
    M. Otting, Civil Action No. 18-cv-8377, U.S. District Court, Southern
    District of New York. fhttps://www.dfs.ny.gov/docs/banking/dfs_occ
    _complaint_with_exhibits_9_2018.pdf. For the CSBS lawsuit filed in the
    U.S. District Court, District of Columbia, see: Conference of State Bank
    Supervisors, (2018, 25 October). CSBS sues OCC over fintech charter. Press
    release. https://www.csbs.org/csbs-sues-occ-over-fintech-charter.
64 New York Department of Financial Services. (2018, 25 October). Statement
    by New York Financial Services superintendent Maria T. Vullo regarding
    the lawsuit filed by the CSBS challenging the authority of the comptroller
    of the currency to create a nonbank special-purpose national bank
    charter for "fintech" companies. Press release. https://www.dfs.ny.gov
    /reports_and_publications/statements_comments/2018/st1810251.

SECTION II

NEW STRATEGIES, TECHNOLOGIES, AND BUSINESS MODELS

CHAPTER SEVEN

The Competitive Threat from Techfins and Bigtech in Financial Services

Michael R. King[1]

Imagine this scenario. A young woman opens an app on her mobile phone. She chats and messages her friends over social media, posts photos, plays games, shops for whatever she needs, orders from a restaurant, buys tickets to a concert, arranges transportation, watches videos, listens to music, and books travel. She pays for all of it using her online account, transfers cash between her money market fund and bank account, takes out an unsecured loan, buys and sells investments, sends and receives money, and buys insurance. All of this within one app.

While this story may once have seemed fictional, it is now a reality and currently available on the WeChat app from the Chinese technology company Tencent or on the Alipay app from its rival Alibaba. Both companies have built online marketplaces and mobile apps that combine e-commerce, social networking, and gaming. They also offer financial products, including payments, deposits, loans, investments, bank accounts, and insurance. Their platform ecosystems now connect more than a billion users with a wide variety of non-financial and financial services manufactured in-house or by third parties. Similar services may one day be available from U.S. companies like Amazon, Apple, Google, or Facebook.

These Chinese technology companies are known as "techfins," a term first coined by Alibaba's Jack Ma in 2016 to describe Ant Financial – the financial services arm of the Alibaba ecosystem. Ma argues that techfins are harnessing technology to redefine financial services and increase financial inclusion. He contrasts this mission with the goal of fintech companies that use technology to profit from selling financial products to customers. Ant Financial's stated purpose is to provide access to capital and financial services to young people, small businesses, and poor nations that are underserved or unbanked:[2]

> "Fintech takes the original financial system and improves its technology," said Ma ... "TechFin is to rebuild the [financial] system with technology. What we want to do is to solve the problem of a lack of inclusiveness."

Ultimately, techfins purport to use technology to create a world where customers have access to financial services just like tap water – you open the tap and water just flows out.[3]

From being a minority view several years ago, the new consensus among bank insiders and industry commentators is that techfins like Alibaba and Tencent, not fintechs, represent a greater threat over the next decade to banks, asset managers, insurance companies, and other financial incumbents.

The other threat comes from a diverse collection of North American technology companies known collectively as bigtech (or big tech).[4] Bigtech companies are Amazon, Apple, Facebook, and Google, where the term highlights that their main competitive strength comes from massive datasets on customer transactions and behavior in their platform ecosystems (Frost et al., 2019). As noted by the Bank for International Settlements (BIS), bigtech is an apt name, as the stock market capitalization of these large technology companies was bigger than that of some of the world's largest financial institutions, including JPMorgan, Bank of America, and Wells Fargo in the United States and the Industrial and Commercial Bank of China and the China Construction Bank.[5]

Whether you are a fan or a critic, it is clear that techfins and bigtech companies are transforming financial services. The main message is that financial incumbents need to pay close attention to these new entrants and consider how to adapt their business strategies in order to survive in the digital age.

The key questions for financial incumbents are as follows: Is the threat from these new entrants real or not? Will the Chinese techfins be able to export their business model abroad? And will bigtech companies push into financial services? To propose an answer, we review the history and strategies of two companies that have moved farthest into financial services – Ant Financial and Amazon. We examine their key competitive strengths to gauge the threat they pose to financial incumbents over the coming decade.

The Rise of Alipay and Ant Financial

Alibaba and Tencent combine the culture of innovation and technical expertise of Silicon Valley start-ups with the customers and scale of Wall Street banks. Both Chinese techfins began with a non-financial business – e-commerce for Alibaba and social networking and gaming for Tencent – that attracted large user bases. They added payments to facilitate the adoption and growth of their marketplaces, then added deposits, investments, credit, and insurance. Now they are using the data and customer insights generated from their platform ecosystems to identify customer needs and cross-sell proprietary and third-party financial products.

The Creation of Alipay

As a pioneer in Chinese e-commerce, Alibaba recognized early on that its online marketplace was being held back by a lack of trust between buyers and sellers (Xie, Siew Kien, & Neo, 2017). Customers were hesitant to pay for goods purchased online, fearing merchants would not deliver them. China featured an underdeveloped payments system, with little penetration of cards and debit cards.[6] It was time-consuming and expensive for consumers to transfer money. Small businesses were held back by a lack of credit, financially constrained, and underserved by the domestic state-run banks. To fill these institutional voids, Alibaba set up Alipay in 2004 as an online payment gateway, similar to PayPal that began operation in 1999. Alipay charged no transaction fees and increased trust in e-commerce by holding customer payments in escrow accounts that would be released to merchants once goods purchased online were delivered. This model proved so successful that Alibaba soon opened Alipay to third parties, both online and offline merchants and service providers.

By August 2008, Alipay had 100 million registered merchants, with daily transactions reaching 2 million. Within a year it reached 200 million users with 5 million daily transactions, then 300 million users by March 2010. Alipay launched a mobile payments app in November 2009, and a consumer version of Alipay launched in January 2010. Alipay grew rapidly and became the dominant player in third-party mobile payments transactions, processing more than 50 percent of all transactions within a few short years.

Alipay's rapid growth was driven by strategic partnerships and product innovations, as follows:

- **Strategic partnerships**: In 2005 Alipay signed partnership agreements with ICBC, China Merchants Bank, and VISA, with the other Chinese banks signing up in the following years. In April 2009, Alipay began working with the e-banking system of the Bank of China, with the cooperation of five major state-owned banks and fifteen national banks. In 2010, it partnered with the Bank of China to allow quick payment with a credit card, adding ten banks in 2011 and improving payment success by credit card from 60 percent to 95 percent.

- **Product innovations**: In 2005 Alipay began a twenty-four-hour customer-service hotline, followed by online customer service and compensation against account theft. In 2008 Alipay began offering voice-controlled payments for mobile users and released its mobile Wireless Application Protocol (WAP) platform. In 2008 Alipay provided a platform allowing Shanghai residents to pay their water, electricity, and telephone bills online, expanding to Hangzhou in early 2009. Alipay became the first service to allow offline payments by scanning barcodes in July 2011 and biometric payments using finger prints in July 2014. In 2013, Alipay launched the digital Alipay Wallet, to facilitate mobile payments by allowing users to electronically store and manage credit cards, gift cards, and discount coupons, to make electronic fund transfers via the Internet, and to make purchases by scanning barcodes and QR codes. Finally, Alipay invested in biometric identity to enable payments using facial recognition.

It is important to recognize that Alibaba did not create Alipay as a strategy to grow its revenues. Instead, Alipay emerged organically as means to solve the pain points faced by its merchants and customers. Alipay did not receive an official license to operate a payments business until May 2011, six years after it began operation. As a regulatory condition for receiving this payments license, Alibaba spun off Alipay into a stand-alone company (called Small and Micro

Financial Services Company), with Alibaba retaining a 33 percent minority stake and Jack Ma as majority shareholder with 46 percent.[7]

A similar customer-centric approach led Alibaba to begin offering other financial services: a money market fund (Yu'ebao), a wealth management marketplace (Zhao Cai Bao), a small-business-lending business (Aliloan), and a credit-scoring business (Zhima Credit or "Sesame" Credit).

- **Money Market Fund (Yu'ebao)**: As e-commerce expanded, Alipay saw that users were holding large balances in their Alipay accounts, which did not pay any interest. Chinese banks did not offer attractive savings rates or investment advice because of the absence of a wealth-management industry for anyone except high-net-worth individuals. In June 2013, Alipay launched a high-interest money market account targeting these consumer deposits called Yu'ebao, which means "spare treasure" in Chinese.[8] Alipay customers could transfer as little as RMB 1 into their Yu'ebao account, which paid an annual interest rate of 5 percent to 6 percent compared to the 3.3 percent rate available on one-year bank deposits. Within six months, Yu'ebao had attracted US$41 billion in investments, and by mid-2017, it had amassed US$165 billion, making it the world's largest money-market fund (ahead of JP Morgan's US$150 billion government money-market fund). Yu'ebao peaked at $250 billion in March 2018, before regulatory pressure led Alipay to impose daily liquidity limits, contributing to a decline in deposits to $168 billion by year-end 2018.
- **Wealth Management (Zhao Cai Bao)**: Most Chinese have little financial literacy and no familiarity with investing and financial products. In April 2014, Ant Financial launched a marketplace for third-party investment products called Zhao Cai Bao.

- **Small-Business Lending (Aliloan, renamed Ant Credit):** Alibaba found that its merchants could not get loans to finance working capital because of a lack of collateral. In 2010, Aliloan began offering unsecured microloans to merchants with the credit limit determined using big-data analysis of merchant behavior in the Alibaba ecosystem. At the time of its U.S. IPO in 2014, Alibaba's prospectus disclosed that it had made US$2.1 billion in microloans to merchants. By year end 2017, this total had reached $5 billion.
- **Credit Scores (Zhima Credit):** The fact that China did not have a comprehensive system of individual credit scores or histories meant that most consumers had limited access to credit. In 2015, therefore, Ant Financial set up Zhima Credit (Sesame Credit), which leveraged big data to provide consumer credit scores based on users' past payment history and their online behavior, including reputation scores on Alipay, Taobao, and Tmall and connections in their social network.
- **Digital Banking:** In 2015, Ant Financial launched an online bank, MYbank, with a mission to serve small businesses and farmers in rural locations with no access to banking services. MYbank is a joint venture with a privately owned banking conglomerate, with Ant Financial holding a 30 percent stake. Within its first two years, MYbank had provided micro-loans averaging RMB 30,000 to 5 million small businesses, with a non-performing loan ratio between 2 percent to 4 percent.

The Birth of Ant Financial

In May 2014, Alibaba announced plans to list its shares in the United States through an initial public offering (IPO). In preparation for this listing, Alibaba was restructured to address regulatory restrictions preventing foreign ownership of a Chinese payment gateway.

Alibaba spun off its five financial units (Alipay, Yu'e Bao, Zhao Cai Bao, Ant Credit, and MYbank) to form Ant Financial Services. Ant Financial's stated mission was to "Bring small and beautiful changes to the world." The ant was chosen as its logo, symbolizing the combined efforts of these small but powerful insects to work towards a common goal, namely using technology to enable financial inclusion. Ant Financial completed a Series A round of financing for an undisclosed amount in June 2015, a US$4.5 million Series B round in April 2016, and then a massive US$14 billion Series C round in June 2018 (led by Singapore's Temasek Holdings and GIC).[9] Ant Financial also raised US$3.5 billion in debt in May 2017 to finance expansion and international acquisitions.

Ant Financial has now grown to become a full-service financial intermediary, providing customers with the products and services needed to manage their financial lives – called FinLives by Ant Financial executives (Wong, 2018).[10] In addition to the existing payment, lending, wealth-management, and banking services, Ant Financial offers the following services to small businesses and consumers, online or via the mobile app:[11]

- **Consumer Lending**: In 2014, Ant Financial set up two consumer lending businesses, Ant Credit Pay (Hua Bei) and Ant Cash Now. Using Zhima Credit scores, consumers can apply for a loan in three minutes, using the Alipay app, and get approval in one second with zero human intervention (the "3-1-0" model).
- **Wealth Management**: In August 2015, Ant Financial established Ant Fortune as a comprehensive wealth-management platform catering to users with little financial expertise. Ant Fortune charged no fees and provided access to Yu'ebao and Zhao Cai Bao. In 2017, Ant Financial opened the wealth-management marketplace Caifu Hao to allow third-party financial institutions to sell wealth-management products.

- **Insurance**: In late 2013, Ant Financial partnered with Chinese insurance company Ping An to launch China's first online insurance company, Zhong An Online P&C Insurance Company. In its first year of operation, Zhong An underwrote 630 million policies for 150 million customers. Ant Financial developed a third-party online insurance marketplace called Ant Insurance Services to provide insurance products to individuals and small businesses from eighty-plus insurance partners. Ant Insurance promises a seamless claims process that takes two minutes to file online, with reimbursement in two hours. Over the first year of operation, Ant Insurance Services insured 392 million customers and 40 million small business owners. Ant Financial has also launched a mutual-aid health insurance plan on the Alipay app that provides basic medical coverage, with the risks and expenses distributed across all members. As of April 2019, it had attracted 50 million members (mostly low-income) with a target of 300 million within two years.[12]
- **Equity Crowdfunding**: In 2015, Ant Financial established ANTSDAQ, the first licensed equity crowdfunding platform in China. It will help entrepreneurs to raise capital from high-net-worth investors who meet minimum wealth and income limits.[13]
- **Global Payments**: Alipay has expanded globally, partnering with Paytm in India, Ascend Money in Thailand, Kakao Pay in South Korea, Mynt and GCash in the Philippines, bKash in Bangladesh, Easypaisa in Pakistan, Touch 'n Go in Malaysia, and Dana in Indonesia. Working with GCash, Alipay has launched a blockchain-based cross-border remittance service.
- **Other Financial Services**: Ant Financial Cloud provides cloud computing services to financial customers. Ant Financial is also investing in artificial intelligence to detect payment risks such as fraud. At its investor day in 2018, Ant Financial reported a throughput of 25,000 transactions per second on its proprietary

blockchain, with production underway in origination verification, remittances, charitable donations, mutual insurance, and hospital e-invoices.

Ant Financial's goal is to understand a customer's needs even before they arrive by exploiting the many data sources on its users. The rate of user adoption of multiple products supports this claim. In 2018, Ant Financial reported that the number of customers using two or more categories of services was 640 million, three or more categories was 480 million, and five categories was 190 million.[14] By Q1 2017, Ant Financial had lent RMB 654 billion ($95 billion) to consumers and small businesses (Frost et al., 2019).

Table 7.1 summarizes the factors that contributed to the domestic success of Ant Financial and Tencent in financial services. Over the past three decades, China underwent economic, demographic, and technological changes that increased demand for financial products from unbanked small businesses and consumers. The Chinese techfins responded by developing online ecosystems that addressed "institutional voids" in China's financial system (Xie, Siew Kien, & Neo, 2017). China also featured a permissive policy and regulatory environment that supported their growth and expansion.

Exporting the Techfin Business Model Abroad

Can the domestic success of the Chinese techfins be replicated abroad? The answer is yes and no.

The features of the Chinese financial system that supported the rapid growth of techfins in China are also present in many emerging market economies (EMEs). Techfins are expanding in EMEs through acquisitions and partnerships, particularly in India, Asia, Latin America, and the Caribbean. These regions feature large,

Table 7.1. Factors explaining the success of the Chinese techfins

---

Economic, Demographic, and Technological Changes

- Rapid economic growth created a middle class of Chinese consumers with rising incomes, increasing wealth, and more leisure time.
- China features a large population of unbanked or underbanked consumers and small businesses whose needs were underserved because of the poor state of the domestic financial system.
- Millennials who were better educated and earned higher salaries were more willing to shop and transact online.
- China's telecommunications infrastructure developed with the arrival of the Internet, personal computers, and mobile phones, allowing techfins to leapfrog into digital banking without the need for expensive branch networks.
- The techfins benefited from other technological developments: cloud computing, big data and analytics, artificial intelligence and machine learning, and QR codes.

Institutional Voids

- China's state-owned economy was inefficient, with businesses and retail customers facing high information asymmetry, high search costs, and a lack of trust between buyers and sellers.
- China's state-owned banking system focused on large companies and government entities.
- China did not have a system of credit scores or ratings, or the history required to create one using traditional metrics.
- Many small businesses and consumers were financially constrained, with little access to credit.
- China's payments infrastructure was antiquated. China did not have a network of credit or debit cards, relying on cash as a primary means of payment.
- Consumers were forced to use expensive and time-consuming methods to transfer money and make payments.
- China's wealth-management industry was undeveloped and focused on high-net-worth individuals, with little attention to lower-income households

Policy and Regulatory Environment

- China's policy and regulatory environment is centrally directed, reflecting the earlier state of development of China's financial system and the nature of the players.
- The stated missions of both Alibaba and Tencent were aligned with government policy to promote economic growth, financial development, and financial inclusion.
- High barriers to entry prevented foreign competition from U.S. tech companies. The techfins could replicate and innovate on foreign business models without fear of foreign competition.
- China's permissive regulatory environment allowed the entry of techfins into payments, investments, and banking.
- Privacy laws in China, or the lack thereof, are more favorable for the data-intensive business models of the techfins.

---

growing, and younger populations with the same high penetration of Internet and mobile phones. The potential for e-commerce and online financial services that leapfrog the existing financial infrastructure is also present. As of 2019, Alipay was already in forty-two countries and supported twenty-seven currencies, while WeChat Pay was in forty-nine countries and supported fourteen currencies.[15]

By contrast, Alibaba and Tencent have made little headway in North America and Europe, where they face competition from bigtech and larger fintechs, as well as opposition from policymakers and regulators. In 2013, Tencent ran high-profile advertising campaigns in European nations with soccer star Lionel Messi. Tencent ultimately withdrew from this market, largely due to the dominance of Facebook and WhatsApp.[16] In 2018, Ant Financial's proposed $1.2 billion acquisition of MoneyGram International was rejected by the U.S. government's Committee on Foreign Investment in the United States over security concerns, despite Jack Ma's visit to the United States to meet with President Donald Trump a year earlier.[17]

As a result of these setbacks, both Chinese techfins have narrowed their ambitions in the near term to serving Chinese tourists traveling overseas and foreign customers who purchase products on Chinese e-commerce sites. For example, in October 2016, Ant Financial partnered with Verifone to allow merchants in North America and Europe to accept Alipay app payments through Verifone's mobile point-of-sale solution.[18] In February 2019, the U.S. drugstore company Walgreens announced a partnership with Ant Financial to introduce Alipay in 7,000 locations across the United States.[19] Tencent has also scaled back its ambitions. While it retains a U.S. branch office in Palo Alto, California, the office is currently focused on recruiting and partnerships, not U.S. expansion.[20]

The Threat from North American Bigtech

While the ambitions of the Chinese techfins to expand in the advanced economies have been curbed in the near term, the question remains whether other bigtech companies are positioning themselves to offer financial services on their platform ecosystems.

In the case of Amazon, the answer appears to be yes. Amazon has spent a decade building a foundation in payments and is now strategically expanding into other financial services to support its e-commerce marketplace, discussed in greater detail below. While we focus on its financial activities in North America, Amazon is aggressively expanding its financial offerings in EMEs, using these markets to pilot products and develop expertise that may be used to offer these services later in developed markets.

Apple, Google, and Facebook appear to be entering financial services in North America and Europe by offering payments (through Apple Pay, Google Pay, and Facebook Messenger, respectively).[21] They are also partnering with financial incumbents. Apple has partnered with American Express, with banks to offer Apple Pay, and will issue a Mastercard backed by Goldman Sachs. Apple's strategy appears to be designed to protect its share of the smartphone market by providing increased functionality on the iPhone and Apple ecosystem.

Facebook's and Google's intentions in North America and Europe are less clear, but they are actively expanding in EMEs.

In 2011, Google introduced an e-wallet and in 2015 partnered with U.S. online lender Lending Club to offer merchant financing.[22] But in 2016 Google closed its comparison-shopping website for mortgages, credit cards, and insurance after only a year.[23] Google has not made any clear statements about its intentions, but it is investing in start-ups. It spun off its investment arm, Google Ventures (GV), in 2009 with Google's parent company, Alphabet, as the sole limited partner. As of 2016, GV, had invested in 245 ventures, of which 13 percent were fintechs.[24] By early 2019, GV had funded more than 400 portfolio companies across all stages and sectors, but the terms "financial services" and "fintech" did not appear.[25] In 2018 Google obtained an e-Money license in Lithuania. And Google has partnered with Indian banks to offer micro-loans through Google Pay, which already offers money transfers and payments.[26]

Facebook has long had an agreement with PayPal that allows users to send money through Facebook Messenger. In 2018 Facebook approached U.S. banks about partnering to provide their services on its platform.[27] But Facebook scrapped its initial peer-to-peer (P2P) money transfer service in Europe after it failed to gain traction. Then in June 2019, Facebook announced plans to launch a digital currency, Libra, to facilitate low-cost money transfers and payments globally using Facebook Messenger and WhatsApp.[28] The digital currency would be backed by a reserve of currencies and U.S. Treasuries, recorded on an open-source blockchain and held in a digital wallet, Calibra, which is owned and operated by a Facebook subsidiary.[29] No banks were listed in the original group of twenty-eight partners, which included VCs, nongovernmental organizations, blockchain companies, payment providers, tech companies, telecoms, and ride-sharing companies. With its global user base of 2.4 billion users as of March 2019, Libra could provide the foundation for Facebook to take a leading position in retail financial services.

While Apple, Google, and Facebook may pose less of a threat to financial incumbents than Amazon, these companies possess the required ingredients to be successful: massive loyal customer bases, well-recognized brands, a history of innovation, a focus on customer experience and design, and expertise in the same technologies driving fintech innovations.

Amazon's Path to Financial Services

The market-intelligence company CB Insights has studied Amazon's strategy in financial services and concluded that it is pursuing a systematic strategy to offer financial services in North America without applying to become a conventional bank (Davis, 2018):

> Based on our findings, it's hard to claim that Amazon is building the next-generation bank. But it's clear that the company remains very focused on building financial services products that support its core strategic goal: increasing participation in the Amazon ecosystem.[30]

Like the Chinese techfins, Amazon first entered financial services by offering payment solutions to increase sales in its marketplace and capture revenues from interchange fees. From this foundation, Amazon has added small-business lending, cash deposits, consumer credit and debit cards, and product insurance.[31] In 2019 there were also rumours of partnerships with major banks to offer regulated financial services such as chequing accounts and mortgages. The pace at which Amazon is introducing financial products appears to be accelerating, suggesting that more is coming.

According to CB Insights, Amazon's strategy has been to build internally and learn through trial and error, rather than to rely on external partnerships, investments, or acquisitions.[32] Amazon develops and tests new features in select markets over several iterations, before launching them more broadly, at which point it is too late for incumbents to respond.

Amazon's entry into payments illustrates its long-term vision. Amazon has spent a decade to develop a full payments infrastructure, including credit and debit cards, e-wallets, cash deposits, and, most recently, biometric payments technology.

• In 2007, Amazon Pay was introduced, allowing customers to pay using credit and debit cards stored in their Amazon account.

- In 2013, "Login and Pay with Amazon" launched in the United States, allowing customers to pay merchants on third-party websites using their Amazon account. This service competes directly with PayPal. It was rolled out in India, and then Europe in 2014.
- In 2017, Amazon Cash allowed users to add cash deposits to their Amazon accounts.
- Amazon Pay Express was added to provide a merchant-payments processing service.
- Amazon's most recent payments initiative is its Amazon Go grocery store, where consumers shop with no checkout required. Customers scan their Amazon app to gain access to the store, then "grab and go" without needing a physical check-out to pay for products.

Along the way Amazon has demonstrated a willingness to fail.

- In 2007, Amazon Flexible Payments Service was introduced to allow P2P money transfers using tokenization but was discontinued in 2015.
- In 2008, Amazon released two e-commerce payments solutions, "Amazon Simple Pay" and "Checkout by Amazon." Amazon Simple Pay allowed third-party websites to accept Amazon account information for payment, but was discontinued in 2015. Checkout by Amazon was an all-in-one solution that allowed online stores to book and process orders like Amazon, including the one-click option, with the payments managed by Amazon. It was discontinued in 2017 and replaced with "Pay with Amazon."
- In 2014, Amazon's point-of-sale card reader for small businesses, Amazon Local Register, was launched but then shut down a year later.

- In mid-2014, Amazon launched a mobile wallet, only to withdraw it six months later.[33]

These failures and subsequent product launches reveal a strategy of experimentation, always with the goal of increasing sales in Amazon's marketplace.

Amazon's other major financial product is Amazon Lending. In 2011, Amazon began providing loans to select merchants on its platform, with the goal of increasing sales by helping merchants finance their Amazon inventories. Amazon Lending offers loans from $1,000 to $750,000 with terms of up to one year, reportedly in partnership with Bank of America.[34] Amazon Lending is by invitation only and is restricted to financing inventories with Amazon, with qualifying merchants selected based on past sales metrics. The application is completed online with rapid turnaround and interest rates reportedly from 3 percent to 17 percent.[35] Over its first six years, Amazon SMB lending provided $3 billion of loans to 20,000 businesses in the United States, Japan, and the United Kingdom.

Key Competitive Strengths of Techfins and Bigtech

This final section reviews the key competitive strengths of techfins and bigtech to assess their potential threat to incumbent financial institutions. While these tech companies feature many competitive strengths, we focus on three that have particular importance for financial services:

1. platform ecosystems and network effects,
2. access to customers and brand recognition, and
3. data insights and customer experience.

Platform Ecosystems and Network Effects

These technology companies are following a "platform ecosystem" strategy built around a core product that is integrated with other in-house or third-party products through an online portal or mobile app (Ceccagnoli et al., 2012; Gawer & Cusumano, 2014). Alibaba's and Amazon's core product is e-commerce. For Tencent and Facebook, it is social media. Apple's core product is smartphones. And Google's is a search engine. In biology the term "ecosystem" describes a community of living organisms and the nonliving components that support them. In a platform ecosystem, the living organisms are the users and merchants while the nonliving components are the products, services, and other features.

The goal of a platform ecosystem is to attract different categories of users to the platform and generate network effects (Evans & Schmalensee, 2016; Rysman, 2009). Same-side network effects occur when an increase in users on one side of the platform attracts even more users on the same side. With cross-side network effects, the growth of users on one side (e.g., customers) attracts more users on the other side (e.g., merchants, advertisers). Each platform ecosystem seeks to offer a unique combination of core and complementary products and features that makes the platform sticky, leading to loyal, repeat visitors. This stickiness creates a barrier to entry, as users may find it difficult to leave the ecosystem or to multihome on competing platforms.

Once this business model is understood, it becomes clear that the techfin and bigtech platform ecosystems will inevitably offer financial services to their users. To be able to engage in e-commerce or P2P transactions, users need an account and an online method of payment. By adding a payment gateway to the platform, the tech company can further monetize its users by capturing part of the interchange fee. Customer and merchant accounts on the platform will also require cash balances, creating opportunities to cross-sell credit, loans, investments, and insurance products.

Access to Customers and Brand Recognition

Most financial products are commodities with many close substitutes. For this reason, banks have invested heavily to build brick-and-mortar branch networks (a tangible asset) and to create a distinctive brand (an intangible asset). The branch network allowed banks to compete for customers based on proximity and convenience. The brand allowed the bank to market a unique value proposition to targeted customer segments. Both sources of competitive advantage have been eroded in recent years, the former by technologies like the Internet and smartphones, and the latter by financial crises and banking scandals and fines.

Technology has eroded the value of a branch network over decades: during the 1970s to 1980s by the introduction of automated teller machines and telephone banking; during the 1990s and 2000s by the arrival of the Internet and online banking; and during the past decade by mobile networks and smartphones. Now consumers have a bank in their pocket, allowing a new generation of customers to bypass physical branches altogether.[36]

In this digital world where geography is less of a barrier, the principal barriers to entry are a financial intermediary's brand recognition and the trust associated with it. These intangible assets were heavily damaged by the 2008–2009 global financial crisis. They were further damaged from 2010 to 2018 by scandals and criminal convictions that resulted in billions of dollars of fines paid by banks globally.

The extent of the damage can be estimated by examining the annual rankings of the most valuable global brands, as compiled annually by Interbrand. In 2006, global financial institutions were eight of the top fifty most valuable brands (led by Citigroup at number 11, American Express at number 14, and Merrill Lynch at number 21). Technology companies were all lower-rated (with Google at number 24, Apple at number 39, and Amazon at number 65).[37] By 2018, these positions had reversed: Apple, Google, and Amazon held the top three spots, and only five global financial institutions were in the top fifty (led by American Express at number 24 and JPMorgan at number 26).[38]

A key metric used to measure the success of techfins and bigtech companies is the size of their user base.[39] Alibaba had 634 million at year-end 2018, while Alipay had over 900 million worldwide. Tencent's WeChat app had 1.1 billion users. In 2018, it is estimated that 45 percent of Americans owned an Apple iPhone. In early 2019, Facebook reported 2.38 billion monthly active users.[40] And since 2016, Google has reportedly been handling 2 trillion searches per year. Clearly these tech companies have been successful in acquiring customers and developing brand loyalty.

Techfins and bigtech companies have suffered significant damage to the trust in their brands over the past two years. In China, Alibaba and Tencent are accused of collaborating with government authorities to monitor Chinese citizens and suppress free speech.[41] Facebook has been hit by disclosures of security breaches, fake news campaigns, and unauthorized use of customer data by third parties.[42] Technology companies have faced critical news coverage, regulatory scrutiny, political inquiries, fines from regulators, and civil lawsuits by privacy advocates. While these events have mostly focused on the ad-based business models of Facebook and Google, all technology companies that collect customer data have been affected. While these companies have updated and publicized their privacy policies, the damage to customer trust remains.

Data Insights and Customer Experience

The media are full of references to the quantity of data that is being collected each day on consumer behavior. Data scientists often cite the same statistic – 90 percent of all data in the world has been collected in the past two years.[43] This data collection has been made possible by the emergence of cloud computing since 2006 and the associated drop in the cost of storage and computing power. The greater availability of data and computing power has awoken the dormant field of artificial intelligence (AI). In particular, the science of getting computers to learn and act without being explicitly programmed – known as machine learning – is being deployed across industries: autonomous vehicles, genome mapping, speech recognition, web search, e-mail spam filters, and recommender systems. It is also being heavily used in financial services.

At the epicenter of this data collection are the platform ecosystems. As mentioned earlier, one of the main competitive strengths of the techfins and bigtech companies is their ability to capture and analyze proprietary data on customer behavior. These platforms are logging each click, key stroke, text message, chat, post, image, and video. These unstructured data sets are being analyzed using machine learning to generate insights on user behavior. The stated goal is to be able to understand a customer's needs even before they arrive. As explained by Alibaba's CEO Daniel Zhang in their 2018 investor day, these data allow Alibaba to turn business-to-consumer (B2C) on its head, with final customer demand generating consumer insights that lead to the supply of new products, or C2B.[44]

But to be clear, the competitive advantage for financial services is not the data per se, it is how these data are used to understand a customer's needs. The techfins and bigtechs are not selling financial services to make a profit from their customers. Their goal is to help customers enjoy their lives and in so doing provide financial services at the moment when users need them (i.e., "turning on the tap of water") to fuel their marketplaces.

This customer-centric perspective (or paradigm) is crucial for understanding the threat to financial incumbents from techfins and bigtechs. These tech companies are not looking to replace the banks, because they do not view the banks as their competitors. Instead these companies want to create a simple and lower-cost experience for their customers. In so doing they are bundling financial services with nonfinancial products. It is this unrelenting focus on the customer experience that distinguishes techfins from fintechs and other financial intermediaries. It is also why financial incumbents should be worried. Soon they may become product manufacturers whose commodity goods are fighting for space on a digital shelf in an online superstore controlled by Alibaba or Amazon.

NOTES

1 I am grateful to Jon Frost, Jesse McWaters, and Richard Nesbitt for input and suggestions. I have also benefited from excellent industry briefings by Lindsay Davis and Matthew Wong of CB Insights. All errors and omissions are my own. Prof. Michael R. King can be contacted at the Gustavson School of Business, University of Victoria, Business & Economics Building 246, 3800 Finnerty Rd, Victoria, BC, V8P 5C2, Canada, michaelking@uvic.ca.
2 Soo, 2016. See also Skinner, 2019.
3 Chen Long, chief strategy officer for Ant Financial, quoted on page 8 in Xie, Siew Kien, & Neo, 2017.
4 FSB, 2019.
5 Carstens, 2018.
6 Chorzempa, 2018.
7 In June 2010, the People's Bank of China issued new regulations that required nonbank payment companies to obtain a license in order to operate in China. Chinese payment companies could not be foreign

owned, which meant that Alibaba had to divest, due to the minority stake held by Yahoo! and Softbank.

8 The Yu'ebao money market fund is managed by Tianhong Asset Management, which is 51 percent owned by Ant Financial.

9 Crunchbase, nd.

10 Ant Financial, nd.

11 The statistics in this section are taken from the Ant Financial strategy presentation by CEO Eric Jing. See: Alibaba Group, 2018.

12 Zhang, 2019.

13 Xiang, 2015.

14 Alibaba Group, 2018.

15 Wu, 2018.

16 Millward, 2016.

17 Roumelio, 2018.

18 *Business Wire*, 2016.

19 Walgreens, 2019.

20 Tencent America, nd.

21 In the United States, 55 million people used mobile payments in 2018, with 22 million users of Apple Pay, 11.1 million users of Google Pay, and 9.8 million users of Samsung Pay. Kats, 2018.

22 LendingClub, 2015.

23 Demos & Nicas, 2016.

24 Medici, 2016.

25 GV, nd.

26 Russell, 2018.

27 Glazer, Seetharaman, & Andriotis, 2018.

28 Murphy, 2019.

29 Facebook, 2019.

30 CB Insights, nd.

31 In January 2018, Amazon announced a collaboration with Berkshire Hathaway and JPMorgan to launch a company aimed at cutting healthcare costs for their U.S. employees. *Business Wire*, 2018.

32 Amazon has acquired companies in order to recruit talent and purchase intellectual property, not the existing business. See: Lunden, 2013.

33 Musil, 2015.

34 Kim, 2018.

35 Guinan, 2019.

36 *Economist*, 2019.

37 Interbrand, 2006.

38 Interbrand, 2018.
39 Unless otherwise noted, these statistics are provided by the market and consumer-data company Statista, nd.
40 Facebook, nd.
41 For two examples among many articles, see: Mitchell & Diamond, 2018, and Schmidt & Feng, 2019.
42 Newcomb, 2018.
43 Marr, 2018.
44 Alizila, 2018.

REFERENCES

Alibaba Group. (2018, 17 September). 2018 Investor Day. https://www .alibabagroup.com/en/ir/investorday.
Alizila. (2018, 17–18 September). Alibaba investor day 2018 – Webcast and highlights. Hangzhou, China. https://www.alizila.com/alibaba-investors -day-2018-live-stream/.
Ant Financial. (nd). About Ant. https://www.antfin.com/index.htm?locale =en_US. Accessed 17 June 2019.
Business Wire. (2016, 24 October). Verifone partnership expands Alipay acceptance to major retailers in North America and Europe. https://www .businesswire.com/news/home/20161024005450/en/.
Business Wire. (2018, 30 January). Amazon, Berkshire Hathaway and JPMorgan Chase & Co. to partner on U.S. employee healthcare. https://www. businesswire.com/news/home/20180130005676/en/Amazon-Berkshire -Hathaway-JPMorgan-Chase-partner-U.S.
Carstens, A. (2018, 4 December). Big tech in finance and new challenges for public policy. Keynote address at the FT Banking Summit, London. https:// www.bis.org/speeches/sp181205.htm.
CB Insights. (nd). Everything you need to know about what Amazon is doing in financial services. https://www.cbinsights.com/research/report /amazon-across-financial-services-fintech/.
Ceccagnoli, M., Forman, C., Huang, P., & Wu, D.J. (2012). Cocreation of value in a platform ecosystem: The case of enterprise software. *MIS Quarterly*, *36*(1), 263–90. https://doi.org/10.2307/41410417.
Chorzempa, M. (2018, 26 April). How China leapfrogged ahead of the United States in the fintech race. Peterson Institute for International Economics. https://www.piie.com/blogs/china-economic-watch/how-china -leapfrogged-ahead-united-states-fintech-race.

Crunchbase. (nd). Ant Financial. https://www.crunchbase.com/organization /ant-financial#section-funding-rounds. Accessed 21 June 2019.

Davis, L. (2018, August 14). Amazon in financial services. CB Insights. https:// www.cbinsights.com/research/briefing/amazon-in-financial-services/.

Demos, T., & Nicas, J. (2016, 22 February). Google shuttering comparison -shopping site for auto insurance, credit cards, mortgages. *Wall Street Journal.* https://www.wsj.com/articles/google-shuttering-comparison-shopping -site-for-auto-insurance-credit-cards-and-mortgages-1456194520.

Economist, The. (2019, 4 May). Special report: Banking – A bank in your pocket. https://shop.economist.com/products/special-report-on-banking.

Evans, D.S., & Schmalensee, R. (2016). *Matchmakers – The new economics of multisided platforms.* Cambridge, MA: Harvard Business Review Press.

Facebook. (2019, 18 June). Coming in 2020: Calibra. https://newsroom.fb.com /news/2019/06/coming-in-2020-calibra/.

Facebook. (nd). Stats. https://newsroom.fb.com/company-info/. Accessed 12 June 2019.

Frost, J., Gambacorta, L., Huang, Y., Shin, H.S., & Zbinden, P. (2019, April). Bigtech and the changing structure of financial intermediation. BIS Working Papers No 779.

FSB (Financial Stability Board). (2019, 14 February). Fintech and market structure in financial services: Market developments and potential financial stability implications. https://www.fsb.org/wp-content/uploads/P140219 .pdf.

Gawer, A., & Cusumano, M.A. (2014). Industry platforms and ecosystem innovation. *Journal of Product Innovation Management, 31*(3), 417–33. https:// doi.org/10.1111/jpim.12105.

Glazer, E., Seetharaman, D., & Andriotis, A.M. (2018, 6 August). Facebook to banks: Give us your data, we'll give you our users. *Wall Street Journal.* https://www.wsj.com/articles/facebook-to-banks-give-us-your-data-well -give-you-our-users-1533564049.

Guinan, K. (2019, 8 November). Amazon Lending business loans review. Finder.com. https://www.finder.com/amazon-lending-business-loans.

GV (Google Ventures). (nd). Portfolio. https://www.gv.com/. Accessed 2 July 2019.

Interbrand. (2006). Most valuable brands – 2006. https://www.interbrand.com /best-brands/best-global-brands/2006/ranking/. Accessed 11 June 2019.

Interbrand. (2018). Most valuable brands – 2018. https://www.interbrand.com /best-brands/best-global-brands/2018/ranking/. Accessed 11 June 2019.

Kats, R. (2018, 9 November). The mobile payments series: U.S. *eMarketer.* https://www.emarketer.com/content/the-mobile-payments-series-the-us.

Kim, E. (2018, 14 February). Amazon has partnered with Bank of America for its lending program: Sources. CNBC. https://www.cnbc.com/2018/02/14/amazon-and-bank-of-america-partner-for-lending-program-but-growth-has-stalled.html.

LendingClub. (2015, 15 January). Google and Lending Club partner to deliver new business financing program. https://www.lendingclub.com/public/lending-club-press-2015-01-15.action.

Lunden, I. (2013, 21 December). Amazon bought GoPago's mobile payment tech and product/engineering team, DoubleBeam bought the POS business. *Techcrunch*. https://techcrunch.com/2013/12/21/amazon-bought-gopagos-mobile-payment-tech-and-productengineering-team-doublebeam-bought-the-pos-business/.

Marr, B. (2018, 21 May). How much data do we create every day? The mind-blowing stats everyone should read. *Forbes*. https://www.forbes.com/sites/bernardmarr/2018/05/21/how-much-data-do-we-create-every-day-the-mind-blowing-stats-everyone-should-read/#7887ea8860ba.

Medici. (2016, 10 February). What is Google doing in fintech? https://gomedici.com/what-is-google-doing-in-fintech.

Millward, S. (2016, 24 May). WeChat's global expansion has been a disaster. *TechInAsia*. https://www.techinasia.com/wechat-global-expansion-fail.

Mitchell, A., & Diamond, L. (2018, 2 February). China's surveillance state should scare everyone. *The Atlantic*.

Murphy, H. (2019, 18 June). What is Libra, Facebook's new digital coin? *The Financial Times*. https://www.ft.com/content/c3746b5c-90de-11e9-aea1-2b1d33ac3271.

Musil, S. (2015, 20 January). Amazon to fold its mobile-wallet app beta on Wednesday. *Cnet*. https://www.cnet.com/news/amazon-to-fold-its-mobile-wallet-app-beta-on-wednesday/.

Newcomb, A. (2018, 24 March). A timeline of Facebook's privacy issues – and its responses. NBC News. https://www.nbcnews.com/tech/social-media/timeline-facebook-s-privacy-issues-its-responses-n859651.

Roumelio, G. (2018, 2 January). U.S. blocks MoneyGram sale to China's Ant Financial on national security concerns. *Reuters*. https://www.reuters.com/article/us-moneygram-intl-m-a-ant-financial/u-s-blocks-moneygram-sale-to-chinas-ant-financial-on-national-security-concerns-idUSKBN1ER1R7.

Russell, J. (2018, 28 August). Google is supercharging its Tez payment service in India ahead of global expansion. *Techcrunch*. https://techcrunch.com/2018/08/28/google-is-supercharging-its-tez-payment-service/.

Rysman, M. (2009). The economics of two-sided markets. *Journal of Economic Perspectives, 23*(3), 125–43. https://doi.org/10.1257/jep.23.3.125.

Schmidt, B., & Feng, V. (2019, 21 February). The companies behind China's high-tech surveillance state. *Bloomberg*.

Skinner, C. (2018). The difference between fintech and techfin. https://thefinanser.com/2018/06/difference-fintech-techfin.html/. Accessed 26 May 2019.

Soo, Z. (2016, 2 December). Techfin: Jack Ma coins term to set Alipay's goal to give emerging markets access to capital.

Statista. (nd). https://www.statista.com/. Accessed 12 June 2019.

Tencent America. (nd). Explore Tencent. http://www.exploretencent.com/. Accessed 17 June 2019.

Walgreens. (2019, 13 February). Alipay, the world's leading digital payment platform, now available at thousands of Walgreens stores nationwide. https://news.walgreens.com/press-releases/general-news/alipay-the -worlds-leading-digital-payment-platform-now-available-at-thousands-of -walgreens-stores-nationwide.htm.

Wong, M. (2018, 11 September). Ant Financial – Unpacking the $150B fintech giant. CB Insights. https://www.cbinsights.com/research/briefing/ant -financial-fintech-giant-growth/.

Wu, J. (2018, 10 December). A surprising number of countries now accept WeChat Pay or Alipay. *TechInAsia*. https://www.techinasia.com/surprising -number-countries-accept-wechat-pay-alipay.

Xiang, T. (2015, 25 November). Alibaba's online equity crowdfunding platform ANTSDAQ launches Beta. *Technode*. https://technode.com/2015/11/25 /alibabas-onilne-equity-crowdfunding-platform-antsdaq-launches-beta/.

Xie, R.S., Siew Kien, S., & Neo, B-S. (2017, 25 August). Fintech and finance transformation: The rise of Ant Financial Services. Nanyang Technical University case ABCC-2017-021.

Zhang, S. (2019, 11 April). China's Ant Financial amasses 50 million users, mostly low-income, in new health plan. *Reuters*. https://www.reuters.com /article/us-china-ant-financial-insurance/chinas-ant-financial-amasses-50 -million-users-mostly-low-income-in-new-health-plan-idUSKCN1RO0H5.

 CHAPTER EIGHT

Creating Strategic Value by Partnering with or Acquiring Fintechs

Jay Wilson

Tennis and banking share a number of similarities. My perspective is heavily influenced from having grown up as an avid junior and college tennis player before spending the first fifteen years of my professional life providing valuation and advisory services to community banks. Both tennis and banking are relatively mature, with the first records of both activities dating back to the late 1800s. Both have evolved over time and been influenced by technology. Competing at Wimbledon today involves genetically engineered synthetic grass, scientifically engineered rackets, and video replay. Technology continues to penetrate the banking industry as well, with customers increasingly asking banks to deliver services digitally through ATMs, the Internet, and mobile apps.

Despite these changes, the core objective of both activities remains the same. For tennis, the core objective is to hit the ball back and forth over the net and within the lines outlined on the court. For banking, the core objective is to provide customers with the ability to make deposits, save, borrow, and make or receive payments.

Many community banks face a unique problem of keeping pace with customer desires and technological innovations. These banks don't want to end up being the tennis player trying to compete in today's tournaments with a wooden racket. This is a significant issue for the banking industry, particularly in the United States, where community banks constitute the majority of banks and are collectively the largest providers of loans to agricultural and small-business borrowers. Furthermore, community banks are often key employers and providers of financing in their local communities, making them an important part of the economy.

In my view, fintech offers community banks the opportunity to equip themselves with the modern technology they need to enhance profitability and be competitive. Technology can also provide their customers with the core banking services that they desire. In order to understand how fintech can help traditional financial institutions compete more effectively, let us first take a closer look at the challenges facing community banks and discuss how fintech can help.

Threats to Community Banks

Four structural forces are changing the landscape for community banks: heightened competition, higher regulatory and compliance costs, a challenging interest-rate environment, and demographic changes in rural America.

Heightened Competition. Despite a decline in their numbers from around 10,000 banks in the mid-1990s, nearly 6,000 community banks with 51,000 locations still operate in the United States, including commercial banks, thrifts, and savings institutions. While community banks constitute the largest number of banks, approximately 90 percent of industry assets are controlled by a small number of extremely large banks with balance sheets greater than $1 billion. Big banks that once hemorrhaged market share are proving to be adept at deposit and asset gathering in larger metropolitan markets (figure 8.1), while community banks still perform relatively well in second-tier and small markets. Technology is

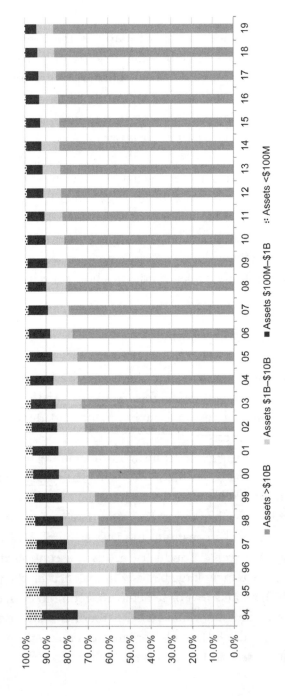

Figure 8.1 Percentage of U.S. bank industry total assets held by bank size category

Source: FDIC.

helping drive this trend, especially among millennials, who do not care much about brick-and-mortar but demand top-notch digital access. The very largest banks, such as JPMorgan Chase & Company, are spending billions of dollars annually to upgrade technology – a level of spending that even super regional banks cannot match. The data show that the efficiency and technology gap between large and small banks is widening.

In addition to increased competition from larger banks, community bankers are being challenged by the rise of fintech, which features a vast array of emerging companies and innovations. Fintech is a challenging strategic threat to assess. Community banks are facing innovations in core banking services (such as payments and lending) from larger, more mature, technology-oriented public companies (such as Square, Paypal, or Amazon) as well as a variety of smaller start-ups. For perspective, a group of community bankers meeting with the Federal Deposit Insurance Corporation (FDIC) in mid-2016 noted that fintech poses the largest threat to community banks. One executive indicated that the payments systems "are the scariest," as consumers are already starting to use fintech applications like Venmo and PayPal to send peer-to-peer (P2P) payments. Another banker went on to note, "What's particularly concerning about [the rise of fintech] for us is the pace of change and the fact that it's coming so quickly." To illustrate: consider that Square's Cash App doubled its user base in 2018 (from 7 million at year end 2017 to 15 million at year end 2018), and Square Capital (its small-business lending unit) lent out $400 million in the third quarter of 2018, representing 33 percent growth from a year earlier.

Higher Regulatory and Compliance Costs. Since the onset of the financial crisis in 2008, community banks have also faced a growing compliance and regulatory burden that has had a negative impact on profitability. To put this growing burden in perspective, consider the following:

- The Call Report, which all banks file quarterly, has increased in length from less than ten pages in the mid-1980s to more than eighty pages today.
- Both the number of new banking acts and the length of those acts has increased in each decade since the 1960s.[1]

Hiring additional staff to handle these regulatory and compliance demands can have a significant negative impact on profitability, particularly for smaller community banks. For example, a study at the Federal Reserve Bank of Minneapolis found a profitability reduction of forty-five basis points for increasing staff by two people for the smallest banks (those with less than $50 million in assets).[2] By leveraging innovations in the regulatory technology (regtech) area of fintech, community banks may be able to meet rising compliance expectations more efficiently and cost effectively.

Challenging Interest-Rate Environment. As detailed below, net interest margins (NIMs) have remained stagnant since the financial crisis. One key factor impacting NIMs was the Federal Reserve's post-financial-crisis zero-interest-rate policy, which resulted in ongoing compression of asset yields at a time when funding costs essentially had reached a floor. Despite increases in the prime rate corresponding with a rising-interest-rate environment since year end 2015, interest rates remain historically low, and margin expansion has been minimal through 2018.

Demographic Changes in Rural America. A study of community banks by the Federal Deposit Insurance Corporation (FDIC) noted that many community banks hold their strongest competitive position in nonmetro areas, as the majority of their offices and deposits are in micro and rural counties.[4] The study went on to note that one

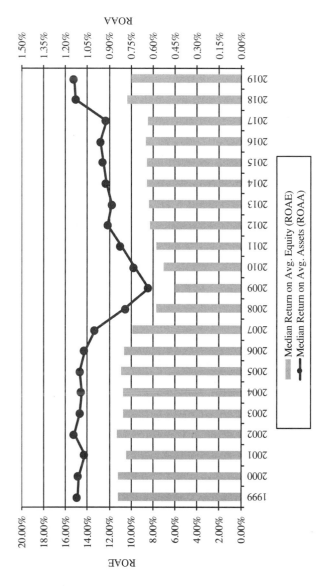

Figure 8.2 Trend in U.S. bank profitability

Source: S&P Global Market Intelligence[3]

downside of this trend is that both population growth and economic growth have been slower in these areas, a circumstance that limits growth opportunities. This trend of depopulation in rural areas does not appear likely to reverse in the near term and challenges the long-run growth potential for community banks. Furthermore, the study notes that depopulation often resulted in a "pinched" age distribution whereby outmigration of younger adults (aged twenty to forty-five) leaves community banks operating in markets where it is difficult to attract younger staff, management, and customers. Community banks will need to continue to adapt and find ways to grow in order to cope with the challenges presented by these demographic trends. These significant competitive and structural pressures have hurt the profitability of community banks (figure 8.3).

As a result, the critical role that a community bank fills as a lender to small business and agriculture is at risk if shareholders decide to sell because of inadequate returns. Confronting this challenge requires the right team executing the right strategy to produce competitive returns for shareholders. Fintech solutions, rather than geographic expansion through organic growth and acquisitions, may be an option. Fintech products and processes can address areas where a bank falls short (e.g., efficiency or revenues opportunities like payments, insurance, or wealth management).

Opportunities for Fintech Partnerships to Help

Many community bank cost structures are wedded to physical branches at a time when customers – especially younger ones – are increasingly interacting with institutions, first digitally and second via a physical location. This transition is occurring at a time

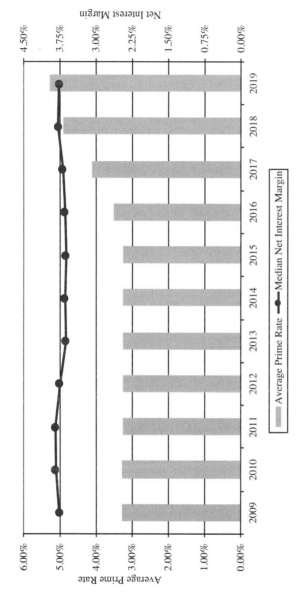

Figure 8.3 Trend in U.S. bank net interest margins

Source: S&P Global Market Intelligence[5]

when core deposits are increasing in value to the industry, as interest rates have risen modestly in recent years. In response, several larger banks, such as Citizens Financial, have increased their emphasis on digital banking to drive incremental deposit growth. For their part, rising funding costs are forcing some fintech companies to consider partnerships with banks. Thus far, both the push into digital banking and formal partnering with fintech companies have been incremental in nature rather than reflecting a wholesale change in business strategy. Nonetheless, community banks will need to adapt in order to compete for and win retail deposit relationships in a meaningful way.

Both banks and fintech companies realize that they need each other to some degree. While many bankers view fintech as a significant threat, others see its potential to assist the community banking sector.

For banks, fintech offers the potential to leverage innovation and new technologies to meet customer expectations for enhanced services. Fintech offers the potential to improve the health of community banks by enhancing efficiency, improving profitability, and returning ROEs back to historical levels. Fintech can also help community banks to compete more effectively against the largest banks and nonbank companies that offer compelling digital solutions.

For fintech companies, the benefits from bank partnerships include the potential to leverage the bank's customer relationships to scale more quickly, to access stable funding, and to gain regulatory and compliance expertise.

Enhancing Noninterest Income and Efficiency

One way to better understand how fintech can assist community banks is to understand the key drivers of profitability for larger banks. This higher profitability can be attributed to their economies of scale – greater revenues from noninterest income (such as fees and commissions) and their lower noninterest expenses (i.e., lower efficiency ratios). Fintech offers community banks several solutions to boost both of these profitability drivers.

Fintechs can enhance noninterest income through innovations in niche areas like payments, insurance, and wealth management. Many community banks have minimal personnel and legacy IT systems in these areas. To overcome these obstacles, community banks can partner with a fintech in these niches, such as a robo-advisor or insuretech company. Such a partnership might be viewed more favorably by a community bank, as it represents a new source of potential revenue and another service to offer their customers. This partnership would not cannibalize community banks' existing trust, wealth-management, or insurance staff, since they have minimal existing wealth-management personnel.

Fintech can also reduce expenses and enhance efficiency ratios for community banks. Branch networks are the largest cost of community banks, making up approximately 47 percent of banks' operating costs. And 54 percent of that branch expenditure goes to staffing.[6] Serving customers through digital banking costs significantly less than traditional in-branch services. The cost of ATM and online-based transactions is less than 10 percent of the cost of paper-based branch transactions in which tellers are involved.[7] In addition to the benefits from having customers shift to digital transactions, community banks can utilize fintech to assist with lowering regulatory/compliance costs by leveraging regtech solutions.

To illustrate the potential savings for community banks, let's assume that a mobile transaction saves approximately $3.85 per branch transaction.[8] If we assume that a community bank has 20,000 deposit accounts and each account shifts two transactions per month to mobile from in-person branch visits, the bank would

save $154,000 per month or $1.8 million annually. These efficiencies would serve to enhance earnings, shareholder returns, and the
bank's valuation.

Moving beyond noninterest income and efficiency ratios, fintech
offers other potential benefits for community banks. For example,
fintech can:

Minimize the Impact of Size/Scale. Fintech can be used to help
   community banks compete against big banks more effectively
   by minimizing the impact of scale as more customers carry their
   branch in their pocket.
Enhance Loan-Portfolio Diversification. Fintech can enhance
   portfolio diversification by offering loans digitally through
   specialized fintech solutions. Community banks can regain
   some market share after years of losing ground in certain
   segments such as consumer, mortgage, auto, and student
   loans.
Enhance Customer Relationships through Omnichannel. Fintech
   can provide an additional touch point to improve customer
   retention. While data are limited, some studies have shown
   that customer loyalty is higher for customers who use mobile
   offerings, with digital banking increasingly preferred by many
   customers.[9] But data have also shown that digital-only customers can be less engaged, loyal, and profitable than those who
   interact with the bank through a combination of channels (digital, branch, etc.). So, community banks that rely more heavily
   on their branch networks should find it beneficial to add digital
   services to complement their traditional offerings in order to
   enhance customer retention while meeting customer preferences
   for how they want to bank.
Value Creation. A key question for bankers and shareholders is,
   "What are the implications of technology for the value of my

bank?" In my own research, I found that the implications for the valuation of a community bank can be quite significant. We found that "triple threat" community banks – those banks with higher fee income, superior efficiency ratios, and greater technology spending – were being rewarded in the public market with better valuations, all else being equal (table 8.1). While we do not advocate for heavy tech spending as a means to an ill-defined objective, the evidence points to a superior valuation when technology is used to drive higher levels of fee income and greater operating leverage.

In analyzing these "triple threat" banks further, I determined that most, if not all, of the "triple threat" banks developed a "niche to riches" type of strategy, with one or more differentiated niches such as wealth management/trust, Small Business Association/ small-business lending, equipment financing/leasing, mortgage, or insurance. These banks augmented that niche with relevant fintech

Table 8.1. Valuation multiples of community banks

| | National Community Banks | Community Bank Peer Group Subset | | | |
		Higher Fee Income[1]	Low Efficiency Ratio[2]	Higher Tech Spending[3]	"Triple Threat" Banks[4]
Price / Earnings	10.9x	11.4x	10.7x	11.5x	12.2x
Price / Book	1.37x	1.45x	1.52x	1.45x	1.83x

Source: Mercer Capital Research, S&P Capital IQ Market Intelligence
Median Valuation Multiples as of 31 December 2018
1 High fee income banks have noninterest income greater than 1% of average assets in the last twelve-month period
2 Efficiency ratio less than 65% in the last twelve-month period
3 Technological expenses greater than 0.20% of average assets in the last twelve-month period
4 "Triple Threat" community banks meet all three criteria: High Fee Income, Low Efficiency Ratio, and Higher Tech Expenses

products. Thus, a digital-technology roadmap must be woven into the strategic plan and be consistent with the community bank's overarching strategy so that the institution will be positioned to take advantage of the opportunity that technology creates to enhance customer service and lower costs.

How to Develop a Fintech Framework

For banks of all sizes, the use of fintech and other enhanced digital offerings represents a potential investment that uses capital but may generate more attractive returns than other traditional growth strategies. While these strategic decisions will vary from bank to bank and may change over time, the stakes are incredibly high for all. In my view, it is increasingly important for bankers to develop a fintech framework and be able to adequately assess potential returns from fintech partnerships. As in other business endeavors, the difference between success and failure in the fintech realm is often not found in the ideas themselves but rather in the execution. Both sides need to navigate the decision process.

I see four primary steps to developing a fintech framework:

1. Evaluate the Bank's Existing Strategic Plan

The best place to start when developing a bank's fintech roadmap is to begin with the bank's existing strategic plan and determine how fintech might complement or enhance it. Fintech may be used to complement or enhance existing services, offer entirely new services, target new markets or customer segments, or reduce back-office costs and improve efficiency. Thus, banks should examine their existing strengths, weaknesses, opportunities, and threats (SWOT) within their strategic plan and consider how fintech might fit within that SWOT analysis.

- Strengths: Fintech products that build a "moat" around the bank's strengths
- Weaknesses: Fintech products that address weaknesses
- Opportunities: Fintech products that seize identified opportunities
- Threats: Fintech products that forestall erosion of existing revenues and customers

Most community banks cannot compete with large banks in terms of branch count and retail footprint. Thus, their fintech investments should match with the community bank's competitive position. For example, does the bank emphasize retail or commercial customers? How can fintech enhance the customer experience? The answer to this question may direct the bank's fintech initiatives as follows (table 8.2):

Table 8.2. Fintech ideas for retail or commercial strategies

Retail Emphasis	Commercial Emphasis
1. Small-dollar consumer lending	1. Underwriting efficiency and turn-around times
2. Online account opening and on-boarding	2. Business cash flow forecasting and management
3. Personal financial management	3. Accounting, budgeting, and payroll tools
4. Automated savings and investment	4. Payments
5. Online residential mortgage	5. Small-dollar C&I lending

2. Identify Attractive Fintech Niches and Companies within Those Niches.

There are a variety of fintech niches to consider, ranging from payments, lending, wealth management (wealthtech), insurance (insuretech), regtech, cryptocurrency and blockchain, and mortgages. Additionally, each niche includes a variety of players, ranging from smaller start-ups to more mature companies. While the vast number of niches and potential partners can be daunting, this breadth of fintech companies allows bankers to be selective and strategic in terms of prioritizing which niches and companies will fit in best with their strategic plan and objectives. One resource to assist banks with this step is to visit the Bank Director's FinXTech Connect, a database of fintech companies that have successfully completed partnerships with banks.[10]

3. Develop a Business Case for Different Strategies.

Fintech is just another capital-expenditure decision. It is therefore important for bankers to evaluate fintech opportunities consistently with other capital-expenditure decisions. An important question to consider is: how does the bank currently make capital-expenditure decisions? For example, how does the bank decide to construct a branch in a new location?

The bank can compare the cost of the fintech investment or partnership to the following:

- the profits generated from a product expansion;
- the profits protected from offering a product delivered by competitors;
- the costs saved from operating more efficiently.

The bank can also use capital budgeting techniques to assess its fintech partners. The techniques can range from the simple to the complex:

- **Simple**: Payback period on investment;
- **Complex**: Rank ordering of various alternatives based on their potential returns on investment and related risks.

Fintech strategies also offer innumerable potential relationships for the bank to assess:

- **Vendor Relationship:** The bank licenses a product from fintech companies.
- **Partner Relationship:** The bank receives greater integration with fintech companies and potential ownership.
- **Investor Relationship:** The bank takes a stake in or acquires the fintech company and shares in the upside and downside.

The bank may also want to consider whether they could build the fintech solution internally. Examining whether to build, license, partner, or invest in a fintech company can be complicated and should involve the use of capital budgeting tools, similar to the framework used for evaluating other capital expenditures.

4. Compare the Different Strategies and Execute the Optimal Strategy.

Once the prior steps are completed, the last step of the decision process may require the bank to establish a rate-of-return threshold and compare that to their estimate of the returns from the fintech endeavor. The range of returns for each fintech strategy (build, license, partner, or invest) for a targeted niche provides a framework to help answer the question of how to proceed. This is the same case when evaluating how to deploy capital for organic growth, acquisitions, and shareholder distributions. The same logic applies for fintech companies.

A detailed analysis, including an internal rate of return (IRR) analysis, helps a bank determine the financial impact of each strategic decision and informs the optimal course. While each option presents a unique set of considerations and execution issues/risks, a detailed analysis helps a bank determine the financial impact of each strategic decision and informs the optimal course. A detailed analysis also allows the bank to compare its fintech strategy to the bank's more traditional growth strategies, strategic plan, and cost of capital.

Partnership Strategy Case Studies and Key Questions

Below we show examples of three community banks that have incorporated fintech into their strategic plan, despite being smaller (in terms of assets) and in some cases located in rural markets.

CBW Bank is a bank located in a rural area (Weir, Kansas, with a population of less than 1,000). CBW Bank is run by a former Google engineer who acquired the bank during the depths of the financial crisis in 2008 and has incorporated fintech initiatives and partnerships into the bank's operations and strategy.[11] Table 8.3 provides an overview of CBW Bank's recent financial performance and some key fintech partnerships.

Nbkc Bank is a community bank that has combined multiple fintech initiatives and partnerships with its traditional branch locations in the metropolitan Kansas City area. Initiatives undertaken by nbkc Bank include starting a fintech accelerator program and partnering with several other fintech companies to enhance their product suite (table 8.4).[12]

Table 8.3. Profile of CBW Bank and its fintech initiatives

Example 1: CBW Bank

Headquarters Location	Weir, Kansas

Examples of FinTech Partners/Initiatives

Yantra	Develops banking and electronic payments systems
Moven	Mobile banking app that lets consumers bank remotely
Ripple	Facilitates a real-time settlement system, currency exchange, and remittance network
Omney	Provides instant payments capabilities to large-enterprise clients

Financial Summary

Total Assets (March 2019)	$56.8 million
Net Income	$5.0 million
Return on Assets	8.82%
Return on Equity	48.73%

Source: Mercer Capital, S&P Global Market Intelligence, and various other press releases and news articles for the bank

Table 8.4. Profile of nbkc Bank and its fintech initiatives

Example 2: nbkc Bank

Headquarters Location	Kansas City, Missouri

Examples of Fintech Partners/Initiatives

Established an Accelerator (Fountain City fintech)	Accelerator provides early access to fintech companies/solutions; fintechs receive seed capital and tap bank executives' expertise
ProPair	An AI company that connects mortgage leads to lending staff
Track	Assists self-employed workers with tax preparation
Greenlight Financial Technology	Provides a smart debit card for kids and young adults that parents manage from their phones

Financial Summary

Total Assets (March 2019)	$719.3 million
Net Income	$15.6 million
Return on Assets	2.38%
Return on Equity	18.88%

Source: Mercer Capital, S&P Global Market Intelligence, and various other press releases and news articles for the bank

Table 8.5. Profile of Radius Bank and its fintech initiatives

Example 3: Radius Bank	
Headquarters Location	Boston, Massachusetts
Examples of Fintech Partners/Initiatives	
Bottom Line Technologies	Offers e-payment, invoice, and document automation solutions
Level Up & NYC Currency Exchange	Shared deposit ATM network to make deposits and withdrawals at ATMs
Aspiration	High-yield checking account through an online investment firm
Prosper	Personal loans between $2 and $35,000
Alloy	Uses an API to automate account opening and manage identity verification through customer lifecycle
Financial Summary	
Total Assets (March 2019)	$1,306.9 million
Net Income	$10.6 million
Return on Assets	0.86%
Return on Equity	9.40%

Source: Mercer Capital, S&P Global Market Intelligence, and various other press releases and news articles for the bank

Radius Bank is a community bank headquartered in Boston, Massachusetts, that has developed a fintech partnership strategy to help the bank build its virtual and digital bank offerings (table 8.5).[13]

The fintech/bank partnership theme also was evident in the 2018 IPO of GreenSky Incorporated, a fintech company based in Atlanta, Georgia. GreenSky arranges loans primarily for home-improvement projects. Bank partners pay GreenSky to generate and service the loans, while the bank funds and holds the loans on their balance sheet. As more partnerships emerge, it will be interesting to see if fintech impacts the valuation of banks that effectively leverage technology to achieve strategic objectives such as growing low-cost core deposits, opening new lending venues, and improving efficiency. One would think the answer will be "yes" if the impact can be measured and is meaningful.

Some common questions for community banks that follow in these banks' footsteps and consider incorporating fintech partnerships into their strategic plans include the following:

- Is the bank comfortable with the fintech company's risk profile?
- What will the regulatory reaction be?
- Who will maintain the primary relationship with the customer?
- Is the fintech partnership consistent with the bank's long-term strategic plan? This was a key topic noted in the Office of the Controller of the Currency's 2016 white paper "Supporting Responsible Innovation in the Federal Banking System: An OCC Perspective."[14]

Acquisition Strategy Case Study and Key Questions

Beyond the strategic decisions around partnering, banks face the conundrum of whether they should acquire or invest in a fintech company.[15] Noncontrol investments in fintech companies by banks represent a hybrid strategy. Many acquisitions or investments often result after the bank has been partnered with the fintech for several years.

Table 8.6 shows that there has been no surge of mergers and acquisitions in which banks buy a fintech company. Out of 276 acquisitions of fintech companies announced from year-end 2016 to mid-2018, only nine (or 3 percent) were acquired by a bank or bank holding company. KeyCorp, which has been one of the nine active fintech acquirers, announced in June 2018 that it would acquire digital lending technology for small businesses built by Chicago-based fintech company Bolstr. At best, activity can be described as episodic as it relates to bank acquisitions, which appear to be designed to supplement internal development.

Table 8.6. Bank acquisitions of fintech companies from 31 December 2016 to June 2018

Fintech Seller	Bank Buyer	Announce Date	Deal Val ($M)
Patrick Consulting Group	Peoples Bancorp Inc.	1/31/17	0.50
Downeast Pension Services, Inc	NBT Bancorp Inc.	4/3/17	5.70
HelloWallet Holdings Inc.	KeyCorp	5/31/17	NA
Sharp BancSystems Inc.	First Baird Bancshares Inc.	6/9/17	NA
Key Merchant Services LLC	KeyCorp	6/30/17	NA
BoeFly, LLC	First Colorado Financial Corp.	8/30/17	NA
WePay Inc	JPMorgan Chase & Co.	10/17/17	NA
Tech and soft dev. resources	Northern Trust Corp.	1/11/18	NA
Digital Lending Platform (Bolstr)	KeyCorp	6/20/18	NA

Source: S&P Global Market Intelligence

For the most part, investments by community (and regional) banks in fintech companies remain sporadic as well, even though fintech companies raised nearly $16 billion of equity capital between year-end 2016 and June 2018. An interesting transaction was a $16 million Series A financing by Greenlight Financial Technology, a creator of smart debit cards, which included investments by SunTrust Bank, Amazon Alexa Fund, and nbkc Bank, among others.

Key Questions for Acquisition Strategy. Should the community bank ultimately decide to invest in or acquire a fintech partner, a number of other key questions emerge, such as:

• What is the valuation of the fintech company? High-growth and early-stage fintech companies present a number of unique and complex valuation issues. Additionally, fintech valuations can be vastly different from those for traditional banks. Fin-tech investors often focus on future revenues, profitability, and growth potential, whereas bank investors often focus on recent historical earnings or near-term earnings expectations and multiples of earnings and tangible book value.

- How should the investment be structured?
- What preferences or terms should be included in the shares purchased from the fintech company?
- Should the bank obtain board seats or some control over the direction of the fintech company's operations?

Conclusion

The world of banking is changing rapidly. Fintech represents an opportunity for traditional financial institutions like community banks to compete better and maintain their relevance. Understanding how fintech will impact an institution and how to respond are critical strategic issues. Many banks are actively surveying the fintech landscape and pursuing a strategy to improve their digital footprint and services through partnerships with fintech companies. Whether through partnerships or potential investments and acquisitions, both banks and fintech companies are coming to the conclusion that they need each other. Banks control the majority of customer relationships, have a stark funding advantage, and know how to navigate the maze of regulations, while fintechs represent a means to meet customer demand, innovate, and also achieve low-cost scaling of new and traditional bank services.

Whatever your strategy, understanding how fintech fits in and adapting to the current environment are incumbent upon any institution that seeks to compete effectively and avoid being the tennis player who shows up on the court today with a wooden racket.

NOTES

1 Ash, P., Kock, C., & Slems, T.F. (2015, 31 December). Too small to succeed? Community banks in a new regulatory environment. Dallas Fed, *Financial Insights*, 4(4).

2 See Feldman, R.J., Schmidt, J., & Heinecke, K. (2013, 30 May). Quantifying the costs of additional regulation on community banks. Federal Reserve Bank of Minneapolis, Economic Policy Paper 13-3.

3 Based on data compiled from 3,666 community banks at 31 December 2019 (defined as 3,232 commercial banks, 229 savings banks, and 205 savings and loan associations in the United States with assets between $100 million and $5 billion), excluding those with unusual loan portfolio and revenue composition.

4 FDIC (Federal Deposit Insurance Corporation). (2012, December). *Community banking study.*

5 Based on data compiled from 3,666 community banks at 31 December 2019 (defined as 3,232 commercial banks, 229 savings banks, and 205 savings and loan associations in the United States with assets between $100 million and $5 billion), excluding those with unusual loan portfolio and revenue composition.

6 Wilson, J. (2017). *Creating strategic value through financial technology.* Wiley: New York.

7 Smith, R.H. (2011, 1 November). Banking's big challenge: Breaking away from the branch model. *American Banker.* https://www.americanbanker.com /opinion/bankings-big-challenge-breaking-away-from-the-branch-model.

8 Huang, D. (2014, 18 December). Mobile's rise poses a riddle for banks. *Wall Street Journal.*

9 Ibid.

10 Bank Director. (nd). FinXTech Connect. See: https://finxtech.com/finxtech -connect/.

11 Quittner, J. (2016, 24 August). Why fintech startups are flocking to a 124-year-old bank in Kansas. *Fortune.* Available at http://fortune.com/2016/08/24 /fintech-bank/. Accessed 5 June 2019.

12 Streeter, B. (nd). Is this community bank's bold digital play the model of the future? *The Financial Brand.* Available at https://thefinancialbrand .com/76594/nbkc-digital-banking-future-fintech-lending/. Accessed 5 June 2019.

13 Miller, Z. (2019, 7 January). "It's not us versus them": How Radius Bank refined its partnership strategy with fintech firms. Radius Bank. Available at https://tearsheet.co/new-banks/its-not-us-versus-them-how-radius -bank-refined-its-partnership-strategy-with-fintech-firms/. Accessed 5 June 2019.

14 Office of the Controller of the Currency. (2016, 31 March). Supporting responsible innovation in the federal banking system: An OCC perspective.

Available at https://www.occ.gov/publications/publications-by-type
/other-publications-reports/pub-responsible-innovation-banking-system
-occ-perspective.pdf. Accessed 5 June 2019.

15 Regulatory hurdles limit the ability of fintech companies to make anything
more than a modest investment in banks, absent purchasing nonvoting
common shares and/or convertible preferred shares.

CHAPTER NINE

A Fintech Founder's Perspective on the Future of Financial Services

Andrew Graham

I am the co-founder and CEO of Borrowell, Canada's leading credit-education company.[1] Our mission is to help Canadians make great decisions about credit. We think it should be easier for Canadians to understand their credit, so they can be confident and in control of their finances. We began with a single product, providing unsecured loans to consumers with good credit histories. Then we started offering free credit scores and connecting consumers with the right products from bank partners. Now Borrowell runs a marketplace that offers credit cards, personal loans, auto loans, mortgages, savings accounts, checking accounts, and insurance.[2] And we recently launched Canada's first artificial intelligence (AI)-powered credit coach, which provides personalized credit monitoring and tips to help users improve their credit, and which is integrated into both our web and mobile app experiences.

We have thousands of new members signing up on our website or mobile apps each week. Our partnerships with other financial institutions have allowed us to reach hundreds of thousands more. In April 2019, we announced that more than 1 million people had checked their credit score with Borrowell, making us arguably the largest Canadian fintech by that measure.[3]

In this chapter I want to share my experience of being a fintech founder and my views on the transformation of the financial-services industry. I have a unique perspective, having worked both for a large bank and now at an entrepreneurial start-up. We have been fortunate at Borrowell to partner with several large Canadian banks, and this has accelerated our growth. At the same time, we have faced the same problems that other start-ups have in acquiring customers and scaling the business. The online lending business is becoming better understood and is more diverse than it first appears, with alternative lenders pursuing different business models and targeting different customer segments. Ultimately, this diversity will benefit borrowers and the financial system, with both big banks and fintech companies playing important roles. We need to see more bank-fintech partnerships, more government support for innovation, and more successful fintech champions. These are the features of a successful and thriving fintech ecosystem.

Launching a Fintech Start-Up

The inspiration for Borrowell came to me while I was working at a bank in Toronto. I was curious about the credit-card market and how consistently profitable it had been for card issuers, which remains true today. Credit cards are heavily used in Canada, and households carry a lot of credit-card debt: about $90 billion in mid-2019. Much of this debt is held by consumers with good credit scores. About 40 percent of people with credit cards carry a balance from time to time and typically pay an interest rate of around 20 percent, sometimes higher.

The world of consumer credit is fascinating. As an economist by background, I was taught to believe in the efficiency of markets, that prices would be set to reflect risk. In reality, this is truer in some markets than others. For example, with car insurance, we all pay different rates based on our driving history. All else being equal, better drivers pay less money than poor drivers. But credit cards don't always work like that. Whether a card holder has a good or a bad credit history, they may well pay the same rate as any other customer. Why would someone with a good credit history put up with that? Well, the choices for unsecured borrowing are not great. Even today, the typical alternative is to go into a bank branch and apply for a loan or line of credit by filling out a stack of paperwork. That process can be very intimidating and take a long time. Credit and financial services in general are complex, and there are a number of reasons why there just isn't efficient pricing for consumer lending.

In 2014, I quit my job and started working on this problem full time, convinced that there was a market opportunity in the consumer-credit space. At that time, there was a ton of activity happening in the online lending world. It was the heyday for new lending platforms. Lending Club and Prosper in the United States and Zopa in the United Kingdom were originating large volumes of consumer loans. My intuition was that there would be a variant on this model that was going to be successful in Canada – one that we could take to other markets as well. Few business ideas focused on the Canadian market can grow to be a billion-dollar business. I believed financial services and lending offered that opportunity because there was just so much credit outstanding.

The original idea for Borrowell was to offer low-cost loans online to help people with good credit refinance more expensive debt. Price was half of the value proposition; the other half was convenience. When we launched, our application form was one page, all of it online. There were no branch visits. The customer entered their name and address on our platform and found out instantly whether they would qualify for an unsecured loan of between $1,000 and $35,000. This instantaneous reply was revolutionary for many people.

The pricing was attractive, too, with the interest rate on the loan determined by an applicant's individual credit risk, with rates as low as a 6 percent annual percentage rate (APR). Then as now, the APR included both the interest rate and the one-time origination fee, which covered the costs of evaluating loan applications, building and operating the processing platform, and providing customer service. The origination fee has remained between 1 to 5 percent of the loan proceeds. The percentage depends on the borrower's credit profile: the better the credit profile, the lower the origination fee. Once the borrower submitted proof of income, verified their bank account, and accepted their loan documents, the proceeds from the loan could be directly deposited into their verified bank account in as little as twenty-four hours from the start of the application.

We have made many improvements to this application process over time and now use a wide array of data beyond credit history to assess risk. But the underlying loan product remains the same. Borrowers can pay it off all at once, at any time. Unlike other lenders, Borrowell does not charge any prepayment fees, so customers can make extra payments or pay off the loan completely without being charged extra fees. This flexible structure is possible because Borrowell originates its own loans, which differentiates us from other online lenders. From the beginning, we have found many buyers for the loans we originate, including Schedule 1 banks and major credit unions. This allows us to keep a lean balance sheet and use our capital to fund Borrowell's technology and growth.

I started working out of Ryerson University's DMZ incubator with Ryerson Futures, an early investor in the company. They provided me with a desk for one year before we moved to the One Eleven innovation hub. These working spaces offered advice and support; neither was a formal accelerator program.

As I developed the business plan, I knew I needed to recruit other people to join me. I approached Eva Wong, who became my co-founder at Borrowell. We had previously founded a nonprofit together, and she was excited to join. We also needed people with technical talent and credit expertise, because, as a first-time lender, Borrowell didn't have a track record to fall back on. We needed to leverage the personal experience of our employees, and so we found early partners who had those different skill sets.

Partnering with the Banks

At the time when we launched Borrowell's online loan platform in early 2015, we had partnered with Equitable Bank, a fast-growing Schedule I Canadian bank that was one of our first investors.[4] Equitable Bank provided funding by purchasing the loans that we originated online. We were not powering software for Equitable Bank, or providing loans to their customers. They were simply an investor. (For an overview of Borrowell's financing history see Box 9.1.)

As our loan volumes increased, we quickly attracted a lot of media attention. Soon we were approached by CIBC, one of Canada's top five Schedule I banks, and started having conversations with them. CIBC was keen to leverage Borrowell's online lending platform, including the intuitive user-experience underwriting approach. I would describe our partnership as a software-as-a-service (SaaS) model. Our value proposition was very clear – we made it very easy for customers to apply for a loan and get an instant decision. We partnered with CIBC to modify the technology that we had built and to develop a customized underwriting model appropriate for their customers. In October 2016 we announced our partnership to offer "one-click" online lending for CIBC clients.[5] Later when we launched our free-credit-score product, we provided that product to their customers as well.

The application process we built with CIBC included our brand *"Powered by Borrowell."* CIBC was responsible for marketing, and Borrowell processed the loan applications. It was a business-to-business

(B2B) relationship – and not a B2B2C relationship, because the borrowers remained CIBC customers, not Borrowell customers. In general, the B2B model in online lending is popular with fintechs at different stages of evolution. In the United States there are many examples of banks partnering with fintechs such as Avant, Kabbage, OnDeck, and Upstart. A number of these fintechs started as direct business-to-consumer (B2C) businesses but have either pivoted entirely or launched parallel lines of business to become B2B suppliers. Many founders have discovered that it can be very hard to run a single-product B2C business, because of the high cost of customer acquisition. I will say more on how Borrowell addressed that problem later.

Regrettably, there are too few examples of Canadian fintechs in partnership with Canada's big banks. Instead, Canada's banks often rely on large, more traditional tech companies like IBM and CGI to help them build their software and IT systems. We see more partnerships between banks and fintechs in the United States and United Kingdom. Some banks in these countries have been very forward thinking, such as JP Morgan with its multifaceted push into partnering with fintechs to get access to emerging technologies. Ultimately, I think partnering with fintechs is going to be a better innovation strategy for banks than trying to do it all themselves.

The Customer-Acquisition Problem

One of the hardest problems faced by any start-up is acquiring customers. When we launched our online loan product in 2015, we thought it would be a slam dunk. There was a huge addressable market. Credit-card debt was a real pain point for consumers with high credit scores. As we expected, getting people to apply for loans wasn't hard – there were many people interested in taking out a loan with Borrowell. The challenge was that our loans were designed for consumers with strong credit histories, yet many of the people applying faced significant credit challenges. We were turning down a high proportion of our early applicants, which was frustrating for them and for us. What we thought would be an easy customer-acquisition story actually proved to be very hard and expensive, because it costs Borrowell money every time someone applies for a loan.

Before I explain more, let me share an anecdote about our loan application process. We worked really hard to make this process fast. There are many processes happening in the background after a borrower completes the application online and clicks on "Get my rate." To determine credit worthiness, we receive about 1,500 data points from Equifax on the customer's credit history, which we combine with other data to make a decision. In the early days, we found that many people who went through this process wouldn't take a loan. When we asked why, we heard over and over again that the approval process was so fast it seemed like a scam. Customers couldn't believe that we had actually checked their credit and processed their loan application in less than a second! Our response was to introduce a slight delay into the process and explain on the screen what our technology was doing: pulling credit, running it through our model, and generating offers. Adding this step had a positive impact on consumer trust. The message is that a fintech can actually be too fast!

We were having a difficult time connecting with customers who would qualify for our loans and had to turn down many who applied. This led to negative feedback on social media. We would receive comments like this on Facebook: "I know three people who tried this and we all received the same response – nothing can be offered." The problem was that many people did not know their credit score.[6] People would call us and say, "I have great credit. Why didn't you approve me for a loan?" And we would look at their credit file and see they had a challenged history of paying bills. But other people reading those comments on social media didn't know that.

We realized that we needed to find better channels to market to Borrowell's target customers. We spent a lot of time thinking about how to get in front of people with better credit. We were launching the CIBC partnership. We were speaking with other financial institutions. We had tried marketing tools like Facebook. But it was proving too expensive to acquire customers that fitted our credit criteria through traditional methods. We debated back and forth what we could do.

Eventually we hit on the answer. In other jurisdictions, fintechs and banks were giving customers their credit score for free. Our experience in Canada was that the level of credit education was low, and there appeared to be a real demand for better access to credit scores. We said, why don't we give people their credit score before we even start the loan conversation? The population of people who want a credit score is wider than people who want loans. If we first give people something of value, then we can decide whether to offer them a loan or not.

In June 2016, in partnership with Equifax, we became the first company in Canada to offer free credit scores.[7] We received a great response. This product went viral, with more than 100,000 Canadians signing up in the first few months. Three years later, more than 1 million Canadians have received their free credit score, and we continue to attract thousands of people each week. Individuals can access their free credit score on their phone or online. The process is instantaneous and doesn't cost the consumer anything. And it doesn't affect a consumer's credit score to check their credit score. And whether their credit score is high or low, we offer them tips for how they can improve it.

It is really interesting how changing the product can change the conversation with customers. At the beginning, we were getting few referrals from existing customers. Most people do not tell their friends that they have applied for a loan, even if they like the experience. We saw this in the customer-response net-promoter scores, which asked, "How likely are you to recommend this product to a friend?" People would give us ten out of ten on the quality of service but then give a low net-promoter score because they were embarrassed to recommend a loan product to a friend. But not with a credit score. What could be more helpful than recommending it to their family and friends as a way to get it for free? So now, a large proportion of new sign-ups come from people who heard about us from others.

We are very excited about the success of this credit-score product. It allows us to start a conversation with a customer and provide real value to them very quickly, and with a low level of commitment on their part; they don't have to provide a credit card, for example. And it generates revenue for us, as some percentage of people who have a good credit score will take out a loan with us or select from the other financial products on our platform.

We went from getting few comments on social media to receiving many, many positive comments. We particularly love the comments where people talk about how this product allows them to take control of their own lives. People wrote, "I was scared to get my credit score. Then I got it and now I feel so much more confident when applying for a mortgage, applying to rent a place, or going for a job interview where I know they are going to check my credit."

The key lesson that I take from this – one that has been powerful in the success of our free credit-score offering – is *to give before you get*.

Despite the success of our free credit-score product, we still had not found the perfect product-market fit with our loans. We were getting thousands of people each week who would come to get their free credit score, but only a small percentage of them wanted loans.

We asked ourselves again what we could do to better serve all these people who were coming to our website.

We saw many customers who wanted other kinds of financial products that we were not offering. So, we started approaching banks and other financial institutions to ask if they wanted to put their products in front of our members. We offered these partners a low-risk acquisition channel where we would get paid based on performance. Those conversations were relatively easy – so much easier than asking, "Hey, can we integrate our technology platform into yours?" The response from the banks was enthusiastic, and we started signing up more partners.

It has been a really exciting transformation for us. We spent all of 2017 building a marketplace of financial products around this free credit score. We have now partnered with more than forty financial institutions to offer credit cards, auto loans, mortgages, savings accounts, checking accounts, and insurance. Now when a consumer gets their free credit score from Borrowell, we can recommend products, services, and tips tailored for them.

Ultimately, this marketplace has become the fastest-growing part of Borrowell's business. Today a large portion of what we do from a revenue and engagement standpoint comes from referring customers to other financial institutions, versus originating Borrowell loans. We've proven that there is huge potential to generate revenue by telling consumers about additional products and services from third parties.

My second lesson is that *it is very hard to be a single-product B2C fintech*. Start-ups really need multiple products to monetize their marketing costs, or they need to develop other channels such as B2B2C.

This experience raises a final point about financial education and literacy. Financial stress in Canada is high. In a recent poll, Canadians were asked a straightforward question: "What's the one issue most likely to keep you up at night these days?" The most frequently given answer, cited by one in four people, was financial issues. At the same time, financial literacy is low, with many people uninterested in talk about financial education. At Borrowell, we have changed the conversation. We provide them with their free credit score, which is easy to get and understand. We use this to start the customer conversation, and then we can provide advice and recommendations. Our goal is to make the benefits of improved credit clear and real.

Let's say a customer comes to our site, and their score is 600, which is below average. We try and help them understand what additional products and services open up to them if their score improves. For example, maybe they'll be able to qualify for a better mortgage. And then we show them three actions they could take to increase their score. This often generates real interest. Customers realize that if they want to raise their score, they have to pay all their bills on time and consolidate their credit into a lower-cost loan. This financial strategy makes sense to them.

My third lesson is that *it is better to offer a product that excites a customer and incorporates a financial-education component* than it is to focus on financial literacy more theoretically.

Scaling a Fintech Business

When starting a business, the overriding goal is to find product-market fit, which means developing a product or service that customers want and will ultimately pay for. This is a really hard challenge. It's not easy to come up with a product, launch it in the marketplace, and have people use it and ultimately pay for it. So, we spend a lot of time in the start-up community talking about finding product-market fit. What we spend less time talking about is what comes later: scaling the business. In many conversations, product-market fit is viewed as the hard part, and scaling is supposed to be the easy part.

I used to think this way. After all, what is a big company, really? A simplistic view is that it's just a larger version of a small company. It turns out this isn't at all correct.

Let me give you an analogy. Mathematicians have developed the "square-cube law," which describes the relationship between surface area and volume as a shape's size increases. When the size of an object is increasing, its volume grows faster than its surface area. If the surface area of a sphere is squared, its volume is cubed. As others have pointed out, this mathematical principle applies to companies as well – things that work at one size do not automatically work at a bigger scale.

What's hard about scaling a business? Let me offer a few examples from Borrowell's recent past.

First of all, technology. In Borrowell's early stages, we would push new features into production very quickly, even if the design or user experience (UX) was rough, so long as they met our security criteria. We wanted to get features out fast and see how users would react. And if the new features didn't work perfectly, it wasn't as important to us as the learning we gained from this approach. Today, Borrowell has tens of thousands of people using our site each day, so the stakes are higher. We had the experience recently of pushing a new feature into production and having it fail, preventing our members from logging in. In the two hours that it took to fix this problem, thousands of people tried to log in but couldn't. That's a problem for a growing business.

Marketing also works differently when scaling than when a company is starting up. In the summer of 2015, a few members from the Borrowell team stood outside a Blue Jays baseball game in downtown Toronto. We gave out ice-cream bars and postcards that gave a sense of what Borrowell is about. That guerrilla marketing idea was possible when we were small, and it worked. As Paul Graham of Y Combinator famously advised, "When you are a start-up, do things that don't scale."[8] But now that we're scaling, our employees cannot stand outside enough baseball games and give out enough ice-cream bars to onboard thousands of customers each week.

And finally, talent management is different at scale. A four-person company is very different from a forty-person company, and is very different again from a four-hundred-person company. When we were a four-person company, we all sat around a table. Communication was easy because the person in charge of engineering was sitting right beside the person running marketing, and so on. In fact, often the same person would be responsible for more than one of these tasks. So, we didn't have to worry about silos or the other challenges that come when the company gets bigger. Scaling a team requires different processes and systems to make it possible for people to communicate.

I learned a theory from Harvard Business School Professor Shikar Ghosh called "The Rule of Three." Professor Ghosh believes that things break and companies need to change at every multiple of three employees. As a start-up goes from being three people to nine people to twenty-seven people to eighty-one people, these are common points where a start-up fails. If the founders don't retool the team and processes, things are going to stop working.

The challenges of scale help explain why partnering between a fintech and a bank can be hard. Organizations that are different sizes operate differently and face different challenges. At Borrowell, we're proud of our partnerships with multiple Canadian banks. When we started the partnership with CIBC, we were a team of twenty-five people interacting with a project team at CIBC many times that size. That difference created a number of challenges. Understanding your partner's objectives, needs, and constraints becomes very important. Partnering with a leading Canadian bank also forced us to grow and put in place many IT systems that really benefited us later. It forced us to roll out enterprise-grade security and user management, for example. This was painful at the time, but it has helped us to grow faster.

Of course, Borrowell is still very much a small company. There will doubtless be new scaling challenges as we grow from where we are today.

Box 9.1. Borrowell Sources of Financing
From 2014 to 2019, Borrowell had raised a total of C$90 million in equity and debt funding over four funding rounds. This funding has come from a range of angel and institutional investors:

- **4 December 2014**: $5.4 million in seed funding and commitments to its loan platform from Ryerson Futures, Equitable Bank (a Canadian Schedule I bank), and Oakwest Corporation Limited (a private investment company owned and managed by the Beutel family), as well as notable individual investors including Roger Martin, John Bitove, and Dan Debow.[9]
- **23 February 2016**: $6.4 million in equity funding and loan capital from Equitable Bank, Hedgewood, Power Financial, Oakwest Corporation, Freycinet Investments, and others.[10]
- **12 July 2017**: $57 million: $12 million in equity funding through a Series A Round and $45 million in new credit facilities to expand Borrowell's credit and loan offerings. The Series A was led by Portag3 Ventures, Equitable Bank, and White Star Capital, with participation by FirstOntario Credit Union. The $45 million in credit facilities was provided by FirstOntario Credit Union and Concentra Bank.[11]
- **17 June 2019**: $20 million of equity and venture debt financing. The series was led by White Star Capital and Portag3 Ventures with participation by Clocktower Ventures, Argo Ventures, and others, including Gaingels, an LGBT affinity group making their first investment in Canada.[12]

The Future of Financial Services

Technology-driven disruption has come later to financial services than it has to other sectors such as retail or publishing. As financial-services innovation has gathered pace over the last decade, thinking about it has evolved. Early on, there was a sense that the fintechs were going to disrupt the banks. In his 2014 "Letter to Shareholders," JPMorgan's CEO Jamie Dimon said "Silicon Valley is coming. There are hundreds of start-ups with a lot of brains and money working on various alternatives to traditional banking."[13] Such views are now rarer among bankers. It seems clear that banks won't be disrupted as, say, department stores have been. Many banks are investing heavily in financial technology and innovation, leveraging the relationships they have with customers. But we will continue to see some breakout fintech players establish themselves and compete globally.

But banks cannot be complacent. The main risk to established financial-services companies may come from large technology companies such as Google, Apple, and Amazon. Facebook's recent announcement that it intends to launch a blockchain-based payment framework, Libra, is a great example. And I think fintech companies have a role to play in being part of that innovation solution for established banks who need to compete against these new entrants. Some banks have pivoted their business model to support fintechs that want to get into B2C banking. Banks such as Cross River and WebBank are providing a very specific service that helps fintechs to meet regulatory requirements.[14]

Smaller community and regional banks face a big challenge. They will have a hard time investing in enough technology to keep up with the larger banks. This is where fintech solutions are going to be powerful. Why should a small bank build their own digital loan software when a company like Avant can do it for them? The banks with the largest IT budgets and scale are able to develop these applications internally. But the smaller community or regional banks really should be looking to partner with fintechs to outsource that IT function.

But I also see banks at the large end of the scale – such as JP Morgan, which has the budget to do whatever it wants – in partnership with fintechs as part of their overall innovation strategy. Even if these large banks can afford to develop it all in-house, they know they are never going to have all the brains and ideas that are going to be happening elsewhere. Google has many smart engineers, and nevertheless they acquire companies to gain access externally to smart people who build things.

Clearly, many more fintech start-ups have received venture-capital funding over the past five years than can be successful in the long run. There has been a lot of capital and a lot of company creation. But there is bound to be a day of reckoning as economic conditions tighten and funding contracts. I think we will see a consolidation among the start-ups, with a few survivors who rise to the top while others follow niche strategies. That will be true in all tech verticals and is true in fintech as well.

The Fintech Ecosystem and Policy

I want to close by sharing my views on the importance of the fintech ecosystem for supporting fintech creation and growth. Let's be clear: we have a fintech challenge in Canada. Despite the success of our technology and traditional financial sectors, few Canadian fintechs have reached significant scale. As Paul Desmarais III of Power Corporation – which is an investor in Borrowell through its Portage Ventures arm – has pointed out, Canada is home to three of the top twenty largest banks in the world, by market capitalization.

However, Canada has produced no "unicorn" fintechs, that is, companies valued at more than a billion dollars.

There are lots of reasons for this, including the relatively small size of the domestic market, which matters more than in many other areas of technology. Crossing borders to find new customers is often harder in financial services due to differing regulation. If you're building an online game, for example, it's relatively straightforward to sell it across the world from day one through the Apple or Google app stores. Set up a fintech offering – for example, online loans – and you need to wade through regulation and registration requirements that are different from country to country or even from state to state.

The demand for financial-services innovation has been weak in Canada compared to that in countries such as the United States and the United Kingdom, which experienced larger challenges in the 2008 financial crisis. As some in the sector like to joke, the worst thing to happen to Canada's fintech industry was that no Canadian banks failed a decade ago. Instead, many regulators and consumers came through that period with a belief that all was well in our financial-services sector.

Another brake on the growth of large fintech companies has been the relative lack of successful fintech-bank partnerships in Canada. That is not good for fintechs, and it is not good for banks. The success and profitability of Canadian banks over the past decade, combined with an oligopolistic market structure, reduce the competitive pressures that could spur more innovation.

Government policy and regulations play a very important role in promoting the fintech ecosystem. I think it is very important for Canadian financial regulators to take a pro-innovation pro-fintech stance. Looking at both provincial and federal financial regulators, in almost every case their mandates are primarily about consumer protection. They are enacting policies to protect the financial system, to protect investors, and to protect consumers. I agree that those are great goals. But in very few cases do regulators have a mandate to promote innovation and competition. Other jurisdictions have created fintech tsars and adopted explicit goals around growing their fintech sector. Canada is a leader in financial services globally and should be a leader in fintech.

Canada should look to other jurisdictions like the United Kingdom for models on how to support and develop homegrown fintech champions. The United Kingdom has built a terrific fintech ecosystem, and they have been very deliberate from a policy perspective, supported by the U.K. Treasury, the Bank of England, the Financial Conduct Authority, and other regulators. They have set out to build a world-class fintech cluster in the United Kingdom, with innovative policies supporting open banking, for example. To emulate their success, Canada should take the same strategic approach. After all, fintechs exist to provide financial services that serve consumers better. That is a goal that everyone should support.

NOTES

1 Borrowell. (nd). Our story. https://borrowell.com/who-is-borrowell. Accessed 28 June 2019.
2 While Borrowell remains primarily consumer-focused, we do offer some products for small businesses.
3 Graham, A. (2019, 2 April). Borrowell officially passes one million members. https://borrowell.com/blog/thanks-a-million-borrowell-officially -passes-one-million-members/.
4 A Schedule I bank is a domestic financial institution that is regulated under Canada's Bank Act. A Schedule I bank may not be wholly owned by nonresidents. Schedule II banks are the Canadian subsidiaries of foreign banks.
5 Borrowell. (2016, 27 October). CIBC partners with fintech innovator Borrowell to deliver "one-click" online loans. https://www.borrowell .com/blog/cibc-partners-with-borrowell/.

6 In 2017, research by CIBC found that 69 percent of Canadians did not
know their credit score, and 45 percent said they had no idea where to
obtain their credit score. See: CIBC. (2017, 2 July). CIBC introduces free
mobile credit score for clients – a first for a major Canadian bank. http://
cibc.mediaroom.com/2017-06-02-CIBC-introduces-free-mobile-credit
-score-for-clients-a-first-for-a-major-Canadian-Bank.
7 Borrowell. (2016, 20 June). Borrowell and Equifax Canada partner to
provide Canadians free access to credit scores. https://www.newswire
.ca/news-releases/borrowell-and-equifax-canada-partner-to-provide
-canadians-free-access-to-credit-scores-583604331.html.
8 Graham, P. (2013, July). Do things that don't scale. Y Combinator. http://
paulgraham.com/ds.html. Accessed 13 June 2019.
9 Borrowell. (2014, 3 December). Borrowell announces $5.4 million in
funding to launch innovative online lending platform. https://www
.newswire.ca/news-releases/borrowell-announces-54-million-in-funding
-to-launch-innovative-online-lending-platform-516607051.html.
10 Borrowell. (2016, 23 February). Borrowell raises $6.4 million in operating
and loan capital from Power Financial, Equitable Bank. https://betakit
.com/borrowell-raises-6-4-million-in-operating-and-loan-capital-from
-power-financial-equitable-bank/.
11 Borrowell. (2017, 21 July). Borrowell raises $57M in new funding to
expand credit education and lending. https://www.globenewswire.com
/news-release/2017/07/21/1055519/0/en/Borrowell-raises-57M-in-New
-Funding-to-Expand-Credit-Education-and-Lending.html.
12 O'Hara, C. (2019, 17 June). Online loan provider Borrowell raises
$20-million in second round of funding. *The Globe and Mail*. https://www
.theglobeandmail.com/business/article-online-loan-provider-borrowell
-raises-20-million-in-second-round-of/.
13 Dimon, J. (2015, 8 April). 2014 annual report – Letter to shareholders.
JPMorgan Chase & Co. https://www.jpmorganchase.com/corporate
/annual-report/2014/ar-solid-strategy.htm.
14 WebBank of Utah lists some of the biggest fintechs as their customers,
including Avant, Klarna, LendingClub, PayPal, and Prosper. See: WebBank.
(nd). Our brand partners. https://www.webbank.com/about-us/about
-us. Accessed 13 June 2019.

CHAPTER TEN

How the Global Asset-Management Industry Will Change

Richard W. Nesbitt and Satwik Sharma

Traditionally, the management of investments was a specialty activity of dedicated professional firms experienced in stocks, bonds, real estate, and all manner of other assets that would produce a return. The management of other people's money (other than deposits) is a relatively new activity for universal banks. Private banks specializing in the management of clients' wealth are found in many countries. Specialized investment-management firms of all sizes have traditionally been the chosen vehicle for investors. As with many things, all of this is in flux, with major trends that will affect who will be successful in the future. Technology is permitting the development of a new class of competitors for investable funds who seek to attract less-well-served parts of this market. In this chapter, we explore forces that are altering the management of investments, how the asset-management industry is expected to change over the next decade, and why it is an attractive business activity for both incumbents and new financial-services players.

The Past Ten Years of Change

For the last ten years, the global economy has seen significant central bank intervention and low investment returns (which are always a function of interest-rate levels). Because of low interest rates, those traditionally requiring fixed-income exposure were forced into the riskier parts of the capital markets. When markets are driven predominantly by liquidity and not fundamentals, returns are more volatile. Some investors are prone to panic when they experience this volatility and at the first sign of a loss get out at the bottom. This is the dilemma of "buy high and sell low," which often describes the behavior of individual investors' in response to market volatility. One of the greatest values to their clients of professional asset managers is to counsel patience for their investments.

The global financial crisis (GFC) of 2008 saw central banks venture forth into a brand-new experiment of quantitative easing (ultra-low rates and the expansion of central bank balance sheets by the purchase of unattractive assets nobody else in the market wanted, to save the banking system). This was only supposed to last over a short period until the economy recovered. Unfortunately, ultra-low rates promoted even more debt issuance by sovereign borrowers and consumers. This response has created a new kind of business cycle: not the traditional one driven by earnings on the income statement and where higher interest rates choke off investment returns, but a new, more intransigent cycle driven by balance sheets and expanding debt levels.

In a balance-sheet-driven business cycle, it is not the level of interest rates that limits growth but the amount of debt in the economy. When balance sheets are unlevered and debt is being added, the economy grows above its natural rate, as debt acts like a supercharger. Once the accumulation of debt reaches a limit and everyone has highly levered balance sheets, this acts as a drag on the economy, forcing it to grow at a rate below its natural growth rate. Investment dollars are then channeled toward debt repayment, starving the economy and slowing growth.

Low and negative returns, especially in the developed world, have led to a greater focus on the management fees being charged. In an era of negligible interest rates and average market returns of 3 to 4 percent, fees of 2 to 3 percent have a material negative impact on returns. In emerging and frontier markets, passive investment products have yet to gain much traction among investors, given significant outperformance against benchmarks by asset managers. Moreover, regulators' requirements for increased transparency during this past decade have compelled asset managers to disclose fees in absolute terms rather than include them within the other costs of the funds, leading to a consistent downward pressure on management fees.

Over the last ten years, underperformance by asset managers, especially those in developed markets, intensified in response to all the difficulties of operating in a world awash with debt. The average mutual fund could not outperform the market (generally because mutual funds are often market clones plus a fee). The belief became that if active managers cannot beat the market, then why not just own the market instead, often for a much lower fee. This has led to the proliferation of exchange-traded funds (ETFs), which are well suited to banks and asset managers, who could provide ETFs with a cheaper fee structure. Exchange-traded products (ETPs) that include ETFs and other passive strategies have also gained tremendous popularity among institutional investors because of the ease and cost efficiencies these products provide in hedging and portfolio construction. Because these funds can closely track an index or a specific asset/sector exposure based on a set of rules, less human power is required and more quantitative models (algorithms) can do the job.

The proliferation of cheap computing has enabled a large amount of the trading in the asset-management industry to be performed by computers using algorithms. This activity could entail managing portfolios on the basis of pre-decided rules to buy and sell securities, or, as in the case of passive products, rules-based portfolio balancing to closely track indices or specific exposures (popularly called smart beta strategies). As with any complex system, over-reliance on computers, models, algorithms, and artificial intelligence could create unintended consequences for the future by impacting market stability. From flash crashes on various stock exchanges to significant drawdowns in complex ETPs, such as the VelocityShares Daily Inverse VIX Short-Term exchange-traded note (XIV) (a passive product that was designed to give the opposite return of the CBOE Volatility Index or VIX), which fell 80 percent in a single day in February 2018, cracks are already starting to appear as more assets are added to the ETP complex in increasingly exotic structures and have begun to attract the attention of regulators in some countries.

Another consequence of a slow-growth economy is that as a share of the economic pie becomes scarce, stocks are largely influenced by commodity prices, and the general business cycle never sees big increases in price. The market's focus is on those companies with strong secular growth characteristics, where valuations just keep trending higher. Investors waiting for the traditional business-cycle-driven upswing of "value" stocks never see it happen, as commodity supply steadily creeps ahead of demand.

Investors who have prospered over the last decade have recognized all of the above trends and changed their investment process and fee structure accordingly. However, many managers have not adapted, leading to poor investment returns and forced consolidations and/or closures of funds. There are now numerous large players using algorithms and quantitative strategies, for minimal fees. The high-quality active stock pickers in asset management that can perform well consistently are still able to command a premium fee. The middle-market players (most mutual funds and traditional institutional pension fund managers, who often provide plus or minus 2 percent relative to average market returns) are increasingly finding it difficult to compete with ETFs and passive products that can provide equivalent or better fee-adjusted performance at scale. Because of poor performance, many hedge funds (which were the darlings of the industry up until 2008, charging 2 percent and 20 percent of profits) are struggling to survive, as they have not been able to perform consistently. Traditionally, pension-fund committees would seek out growth- and value-style managers. However, as value managers' performance has disappointed fund sponsors, the trend has been to hire "alternative" managers instead. These were initially the hedge-fund managers, but more recently have been what are termed "alpha managers." The asset-management industry is starting to consolidate as the pressure on fees and returns intensifies.

The industry has changed in the last twenty years towards more passive investing through index funds (ETFs), where regular dialogue with the management of each constituent company does not happen as frequently. Similarly, a large majority of mutual funds and the active-management industry produce portfolios that very closely mimic the index. This type of investment strategy requires less company research and is more about understanding macro factors that influence the overall stock market. It generally has a lower information quotient, as it has a great number of participants betting on very poor-quality information. However, larger passive-asset managers have become increasingly vocal about fostering higher standards of corporate governance, ESG (environmental, social, and governance) monitoring and adoption, and longer-term thinking as a broader goal for all public companies. Given their scale and their investments in almost all publicly listed companies, these asset managers are well positioned to create a lasting impact on the issues.

Increasing Attractiveness of the Wealth-Management Business

In 2017, McKinsey & Company estimated that the global wealth-management industry accounted for 13 percent of the $5 trillion in revenue for the banking industry.[1] Following the 2008–2009 global financial crisis, global banks realized the merits of growing a wealth-management business because of the relative "stickiness" of assets in that business. It was observed that, barring exceptional circumstances, customers of wealth management did not withdraw assets and change their wealth advisors based on short-term volatility in the financial markets. Thus, this business provides banks with a relatively predictable and stable fee revenue stream as compared to the highly cyclical commission-based fees that banks earn from other products and services, such as lending and capital markets. The unique qualities of wealth-management businesses also make them attractive to large banks. Instead of lending customers your money and posting capital against the risk posed by this activity, banks instead take in other people's money and invest it, at the client's risk, on their behalf, for a fee.

Since 2008, banks across the developed world have grown their wealth- and asset-management businesses in comparison to other parts of the bank (for example, see figure 10.1).

Banks have also been active in building the wealth-management business inorganically through acquisitions. In 2018, Bank of Nova Scotia acquired two wealth managers, MD Financial for $2 billion, and Jarislowsky Fraser for $800 million. Goldman Sachs, another investment bank that has been steadily growing its wealth-management franchise, made its largest acquisition in twenty years in 2019 to acquire wealth manager United Capital for US$750 million.

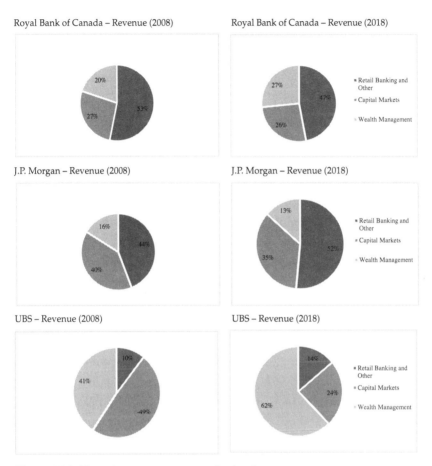

Figure 10.1 Changing revenue sources by bank

Growth of ETFs and Passive Investing

In the aftermath of the global financial crisis, central banks in the developed world used quantitative easing (QE) as a policy instrument to ease interest rates so that lending to the main economy continued. An unintended consequence of this action was persistently low interest rates in the decade that followed. This activity has also led to lower risk premiums, with a resulting lowering of average market returns. As per a 2018 Morningstar analysis of 4,600 U.S. funds with an aggregate assets under management (AUM) of $12.8 trillion, only 24 percent of all active funds – those holding stocks, bonds, or real estate – outperformed a comparable average passive fund over the ten years through December 2018.

In an environment of lower market returns, investor focus has been directed towards lowering the costs of investing (i.e., paying lower fees for investment products and brokerages). This has been the primary driver behind the rise of passive investments in the last decade. Passive funds also include what have come to be known as smart beta strategies. These strategies passively track an index but include an active, rules-based component. Securities are selected and weighted by criteria other than market capitalization alone, a strategy that creates the possibility of outperforming the market.

Figure 10.2 shows the split of the U.S. equity assets under management from 2008 to 2018. Passive funds have grown at more than twice the rate of active funds to make up nearly half the AUM in 2018. As a matter of fact, in December 2018, assets in passively managed large cap funds surpassed assets in actively managed large cap funds in the United States.[2]

This does not mean the demise of the active fund-management industry, however. Investor demand for products that can outperform the market is unlikely to disappear. A Boston Consulting Group (BCG) analysis of the drivers of inflows confirmed that, in the United States, only active funds with five-star ratings or new products were capturing significant net inflows, while one- to four-star funds in aggregate had suffered net outflows over the past few years.[3] Some active managers have responded to the shift to passive by better aligning fees with performance. For example, a leading global asset manager has cut its base management fees for active

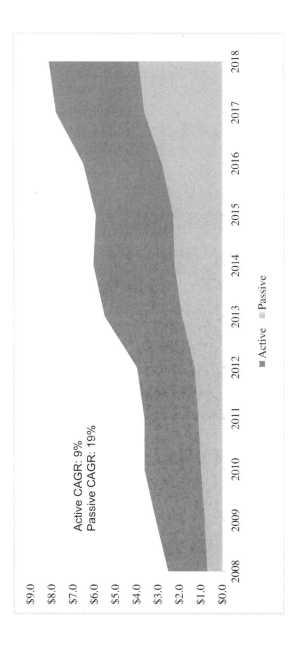

Figure 10.2 U.S. equity funds AUM ($ trillions)

funds by ten basis points but will increase them by twenty basis points if they outperform benchmarks by 2 percentage points or more. Such fee constructs would become increasingly prevalent as managers further align performance with pay.

Demographic Change

Changing demographics have played an important role in shaping the direction of multiple industries, and wealth management has been no exception. Three of the most consequential trends in the developed world have been the rise of millennials, an aging population, and the rise of women investors as a class.

Rise of the Millennials

Millennials, often described as a generation of people born between 1981 and 1990, are poised to be a changing force in several industries because their unique preferences and social situation are quite different from those of any previous generation of consumers and investors. Over the next several years, this millennial cohort will provide the largest growth in the investing population, with significant implications for the asset-management industry (see figure 10.3).[4]

Among other preferences, millennials espouse a strong concern for social and environmental sustainability.[5] This has been the central force behind the rise of impact investing and the use of environmental, social, and governance (ESG) factors in evaluating investable companies. According to a recent survey by Morgan Stanley, millennials are twice as likely to invest in a stock or a fund if social responsibility is part of the value-creation thesis. In addition, millennials are also the generation that has transitioned from their education to a workplace that is marked by relatively jobless

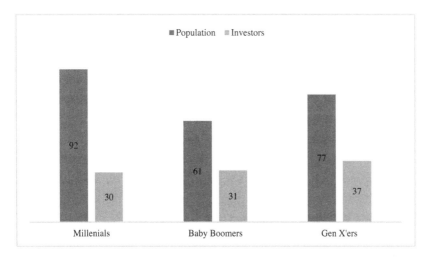

Figure 10.3 Generational differences in investing population (in $millions)

growth, the gig-economy of part-time work, and rising frustration with globalization, which is increasingly blamed for abetting the growth of wealth inequality. Millennials are more leveraged than the baby boomers at the same stage of life, a circumstance that has delayed important life milestones such as getting married, raising a family, buying homes, and, eventually, creating wealth. As a result, asset managers have had to innovate to provide products at the lowest cost and the lowest denominations to encourage millennials to invest. This is one of the biggest driving forces behind the rise of automated investing, colloquially called "robo-advisors."

Aging Population and Wealth Transfer

According to Accenture,[6] the Greatest Generation (born in the 1920s and 1930s) will transfer nearly $12 trillion to baby boomers (born from 1946 to 1964). The baby boomers in turn will transfer nearly $30 trillion in financial and nonfinancial assets to their heirs in North America alone. As a result, boomers remain vital to the wealth-management industry as the generation that is still accumulating wealth and eventually transferring it to the next generation. Wealth-management firms have thus been focused on understanding the requirements of this cohort and creating products to help with this transition. The boomers' attitudes toward aging are different. They expect to remain healthy, travel, and continue working much later than previous generations. They take a more active, hands-on approach to the transfer of wealth to their heirs, and require a high-touch, personalized service from wealth advisors. Wealth-management firms need to provide increasingly sophisticated and customized estate planning, trust structuring, and inheritance services at scale to be able to attract and retain clients in this generation. As a result, the role of the advisor has changed from that of a provider of multiple products to a provider of a comprehensive investment and inheritance strategy. This development has spawned new business models, such as family offices that take an intergenerational approach to provide end-to-end solutions addressing the needs of multiple generations of a family.

More Female Investors

According to the Boston Consulting Group, between 2010 and 2015 private wealth held by women grew from $34 trillion to $51 trillion. Women's wealth as a share of all private wealth rose from 28 percent to 30 percent over the same time period. By 2020, women are expected to hold nearly $72 trillion in wealth. This has made women an important investor class and a key determinant in the flow of funds to asset management. Wealth managers have had to innovate to appeal to this segment of investors. In recent times, the industry has seen a rise of women-focused asset managers. From innovation in product and investing styles, to a focus on social impact and governance, to early-stage venture-capital funds (VCs) that allocate capital specifically to women entrepreneurs, a whole ecosystem is developing to serve the female investor better. Examples include the Female Founders Fund created by entrepreneur Anu Duggal in 2014 to make early-stage investments in women-led companies. Its first fund was about $6 million in size and invested in thirty companies. Notable investors in the Female Founders Fund include Melinda Gates and Stitch Fix founder Katrina Lake.

Focus on Environmental, Social, and Governance and Social-Impact Investing

With a change in decision makers, environment, social, and governance (ESG) and social-impact investing have gained further acceptance as mainstream investment philosophies. In the long term, these could be extremely valuable approaches to creating market-based incentives for businesses to share responsibility in finding solutions to broader issues such as climate change, diversity and inclusion, sanitation, nutrition, health, and so on.

The growth of passive investments has given rise to the concern that index funds need to be invested in companies in proportion to their weight in underlying indices, a strategy that may impede their ability to enforce acceptable standards of corporate governance or ESG governance in investee companies. However, large index providers such as BlackRock and Vanguard have demonstrated awareness of these concerns and, in partnership with other institutional investors, have proactively created guidelines for governance and proxy voting.

Catherine Chen, CEO of a new ESG investment manager Avant-faire, describes ESG as follows:

A new way to look at ESG investment is to use a thematic approach known as impact investing. Each impact investment is based on a specific impact investment theory or philosophy for investment evaluation, reporting and disclosure. ESG investing is becoming important for both asset management and global risk mitigation.

First, ESG/Impact investing is related to the United Nations Sustainable Development Goals[7]and the Paris Agreement (Accord de Paris) under the United Nations Framework Convention on Climate Change.[8]Human society is facing ever changing challenges in nature, resources, and humanity issues. In humanity advancement and sustainable habitation, ESG/Impact investing is the solution to address social pain points by deploying capital. We see impact investment joining forces of finance and wealth to make meaningful and practical investment products.

Second, ESG/Impact investing could facilitate PPP (Private Public Partnership) investment, and more efficient and timely construction of social infrastructure. The UK Government said it would work with the pension industry to support the launch of social impact investment strategies and encourage more investments into areas addressing social issues. (June 2018). The French Reserve Fund announced it would substantially increase allocation to impact investing from its current mandate which was just over 1% of its EUR 36 billion portfolio. (February 2018). The Swiss Investing Fund for Emerging Markets was set up by the Swiss Government in 2005 to make impact investments in emerging countries. It has invested a total of about USD 900 million since its establishment and USD 87 million in 2017 in impact projects. Germany's Federal Ministry for Economic Cooperation and Development, Germany's Development Bank, and the International Finance Corporation offered a mandate of more than USD 100 million in 2010 to a private impact investment manager to provide debt financing to microfinance institutions in Asia (including Central Asia) to expand their portfolio of loans to micro and small businesses.

Third, in terms of the global wealth distribution, half of the wealth in the world belongs to the top 1% of the population. In addition to family offices and institutional investors, large foundations and charities are another source of global wealth that realize their share of social responsibilities. The efficient and effective use of capital mostly comes from these entities with impact investing being their preferred investment approach for many years, such as the Rockefeller Foundation, the Ford Foundation, and the Gates Foundation.

Lastly, social value is changing. As discussed above, individuals and espe-cially millennials have an increasing focus on individual contribution to the society, pursuit of happiness and healthy life, free education, aging population and greener planet. Impact investing tackles these issues by establishing specific investment objectives and deploying capital. Over a longer term the intrinsic value of assets will be more associated with ESG factors. Economic values and social values would converge.[9]

Companies Choosing to Stay Private for Longer

Given the deepening of private markets through access to early-stage venture and private capital, companies are often choosing to stay private longer. The increasing regulatory burden, scrutiny, and relatively higher reporting requirements for public compa-nies have added to this trend. Companies increasingly feel that the quarterly reporting requirement puts undue pressure on short-term performance, taking valuable effort and focus away from long-term strategy and operations. As a result, the number of publicly traded companies listed on U.S. stock exchanges has declined by almost 50 percent since peaking in 1996. This phenomenon is not limited to the United States. It is also happening in other developed econo-mies, which have seen the number of listed companies fall by 20 to 60 percent from the peak in the last two decades. Dell is a notable example of a public company that chose in 2013 to become a private corporation, arguing that this was necessary to meet their future challenges. In 2019, completing a full circle, Dell became a public company again. Another recent example of this trend is the pro-posed acquisition of WestJet Airlines by Onex, a private equity firm. Ed Sims, president and CEO of WestJet, stated that, among other reasons, the company chose to accept the relatively patient capital offered by Onex as an alternative to public market capital and the concomitant relentless pressure of quarterly earnings reports.

In response, larger institutional investors have started to diversify to invest across both public and private markets, further deepening private markets and accentuating this trend. For example, Fidelity Investments, an asset manager with a long history of providing great public-market investment management has invested in pre-IPO private companies such as Uber and Tesla over the last few years. Sovereign investment funds and large pension funds have moved into the private markets as they seek yield beyond what they can generate in the public markets.

Technology is expected to help this trend further through the creation of private exchanges that help fund businesses at any stage of development. From online accelerators (e.g., Y Combinator, Techstars, etc.) to private exchanges (Forge), an ecosystem has developed that provides capital to companies and liquidity to investors at every stage of development.

Over time, this shrinking of the universe of public companies has proven to be a loss for active managers and retail investors alike, and, some argue, has led to a reduction in shareholder democracy. This trend also may have significant long-term social and ecological ramifications. Given the greater propensity of companies to remain private, and the preponderance of wealthy accredited investors in private funds, the shrinking of the universe of public companies may indirectly feed the rise of wealth inequality in society. The trend also threatens the concept of exchanges as a financial marketplace, reduces transparency in the economy, and impedes the ability of regulators to create a level playing field for all investors.

Impact of the Growth of Asia

The rise of the Asian economies has been a well-documented trend for many decades now. More recently, attention has shifted to the growth of China as an economic and military powerhouse. The latent potential of India to traverse a similar growth trajectory over the next several years is often forecast. While the growth of China over the last three decades has made it one of the main engines and integral components of global economic growth, Chinese asset managers have not been able to play as consequential a role as those in Western developed economies. A primary reason for this is the strong grip of the Chinese government on the country's financial institutions, with the result that global investors have less confidence in these institutions. In addition, questions around intellectual property rights and the current caution around state-owned or state-affiliated Chinese entities stifle appetite for any asset-management-centric technologies that are developed in China. Thus, while the growth of the Chinese economy and related investment opportunities would be of interest to investors, China by itself does not yet play a significant role in changing the nature of the business of asset management. Similarly, India is an important investment destination for global investors, given its young and growing population and a GDP growth rate that is among the highest in the world. India has its own set of issues, including poor infrastructure, a gargantuan bureaucracy, and corruption, which raise questions around investor protections and contractual guarantees. However, India's growth potential, highly attractive demographics, independent courts, and a democratic polity have given sufficient confidence to longer-term investors such as pension funds that have invested substantially in infrastructure funds. Such investments, however, are yet to be tested in a declining market environment.

In addition, China and India are both highly consequential to the wealth-management industry because of the fast-growing personal wealth and rise in the number of high-net-worth individuals (HNWIs) and ultra-high net-worth individuals (UHNWIs) in

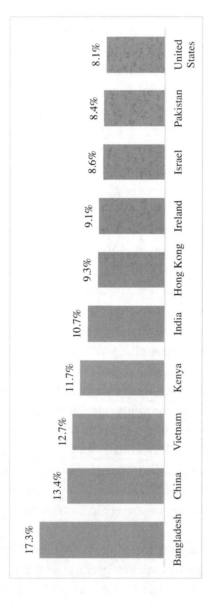

Figure 10.4 Growth rates in ultra-high-net-worth population from 2012 to 2017[10]

these countries (figure 10.4). The asset allocation and investments made by this group of investors will have an increasing impact on fund flows and the growth of industries across the world. Banks and institutional investors in developed economies are increasingly tapping into the growing population of rich individuals who are equally interested in diversifying their investments to include assets across the world.

This trend has made Asian investors an important source of funds for investments, especially in real estate, in key international destinations such as London, Sydney, and Vancouver. While this investment has helped to create jobs and sustain local economies, over time it has also led to the creation of asset bubbles in these cities and resistance from the local population that found itself priced out of the market. Policymakers have responded in order to maintain the balance between growing the economy and cooling the escalation in asset prices. For example, in Vancouver, the government instituted a 15 percent foreign buyers' tax on real-estate transactions that helped to reduce the pace of price rise in local markets. Similarly, in 2018, the government of New Zealand banned most foreigners from buying homes, in a bid to reign in runaway house prices. In addition to the impact on local markets, another reason why international investment flows have been under increasing scrutiny is because of concerns around money laundering and money sourced from illegal activities. Regulatory controls on money laundering may at times not be as robust in some international jurisdictions, which may help bad actors in channeling funds through those jurisdictions. The battle against money laundering will persist well into the future as new creative ways are found to avoid laws and regulations. Banks will be on the front line of this fight, and regulators will rely on banks to play a cross-economy role.

Use of Technology in Asset Management

In the previous sections, we highlighted the major factors that are impacting the asset-management business today and are expected to continue to impact it in the future. These factors are:

- changing demographics;
- growth in passive investing;
- growth in private markets and reduction in public markets;
- global changes in wealth distribution and growth.

This section is dedicated to the impact of technology on the wealth- and asset-management business. We divide the impact of technology into three main categories to examine important underlying themes:

Technology's Direct Impact on Asset- and Wealth-Management Firms

Some asset managers foresaw the impact of technology on their business earlier than others, and started investing for the future. That foresight is evident today in the market leadership of companies like BlackRock. In the late 1980s, the banks generally had much better technology than the buy side, and this exacerbated an information asymmetry. BlackRock's founders wanted to better understand portfolio risks and protect against downsides but couldn't find any products that were suited to their needs. This led BlackRock to invest in and develop Aladdin, its robust investment platform and risk-management system. Consistent investment in the technology created additional opportunities for BlackRock. By the early 1990s, institutional clients were expressing an interest in using Aladdin to oversee their full portfolio, not just the assets that BlackRock managed on their behalf. Today, Aladdin has grown to cover virtually every asset class and is used by BlackRock and more than 200 insurance companies, pension funds, and asset managers in nearly fifty countries. Because of this scale, BlackRock is able to invest in the technology continuously to improve the platform at scale and realize its benefit as an overall ecosystem.

Recent years have seen multiple fintech start-ups challenge banks and other financial institutions by creating new verticals, ultimately forcing institutions to adapt to compete with these upstarts. Over time, a large proportion of the traditional mutual fund industry may end up with robo-advisors. This part of the industry was geared to those with minimal investment assets (i.e., less than $100,000). Small accounts are very expensive to manage and are well-suited to being managed and serviced by robo-advisors. This trend could grow further to service relatively richer investors, but it has serious limitations when investor requirements become more complex.

Wealthy investors (those with investment accounts above $10 million), ultra-wealthy investors (those with investable assets above $50 million), and uber-wealthy investors (those with investments above $100 million) prefer personal asset managers whom they can talk to about their investments, given the complex nature of their requirements. Every individual is unique in how they approach life, and robo-advisors can only deal with the traits common to all. Human interaction in this part of the wealth curve will be required for a long time to come. Also, the best advisors would put the client's returns ahead of their profits. This means outcomes-based pricing rather than commissions on products sold. Wealth managers catering to the wealthier section of the investor population could be expected to fare better than those catering to smaller investors in a persistent low-return environment.

New Tools Being Used for Investing by Institutional and Retail Investors

The post GFC period has proven to be the perfect storm for asset management. While central-bank-infused liquidity has been a driver of market returns, low volatility in the markets has reduced the alpha generated by active management, thereby pushing investors further into passive investments. The consistent outflow of funds from active management and inflow into passives is a testament to this fact. In such an environment, it has become imperative for asset-management firms to reduce internal costs and drive efficiencies throughout the organization, including research, back-office, and distribution. Recent years have seen several fintech companies create solutions for the asset-management companies.

Research: Traditionally, research analysts have relied upon tools such as the Bloomberg Terminal, Factset, CapitalIQ, and Thomson Eikon (now Refinitiv) terminals. These terminals provide live financial data and a wide array of analytics that are valued by research analysts. These terminals are also extremely expensive, with a single Bloomberg subscription costing upwards of $20,000 per year. With advances in automation and data science, fintech upstarts are trying to enter the data-provider market by offering Internet-based tools that can provide the same data and analytics for a fraction of the cost. One such company is Sentieo, an investment-research software suite that uses AI to scan financial documents, analyze alternative data sets, and create visualizations. By late 2018, the fintech SAAS start-up had 700 customers, including top hedge funds, plus mutual funds, Fortune 500 companies, and investment banks that pay around $6,000 to $12,000 per year for a terminal.[11]

Back-office Automation: A lot of functions in the back office are repetitive. Filing a regulatory report on a set-time basis to market authorities, disclosing information to end clients, and performing reconciliations are jobs that can be undertaken by robotic process automation (RPA) or machine-learning technology. Optimas – a Boston-based consultancy – estimated that around 90,000 jobs in asset management would disappear as a consequence of AI by 2025.[12]

Distribution: The advent and penetration of the Internet and social media have provided a highly scalable distribution channel for asset managers. Younger generations of investors are even more inclined to transact online rather than through a dedicated wealth manager. In examining this trend, while we have discussed robo-advisors above, there is another aspect to the distribution of financial products that is important for the retail investor – brokerages. Brokerages help investors purchase individual stocks, mutual funds, ETFs, and other listed financial securities for their portfolio. In that, they compete directly with robo-advisors for "do-it-yourself" or DIY investors. In recent years, banks have acquired brokerages because of their highly profitable commission-based fee structure. However, with investor pressure on limiting investment costs, new fintech start-ups have been launched that offer zero-commission brokerages. One such start-up is Robinhood, a commission-free stock-trading app. It has gained significant appeal among millennial investors, who value the zero-commission fee and the simple and stylish user interface. It has also attracted attention by offering a bouquet of assets other than those listed on exchanges, including cryptocurrencies (Bitcoin, Litecoin, and Ethereum). Since its founding in 2011, Robinhood's user base has grown to more than 4 million users in 2018.

Social media has been a big influencer on our business in ESG/impact investing. The most important positive impact is to provide us a new channel to address investors' concerns and educate them on ESG/impact investing. Social media also creates more global awareness on ESG, and helps to enhance our coverage in regions in which we are yet to have exposure. The negative impact would be having more "green washing" investment managers offering gimmick products in the market.

> *In the future, we expect heightened social and traditional media interest in taking initiatives to discuss more in-depth topics of impact investing. We believe that complying with the Paris Agreement and working towards the SDGs are important missions for all global citizens. It will be helpful if more of the general public become aware of the urgencies.*[13]

Impact of Technology on Underlying Investments

Not surprisingly, technology has also had a far-reaching impact on the underlying investments of asset-management firms. New asset classes such as cannabis, cyber-threat prevention, and cryptocurrencies have been spawned in the last few years. Technology is also leading to the creation of new industries. Tesla was among the first large-scale manufacturers of electric cars. As a market leader, it has opened up a whole industrial ecosystem around the electric car and has disrupted the industrial ecosystem for the incumbent internal-combustion engine. This has an impact not only on immediately connected companies (e.g., those providing battery commodities, crude oil, etc.) but also on seemingly unconnected industries such as real estate (e.g., through the repurposing of urban infrastructure to accommodate a wider adoption of electric and self-driving vehicles). Technological innovations have thus made it extremely difficult for investment analysts to be focused on just one industry, given the interconnectedness and first- and second-degree impacts of technology on multiple sectors. The solution, interestingly, is also provided by technology.

Artificial intelligence and machine learning will prove to be game changers for active management and for the broader markets. These technologies have the power to propel markets further toward perfect efficiency by enabling real-time impact assessment of new developments. Coupled with other advances such as quantum computing, these would also enable fund managers to employ a multitude of fast and accurate quantitative analysis tools that would generate analysis faster and more accurately than human analysts could do. As a result, the need for junior research talent would decrease over time, and active-fund-management teams would increasingly comprise a small group of human decision makers supported by highly complex and capable computer-based analysts. The industry appears divided over the eventual outcome – a complete dominance by or a complete failure of AI machines in investing. The truth most likely is somewhere in between. Humans and machines will combine to create an investing partnership that leverages their combined strengths.

While current applications of AI and machine learning focus on real-time analysis of a large volume of data to draw quantitative insights, even more interesting would be a future where AI algorithms will start processing qualitative information, apply qualitative investment criteria, and generate superior long-term investment decisions while checking for behavioral biases that human investors often exhibit in decision making. Imagine a scenario where the S&P Index is down 800 points in a flash crash and has severely impacted some of your positions, but the AI system at your desk evaluates your prior responses to similar drawdowns and stops you from making an emotionally charged, suboptimal trading decision.

However, some asset managers believe that the impact of positive behavioral biases on decision making will be hard to be emulated by machines, thereby giving human investors an edge over machines in investing. Proponents of value investing believe that even today, although there is access to a tremendous amount of data and computing, that hasn't created alpha uniformly for investors. With increasing numbers of algorithmic investors, the volatility around key announcements in the stock markets (such as earnings, M&A, activist campaigns) has increased, providing fertile investment opportunities for the patient and thoughtful human investor. It remains to be seen if we'll actually be able to create machines that can remove inherent human biases from the investing decision.

Looking further into the future, quantum computing would further automate the role of the investment analyst. Quantum computers work by harnessing the power of subatomic particles to speed up processing. Under some circumstances, they can be nearly 100 million times faster at solving problems than conventional computers. The earliest such computers were developed in the 1980s, but now they're entering commercialization at scale. The use of quantum computing in the investment industry has been considered for several years as a natural progression and extension to high-speed, algorithmic trading and decision making. As an example, if an investment manager wished to construct a portfolio of thirty stocks from a universe of sixty, there would be 100,000 trillion possible combinations. A quantum computer would be able to calculate the most appropriate risk-optimized portfolio significantly faster than a conventional computer.[14]

Conclusion

For active fund managers, knowing the companies you invest in is the single most important part of your job. It requires countless hours of research and analysis to ensure that the investment premise is correct, in order to be able to react the moment that is no longer the case. This is what successful active managers are known for and is the only way to produce best-in-class returns. Technology has been a game changer for the industry because it allows for much quicker analysis of the quantitative data. However, the qualitative part of the analysis tends to require more human interaction and is still the biggest part of the investment process.

The most significant driver of change, beyond even the impact of technology, will be the dramatic and global demographic shifts that are already occurring. As the boomer generation retires, more money will be required to be withdrawn from accounts, as opposed to being invested. In general, this generation has not saved as much as they should have, and the average North American has less than $100,000 put away for retirement. As a result, these people will have to work longer, or become a burden for their children.

Artificial intelligence and machine learning will be game changers for the asset-management industry. These technologies will save many person hours in the research process, so those who have them first will profit the most. As with anything, once these technologies become mainstream it is hard to see the advantage one manager will have over another. Traditional skills will then reassert themselves as the key determinant of successful investment management. The overall effect will be interesting, because if everyone has the ability to process all information instantly through AI, then the markets will become, in theory, super-efficient, and it will become extremely hard to make money beyond the market return. On the other hand, even today, two people can read the same research and reach two different conclusions, so it is not yet clear how this all works out in a world of machine learning. What is clear is that many junior research jobs will disappear. Success will be all about predicting the future and making prudent portfolio decisions, both of which are always hard to do. For now, AI has produced enhanced quantitative capability with an ability to learn and be more adaptive to changing markets through the use of generic algorithms. The serious game will start when the machines can truly process qualitative information, apply qualitative investment criteria, and generate superior long-term investment decisions or find a way to identify the most optimal candidates for investment at an earlier stage.

Finally, we see the wealth-management industry bifurcating into two distinct segments. First, the segment of largely millennial retail investors who are better served through online platforms such as robo-advisors. The second segment would be those with a significant amount of wealth, who, because their needs are more complex, generally prefer an asset manager whom they can talk to about their investments and for whom the relationship usually goes beyond just their current investment account. Each individual has unique needs, and robo-advisors can only deal with the most basic, common traits of investors. Till we see further refinement in technology to provide mass customization of investment advice at a large scale, human interaction in this significant asset part of the wealth curve will be imperative.

NOTES

We gratefully acknowledge contributions by Catherine Chen, founder and managing partner of Avantfaire, and Mary Throop, founder and partner of Summerhill Capital Management, and the assistance of other leaders in the global asset-management business.

1 McKinsey & Company. (2018). New rules for an old game: Banks in the changing world of financial intermediation. *McKinsey Global Banking Annual Review 2018*.

2 Gittelsohn, J. (2019, 12 February). Passive funds overtake stock-pickers in the U.S. large cap market. *Bloomberg*. https://www.bloomberg.com/news /articles/2019-02-12/passive-funds-overtake-stock-pickers-in-u-s-large -cap-market.

3 Beardsley, B., Donnadieu, H., Fages, R., Hapelt, C., Heredia, L., Morel, P., et al. (2017, 11 July). Global asset management 2017: The innovator's advantage. BCG (Boston Consulting Group) report.

4 Accenture Consulting. (2017). Millennials and money: The millennial investor becomes a force. https://www.accenture.com/_acnmedia /PDF-68/Accenture-Millennials-and-Money-Millennial-Next-Era-Wealth -Management.pdf.

5 Tett, G. (2018, 20 September). Millennial heirs to change investment landscape. *Financial Times.* https://on.ft.com/2MTsBDP (Millennial Heirs to Change Investment Landscape).

6 Accenture. (2015). The "greater" wealth transfer – Capitalizing on the intergenerational shift in wealth. https://www.accenture.com /t20160505t020205z__w__/us-en/_acnmedia/pdf-16/accenture-cm -awams-wealth-transfer-final-june2012-web-version.pdf.

7 United Nations. (nd). Sustainable development goals. https://sustainable development.un.org/?menu=1300.

8 United Nations. (nd). The Paris agreement. https://unfccc.int/process -and-meetings/the-paris-agreement/the-paris-agreement.

9 Quotation from Catherine Chen, CEO of new ESG investment manager Avantfaire; extract from material shared with the authors.

10 Source: Wealth-X. (nd). https://www.wealthx.com/.

11 Constine, J. (2018, 30 October). Sentieo raises $19M to be the AI-powered Bloomberg terminal. Techcrunch. https://techcrunch.com/2018/10/30 /sentieo/.

12 Pierron, A. (2017, 1 March). Artificial intelligence in capital markets: The next operational revolution. www.opimas.com/research/210/detail/.

13 Quotation from Catherine Chen, CEO of new ESG investment manager Avantfaire; extract from material shared with the authors.

14 Walker, O. (2018, 20 October). Nasa says quantum computing is the future for funds. *Financial Times.* https://on.ft.com/2WbQyv1 (Nasa Says Quantum Computing is the Future of Funds).

CHAPTER ELEVEN

Next-Generation Financial Advice: Reimagining Wealth Management in the Age of Technology

Chuck Grace and Andrew Sarta[1]

Introduction

Historically, banks and other financial institutions have been enthusiastic participants in innovation and the adoption of new technologies. Over the next few years, however, their commitment and agility will be tested. The world is pursuing financial technologies ("fintech") at a dizzying pace, with global investment in fintech estimated at $57.9 billion for the first six months of 2018, surpassing the total for the 2017 fiscal year (KPMG, 2018). While all change brings some trepidation, industry players need to understand that with fintech, *a failure to act is a bad option*. Changes in financial services are well underway, and the pain will be felt most by those financial institutions that fail to respond to change.

This chapter focuses on the area of fintech concerned with providing financial advice – popularly known as robo-advice. When robo-advisors first emerged a decade ago, many experts sowed fears of disruption and predicted doom for traditional financial-advice organizations (Ludden, 2015). The term "robo-advisor" comes with a popular narrative that suggests the presence of actual robots that not only look like humans but are here to replace human advisors.

There's also a sense that these "machines" require science-fiction-grade technology that is not yet available and that will be impossible to regulate when it is deployed.

While this narrative makes for a compelling story, our research has found it to be untrue. We have held working sessions and interviews with key players from the wealth-management industry. The overwhelming consensus that emerged is that the required technologies are not tomorrow's technology but are already available. And they could be deployed to deliver better financial advice to clients today.

This point is important. All stakeholders agree that digital technology creates an opportunity for better financial advice. Technology can enhance the value proposition of human advisors – not take away their jobs. Some tasks are better performed by machines, while others only succeed in the hands of humans. For instance, the task of onboarding clients or rebalancing asset portfolios can be effectively executed digitally. However, identifying financial aspirations or ensuring the well-being of clients during emotion-laden recessionary periods is best handled by human advisors. If technology and humans are integrated into the financial services industry in the right way, our research suggests that the combination will lead to better outcomes for clients by, in part, addressing a broader spectrum of their needs.

We argue that the future of the investment industry will be a hybrid model that partners a human advisor with technologies (such as data analytics and machine learning) that increase the value of financial advice and enhance the client experience. We call this *Next Generation Financial Advice.*

Innovation and technology are not new to wealth management and financial advice (Investor Economics, 2016). Given the complexity and time-sensitive nature of most financial instruments, the wealth-management industry has relied for decades on technological innovation to promote growth and increase competitiveness. What is new is the rapid pace of innovation, driven by the power and diversity of new technologies. Today, the delivery of financial services isn't just confronted with technological breakthroughs in artificial intelligence (AI) or big data; it is simultaneously confronted with breakthroughs in social media, analytics, user-experience interfaces (UX), blockchain, biometrics, and the Internet-of-Things (IoT), among others.

For financial advisors, technology is a tool – nothing more. It doesn't wake up in the morning hoping to disrupt organizations. It facilitates innovation only when people use this tool to pursue their ambitions. One of the things that still differentiates humans from machines is a conscious ability to thoughtfully and imaginatively choose those ambitions. We can either wait for the technological options to overwhelm us or we can seek to define, in advance, the best use of those tools.

We identify six broad opportunities that are guiding *Next Generation Financial Advice*. We foresee a remodeling of financial advice that leverages the power of digital technology to free financial advisors from computationally heavy and time-consuming activities in order to focus on relationship-building activities that deepen trust with clients. The opportunities outlined are shaped from research conducted by the Ivey Business School over 2017 and 2018 (Grace, Young, & Sarta, 2017). We define financial advice in broad, holistic terms that extend well beyond the scope of the first generation of robo-advisors that have attracted most of the media's attention. It is also important to note that, while wealth management broadly considers both the management of investment products (such as tangible assets, individual securities, or mutual funds) and financial advice (such as recommending the appropriate asset mix to consumers), our primary focus is on the services associated with financial advice.

1. Digital Offers an Opportunity for Stronger Client Impact

The consensus from our research is that integrating digital technology into the world of wealth management will lead to better outcomes for clients. The question of the value of digital advice needs to be reframed to ask how can we best meet a client's needs, not how can we most effectively digitize an advisor's brain.

While some participants worry, in a practical sense, about what this evolution may mean for their industry, they agree that some tasks can simply be done better by machines. Technology can lead to cheaper, more efficient outcomes for clients, who will also get the added benefit of ease of access.[2] With digital solutions, clients can stay on top of their finances and be disciplined in their savings and investments (McWaters & Galaski, 2017). They can also get answers to their questions much faster than they would if they had to book an appointment with their advisor.

At its root, stronger impact requires that we address the broadest range of client needs – a holistic view. We must integrate the complex nature of their financial realities while balancing a dynamic, and sometimes contradictory, range of priorities and goals. Today, in Canada, advisors are sometimes conflicted in their advice for reasons too broad to list here (Foerster et al., 2017; Grable, Hubble, & Kruger, 2018; Montmarquette & Viennot-Briot, 2016; Thaler & Sunstein, 2009). However, digital advice, fueled by the right data, offers an opportunity to cut through the web of conflicts (structural, corporate, regulatory, and professional) to focus exclusively on the client's best outcome.

The use of technology also provides an opportunity to incorporate financial education into the design, leading to more informed clients who are better able to make decisions or ask relevant questions. Broad access to easy and intuitive mobile applications ("apps") would increase access to financial advice for consumers who are currently underserved by today's wealth-management paradigm, where it is only economic for financial advisors to focus on high-net-worth clients. Finally, the automation of investment advice will lead to robust, predictable recommendations that are personalized for each customer – something the industry has struggled to achieve with human advisors (Grable, Hubble, & Kruger, 2018).

2. The Future of Financial Advice Is Hybrid

There will always be a role for human advisors in the financial-advice equation because there are certain things machines simply have not demonstrated the potential to do well (Heidrick & Struggles, 2018). For instance, a digital platform will not be able to hold a client's hand when the stock market drops by 20 percent. Nor will it truly understand what someone is saying using natural-language processing alone. The ideal scenario appears to be one where financial advisors use digital technologies to perform the computations and broad analysis of data, while the advisors focus on (i) interpreting the analysis to determine what is in the best interest of the client, and (ii) managing the behavioral aspects of the relationship, such as reassuring clients during periods of market volatility.

Humans remain uniquely skilled at subjective tasks – those automatic, intuitive, and instinctual tasks that let us navigate the world successfully and read between the lines in client conversations. We move quickly and effortlessly between thoughts. We are highly visual. And we are great storytellers. Researchers in behavioral finance and economics refer to these attributes as "System 1" thinking, which is fast, instinctive, and emotional (Evans & Stanovich, 2013). Our deliberative, analytical mind – or objective side – works with data and logic to perform complicated actions using "System 2" thinking, which is slower, more deliberative, and more logical. Humans are often skilled at these logical tasks, but machines have proven to be faster, tireless, more precise, and capable of evaluating large quantities of data more effectively than humans (Kahneman, 2011).

Research is beginning to show that this combination of a human advisor paired with a digital assistant is more effective than either one by itself (McAfee & Brynjolfsson, 2017). This divvying up of responsibilities would give advisors more time to do what robots cannot – namely, develop human relationships – while improving service and achieving better client outcomes. The goal is to augment or "nudge" what advisors can do in order to provide a better customer experience (Thaler & Sunstein, 2009).

Technology will free the advisor from having to perform a growing number of routine tasks, like rebalancing a portfolio or optimizing the asset mix.[3] But technology also means advisors will be able to focus on managing client relationships and providing advice based on data-driven outcomes. Advisors will also need to review the recommendations generated by algorithms before anything goes to a client to ensure they are actually the best option. And as the role of the advisor changes, licensing and training of financial advisors will also need to change in order to train them in the areas where humans provide the greatest value. Table 11.1 provides examples

Table 11.1. Examples of subjective versus objective tasks in financial advice

	Subjective Tasks: Humans Do Well	Objective Tasks: Machines Do Well
Goal Setting	Prioritization, balancing trade-offs, confirming values, clarifying aspirations	Empirical options
Savings Discipline	Creating a call to action (inertia), helping with financial literacy	Projections, scenarios, holistic view, visualizations
Asset Mix	Confirming risk tolerance	Risk required, risk capacity, optimization, rebalancing
Fees & Taxes	Handling exceptions	Optimization, product due diligence
Catastrophic Risk	Articulating product options, overcoming inertia	Projections, scenarios

of financial advice activities that machines do better than human advisors, with algorithms focused on objective tasks and humans focused on subjective tasks.

3. The Required Technology Is Proven, Economical, and Widely Available

While new iterations of current technology will continue to evolve, we argue that the basic technology to offer *Next Generation Financial Advice* is already available today. It is already being used in different parts of society and the economy.[4] In fact, the participants in our research noted that the required technologies are far from leading edge by today's standards.

Our research identified the following key technologies for achieving enhanced client outcomes:

- *Cloud computing:* for increased connectedness to portfolio performance
- *Digital onboarding:* for increased convenience and enhanced compliance
- *Psychographic profiling tools:* to enhance personalization and client tendencies
- *Social media tools:* for increased communication with clients
- *Machine learning:* for increased predictive outcomes in client behavior
- *Online portals (or multi-sided marketplaces):* for an efficient gateway to third-party service providers
- *Account aggregation tools:* for an increased view of a client's entire financial data
- *Lean digital manufacturing technologies:*[5] for increased back-office efficiency

Our research found, however, that most of these technologies are currently being applied in isolation by investment advisors and their employers. The power of these technologies to achieve superior client outcomes will only be realized when they are integrated into a comprehensive platform (McAfee & Brynjolfsson, 2017). In other words, holistic advice requires technology integration and open platforms.

At this stage, the main concerns surround data security and privacy, both of which cut to the root of trust – the cornerstone of financial advice. The lack of proper infrastructure to share information between players and the current regulatory silos pose a data-aggregation challenge. This conclusion is consistent with existing research that suggests no single agency or formalized group has the clear legal authority or mandate to manage all aspects of systemic risk (Le Pan, 2017).

4. Successful Organizations Will Collaborate around the Client Experience

While the technology needed to deliver hybrid advice may not be leading edge, its deployment – particularly by start-up robo-advisors – is disrupting the industry status quo. The information technology (IT) systems currently used by most incumbent financial institutions were designed for traditional siloed ways of doing business. These systems provide an end-to-end solution to fulfill the sale of a certain type of product, such as a mutual fund or a guaranteed investment certificate. Different products are sold through different divisions and, therefore, the IT systems have little connectivity. It is not uncommon for a customer to have to log in to different systems to access different product relationships with the same institution, such as a bank website for checking and savings accounts, and a broker-dealer website for trading in securities, bonds, and mutual funds.

In contrast, modern IT systems developed by new fintech entrants (including robo-advisors) are typically more flexible, modular, and open (McAfee & Brynjolfsson, 2017). They leverage more robust application programming interfaces (APIs), allowing data to flow across multiple product lines and even across organizations. This open architecture makes it relatively easy to generate a comprehensive view of a customer's financial situation. Thus, the financial advisor can recommend solutions that address a customer's needs more holistically than is possible with siloed IT systems. For example, account aggregation can provide insight into assets held at other financial institutions to ensure that the client's risk and tax situation is being optimized across their entire portfolio, not just the portion held by a given financial institution.

In addition to enabling a holistic view of a customer's data, fintech companies can generate better insights and advice by applying value-added analytics to these data sets. Personal financial management tools provide human advisors with insight into a client's spending behavior; they can identify opportunities to increase savings or assess how realistic a client's lifestyle goals might be. These data analytics are being used to automate actions that improve a client's financial well-being. Automated saving and portfolio rebalancing are popular examples of these features in action. The computer algorithm learns how each customer responds to data insights and provides more effective nudges to jumpstart the desired customer behavior. As more data are collected, the nudges become more effective through a process of continuous improvement by the algorithm.

This situation points to mutually beneficial opportunities for incumbents and fintechs to collaborate. Incumbents may have trouble keeping up with the pace of innovation in such learning algorithms, highlighting a capability gap. For their part, fintech start-ups need access to the large data sets held by incumbents to train these learning algorithms, in addition to incumbents' regulatory expertise. Such a scenario offers plenty of opportunity for partnerships to improve client outcomes. Most fintech-incumbent partnership opportunities fall into two categories:

1. Start-ups that have developed novel applications that include a function core to traditional banking competencies (e.g., shopping for a home or car that requires a loan);
2. Start-ups that have developed highly specialized applications that enable a key aspect of the overall client experience (e.g., personal financial management, account aggregation).

Engaging in fintech partnerships will become increasingly important for incumbents to enable them to reach new customers in new ways and remain relevant. Fintechs pursuing business-to-business (B2B) models, such as robo-advisors that license technology to incumbents, are more likely to succeed by leveraging the scale of incumbents. The world of financial advice is shifting toward a model where incumbents and start-ups take advantage of each other's strengths while overcoming their independent weaknesses (Ernst & Young, 2018). The partnership of U.S. robo-advisor Acorns with Lincoln Savings Bank to offer a savings account with a debit card is an example of an improved customer experience made possible by pairing a micro-investing app with an FDIC-registered bank.[6] For their part, the U.S. robo-advisor Betterment and the Canadian robo-advisor Nest Wealth are both licensing software to incumbents in order to free human advisors from tasks that can be automated so they can refocus on building client relationships.[7]

5. Open Data (Banking) Will Accelerate Innovation

The assumption among both incumbents and start-ups has long been that regulators were an obstacle for digital advice and needed to "get out of the way." But our research found that many processes that companies look to automate are already permitted under current regulations. Currently there are no regulatory impediments to robo-advisors' use of technology to onboard clients. The regulators who participated in our research maintained that, if the financial advice generated by an algorithm is wrong, the company providing that advice is liable, just as it would be when a human advisor makes a mistake.

As a result of that liability exposure, the regulators were not overly concerned with the perceived lack of audit trail associated with digital financial advice. In fact, *Next Generation Financial Advice* may actually be a better option, because it can provide an electronic record of what was presented to the client and why, instead of the "he said/she said" situation that might occur with a human advisor. Regulators generally felt that the adoption of digital technologies was more of a business issue than a regulatory one. It is up to individual firms to figure out the regulations that govern any changes to their business models – just as they do today with other human-centric issues.

Open banking, where consumers have greater control over their data, was identified as a cornerstone issue.[8] Strategy in a digital age pivots on data, and any fences built around data will limit the effectiveness of computer algorithms. It is difficult to provide innovative solutions when fintech start-ups cannot access the data they need to create the right solutions. Open data are needed to make sure the algorithms are legitimate and verifiable. This access poses a supervisory challenge in terms of privacy and security concerns, but also an opportunity to encourage innovation. The United Kingdom's

Open Banking initiative is leading the way in this area and is stimulating regulatory conversations globally on the question of who should have access to customer data and what data are reasonable (Open Banking Working Group, 2018). Similar legislation has been passed by the European Union and Australia, and versions of it are being reviewed in the United States, China, and Southeast Asia (U.S. Department of the Treasury, 2018).

Policymakers recognize that "open banking" is a widely touted catalyst for promoting more innovation and increased competition by the fintech community.[9] While it is too early to understand the outcomes of the U.K. initiative, open banking has implications well beyond start-ups. The implications are much, much broader for incumbents, who currently house much of the data. The implications extend not just to financial advice but to privacy and data security as well. Central to this conversation is the question "Who owns the data – the client or the firm that stores the data?"

Without access to data, fintech innovators, both small and large, will stall, and any benefits to retail customers will evaporate. Standardized processes for securely accessing data with a client's permission should be viewed as table stakes for *Next Generation Financial Advice* to be achieved.

6. Hybrid Services Require New Models

We have argued that many of the perceived barriers to *Next Generation Financial Advice* are not really barriers at all. Technological innovation is moving forward at a rapid pace, and most of the required tools are already available. Instead, the main obstacles to moving digital advice forward appear to be a lack of adoption by customers, combined with inertia by incumbent financial institutions. Robo-advisors are currently managing only a small fraction of assets under management (AUM) globally – below 2 percent in North America and less in Europe and Asia. The reality is that fintech new entrants are simply not attracting enough customers to transform this industry (Breznitz, Breznitz, & Wolfe, 2015).

True progress towards achieving *Next Generation Financial Advice* must be driven by the financial incumbents who have the large customer bases, the financial and regulatory expertise, and the funding to invest in new technologies and IT systems. These incumbents need to integrate digital infrastructures into every aspect of their operations. And regulators need to contribute by creating an environment that supports change, with the goal of providing a better service to retail customers. Fintech start-ups, for their part, need to focus on the business side of their firms, not just the technology. In particular, they need to understand what is needed to make their start-ups viable from both a business-model perspective and a regulatory perspective. We refer to this requirement as putting the "fin" in fintech.

Most incumbents are working on developing digital financial advice but are struggling to make progress. In our research, all of the participants surveyed identified hybrid digital advice as the number-one priority, or in the top five priorities, for their firm. But the implementation of hybrid digital advice is proving to be a bigger and more complex task than imagined. We have identified a myriad of complex issues confronting the different market players in this industry (table 11.2). Many, but not all, of these complex issues are internal to the specific players.

In the context of *Next Generation Financial Advice*, the failure of disrupters to gain traction and the complexity faced by incumbents point to the fact that something fundamentally different is occurring in the marketplace for financial advice. The traditional models of disruption and innovation do not seem to work.

Table 11.2. External and internal barriers to change

	Smaller Firms, Start-ups, and Disrupters	Large Incumbent Firms	Common to Both
External Barriers	• Lack of APIs • Talent acquisition	• Talent acquisition • Vendor capacity	• Data mobility • Regulatory silos • Digital adoption
Internal Barriers	• Ability to scale • Funding	• Leap of faith • General inertia • Data architecture • Adviser resistance • Economic incentives • Channel conflict • Risk aversion • Change management	• Complexity • Development capacity • Sequencing

Most of our understanding of innovation, be it radical, disruptive, or architectural, comes from contexts where products reign supreme, not from service industries. The theory of architectural innovation was developed by Henderson and Clark (1990), who studied the semiconductor lithography industry, while the theory of disruptive innovation came from Christensen's (1997) famous study of the computer-disk-drive industry. There is reason to believe that technological innovation in the financial-services industry may be different. While innovations in tangible products often coalesce around dominant designs that emerge in a discontinuous way, it is difficult to imagine a dominant design emerging for an intangible service such as financial advice.

The lack of fit between established theories of innovation may also be due to the type of innovation that we are now witnessing. We are seeing the emergence of *intelligence-based* innovation, centered on decision making. Intelligence-based innovation appears to challenge existing services before it displaces them – if they are displaced at all. Innovations in services must essentially prove their value to customers before they are adopted and displace existing customer offerings that are viewed as less attractive.

The needs of the customer are well known. Clients want personalized, hassle-free, effective, competitively priced, and trustworthy financial advice. While recent innovations in financial advice promise to satisfy these customer needs, it is not clear that one dominant design will emerge that meets all of these objectives. Rather than consolidating around a new model, the industry is likely moving in the opposite direction, where modes of financial advice will continue to fragment. For example, we have seen that direct investing options can coexist alongside full-service financial advice. And the investment products offered to customers will continue to fragment, as seen in the explosion of exchange-traded funds (ETFs) and the emergence of funds targeting different investment objectives, such as corporate socially responsible (CSR) mutual funds.

In this context, the ability of organizations to adapt becomes critical for success. Adaptation is not a task solely for incumbent financial institutions. Nor does it suggest that start-ups provide the models to emulate. When an organization adapts, it does not simply change – it changes in such a way that it aligns to the external environment and markets in which it operates. Adopting new technology may be part of the equation, but adopting technology without consideration for alignment to the external environment is unlikely to be fruitful. The challenge with environments and markets, however, is that they are not monoliths; they are multifaceted, complex, and dynamic.

Conclusion: Redefining the Value of Financial Advice (and Trust)

The future of *Next Generation Financial Advice* will be a hybrid model where financial advisors embrace technology, incumbents partner with fintech start-ups, and everyone stays focused on the end game: namely, facilitating better client outcomes. Within this world, we see two potential strategies – one at the societal level and the other at the market level.

At the societal level, incumbent firms compete by fostering a relationship of trust with their clients. Trust reigns supreme in financial advice. Clients are willing to entrust their life savings to financial advisors who have a track record of being reliable. Clients really need to know one thing – that their savings are protected or, as our expert panelists suggested, that "they are going to be okay." Human advisors currently dominate in building these relationships, as computers are not adept at sensing emotion and comforting clients. The importance of trust increases with the size of the individual client's portfolio. High-net-worth clients are likely to place greater value on human-centered advice, as the complexity of their needs instills a need for greater trust.

Understanding the evolution of trust becomes a critical element in informing strategic decision making for firms providing financial advice. This dimension likely favors incumbents. Trust is built up over long periods of time and is related both to demographic changes and to economic cycles. Mature, highly regulated environments (such as North America and Europe) are witnessing slower migration from traditional, human-centered advice to digital-only robo-advice, as trust has remained resilient between clients and incumbents. In less mature environments, such as the Chinese market, relationships with financial advisors are less established, and clients are exhibiting a greater willingness to adopt digitally based advice solutions. Younger generations are proving much more willing to adopt digital solutions, particularly millennials, who will soon be the largest group of savers. At the same time, technological changes are occurring that may alter these relationships in the future. The speed of disruption by new technologies will be related to the length of relationships between clients and financial advisors.

At the market level, start-ups compete on the basis of their value proposition to customers. On the one hand, start-ups use technology to offer personalization and convenience. On the other hand, the lower fees offered by start-ups are forcing incumbents to justify the value they offer to clients. In competitive markets, the value equation is being recalculated, and industry players either need to increase the services rendered for the same price or offer the same services at a cheaper price. To date, the latter approach has prevailed, with fee compression emerging as an industry trend. While this certainly benefits clients, it may result in a race to the bottom for industry players as revenues decline. Long-term value in the industry may rest on the ability for organizations to use technology to deliver truly personalized, holistic, and convenient financial advice at the right value and not exclusively the lowest cost.

These relative competitive strengths – with incumbents developing trusting relationships versus start-ups offering low-fee customization – point directly to opportunities for partnerships. They also highlight the benefits of the hybrid human-technology model that we believe will shape the future of financial advice. The incumbents in financial advice are trusted, established organizations that specialize in addressing the emotional aspects of investing while perhaps falling short of the capabilities needed to offer personalized, low-cost financial advice. Fintech start-ups, conversely, hold capabilities that appeal to clients' needs at the market level while struggling to appeal to long-standing trust-based relationships held by incumbents. When these strengths are combined, a clear strategy emerges. In the short term, partnerships and hybrid advice offer a strategy to address this complex environment. In the long term, those organizations that are able to leverage and learn from such partnerships are likely to achieve sustained relevance as they offer financial advice that is personalized, trustworthy, cost-effective, and convenient.

NOTES

1 The authors would like to thank Michael King (editor), Amy Young, and participants at two Ivey workshops on the future of digital advice in March 2017 and November 2017 for their input and comments. We acknowledge financial support from the Scotiabank Digital Banking Lab at Ivey Business School. All errors and omissions remain our own.

2 In the United States, Charles Schwab's Intelligent Advisory platform (a Robo/Human Hybrid) is priced at an annual fee of 28 basis points (0.28%) of assets under management to a maximum annual fee of $3,600. With its fixed-price subscription model of $80 a month, or $960 annually, Canada's Nest Wealth has established a new benchmark for the value of financial advice.

3 To the extent that an advisor defines their value proposition by one of the objective tasks, there is a distinct possibility that the number of required advisors will shrink as those tasks are automated. At the Money Management Institute's Wealth Summit in October 2017, panelists estimated the shrinkage at 25 percent, over five years.

4 A January 2016 article by Fulvia Montresor for the World Economic Forum estimated that by 2025, 10 percent of people will wear clothing connected to the Internet and that 3D-printed cars will be in production. She noted that the United Nations has set a goal to connect 100 percent of the world's inhabitants to affordable Internet by 2020 and references a study out of the University of Oxford that suggests a 58 percent probability that the occupation of "personal financial advisor" will be automated. (See Montresor, 2016).

5 Lean digital manufacturing refers to the systematic elimination of waste and redundancy in business processes. In financial services, the vast majority of business processes are digital but still reliant on older, inefficient legacy platforms.

6 Acorns Support, 2020.

7 See Betterment Securities, nd, and Nest Wealth, nd.

8 The Open Banking Standard defined open data as data that anyone can access, use, and share. Open banking regulates the use of open application

interfaces that enable third-party developers to build applications and services around the financial institution.

9 In its 2018 budget, the Government of Canada asked for comments on whether open banking had the potential to benefit from a broader range of financial products and services, and in September 2018, Minister of Finance Morneau launched an Advisory Committee on Open Banking. On 19 June 2019, the Standing Senate Committee on Banking, Trade and Commerce released its report *Open banking: What it means for you*. The report discussed open banking and made recommendations for reforms in the interests of Canadian consumers and financial-services providers.

REFERENCES

Acorns Support. (2020). What is my actual bank as an Acorns Spend customer? https://www.acorns.com/support/spend/what-is-my-actual-bank-as-an-acorns-spend-customer-/. Accessed 28 June 2019.

Betterment Securities. (nd). Betterment for advisors. https://advisors.betterment.com/. Accessed 28 June 2019.

Breznitz, D., Breznitz, S., & Wolfe, D. (2015). *Current state of the financial technology innovation ecosystem in the Toronto region*. Innovation Policy Lab at the Munk School of Global Affairs. Retrieved from www.munkschool.utoronto.ca.

Christensen, C. (1997). *The innovator's dilemma: When new technologies cause great firms to fail*. Brighton, MA: Harvard Business Review Press.

Ernst & Young. (2018). The evolution of robo-advisors and advisor 2.0 model.

Evans, J.St.B., & Stanovich, K.E. (2013). Dual-process theories of higher cognition. *Perspectives on Psychological Science 8*(3): 223–41. https://doi.org/10.1177/1745691612460685. Medline:26172965.

Foerster, S., Linnainmaa, J., Melzer, B., & Previtero, A. (2017). Retail financial advice: Does one size fit all? *Journal of Finance*. Retrieved from https://doi.org/10.3386/w20712.

Grable, J., Hubble, A., & Kruger, M. (2018). Do as I say, not as I do: An analysis of portfolio development recommendations made by financial advisors. www.centerforfinancialplanning.org.

Grace, C., Young, A., & Sarta, A. (2017, November). Financial advice in Canada: A way forward. Retrieved from www.ivey.uwo.ca.

Heidrick & Struggles. (2018, March). The future of digital financial advice. Retrieved www.cfp.net.

Henderson, R., & Clark, K. (1990). Architectural innovation: The reconfiguration of existing product technologies and the failure of established firms. *Administrative Science Quarterly, 35*(1), 9–30. https://doi.org/10.2307/2393549.

Investor Economics. (2016). *Fintech Advisory Service – Canada*. Fall.

Kahneman, D. (2011). *Thinking, fast and slow*. Toronto: Doubleday Canada.

KPMG. (2018). The pulse of fintech 2018.

Le Pan, N. (2017). Opportunities for better systemic risk management in Canada. *CD Howe Institute Commentary, 490*.

Ludden, C. (2015). The rise of robo-advice: Changing the concept of wealth management.

McAfee, A., & Brynjolfsson, E. (2017). *Machine, platform, crowd: Harnessing our digital future*. New York: W.W. Norton & Company.

McWaters, J., & Galaski, R. (2017). Beyond fintech: A pragmatic assessment of disruptive potential in financial services.

Montmarquette, C., & Viennot-Briot, N. (2016). The gamma factor and the value of financial advice. Centre interuniversitaire de recherché en analyse des organisations. 2016s-35. https://www.cirano.qc.ca/files/publications/2016s-35.pdf.

Montresor, F. (2016, 19 January). The 7 technologies changing your world. World Economic Forum. https://www.weforum.org/agenda/2016/01/a-brief-guide-to-the-technologies-changing-world/.

Nest Wealth. (nd). Nest Wealth Plus. https://www.learn.nestwealth.com/plus/. Accessed 8 May 2020.

Open Banking Working Group. (2018). The open banking standard – Background document no. 2.

Thaler, R.H., & Sunstein, C.R. (2009). *Nudge: Improving decisions about health, wealth, and happiness*. New York: Penguin Publishing Group. https://books.google.ca/books?id=bt6sPxiYdfkC.

U.S. Department of the Treasury. (2018). A financial system that creates economic opportunities: Nonbank financials, fintech and innovation.

CHAPTER TWELVE

Treasury and Technology

Peter Levitt and Tom McGuire

Much of industry commentary on technology in banking deals with ways in which financial technology (or fintech) companies are disrupting traditional banks with cutting-edge innovations in digital offerings, mobile payments, social media, artificial intelligence, Bitcoin, and the like. Less visible, but arguably just as important, are how technological innovations are changing more traditional aspects of banking, including the Risk, Finance, and Treasury functions.

This chapter focuses on the technological evolution in banking as seen from the bank's Treasury department. It provides a high-level overview of the role of the Treasury function, which is to manage the bank's balance-sheet resources (capital, funding, and liquid assets) and the associated risks (funding, interest rate, foreign exchange, and liquidity) to enable the bank to achieve its overall strategy. The chapter summarizes how technology is currently used by Treasury and highlights some specific use-cases for technological improvements. It reviews a number of unique challenges in implementing new technology for this part of the bank. Finally, it outlines how to develop and implement a technology strategy for the Treasury function.

The Role of Bank Treasury

The Treasury department is essentially the circulatory system of the bank. Treasury manages balance-sheet resources (capital, funding, and liquid assets) and balance-sheet risks (liquidity, interest-rate, and foreign-exchange risks) to enable the bank to achieve its overall strategy. This goal is accomplished within a predefined risk appetite, regulatory requirements, and other constraints such as management-determined targets and limits, as well as rating-agency standards, to name a few. In this role, Treasury can be seen as "engine room central." It intermediates between the bank lines of business (and their clients) that supply or require funds and that create or mitigate balance-sheet risks. It also intermediates between the bank and capital markets. The Treasury function is at the core of a bank's role as a financial intermediary that drives the economy and enables the ambitions of individuals, organizations, communities, businesses, and corporations.

Treasury has the primary accountability – supported by an asset/liability committee (ALCO) composed of senior executives from across the bank – for the safety and soundness of a bank's balance sheet. In this role, Treasury manages balance-sheet resources and, importantly, the bank's interest-rate, foreign-exchange, and liquidity risks. Table 12.1 summarizes the various Treasury responsibilities that are discussed in this section.

Table 12.1. Treasury responsibilities

Capital Management	Liquidity Management
• Funding and Funding Risk	• Liquidity Risk
• Interest-rate Risk	• Funds Transfer Pricing
• Foreign-exchange Risk	• Resource Management
• Stress Testing	• Advise Bank Lines of Business
	• Recovery and Resolution Planning

Raising Funding and Managing Funding Risk

One important aspect of Treasury's responsibility is raising funds for the bank's operations in the form of deposits, secured and unsecured borrowings (including subordinated debt), and preferred shares and common equity. Most large banks augment their deposit funding by issuing debt securities to shorter-term money markets and longer-term-debt capital markets. The Treasury group is responsible for raising this market funding and invests in the technology to facilitate these transactions, including systems for managing funding instruments, hedging these instruments, and securitizing and issuing mortgage-backed securities, covered bonds, and other asset-backed securities. Treasury also manages the legal infrastructure of funding, such as filing prospectus materials with securities regulators and exchanges.

An important element when managing funding risk related to capital markets is to create a well-diversified funding portfolio across geographies, investor types, instruments, and term structure. The Treasury team also invests time and resources in fixed-income investor relations. Treasury staff travel to meet with their global investor base to ensure that credit analysts and portfolio managers understand the bank's strategy and risk posture. This outreach is essential to maintain the support of these investors and to maintain access to this vital supply of a critical balance-sheet resource. This investor-relations function has become even more important in recent years, as global systemically important banks (G-SIBs) are required by regulation to issue minimum levels of debt convertible into equity to meet their total loss absorbing capacity (TLAC) requirements. TLAC is a component of the bank-resolution requirements as established by the Financial Stability Board in the wake of the 2008–2009 global financial crisis.

Capital requirements for banks are set to meet both external regulatory requirements and internal management targets. Capital models are comprehensive and complex and rely on a strong partnership with the bank's risk-management function. The most common global capital measures are risk-based capital requirements (Common Equity Tier 1, Tier 1, and Total Capital) and leverage-based requirements (leverage ratio, and supplementary leverage ratio in some countries). Treasury ensures that the bank has sufficient capital on hand to meet minimum capital requirements and provides guidance on business strategy if there is risk that the growth in capital requirements will outpace the growth in capital formation through retained earnings. Treasury also advises on capital-optimization opportunities and capital sufficiency for potential acquisitions. Treasury will raise funding from investors when required to maintain target capital ratios. The issuance of additional Tier 1 capital in the form of preferred shares, and Tier 2 capital in the form of subordinated debt (in both cases, convertible to common equity under bank-recovery scenarios) is a fairly routine matter, while issuance of common equity is rare.

Managing Interest-Rate Risk

Interest-rate risk arises from the repricing characteristics of assets (such as mortgages) and liabilities (such as deposits) whose prices are influenced by changes in interest rates, changes in the shape of the yield curve, changes in cash flows from assets and liabilities, and changes in customer behavior. For most large banks, net interest income (NII) represents more than 50 percent of total revenues, with the remainder generated from noninterest income such as fee income and trading profits. NII can also exhibit significant volatility when interest rates change, if interest-rate risk is not properly hedged.

To manage this risk, Treasury functions use sophisticated asset/liability-management (ALM) models that perform detailed interest-rate sensitivity analysis of comprehensive cash flows for the entire balance sheet, and related off-balance-sheet risks. ALM models run many rate-shock scenarios and measure principally earnings at risk (EaR) and economic value of equity (EVE). EaR is focused on nearer-term impacts of rate changes on NII, typically with a twelve-month time horizon. The measurement and management of this risk help the bank deliver on the promise of stable and predictable earnings for shareholders. EVE effectively measures the present value of the balance sheet under a defined-rate scenario, and is a measure of future earnings over the life of the balance sheet. This metric is key to managing long-term valuation of the balance sheet.

Bank Treasury functions run active hedging programs that transact on a daily basis, relying on interest-rate swaps, forward contracts, and bond trades to achieve a target risk profile. Note that many balance-sheet items, such as nonmaturity (demand) deposits and equity, do not have defined interest-rate characteristics, so ALM models must by necessity define the assumed duration of demand deposits and the target duration of equity.

Managing Foreign-Exchange Risk

Treasury monitors and manages foreign-exchange risks from a number of sources. Foreign-exchange risks arise from holding assets and liabilities denominated in currencies other than the bank's own currency of account and from variations in the values of one currency versus the other (foreign-exchange rates). They also arise from earnings generated in a currency different from the bank's currency of account, such as the earnings from a foreign subsidiary, or through variations in a bank's investment in a foreign subsidiary. It is common for global banks to have a mismatch between the capital ratios of foreign subsidiaries (capital invested in a foreign subsidiary over the capital requirements of that subsidiary) and the capital ratio of the consolidated bank. These mismatches create volatility in the consolidated bank's capital ratios when foreign-exchange rates change. Treasury hedges this exposure through a net investment in foreign operations (NIFO) hedging strategy.

Managing Liquidity Risk

Among the most important responsibilities Treasury fulfills is making sure the bank has sufficient liquidity on hand, or assets that can be converted into cash on short notice, to ensure that the bank can meet all obligations when due. The most frequent reason for banks to fail is their inability to manage through a liquidity crisis, and the Treasury function in a bank invests significant resources in managing this risk. Treasury manages liquidity risk through a combination of monitoring, forecasting, reporting, stress testing, and contingency planning.

As part of liquidity risk management, a Treasury's investment function manages a pool of high-quality liquid assets (or HQLA). High-quality liquid assets are highly rated short- and medium-term securities issued by governments (federal, provincial, municipal), mortgage-backed securities, central bank reserves, and relatively smaller amounts of corporate bonds and equities. In some banks, Treasury's investment function also manages a portfolio of longer-term bonds and equities to enhance the bank's overall investment return rather than contribute to the bank's liquidity.

Liquidity risk management starts by measuring the survival horizon of a bank under a range of moderate and severe stress scenarios. These scenarios typically assume there is a "run on the bank," in which unusually large volumes of deposits are withdrawn over a short period of time, exacerbated by other factors such as loss of access to wholesale funding markets, increased drawdown of com-mitted lending facilities, and increased collateral demands from counter-parties. These demands on liquidity are funded through the liquidation of high-quality liquid assets augmented by the bank's capacity to raise short-term and secured funding, a remedy that may still be possible in periods of duress. The relationship between the bank's access to liquidity and the liquidity demands in a stress scenario defines a bank's survival horizon. A bank cannot survive beyond the point at which it runs out of cash (unless it is supported by a central bank as lender of last resort).

Global bank regulations define two standard liquidity-risk met-rics, the liquidity coverage ratio (LCR) and the net stable funding ratio (NSFR). The LCR defines a severe thirty-day stress scenario, and the NSFR defines the structural requirements for long-term sta-ble funding on a bank's balance sheet. In addition to these require-ments, many national regulators impose additional liquidity metrics (such as 2052A in the United States and the net cumulative cash flow in Canada). Individual banks will also operate their own propri-etary survival horizon models.

Treasury assists the bank's businesses in managing their balance-sheet resources, including pricing, analytics, and efficiency. Through funds-transfer pricing (FTP), Treasury provides daily cost-of-funds/credit-of-funds information to all businesses, a primary input to product-pricing models. FTP in advanced bank models acts as a risk-transfer mechanism, centralizing balance-sheet risks in Trea-sury and moving them out of the lines of business. To be successful, FTP rates need to reflect balance-sheet hedging costs and rewards, such as liquidity premiums and option costs.

These Treasury activities – funding, managing risks related to financial resources, and advising business lines – all enable a bank to provide a vital service to the economy and society – credit inter-mediation and maturity transformation, whereby a bank takes in customers' money through short-term deposits or other obligations and then lends or converts them into assets at longer term to other customers.

Technology Systems in Treasury

Treasury's responsibilities entail a host of low- and high-end technological capabilities.

Over many years, each bank has developed proprietary and customized IT systems to run the various calculations described above, including producing risk metrics and generating reports for management and regulators. These IT systems are used for scenario analysis, forecasting, and stress-testing exercises. The complex web of IT systems must ultimately generate the financial statements and other reports required by publicly listed companies for shareholders and other stakeholders.

In the Treasury department, IT systems are used for managing capital and funding positions, for funds-transfer pricing, for modeling and managing the various risks (interest rate, foreign exchange, and liquidity), and for stress testing and scenario analysis. In carrying out these activities, Treasury also uses, and sometimes designs and validates, an array of models that themselves can be run through various IT systems spread across the organization.

Like other business activities within a bank, Treasury activities can be executed manually – for example, through the use of Excel spreadsheets – or they can be executed more systematically through computer algorithms and application programming interfaces (APIs). Manual processes are more labor-intensive and more prone to human error. The more systematic and repeatable the processes and related technology, the more robust, consistent, and reliable the results. Hence, there is a compelling case for Treasury to use advanced technology to execute its responsibilities quickly and systematically.

Large and established banks often rely on legacy technology, and in some cases, this means that not all systems are fully integrated with each other. Acquisitions of other financial entities frequently result in the acquisition of incompatible, inconsistent IT systems that must be integrated or eliminated over time.

When using different IT systems, banks frequently are forced into overlaying manual "workarounds" to accommodate new requirements or modifications that the IT systems-in-place cannot handle in their current configuration. These workarounds are labor-intensive and prone to human error. Moreover, different systems may be used for different purposes, resulting in management information or formal reporting that is not consistent, thereby requiring time-consuming checks and reconciliations.

Use-cases of new technology to improve the end-customer experience are widely known: easier banking, electronic money transfers and bill payments, on-line shopping, online loan approvals. The list goes on. The use-cases for the behind-the-scenes Treasury, Risk, and Finance functions may be less familiar but are equally important for the bank's success. Table 12.2 outlines examples of technology use-cases to enhance the bank's Treasury function.

Table 12.2. Technology use-cases for Treasury

* Real-time data
* Digital dashboards (iPad Treasury)
* Real-time intraday liquidity monitoring
* Dynamic pattern recognition in funding and liquidity behavior
* Interest-rate-risk scenario analysis
* Liquidity-pool-efficiency checks
* Payments pattern detection
* Quick, ad hoc scenario analysis

Unique Technology Challenges in Treasury

Treasury's responsibilities give rise to numerous challenges in developing and implementing new technologies that are unique to this area of the bank. Table 12.3 summarizes the various challenges that contribute to the complexity of implementing new technologies in the Treasury function.

First, the breadth and depth of the Treasury function make it difficult to develop an information technology (IT) system to encompass all of these requirements. Treasury touches all aspects of a bank's operations. It is accountable for managing all balance-sheet risks and related off-balance-sheet exposures. This responsibility requires accumulating granular data at the client or account level for every dollar of exposure on or off the balance sheet.

Massive data accumulation creates unique technology challenges for the Treasury function. Banks require powerful and stable computer systems to collect, store, process, and secure tremendous volumes of data. Data pass to and from the bank among many sources, including retail and commercial customers, trading counterparties, vendors, and regulators. Banks use these data for a host of purposes. For example, the data enable customer transactions, including drawing funds, paying bills, taking out loans, and purchasing goods and services. Banks collect, store, and process data through

Table 12.3. Technology challenges in Treasury

- Breadth and depth of requirements
- Significant regulatory burden
- Complexity of modeling
- Complexity of valuations and hedging
- Behavioral modeling
- Projecting forward balances
- Level of finance integration across functions

these activities using a host of technological platforms, both in physical branches and electronically (online or through mobile devices).

Second, banks are subject to significant regulatory requirements. Treasury must manage a multitude of laws and regulations, including solvency and capital requirements and liquidity requirements (LCR and NSFR). These regulations are complex and involve significant use of technology and modeling capabilities for things such as determining risk-weighted assets (RWAs) for capital adequacy, and economic value of equity (EVE) or earnings at risk (EAR) for structural interest-rate risk management.

Adding complexity to this situation, banks operate as global enterprises and must simultaneously comply with the regulations of many countries, both individually and at the consolidated bank level. Despite the efforts of the Basel Committee on Banking Supervision to achieve global consistency in bank regulation, country regulators for a number of reasons have elected to implement unique, and sometimes inconsistent, risk-measurement and reporting requirements, increasing the burden on the IT systems used by Treasury.

Third, certain Treasury functions related to balance-sheet risk management require technology to support modeling of significant complexity. For resolution planning, for example, balance sheets and related risk metrics must be projected five years into the future. For liquidity-risk modeling, Treasury examines the performance of balance-sheet liquidity under multiple scenarios that cover a range of different severities. For structural interest-rate risk management, numerous quantitative and qualitative shocks to the yield curve are performed, and in each case the impact on projected earnings and the economic value of equity must be determined.

A key challenge for Treasury technology is to find a way to perform all these functions with a common database and common technology. Vendor solutions can provide robust capabilities. However, vendor solutions can be expensive to operate and lack flexibility and the capacity to customize models that individual banks need to develop a competitive advantage over their peers.

Fourth, valuations and hedging are complex activities. Bank balance sheets are made up of financial instruments that need to be valued in order to measure risk. This valuation must reflect changes both in exogenous variables and to hedge exposures. Some well-known, everyday products are in fact complex composite financial instruments. Take, for example, a mortgage. A mortgage is made up of simple and known cash flows (such as principal and interest payments), unknown and interest-rate path-dependent cash flows (such as periodic principal pre-payments), and embedded options (such as the right to pay down some or all of the principal at any time). This pre-payment option is typically exercised when interest rates have moved, so that such pre-payment is economically advantageous for the borrower.

Treasury relies on models and technology that can take complex financial instruments, break them down into their component parts, and value them under different scenarios. Such valuation models must include features such as determining the value of embedded interest-rate options, determining the effective duration and convexity of instruments, and developing an appropriate hedging strategy. These hedging strategies need to be adapted to reflect the hedging instruments available in each country and the sophistication of people and technology in the firm. They must also provide the capacity to account for and report accurately in a hedge accounting framework.

Fifth, the Treasury function must model and take account of customer behavior. Many bank products have cash flows that depend on the behavior of clients under different scenarios. Treasury's hedging of the balance sheet requires behavioral modeling, which, in turn, is used to drive key assumptions in asset-liability management (ALM) and other models. Behavioral modeling relies on significant time-series data, supported by data scientists using advanced statistical modeling, and supplemented with professional judgment. Unique technologies are deployed for this purpose by leading banks as a source of competitive advantage in the industry.

Sixth, the Treasury function projects forward balances. Treasury operates in an environment where daily activities (such as cash management, funding, and hedging interest risk) compete for resources with functions that rely on a forward-looking view of the balance sheet. Funding plans, for example, are contingent on access to debt capital markets to raise funds to cover balance-sheet needs, and rely on technology to project balance sheets many months or years into the future.

Similarly, developing a capital plan requires not only projected balance sheets but also forecasts of risk-weighted assets, future-dated regulatory requirements, and business strategies (including potential M&A activity). Treasury must ensure that the bank has the capacity to fully comply with all capital requirements over time. Technology platforms are deployed for this purpose but are complex and proprietary.

Seventh, the Treasury function features a high level of finance integration with the rest of the bank. The Treasury department reports to the bank's chief financial officer (CFO) and works closely with colleagues in the Finance and Risk departments. This reporting structure may exist even though in many cases the technology platforms of these areas are quite independent. Increasingly, banks are working to increase the level of integration between Finance, Risk, and Treasury so that common databases, forecasting, and other tools can be operated more efficiently.

Financial reporting relies on the funds transfer pricing (FTP) function in Treasury to determine product and business profitability, information that ultimately flows into segmented financial results reported to shareholders. The interface between the Treasury FTP function and financial reporting often relies on manual intervention. As banks modernize their finance technology, they will increasingly look at things like broadening the purpose of the general ledger to include capabilities like modeling FTP rates, gross margins, RWAs, and other balance-sheet items.

Developing and Implementing a Treasury Technology Strategy

Implementing new technologies creates a host of challenges for Treasury executives. As outlined above, they must navigate and manage a dizzying number of considerations and unique challenges, with uncertain outcomes but potentially large implications if done right or wrong. To be successful, the Treasury area must develop a coherent, comprehensive technology strategy.

While the need to have a specific technology strategy for the Treasury function may seem obvious, devising a comprehensive strategy can be very difficult in practice for Treasury executives in the crush of dealing with day-to-day time-sensitive requirements. For example, this could mean triaging time and resources to meet immediate needs – such as regulatory or business changes – and also maintaining focus on the planning and resourcing needed to accomplish long-term solutions.

A comprehensive strategy should take into account an accurate view of the status quo, all technology needs of the Treasury department, and an understanding of how they fit into the overall bank IT strategy. It must include a rigorous prioritization of IT needs, since all fixes cannot be undertaken at once. Surveying the Treasury's IT needs will require interviewing staff and business partners throughout the firm to assess the highest priorities, greatest needs, and biggest deficiencies.

More concretely, developing a Treasury technology strategy includes the following steps:

1. Establish a governance process
2. Gain consensus on the target end state
3. Establish the IT budget
4. Devise the implementation plan
5. Execute the plan

Establish a Governance Process

The first step in developing a Treasury technology strategy must be to put in place a thorough governance process. Essentially, a governance process clarifies and maps out who makes what decisions and how these decisions are made. Technology governance must be integrated into the bank's overall governance process involving senior management and the Board of Directors.

Gain Consensus on the Target End State

The second step is to gain consensus on the target end state for the IT system. Perhaps the most difficult challenge of devising Treasury IT strategy is achieving consensus on what initiatives the company should pursue and why. Possible uses of new technology are virtually limitless – for example, providing better, more granular, and timely data, better customer experience, and greater efficiency and decision-making capability, to name just a few – and yet a company has limited resources by way of time, staff, and budget. Business people and shareholders will naturally want to prioritize those initiatives that will increase profitability with the most certainty.

In reality, proving that a new IT capability will definitively result in a specific dollar amount of incremental income or savings can be extremely difficult in practice. In most cases, implementing new technology in a bank entails multiple steps from concept to roll-out, any one of which can go awry, thereby undercutting whatever assumptions were made in estimating incremental income.

In some cases, new technology will not directly result in additional income or savings but will instead provide better data and insight, enabling better decision making, which in turn may produce a better financial outcome. And as every CFO knows, proving a counterfactual of how much greater expenses will be if new technology is not undertaken can be especially tricky. Nevertheless, management has no choice but to do its best in making such decisions.

Establish the IT Budget

The third step is setting the IT budget. Like all companies seeking to maximize bottom-line profitability, banks seek to minimize expenses. However much a company decides to spend, there are usually not enough budget dollars available to satisfy all technological needs, including research and development for new capabilities and product offerings. Prioritization is therefore essential in managing the supply and demand of IT dollars.

The bank will have a governance and priority-setting process wherein all parties across the bank are given an opportunity to make their case for IT spending, resulting in fully informed decisions as to what technological projects will be undertaken, delayed, or not approved. The result of this prioritization process should be a list of projects to be undertaken, ordered first through last. This process will also generate a list of IT requirements that don't make the cut for funding but that are acknowledged for funding consideration at a later date. A list of known but unfunded projects also serves to inform management and the board as to what risks relate to forgoing what projects.

Considerations to be taken into account when determining how much in aggregate is appropriate to spend on technology, and what specific projects to fund include the following:

- whether to upgrade current outdated IT systems, or replace them outright;
- what new initiatives or capabilities ought to be undertaken or developed (rather than just fixing or replacing current ones);
- how much should be spent on research and development, agreeing on technology use-cases and metrics for measuring success;
- whether the size of the business and profitability outlook justify investing the dollars required (i.e., assessing the economies of scale);
- what level of investment is necessary to exceed competitors' capabilities (or simply to keep up); and
- what trade-offs to make between projects to meet regulatory requirements versus those expenses that will improve financial performance and/or the customer experience.

None of these judgments are clear cut, and the factors influencing these considerations are in constant flux: requirements change, customer preferences may not be obvious, and direct and indirect knock-on effects abound. There is a constant risk of being penny wise and pound foolish; avoiding small, near-term costs may result in larger costs down the road.

These considerations and trade-offs reinforce the need for a robust governance process whereby all stakeholder concerns are presented, deliberated, and decided upon – not an easy task, especially in large, complex banks with multiple businesses in multiple jurisdictions.

Devise the Implementation Plan

The next step is to transform the list of prioritized IT needs into a clear, realistic and universally understood implementation plan that can be accomplished within the allocated budget. The implementation plan must clarify roles and responsibilities, identify interdependencies among participants and sub-tasks, and address all questions as to who, what, and how. The implementation plan must be designed so as to accomplish the desired upgrade in technology without disrupting the customer experience or hindering the delivery of necessary services in the meantime.

As the plan is devised, management will have to answer a host of implementation questions including:

- whether to upgrade current systems or replace them completely;
- whether to build in-house systems or purchase and tailor vendor-provided solutions (build versus buy);
- whether to perform various tasks and services internally or to contract a third party externally (insource versus outsource); and
- how to migrate and transition old technologies and data as seamlessly as possible.

Execute the Plan

At the end of the day, a strategic plan is all about execution. While it's relatively easy to describe at a high level how new technology may be implemented, the hard part is actually doing it while not disrupting current operations or client service. Treasury cannot, for example, take a time-out from meeting interest payments, satisfying regulatory requirements, or managing the daily routine of allocating financial resources in response to supply and demand across the bank.

In advance of implementation, it is impossible to know with complete certainty whether an IT strategy is right. IT strategy requires constant reassessment, revision, and monitoring of the market, including customer needs and competitors' capabilities. The key is striking the right balance in embracing technological evolution to enhance customer service, improve efficiency, and keep up with or exceed competitor banks, while minimizing costs and not veering off strategy.

Done right, technological evolution can help banks succeed in meeting customer needs, retaining their loyalty, and increasing efficiency and advancing their societal role of providing credit intermediation. Done wrong, technological evolution can waste money, disrupt the customer experience, lead to the loss of customers, and damage the bank's franchise. The stakes may be high, but technology to support the bank's Treasury function can deliver a sustainable competitive advantage for a bank, increasing the bank's profitability and valuation.

CHAPTER THIRTEEN

Technology and Reimagining the Future of Housing

Evan Siddall and Vicki Martin

Introduction

Housing is a unique asset that we can consume, invest in, and trade in the marketplace. These characteristics can compound and amplify, making housing prone to exaggerated cycles. Moreover, behavioral and psychological factors can further aggravate price movements: fear of housing insecurity, speculation based on extrapolated expectations, and the fear of missing out that all of that can cause. Many commentators have referred to the resulting "financialization" of housing, which is further promoted by government policies that favor home ownership in some countries.

These factors and the lessons of the global financial crisis still loom large ten years later. They rest at the heart of regulatory intervention, and they serve to distract incumbents from disruptive fintech start-ups – new ventures that threaten our payments and mortgage systems. Millennials' behavior provides fertile territory for these innovations. The comfortable banking oligopoly in Canada faces competitive threat from new business models and from foreign institutions attracted by opportunities in our stable financial system. Even more impactful, innovations in housing are needed to address affordability pressures, and technology offers hope for resolving these concerns.

The unique linkage between housing markets and our banking system was quaintly portrayed by the plight of George Bailey's character in Frank Capra's 1946 film, *It's a Wonderful Life*. As Bailey's neighbors participate in a run on George's savings and loan, he pleads with them for calm. But emotions run high amid fear of losing savings and facing foreclosures. Household leverage increases these risks and causes pro-cyclicality: the more people panic, the more likely it is that others will panic, too.

In a small way, the movie highlights how closely housing is tied into our banking system. We deposit our short-term savings with lenders, lending them money that they in turn lend to our neighbors as long-term mortgages. Banks today are more complex than in 1946, but mortgage lending remains a core function, the "maturity transformation" of short-term savings into long-term lending at its most basic.

Banks' mortgage-financing activities tie them tightly to the odd psychology of housing markets. Of course, it was housing that brought the world to its knees in 2008–2009. Housing is woven into our financial system because of the centrality of mortgage financing: about 50 percent of Canadians' net worth is invested in our homes. Securitization funding is another linkage that can serve to transmit risk throughout a financial system. As a result of these factors, of the forty-six financial crises for which we have housing data, more than two-thirds were preceded by housing boom/bust cycles.[1]

Evolution of the Mortgage Market

Mortgages are mentioned in English common-law documents that date back more than 800 years. Mortgages originated in England in what were originally conditional sale agreements. Home buyers would get loans directly from the seller but were not able to occupy the house until the entire amount was paid. Mortgage terms were quite draconian: if prospective buyers failed to keep up with payments, they would forfeit both their prior payments and any right to the house. The debtor could, however, sell the underlying property in order to recover the money paid from the sale proceeds.

Here in Canada, modern mortgages in the early 1900s typically required only monthly interest payments. Often of only five years' duration, these original mortgages attracted substantial rollover risk of the amount owing at expiry. Economic events, notably including the Great Depression, led naturally to many defaults. Borrowers were unable to maintain current interest payments on properties with negative equity. After that, mortgages tended to have a longer duration – twenty or thirty years – and were fully amortizing. As such, mortgages paid fixed monthly amounts combining interest plus some repayment of principal, as they do today.

Interestingly, mortgages were originally provided in Canada mainly by insurance companies. While a prohibition on banks' providing mortgages was lifted with the introduction of the Bank Act in 1954, it wasn't until a 1967 amendment removing a 6 percent interest cap that banks entered the market fully, a market that they dominate today.

The rise of inflation in the 1970s altered mortgages into the products we know now. As interest rates climbed, lenders and borrowers found themselves locked into fully amortized loans that didn't reflect interest-rate changes. The creation of the partially amortized mortgage, which protects both lenders and borrowers from fluctuations in the market, means that instead of twenty- to thirty-year terms, one-, three-, or five-year terms amortized across twenty to twenty-five years have become a better option. Partially amortized mortgages are now the most common mortgage type in Canada.

The Canadian Mortgage Market

Mortgages totaling approximately 1.5 trillion dollars are outstanding in Canada, comprising uninsured conventional mortgages and high-ratio mortgages with loan-to-value ratios of above 80 percent. Under the Bank Act, federally regulated financial institutions have been required to purchase government-guaranteed mortgage insurance since 1954.[2]

Insurance is provided by Canada Mortgage and Housing Corporation (CMHC), a federally owned crown corporation, and two private mortgage insurers, Genworth Canada and Canada Guaranty. As shown in figure 13.1 below, CMHC's market share has gradually declined since the financial crisis to below 50 percent; as of 2018, Genworth's share was around one-third, and Canada Guaranty accounted for the remainder.

Canada has a rather distinctive mortgage-finance system. In many ways, it is crisis-resistant because of the concentration of activity in a few well-capitalized banks, a rigorous regulatory environment, an immaterial level of sub-prime lending, and a low proportion of variable-rate mortgages. Mandatory mortgage insurance also socializes housing market risk, insulating lenders. However, with mortgage insurance having removed lenders from this exposure, some argue that moral hazard is introduced and has contributed to household debt-to-income levels bordering on 180 percent, as shown in figure 13.2 below.

Mortgages have remained largely secure in credit quality, and arrears rates (the proportion of mortgages having past-due payments of longer than ninety days) have rarely exceeded 0.33 percent. Indeed, even during the financial crisis, arrears rates remained well below 1 percent. Unlike in some U.S. jurisdictions, mortgages in Canada generally include a legal promise to pay, with recourse against the borrower, not just the property. People cannot merely

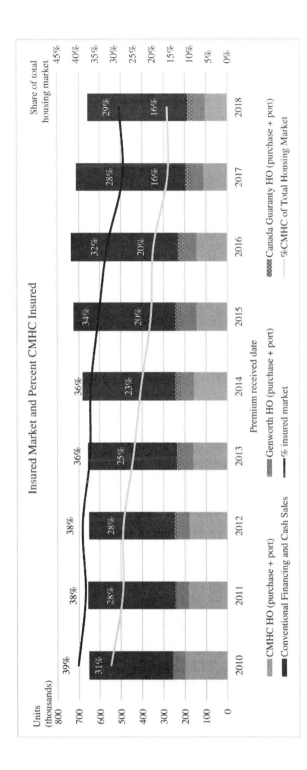

Figure 13.1 Insured market and percent CMHC insured

Sources: CMHC HO transactional purchase new insurance written, CMHC starts & completion survey, Genworth's financial supplements, Canada Guaranty's financial supplements (Total Housing Market is measured as the sum of three components: LS, Estimates of private sales, & completions)[3]

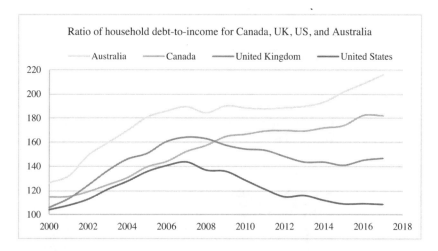

Figure 13.2 Ratio of household debt to income for Canada, the United Kingdom, the United States, and Australia[4]

hand the keys to their home to a lender when they face negative equity in their houses.

A final factor in Canada is the preponderance of fixed five-year mortgage terms. Only 30 percent of mortgages are variable rate. Consequently, any given year sees around 20 percent of mortgages renewed. This factor reduces the risk of interest-rate shock to Canadian borrowers.

Canadian Mortgage Origination

The "Big Six" banks originate around 75 percent of mortgages in Canada. Credit unions and *caisses populaires* originate an additional 14 percent, while monoline mortgage-finance companies are responsible for a further 6 percent, leaving about a 1 percent market share to smaller private lenders and mortgage-investment companies, many of which offer sub-prime loans.

Mortgage-insurance premiums have increased in recent years in response both to the tighter regulatory capital regime of the Office of the Superintendent of Financial Institutions (OSFI) and CMHC's pricing decisions, which reflect increasingly sophisticated risk management and stress testing. As the market leader, CMHC has functioned as the price setter in the mortgage-insurance market.

The practice of underwriting mortgages needs to attend to the risks that could cause a borrower to default on the loan. Several factors are considered, including the value of the subject property, the borrower's debt-service burden and ability to pay (including income quality or reliability), her or his credit score, and other factors.

Interestingly, the single most important factor observed in driving mortgage-insurance claims is unemployment. Along with marital breakdown, this risk is very hard to predict over the future life of the mortgage. Indeed, debt-service ratios at origination, as well as income quality, while important for understanding a borrower's current ability to service the loan, are non sequiturs in the context of future job loss – the greatest risk.

Risks Inherent in Mortgage Finance

Canadian households did not suffer the deleveraging that occurred elsewhere, and indebtedness now approaches historic highs. As a measure of financial risk, this figure is problematic. While arrears remain low, the burden of financial leverage limits our economic freedom in facing a crisis and threatens a repeat of pro-cyclical behavior. Worse, Canadians have effectively borrowed future income to buy housing today. This is income that will be used to pay interest in the future, rather than being spent on more economically productive consumer goods. Housing has mined our economic future.

We are more aware of the inherent systemic risks associated with housing following the global financial crisis. The negative effect of falling house prices on consumption can last a long time, as suggested by the U.S. experience after the Great Recession. Consequently, if rising home prices create perceptions of greater wealth that eventually prove to be unfounded, the related increase in consumption will be unsustainable. The impacts on financial stability may be particularly severe if that consumption is financed by other credit.

Research by International Monetary Fund economists Atif Mian and Amir Sufi has shown that high levels of indebtedness coupled with elevated house prices precede economic contractions. They call the relationship "so robust as to be as close to an empirical law as it gets in macroeconomics." Notably, the authors have proposed shared-equity mortgages as a more coherent form of home ownership program.[5]

Research also associates stable housing with improved economic and social outcomes. Health and education measures are positively correlated with secure housing. As Michael Desmond wrote in his 2016 Pulitzer Prize-winning book, *Evicted: Poverty and Profit in the American City*, "Without stable shelter, everything falls apart."[6]

Housing affordability is a political issue in many jurisdictions and will persist until house prices and incomes realign. Since this adjustment requires reduced indebtedness – which likely awaits higher interest rates – and higher incomes, policymakers are exploring transitional programs. Some of these, such as those that encourage rental, can mitigate demand – while also reducing vacancy rates, however. Others are misguided programs that worsen affordability: down-payment assistance, non-amortizing (interest-only) mortgages, and so on.

Mortgage Funding and Securitization

Mortgage lending is funded in various ways in Canada that vary according to the business models and the different regulatory frameworks that apply to various types of lenders. Consumer deposits represent the least expensive and most pervasive source of funding. Beyond that, term deposits, "bail-in" debt, and wholesale funding (commercial paper and overnight repurchase agreements) are common forms of funding, in addition to equity capital.

Furthermore, qualifying lenders – comprising almost all of the approximately 600 mortgage lenders in Canada ("Approved Issuers") – can borrow against pools of insured mortgages that are then sold to investors with the support of a timely payment or liquidity guarantee from CMHC. Securitized mortgages are either simple pass-through (amortizing monthly-pay with prepayment risk) National Housing Authority (NHA) mortgage-backed securities (MBSs) or structured Canada Mortgage Bonds (CMBs) that make use of total return swaps to convert underlying mortgage payments into investor-friendly semi-annual interest payment bullet bonds.

Generally, CMBs are bought by institutional investors and NHA MBSs are bought by banks – from smaller lenders – since they are less expensive "high-quality liquid assets" required to be held in compliance with the OSFI-mandated liquidity coverage ratio.

Securitization fees and guarantee limits are set each year by the minister of finance. CMHC allocates these amounts evenly among approved issuers each year as a result of previous policies favoring lender competition. Legacy government policy was to help smaller lenders compete with "Big Six" banks by giving them a disproportionate share of securitization amounts.

A nascent private residential mortgage-backed security (RMBS) market exists in Canada. Mortgage-financing company MCAP has issued $712 million in three separate RMBS offerings in recent years. While federal authorities have increased guarantee fees, strengthening the incentive for private securitization, CMBs still represent a very attractive funding vehicle versus anything other than retail deposits.

CMHC also administers Canada's covered-bond framework, which allows lenders, generally larger banks, to issue secured debt to investors in the form of bonds "covered" by security in underlying mortgages. A common form of borrowing in Europe, this mechanism has opened up $193 billion in new funding via European markets since 2013 for eight qualifying Canadian banks.

Technological Innovation at CMHC

CMHC is exploring new approaches to underwriting and mortgage-insurance adjudication, using technology, analytics, and artificial intelligence.

In 1996, CMHC introduced its mortgage-insurance adjudication system called "emili,"[7] a risk-management tool that approves or refers the loan application based on an analysis of different risk factors. This software program contains a number of different evaluation modules, and sits at the heart of CMHC's insurance operations. Largely a workflow-management program, emili auto-adjudicates approximately 60 percent of applications, with the balance referred to CMHC's underwriting team for further assessment. Genworth Canada also uses an automated system. As with CMHC, any applications not automatically approved are referred to an underwriter.

Given the shortcomings noted above in our ability to assess the likelihood of future claims, CMHC has initiated a project to modernize its decision-making software. We are exploring how to supplement our modeling to account for behavioral factors using predictive analytics. We foresee that emili will be a ubiquitous software-as-a-service cloud-based platform through which risks are better managed and data are standardized and aggregated. This initiative will result in more integrated through-processing and is a response to the post-crisis attentiveness to housing prices and systemic financial risk.

The new version of our underwriting system may also utilize CMHC's proprietary risk models, HOLLEA and MOLLEA, which are used for our annual stress testing and other risk-management activities. By integrating systemic factors into mortgage underwriting, using loan-level data, CMHC is building a more robust underwriting and risk-management framework.

Mortgage Regulation

At the federal level, the regulation of mortgage origination and funding falls into two categories. Banks and other federally registered financial institutions are subject to micro-prudential oversight by OSFI. And the parameters that govern mortgage insurance (called the "sandbox") are issued by the minister of finance and comprise our version of macro-prudential regulation. A broader group of lenders is also caught within the federal web by virtue of CMHC-sponsored securitization.

OSFI regulates federally regulated financial institutions: generally banks and a few others, including mortgage insurers.[8] OSFI's B-20 Guideline[9] prescribes standards for underwriting and risk management in mortgage lending, and B-21 extends these practices to mortgage insurers.[10] Credit unions and *caisses populaires* are mostly provincially regulated and, as such, subject to varying levels of active oversight. Moreover, some lenders are unregulated, including a growing number of private mortgage-investment companies.

The foundation of Canada's regulation of mortgage activity at a macroeconomic level is mandatory mortgage insurance. First introduced in 1954, it initially required a 25 percent down payment. Since then, the loan-to-value ceiling has been eased, with the current minimum of 5 percent (95% LTV) enacted in 1992 for first-time home buyers and in 1998 for all buyers. In October 2016, a 10 percent requirement was added for the portion above $500,000.

Successive finance ministers have reduced the size of the mortgage-insurance "sandbox" by imposing ever-stricter requirements. Over the past eleven years, requirements have been tightened on six successive occasions. As of spring 2019, in addition to meeting OSFI's underwriting expectations, mortgages must have the following characteristics to qualify for mortgage insurance:

- house prices of $1 million or less; owner-occupied
- a minimum down payment of 5 percent plus 10 percent on the portion above $500,000
- a gross debt-service ratio of not more than 39 percent of income and total debt service of 44 percent, calculated using the posted five-year fixed Bank of Canada rate, which is a premium of approximately 2 percent above the negotiated mortgage rate (mortgage-rate stress test)
- a minimum credit score of 600
- not available for refinancing – removal of equity
- a maximum mortgage amortization of twenty-five years

Post-Crisis Regulatory Environment

The financial crisis has cast a long shadow, as pre-crisis excesses are still being worked out. Prudential regulators like OSFI have used new liquidity requirements and stricter capital rules to address the shortcomings that contributed to the near collapse of the global financial system just over ten years ago.

And whereas central banks in the United States, United Kingdom, and Europe grew their balance sheets to provide liquidity to a starved system, that wasn't necessary in Canada. CMHC's Insured Mortgage Purchase Program, authorized at $125 billion, was deployed to the extent of $69 billion for similar purposes. However, all of those funds were repaid in the ordinary course, and Canadians were largely unscathed.

The latest insured-mortgage parameter changes included enhancing the stress test by applying it to the most popular five-year fixed mortgages. The extension of the stress test was mimicked by OSFI and applied to all mortgages, including uninsured conventional mortgages, effective January 2017 via an amendment to Guideline B-20.

These changes were associated with a slowing of housing activity in Canada, although other factors were also at play. It is not possible to isolate the effect of the rule changes from other federal and provincial measures that include taxes on foreign-investor activity and on vacant housing, rent controls, natural market fundamentals, and the impact on expectations and behavior that could amplify these effects. Some industry participants were nonetheless quick to criticize the stress test as a culprit in reducing real-estate prices and activity, as if that were an "unintended consequence," which it was not.[11]

A Changing Competitive Dynamic

Domestic banks' residential mortgage-lending franchise is at risk. We foresee increased competition in coming years due to several factors: reduced funding cost advantages, emerging competition via payment platforms (Apple Pay, Google Wallet), and disruptive fintech business models.

Regulatory restrictions leave an unsatisfied demand for nonconforming high-ratio mortgages (above 80 percent loan to value), which are offered by financial institutions that are not federally regulated. CMHC's successive insurance-premium increases have also increased the opportunity for competition. Thus far, however, low funding availability has limited the extent of noncompliant Alt-A mortgage lending in Canada. In particular, since mortgages must be insured to qualify for securitization, conventional funding methods are more limited.

Moreover, business models that are based on regulatory arbitrage or marginal opportunities created by the sandbox parameters have proven to be vulnerable. Home Capital was one such Alt-A lender whose business model came under pressure following action by securities regulators. Home competed aggressively for Alt-A credits and relied on deposit funding which ran in the face of regulatory action and a resulting liquidity squeeze.[12]

Banks are under increased pressure in many lines of business from start-ups and new nonfinancial entrants. Banks seem to have a competitive funding advantage via access to insured deposits. In addition, extensive regulation benefits larger banks, for which scale economics permit improved management of credit, interest rate, and funding risk.

However, the lessons from other industries – hotels, taxis, recorded music – show that "asset light" business models can attack incumbents – and quickly. Notably, the opportunity to make use of data using technology may shift the competitive balance even further.

In under ten years, Airbnb has revolutionized the way we travel, impacted housing stock, and turned our homes into micro businesses. Amazon has turned retail on its ear, drastically changing both commerce and commercial real-estate markets across North America. And behemoths like Apple and Google threaten banking and payments. Mortgage lending cannot be immune.

We should expect that someone today is sitting in their garage charting out an entirely new way of looking at our housing system. The curse of the incumbent is a lack of imagination. As Bill Gates said, "We always overestimate the change that will occur in the next two years and underestimate the change that will occur in the next ten."[13]

Banks are worried. Funds are pouring into disruptive fintech start-ups: the sector attracted over US$40 billion of capital from 2014 to 2017 inclusive.[14] Online lenders in the United States like Clara, Better Mortgage, and Lenda are already offering e-mortgages, as is Quicken Loans via its Rocket Mortgage product. In the fourth quarter of 2017, Quicken Loans issued US$25 billion in mortgages, overtaking Wells Fargo as the largest U.S. mortgage originator.[15] And start-up mortgage lenders like Mogo Financial want to do the same in Canada.

Canada's staid and comfortable housing-finance system has many ingredients for disruption. In the short term, new models will provide significant improvements in the efficiency of housing-finance systems and processes. In the longer term, we can expect foundational changes, including new sources of mortgage funding and unique, progressive models of property tenure.

Aware of these pressures, CMHC is exploring five opportunities in the potentially most fertile areas: automated through-processing, blockchain-enabled mortgage funding, use of artificial intelligence in underwriting, peer-to-peer lending, and novel forms of property tenure. These are just a start – known unknowns; there will be much more that can't be seen today.

Automating Mortgage Processing

Mortgage originators were early adopters of fintech in Canada. Web-based applications have been used for decades, enabling mobile sales forces to serve their clients in a variety of applications. Sophisticated lead-generation systems, mobile tools, and customer-relationship programs have enabled lenders to engage with potential borrowers in innovative ways.

However, the mortgage-application process itself remains onerous and ripe for disruption, often taking over a week to gather documentation. Soon, the entire mortgage-application process could be authorized by biomarkers, with all necessary information accessible by the lender within seconds. No longer needed to collect and verify documentation, mortgage originators will have to evolve or become extinct.

Every stage of the mortgage-financing "supply chain," from origination and underwriting through conveyancing and servicing to securitization and claims management, is currently being explored in a search for the efficiencies offered by readily available technologies. Already a variety of technologies, including customer-relationship management tools, artificial intelligence (AI), and blockchain, are being used to significantly streamline the servicing of mortgages, with the promise of enhanced customer service and lower costs. Increased pricing differentiation may also result, given the low cost of qualifying higher credits versus the more human intensity needed for financially weaker applicants.

Distributed Ledgers and Funding

Mortgage markets are also intrigued by automated distributed-ledger technologies (DLT) like blockchain. While predictions that Bitcoin will replace currency are likely far-fetched, DLT can offer measurable gains in reliability, security, and the efficiency of financial processes. Immediate deployment of DLT may be hampered by security, scalability, standardization, and privacy concerns; however, the technology has real promise. Seventy-seven percent of incumbents expect to adopt blockchain as part of core processes by 2020.[16]

Indeed, a CMHC-Accenture team has mapped the entire mortgage life cycle, from origination through to servicing of securitized mortgage bonds, to assess these opportunities. CMHC is co-investing with Accenture in a blockchain proof of concept involving mortgage funding. While the focus thus far has been on operating efficiencies, a full migration of securitization to distributed ledger technology is foreseeable, where authentication no longer requires human intervention but is verified using blockchain. This could significantly increase the speed of the mortgage transaction, and could also decrease costs.

Artificial Intelligence Underwriting

Most mortgage underwriting systems are auto-adjudicated, with only a small number referred to a human underwriter for manual assessment. AI applications make quality lending decisions based on data and logic. As mentioned earlier, CMHC's second generation emili underwriting system will be recoded from the archaic programming language COBOL using a modern decision-rules engine. A new cloud-based application can also avail itself of AI.

AI could enable bespoke customized mortgage products, with varying repayment terms, interest rates, and amortization periods based on the borrower's earnings, spending habits, and financial-planning needs. Risk-based pricing will become much easier to assess and administer, and can be used to reward the truly low-risk borrowers. However, the borrowers identified through analytics as being higher risk will likely face even greater barriers and be further excluded.

The potential exists for reinforced bias in AI systems, whereby certain ethnic or socioeconomic groups may be disadvantaged. AI and open banking will allow additional "soft" information to be incorporated into decision making, such as the borrower's educational history, where the borrower spends their time, who they communicate with, and what sorts of pastimes they have – introducing new forms of potential discrimination. AI systems could, however, also reduce human bias by removing human decision making.

Finally, the remote nature of some Canadian communities, such as those in the north, could test the limits of machine-based underwriting. Homes outside major urban centers generally take longer to sell and are therefore weaker security for lenders. Adjusted mortgage pricing may be introduced in these regions.

Peer-to-Peer Lending

Just as individuals increasingly own distributed energy systems, and entertainment companies have been disintermediated by YouTube stars and social media influencers, financial institutions similarly face an increasingly decentralized future. Cost-effective peer-to-peer lending platforms already exist in other areas. For example, Lending Loop helps investors lend directly to Canadian businesses and has funded close to 700 loans and $50 million since starting in 2015. Wealthsimple has established itself as an online investment manager and has grown its market share significantly.

Whereas Canada's mortgage marketplace is strictly regulated federally, peer-to-peer lending is currently regulated under provincial securities laws. A Cooperative Capital Markets Regulatory System[17] would help make it more cost effective for fintech firms to develop products and services that comply with securities legislation across the provinces.

Funding may be a further constraint. For some existing peer-to-peer lending programs in other jurisdictions, such as the United States, demand for the loans has begun to outstrip the available investment dollars. As such, they have started to look to securitize their portfolios. We are only beginning to explore this possibility in Canada. Peer-to-peer mortgage lending may be better suited to nonprofit and government entities, given the lower margin in mortgage lending versus the current peer-to-peer focus on higher margin lending.

Changes in Property Tenure

While Canadians will continue to want to own real estate, the manner by which they acquire shelter is already changing. Fintech will enable new models and will radically reduce transaction costs to accelerate these changes. These will appeal to the millennial "sharing generation," while reaping the benefits of increased asset utilization.

Futurist and Stanford University lecturer Tony Seba predicts that private car ownership will drop by 80 percent by 2030, a trend that is reflected in growing ride-sharing applications such as Uber and Lyft.[18] Just as car manufacturers are preparing for this shift, markets must anticipate the future of housing. Will millennials, generation Z, and Gen Alpha continue to want to own the traditional white picket fence, or will they be looking for a new housing model? And who will deliver it?

Fractional Ownership

An individual's property can be reimagined as a bundle of tradable rights (to occupation, ownership, lease interest, mortgage interest, and to gift an interest). These interests can be unbundled, just as coupons are stripped from bonds and sold separately. Technology enables fractional models by automating marketing, transaction, and administrative processes. One such model is offered in Australia by BrickX, where a home is owned via a trust, and BrickX sells shares in that home to others.

Multiple parties can also legally purchase interest in homes as tenants-in-common. This is becoming more popular in other jurisdictions, such as California. While difficult to finance through mainstream lenders, mortgage products for these models are offered elsewhere.

It is a small step from common joint tenure or "condominiumization" to fractional models. Web-based applications such as weown.

ca can aggregate co-occupants, to whom mortgage lenders can offer specialized products for these types of borrowers.

Along these lines, the 2019 federal budget announced that CMHC will offer a new shared-equity mortgage product to qualified applicants. The First Time Home Buyer Incentive makes available a 5 percent (for resale homes) or 10 percent (for newly built homes) shared-equity mortgage that bears no monthly interest burden and only requires the owner to share a proportion of gains or losses with CMHC.

The $1.25 billion program (supplemented by a $100 million lending facility for existing shared-equity mortgage providers) will be available to first-time home buyers who qualify for mortgage insurance and who have mortgage debt of no more than four times a maximum annual household income of $120,000. The program will attract people into the housing market and will also result in some substitution from mortgage-insurance volumes. We expect a modest reduction in mortgage-insurance activity as a result.

Hybrid Tenures

Two primary residential tenures exist in Canada at present: leased interests and "fee simple" ownership. People may currently be purchasing homes to access some of the benefits, such as the right to tenancy, but are willing to forgo other rights in the bundle, such as the rights to sell the property at an appreciated value in the future.

As noted earlier, shared-equity rental programs exist in Canada and are being expanded by the federal government. Technology will likely enable more tenure types along the spectrum, and CMHC is monitoring emerging models.

Hybrid tenures may also allow a graduated entrance into the real-estate market, affording young adults an opportunity to invest in the benefits of home ownership.

Housing as a Service

As technology changes the way we work and enables more remote capabilities, it may begin to change our need for fixed housing in one geographical region. As a result, housing as a service may begin to grow in popularity. WeWork, a popular co-working space provider, has introduced WeLive, whereby people can live in a variety of locations around the world for a monthly subscription fee. The company has even introduced WeGrow, a school with a similar global vision.

Another co-living company, Common, has formed a new venture called Kin with a large New York developer to provide co-living spaces for young families that include playrooms, on-demand child care, cleaning services, and family programming.

These types of housing models may be attractive to a more mobile workforce and may reduce rates of home ownership in Canada, with implications for our economy and society.

Property Tech (Proptech)

Existing conventional tenure types are confined by a bricks-and-mortar construct. Technology enables us to digitize uses and add temporal features, thereby accessing a "long tail" of heretofore unavailable value. Proptech is a potential game-changer. Google's Sidewalk Labs has explored modular buildings, including in Toronto, where the walls are like Lego blocks, and buildings can be repurposed.

By making space fluid, proptech is also changing how we define property. These changes can have a fairly significant impact on mortgage financing, since the underlying security will evolve in tandem.

A Networked Future

In his book *The Seventh Sense*, Joshua Cooper Ramo warns about the risk of networks, while arguing that only connected organizations will thrive.[19] Distributed networks will use data and computing power and risk being concentrated in a few hands, such as Google, Amazon, and Facebook. In the United States, Zillow and other models are attempting to build data-rich real-estate networks.

CMHC's five-year 2019–2024 Strategic Plan, *Our Housing Affordability Strategy*, puts technology and data at the center.[20] In executing on our strategy, we now have agile "skunkworks" teams examining the following initiatives that could enhance the housing network in Canada:

- offering an AI "chatbot" to improve the usability of our website and help guide proponents through our program-application processes, using Microsoft Cognitive Services;
- reimagining our antiquated emili mortgage underwriting system as a cloud-based systemic risking engine, and potentially a means of aggregating standardized housing data;
- creating an Analytics Center of Excellence to employ data science and analytics applications like Tableau and Sisense to our business- and housing-affordability solutions; and
- exploring the use of artificial intelligence software in our business, including open-source software like TensorFlow, Keras, and Microsoft Cognitive Toolkit.

CMHC has taken modest steps to prepare for an uncertain future. We are starting to think about how our programs and policies need to be developed differently. Given the speed of change, regulators will need to ensure that their policies are principle-based versus rule-based, and are system agnostic. As with payments, we need to anticipate how different business models require unconventional regulation. This will ensure the durability of their policies, and will provide a framework for emerging models that we have not yet had time to consider.

Conventional mortgage facilitators will find their functions undermined as machines more efficiently perform rote, repeatable tasks. More ominously, machines' increasing ability to perform cognitive tasks requires humans to migrate to more intense and ambitious cognitive activities. This trend will apply to mortgage brokerages, real-estate agents, lawyers, appraisers, and inspectors alike. The ability of technology to offer consumers cheaper, individualized, more efficient, streamlined systems is therefore a threat to our entire mortgage system.

The most agile, flexible, forward-looking, and consumer-centric organizations will be in the best position to take advantage of the exciting new developments in the fintech and open-banking spaces.

Conclusion

In summary, we foresee a much different mortgage market within just a few years. Where value exists in digital fractionalization, the nearly costless use of technology will create new economic opportunities. Moreover, significant insight exists via standardized data and big data capabilities that use analytics, AI, and data mining to manage risks and create new opportunities. In a sense, the comfortable banking oligopoly in Canadian mortgages is vulnerable. However, incumbent banks are anticipating these forces and investing in defensive and cannibalistic start-ups themselves.

We are sure that the comfortable Canadian mortgage market is under pressure from these powerful trends. Yet the future is as murky as the richness of our imaginations.

CMHC has set an audacious goal that by 2030 everyone in Canada will have a home that they can afford and that meets their needs. Closing this gap is a daunting challenge. Building sufficient housing is part of the solution – but a very expensive path. In fact, technological innovations will support behavioral changes that offer true hope for universal security of shelter in Canada. We hope and believe that technology will be the means by which we reimagine the future of housing in Canada.

NOTES

1 Crowe, C., Dell'Ariccia, G., Igan, D., & Rabanal, P. (2011, April). How to deal with real estate booms: Lessons from country experiences. IMF Working Paper.
2 For comprehensive overviews of the Canadian mortgage system, refer to: Crawford, A., Meh, C., & Zhou, J. (2013, December). The residential mortgage market in Canada: A primer. Bank of Canada, Financial System Review. https://www.bankofcanada.ca/wp-content/uploads/2013/12/fsr-december13-crawford.pdf; and Lascelles, E. (2010, 17 June). Canadian mortgage market primer. TD Securities Economics Strategy: Market Musings. https://www.td.com/document/PDF/economics/special/td-economics-special-el0610-cdn-mort-market-di.pdf.
3 Genworth MI Canada Inc. (2019, April). Financial supplements. http://investor.genworthmicanada.ca/English/financials-and-filings/quarterly-reports-archive/default.aspx; Canada Guaranty Mortgage Insurance Company. (2019, April). Quarterly portfolio metrics report. https://www.canadaguaranty.ca/portfolio-metrics/; Canada Mortgage and Housing Corporation. (2019, April). Mortgage loan insurance business supplement. https://www.cmhc-schl.gc.ca/en/about-cmhc/corporate-reporting/quaterly-financial-reports; Canada Mortgage and Housing Corporation. (2019, April). CMHC starts and completion survey. https://www03.cmhc-schl.gc.ca/hmip-pimh/.
4 Organization for Economic Co-operation and Development. (nd). https://stats.oecd.org/.
5 Mian, A., & Sufi, A. (2014). *House of debt: How they (and you) caused the Great Recession, and how we can prevent it from happening again.* Chicago: University of Chicago Press.
6 New York: Crown.
7 CMHC. (2018). About CMHC's emili. http://192.197.69.106/en/corp/nero/jufa/jufa_035.cfm. Accessed 31 July 2019.
8 While OSFI does not regulate CMHC, *per se*, it conducts an annual review of the activities of crown corporations and risk management and reports

the results of its supervisory assessment to the minister of finance and the minister responsible for CMHC. OSFI's purview was extended to CMHC in 2012 following an investigation of the company's risk management by then Minister of Finance Jim Flaherty, following the financial crisis. Since then, CMHC has conducted its affairs as if it were subject to OSFI's direct oversight.

9 OSFI. (2017, October). Residential mortgage underwriting practices and procedures – effective January 1, 2018. http://www.osfi-bsif.gc.ca/Eng /fi-if/rg-ro/gdn-ort/gl-ld/Pages/b20_dft.aspx.
10 OSFI. (2019, March). Residential mortgage insurance underwriting practices and procedures. http://www.osfi-bsif.gc.ca/Eng/fi-if/rg-ro /gdn-ort/gl-ld/Pages/b21.aspx.
11 For further insight into this debate, refer to our letter to the House of Commons Finance Committee: CMHC. (2019, 23 May). CMHC statement – Letter to the Standing Committee on Finance (https://www.cmhc-schl .gc.ca/en/media-newsroom/news-releases/2019/cmhc-statement -letter-standing-committee-finance-fina); and additional commentary as follows: Siddall, E. (2019, 5 March). Are current mortgage rules too strict? No. *Toronto Star.* https://www.thestar.com/opinion/contributors /thebigdebate/2019/03/05/are-current-mortgage-rules-too-strict-no.html; and Siddall, E. (2016, 17 October). The intended consequences of new housing policies. *Globe and Mail.* https://www.theglobeandmail.com /report-on-business/rob-commentary/the-intended-consequences -of-new-housing-policies/article32383166/. Counterpoints are offered by admittedly self-interested commentators as follows: Hudak, T. (2019, 30 April). Ottawa's stress test is demolishing Canadians' housing dreams. Which party will rebuild them? *Financial Post.* https://business .financialpost.com/opinion/ottawas-stress-test-is-demolishing-canadians -housing-dreams-which-party-will-rebuild-them; and Alexander, C. (2019, 5 March). Are current mortgage rules too strict? Yes. *Toronto Star.* https:// www.thestar.com/opinion/contributors/thebigdebate/2019/03/05/are -current-mortgage-rules-too-strict-yes.html.
12 For more on Home Capital's near collapse, please see: McFarland, J. (2017, 13 May). Mayday at Home Capital. *Globe and Mail, Report on Business.* https://www.theglobeandmail.com/report-on-business /home-capital-saga-real-estate/article34972594/.
13 Brown, D. (2019, 4 December). This perfect Bill Gates quote will frame your next decade of success. Inc.com. https://www.inc.com/damon -brown/this-perfect-bill-gates-quote-will-frame-your-next-decade-of -success.html.

14 PricewaterhouseCoopers. (2017). Redrawing the lines: Fintech's growing influence on financial services. *Global FinTech Report 2017*.

15 Sharf, S. (2018, February 5). Quicken Loans overtakes Wells Fargo as America's largest mortgage lender. *Forbes*.

16 PricewaterhouseCoopers. (2017). Redrawing the lines: Fintech's growing influence on financial services. *Global FinTech Report 2017*.

17 The Cooperative Capital Markets Regulatory System. (nd). Welcome. http://ccmr-ocrmc.ca/. Accessed 31 July 2019.

18 Seba, T. (nd). Rethinking transportation 2020–2030. https://tonyseba.com /portfolio-item/rethinking-transportation-2020-2030/. Accessed 31 July 2019.

19 Ramo, J.C. (2016). *The seventh sense: Power, fortune and survival in the age of networks*. New York: Little Brown.

20 CMHC. (2019). 2019–2023 summary of the corporate plan. https:// eppdscrmssa01.blob.core.windows.net/cmhcprodcontainer/sf/project /cmhc/aboutus/corporate%20reporting/pdfs/summary-corporate-plan -2019-2023-cmhc-en.pdf. Accessed 31 July 2019.

SECTION III

SUCCEEDING IN THE FINTECH ERA

CHAPTER FOURTEEN

The Business Case for Gender Diversity in Financial Services

Brenda Trenowden

Gender diversity in the workplace is a business-performance issue, not just a social issue. It is particularly important in banking and financial services. This industry is facing huge challenges, with increasing geopolitical instability, changing and unpredictable regulation, digital disruption, and cybercrime, and – importantly – an unrelenting battle for talent. With all of these forces, it is easy to let diversity slip down the agenda. But this is precisely the time when leaders really need to focus on this issue. Research shows that businesses with more diverse boards and management teams are more effective than teams with a homogeneous group at the top. Diversity addresses the challenges around groupthink and helps businesses to solve the many complex problems they are facing.

I have been delivering this message in my discussions with CEOs, board chairs, and other leaders since becoming the global chair of the 30% Club in 2015. The 30% Club is a global group of women and men who are campaigning for better gender balance on company boards and throughout organizations. We believe the only way to achieve real, long-term sustainable change is through a voluntary, business-led initiative where companies commit because it makes good business sense. From its roots in the United Kingdom, the 30% Club has spread to fourteen countries/regions and continues to expand.

In this chapter, I first outline the business case for diversity and why it is important for the financial-services sector. Second, I discuss how organizations need to collect data to diagnose their own particular issues and to set targets. Third, I talk about the importance of engaging stakeholders in companies, such as shareholders and institutional investors. And finally, I outline actions leaders can take to help their organizations become more diverse and inclusive and ultimately reflect a better gender balance.

Research on Performance and Diversity

A large body of research documents the significant correlation between increased gender diversity and financial performance. There are also benefits for talent attraction and retention, innovation and productivity, and customer engagement. While the question of causality remains open, it is clear the correlation is very strong.

A 2016 Peterson Institute study of nearly 22,000 global companies in ninety-one countries found that companies that went from zero female representation on the board and in the executive suite to 30 percent representation experienced, on average, a 15 percent increase in net profit margins.[1] A 2018 McKinsey & Company study of 1,000 companies in twelve countries found that organizations in the top quartile when it comes to gender diversity among executive leadership teams were 21 percent more likely to outperform on profitability and 27 percent more likely to have superior value creation.[2] The highest-performing companies on both profitability and diversity had more women in line (i.e., typically revenue-generating) roles than in staff roles on their executive teams. Companies in the top-quartile for ethnic/cultural diversity on executive teams were 33 percent more likely to have industry-leading profitability. And companies in the bottom quartile for both gender and ethnic/cultural diversity were 29 percent less likely to experience profitability above the industry average. A 2016 Credit Suisse study similarly documented that companies with a higher participation of women in decision-making roles generate higher market returns and superior profit outperformance using a number of measures.[3] These studies are part of a larger body of research that makes the case for greater diversity from a financial performance point of view.

The global nonprofit Catalyst categorizes the business benefits of diversity in terms of three pillars. The first pillar is improved financial performance. In addition to the research highlighted above, Catalyst has summarized the research linking diversity and financial performance across a variety of academic and business studies. Their summary is available online and highlights the links between diversity and indicators of profitability and financial health, including accounting returns; cash flow return on investment; earnings per share; earnings before interest and taxes (EBIT) margins; gross and net margins; investment performance; profitability measured by Return on Assets (ROA), Return on Equity (ROE), and Return on Sales (ROS); revenue and sales growth; share price performance; and market valued measured by Tobin's Q.[4]

The second pillar is the importance of attracting and leveraging talent. Employers need to cast a wider net and consider underrepresented groups when hiring. These findings apply to diversity along many dimensions, of which gender is just one. Catalyst summarizes research showing that companies with higher levels of gender diversity and with HR policies and practices that focus on gender diversity[5]

- are more successful at retaining talent,
- have teams with increased job satisfaction and knowledge sharing,
- have employees who report experiencing trust and increased engagement at work,

- are more innovative and earn a premium for their innovation,
- exhibit less groupthink and better decision making, and
- have fewer instances of fraud and higher ratings on corporate social responsibility.

The third pillar is better reflecting the marketplace. Teams are as much as 158 percent more likely to understand target consumers when they have at least one member who represents their target's gender, race, age, sexual orientation, or culture. When a workforce reflects the racial/ethnic diversity of its consumer base, employee productivity increases. Women control US$20 trillion of consumer spending and represent a bigger growth market than China and India combined. Women make over 90 percent of most household purchase decisions and even 60 percent of automobile purchase decisions. Because of this it makes sense for companies that are consumer facing to have more women on their boards, on senior leadership teams, and indeed on all of their teams.

We are starting to see that it just makes good business sense to think about gender diversity. It is time to reframe the discussion. Instead of asking, "What are the benefits and why should companies be doing this?" we should be asking, "What are the costs and what are the risks of not doing this?" That is the way that we should all be looking at it.

Setting Targets

In business, and particularly in financial services, we know that "what gets measured gets done." As a result, the 30% Club decided that we would start at the top and set targets that were transparent, measurable, and ambitious. We set a target of 30 percent female representation on boards by 2015 for the largest 100 companies in the

United Kingdom, the FTSE 100. You may wonder why we did not choose 50 percent. Back in 2010 when we got started, the FTSE 100 companies only had 12.5 percent female representation on boards, and there were twenty-one all-male boards. Our view was that if we set the target too high in too short a time period, then people would lose interest and we would lose momentum. The research also pointed to 30 percent as the tipping point for any underrepresented group. For example, if there is one woman on a board of ten, everything she says is seen as "the female voice." If there are two women, people get them confused with each other. Once there are three, they become "normalized" and can be heard as individuals, like any other board member. This is why we chose 30 percent as our goal. And, to be clear, we view 30 percent as a minimum, not an end goal.

Shortly thereafter the U.K. government got behind this target, conducting a study looking at how the United Kingdom could become more competitive and more productive. Part of the answer was having more women in senior positions. The U.K. government therefore launched the Davies Review, which set a target for a minimum of 25 percent female board member representation by 2015.[6] While the target was lower than 30 percent, the main point was that it began to generate momentum. We had our campaign, these enlightened chairs, and government policy behind us.

I will say that the toughest part was when we started writing to companies. We didn't receive many responses, and we also received some quite rude responses. We decided to change tactics and ask chairs at supportive companies to go out and lobby their peers. It became like a competition. No one wanted to be the last company in the FTSE 100 with an all-male board. The last was Glencore, and they finally added a female board member in 2014 (they now have two).

We also received a lot of media coverage in the United Kingdom. A week didn't go by where we weren't called and asked to comment on this issue in the papers, or on television or radio. We also gained momentum by expanding the 30% Club internationally. We hadn't planned this expansion, but we received a lot of interest from groups around the world. In response, we helped to set up groups from Australia to the United States and Canada.

By the end of our first campaign in 2015, female representation in the United Kingdom had increased from 12.5 percent to 26 percent. We also eliminated all-male boards from the FTSE 100. This was a huge achievement, and it was accomplished through voluntary means, not through the use of quotas. Today we are pleased to say that the FTSE 100 has 31 percent female representation overall and 63 of the 100 companies have boards that are at least 30 percent female.

Engaging Stakeholders

Since 2016 we have been focused on executive management and the talent pipeline. Our new campaign is concentrated on signing up CEOs committed to the 30 percent target within their leadership teams by 2020. This is a more challenging target for most companies, as it takes time to build the pipeline, and most companies have very long-standing routes to executive leadership. This requires strong commitment from the CEO and very deliberate and sustained action from the senior leadership and managers. Given all of the other short-term priorities that leaders are dealing with, it can be difficult to get them to focus on this issue.

We believe that one of the most powerful incentives is pressure from shareholders. In the United Kingdom, our 30% Club Investor Group comprises thirty-five asset owners and managers with approximately £11 trillion in assets under management. We also have active investor groups in Australia and Canada (with more to come). These groups are very clear that better gender diversity on the boards and executive teams at the investee companies will lead to better long-term performance. They see this as a stewardship and governance issue that companies need to address.

The 30% Club has developed a statement of intent that members of our Investor Group sign. It states that they will actively engage with investee companies on corporate governance issues, including the process for identifying suitable candidates for board and senior executive roles. They expect transparency and evidence of a commitment to diversity in senior management. And if, after engaging with board chairs and nomination committees, they are not satisfied, they may choose to vote against re-election of the chair of the board and the chair of the nomination committee. The group also collectively reviews the top listed companies to identify outliers. We like to "name and fame" top performers, and we will constructively engage with the laggards. To date we have had a number of successes from this initiative.

Where to Start

Many companies do not know where to start when it comes to addressing gender diversity. Here are some steps they can take.

Recognize Hidden Biases

The first step is to recognize hidden biases. We need to be aware of our biases and challenge ourselves, while creating a safe environment to challenge each other. Many companies fall into what we call the "merit trap." They are convinced that they operate as a meritocracy. Merit, however, is often used as shorthand for a package of attributes that we innately recognize as good qualities. This creates obstacles for women who are working in male-dominated environments where there are deeply held beliefs and norms about what qualities are suitable for leadership. The same bias applies for men working in female-dominated environments.

One study found that companies that were the most vocal about being meritocracies were actually the most biased in their promotions. These companies believed that they were objective, but they didn't stop and examine their biases. Beware of companies that trumpet their strong sense of meritocracy – their unquestioned bias means they are likely to be the opposite of meritocratic. Often statements such as "He's a great fit for the team" or "She's a great cultural fit" can be translated as "He or she looks, sounds and acts just like me." Because merit is judged on two criteria, past performance and potential – and because evaluation of the latter is a very subjective affair – women often lose out, especially in male-dominated environments where there are strongly held beliefs about who is suitable for leadership.

There are two ways to address this hidden bias problem: through leadership and through training. First, we have all heard how important leadership is and how culture has to be set from the top. In terms of leadership, the CEO has to believe that better gender balance will lead to better business decisions, and they have to talk about it with their team and in public forums. They have to prioritize it and they have to set targets as they would with any other business goal. If the CEO doesn't believe in it, or isn't perceived to believe in it, then nothing will change. Second, companies need to invest in training their middle managers. Many companies promote their top sales people or top technical people into management roles as a reward for outstanding performance. More often than not, these new managers receive little or no training from their employer and have no proven track record of being an effective manager. They may not even be interested in managing. As a result, most are not effective at understanding differences in the learning styles and working approaches of their team members, and they fall into the trap of sponsoring and promoting people like themselves.

One large bank that spent a lot of time reviewing exit interviews and post-exit interviews of "regretted" female leavers found that the majority left out of frustration with their managers – they were not being heard, were not understood, and were regularly overlooked for promotions. As a result, they left for better opportunities elsewhere (not for work-life-balance issues, as the company originally thought).

Having a positive and inclusive corporate culture is critical to the success of diversity initiatives and, ultimately, to the success of an organization. Organizational culture is usually defined as the underlying beliefs, assumptions, values, and ways of interacting that contribute to the social and psychological environment of an organization. To put it more simply, employees often describe it as "the way things are done around here." As a popular saying goes, "We are what we repeatedly do." Unfortunately, those things that we repeatedly do aren't always positive – things like hiring and promoting in our own image, building networks exclusively through sporting events or sessions after work in the pub, or encouraging winning at all costs.

The CEO has to have a strong sense of the culture that he or she wants to promote. They have to have a vision for the organization, and they must be very clear on how the culture links to the strategic objectives. This then needs to be communicated authentically. The right behaviors need to be promoted and rewarded publicly.

Personally, I think that a shared sense of purpose and sense of belonging are the two things that can really create a competitive advantage in terms of organizational culture. People want to go to work feeling that what they are doing is meaningful and that they have a role to play in the overall corporate strategy. They want to know that they are making a meaningful contribution. People also want to feel an emotional connection to the firm they work with and a sense of belonging. They want to be part of the team. This is human nature. Research has shown that improving the sense of belonging in under-represented groups reduces stress levels and improves physical health, emotional well-being, and performance. It creates an authentically inclusive culture where everyone can be the best version of themselves and truly thrive.

Diagnose the Problem

The second step is diagnosing where the problem lies. There is not a single model that fits every company. Every company is different, and each company has to spend time on metrics and measurement to understand their own particular challenges. Typically, companies will delegate this issue to the Human Resources (HR) department. Instead, business leaders need to be accountable for driving the initiative themselves. They need to ask their HR teams to gather the data to identify the areas where biases are more prevalent and then analyze it to determine the root causes.

One large U.K. bank thought they might have a problem in the investment bank at the vice-president (VP) level. They collected data on how long women and men at the VP level spent in the role before they were promoted. The data showed that women were spending six years longer in the role than men before promotion. The company recognized that they had a very significant gap, and this was an important step for them. They then spent the time to understand why this was happening. They examined the targets in that division and the promotion processes. They talked to the women and the men, and met with the managers. I've since asked several companies for that same statistic, and most companies replied that they didn't have those data and that they were too difficult to collect. If a company really cares about gender diversity, they will get the data and challenge themselves. The United Kingdom has just completed its second year of collecting and reporting data on gender pay gaps. While some of the reported numbers have had errors, and many companies have been slow to report, the exercise has been successful in shining a light on the problem and forcing companies to speak publicly about what they are doing to address it.

Provide Gender-Neutral Job Descriptions

A third step is to objectively scope out roles and provide clear job descriptions. It can be helpful to limit job descriptions to "musthaves," rather than including a long list of "nice-to-haves," because studies show that while men are likely to apply for jobs for which they meet only 70 percent of the qualifications, women are much more likely to hesitate unless they meet 100 percent of the listed requirements. Making sure that job descriptions are gender neutral is also a simple way for companies to ensure that they are attracting the broadest talent pool. One large accounting firm advertised a role for an industry leader with a specific set of skills and experience and found that only men were applying for the role. One month later, they reposted the exact same advertisement, but without the term "industry leader," and found many women applying as a result of that one small change. Seemingly, only the men saw themselves as "industry leaders," whereas the women, despite having the requisite skills and experience, did not associate themselves with that term.

This example highlights the fact that there are masculine words that men respond to and feminine words that women respond to. Words and phrases like "aggressive" or "mission critical" are masculine, and words like "partnership" and "passion for learning" are feminine. For some time now, there has been software available to screen for gender-coded language in job advertisements, allowing ads to be made gender neutral by removing words that may discourage female applicants.[7]

Change Hiring Practices

A fourth step relates to hiring practices, including the use of blind curriculum vitaes (CVs), hiring for teams, diverse interviewers, and shortlists that require female candidates. Research has shown that if you use a blind CV that removes any reference to gender, then it is easier for recruiters to bypass their biases. Where practical, another de-biasing strategy is to hire for teams rather than for specific roles. This involves working out what skills and attributes are missing from the current team and looking to fill those gaps rather than recruiting an individual that fits with the uniformity of the group. To ensure more diverse choices, recruiters should also use a diverse group of interviewers and interview individually, comparing assessment scores afterwards. This encourages more objective assessments and avoids allowing one or two individuals to influence the others. When executive-search firms are used, the firms should be mandated to include two or more women on the shortlist. A study by *Harvard Business Review* found that, "if there is only one woman in the candidate pool there is statistically no chance of her being hired ... but that changes dramatically if she is joined by one other woman."[8] And if the executive-search firm says it cannot find suitable female candidates, then it is time to change search firms, because they are probably not looking hard enough.

Match Women with Senior Sponsors

A fifth step is to match women with a sponsor higher up in the organization. Many people are familiar with the concept of mentorship, but they may not understand the difference between a sponsor and a mentor. A mentor is someone who coaches a candidate and provides career advice. Many companies have formal mentoring schemes that junior staff can enroll in. A sponsor is someone who advocates on a candidate's behalf. Typically, they should be in the same company and be someone who has influence in the organization. At review meetings when the management team are talking about promotions, the sponsor will speak up on the protégé's behalf and will seek out opportunities to help the protégé build their profile. In return, the protégé has to be loyal and has to perform. A smart sponsor picks out good people, sponsors them, and builds a following of loyal people throughout the organization. The sponsor is helping them and bringing them up through the organization, and in exchange the protégés are not only loyal to the sponsor but will provide them with information and be available for them when needed. It's a mutually beneficial relationship. The problem is that most financial firms tend to have men at the top, and these sponsorship relationships happen much more naturally among men. Firms concerned about gender representation will create sponsorship plans for talented women as well, and help pair them with an appropriate sponsor.

Provide Female Role Models

A sixth step is to provide role models. In organizations, the expression is "You need to see it to be it." Firms that do not have senior women at the top will have difficulty attracting and keeping women. Female candidates will not see a possibility for them at the top when looking at an employer. Research has shown that many young people leave companies after three years when they do not see any role models like them at the top, or anyone that they can relate to and respect. This finding applies to women and other under-represented groups. Role models are very important and are related to unconscious bias. If I close my eyes and picture a CEO or a board chair, I imagine a gray-haired man in a suit. Even though I may be actively seeking to increase female representation at the top, I still have that automatic response because of gender stereotypes and gender norms.

Conclusion

Gender diversity in financial services is not just a social issue; it is a business performance issue. All stakeholders have an interest in seeing more diversity at the top of companies to promote better decision making and avoid groupthink. The 2008–2009 global financial crisis highlighted the costs of a lack of diversity of opinions when faced with a challenging external environment. The banking and financial-services industry will undoubtedly face many challenges in the coming decade. These challenges can be overcome with better decision making by diverse teams of individuals.

Promoting gender diversity has to be a priority for the leaders in an organization. They have to be committed and accountable. They need to look at the company's values and systems, including recruitment, promotion, mentoring, and sponsorship; training of managers; and role models. Most importantly, they need to have targets and measurements in place to make people accountable. Ultimately, the goal should be to promote an inclusive culture and create change in organizations where women are under-represented in senior roles, because the cost of not doing so is significant.

NOTES

1 Noland, M., Moran, T., & Kotschwar, B. (2016, February). Is gender diversity profitable? Evidence from a global survey. The Peterson Institute, Working Paper16-3.
2 Hunt, V., Prince, S., Dixon-Fyle, S., & Yee, L. (2018). Delivering through diversity. McKinsey & Company.

3 Dawson, J., Kersley, R., & Natella, S. (2016). The CS gender 3000: The reward for change. Credit Suisse.
4 Catalyst. (2018, 1 August). Appendix: Why diversity and inclusion matter: Financial performance. https://www.catalyst.org/research/why-diversity -and-inclusion-matter-financial-performance/.
5 Catalyst. (2018, 1 August). Quick take: Why diversity and inclusion matter. https://www.catalyst.org/research/why-diversity-and-inclusion-matter/.
6 U.K. Government. (2011, 24 February). Women on boards. https://www .gov.uk/government/news/women-on-boards.
7 Matfield, K. (nd). Gender decoder for job ads. http://gender-decoder .katmatfield.com/. Accessed 31 July 2019.
8 Johnson, S.K., Hekman, D.R., & Chan, E.T. (2016, 26 April). If there's only one woman in your candidate pool, there's statistically no chance she'll be hired. *Harvard Business Review.* https://hbr.org/2016/04/if-theres-only -one-woman-in-your-candidate-pool-theres-statistically-no-chance-shell -be-hired.

CHAPTER FIFTEEN

Bank Strategy and Innovation Utilizing Technology

Richard W. Nesbitt[1]

Recently a CEO was overheard stating that their bank needed to develop an artificial intelligence (AI) strategy for their firm. This was going to take a lot of time, and management needed to get right on it. But wait! Does the CEO have a Microsoft Office strategy? Of course not. The bank uses Microsoft Office as a tool just as it might use any other fixed or virtual asset to accomplish its strategy. Similarly, AI may one day be a tool used in banking to accomplish its strategy.

This chapter examines the role of technology in the strategy of a bank. To discuss this question, we must first define what we mean by strategy. Entire libraries – both physical and digital – could be filled with the books written on strategy. Many consulting firms exist to tell executives how to develop strategy. Business schools have large departments devoted to the research and study of strategy. We cannot do justice to this topic in a single chapter. Instead, this chapter gives the reader a glimpse into how senior executives at a bank think about formulating strategy. We relate this function to the role of technological innovation, which today is a "hot" topic among executives in banking and many other industries.

What is strategy? In its simplest form, strategy is the answer to three distinct questions:

1. Where is the organization today?
2. Where would the organization like to go in the future?
3. How will it get there?

Technological innovation is not strategy. The role of technology is to provide answers to the third question above – namely, how an organization achieves its objectives. This chapter identifies two forces, risk management and customer/competition, that define a bank's strategy and ultimately dictate its future success. Technology does not define where we are today, nor does it set the direction for where we would like to go. Technology is a tool of strategy. It is not an end in itself, despite what futurists would have us believe.

Banks have a long history of innovation. They have been employing technology as a tool to improve customer service for many decades. For example, banks developed automated teller machines (ATMs) for customer convenience and cost efficiency, and online and then mobile banking to provide customers with products and services electronically. Banks innovated to allow customers to deposit checks online, thereby freeing them from the chore of making multiple visits to their bank branch. For decades, bank branches were customers' main point of contact and source of financial information. But now many people bank online and only visit their branch infrequently for specific activities.

These early banking innovations, along with many others happening today, are fundamental to explaining the current landscape in financial services. Technology will allow banking to continue improving customer experiences well into the future. Without digital banking, there would be no discussion of new topics such as open banking, as it would not be feasible for customers to share their account information manually except with great difficulty. There would be no new payment methods or, for that matter, innovations such as a secure form of digital cash. The future of our banking system would look radically different from the path it is on today.

The Essential Nature of Banks

Technology is a tool for achieving strategy, not a goal in and of itself. With this clear view of where technological innovation fits, the answer to the first two strategic questions – where we are and where we are going – requires an understanding of what really makes banks work.

A bank's strategy and operations are most affected by two fundamental forces that dominate the time and attention of senior management:

1. **Risk Management**
   • Banks are risk-taking entities. They are highly leveraged, highly cyclical, and therefore highly regulated.
2. **Customer/Competition**
   • Banks have two major customer segments: businesses and individuals.
   • Banks engage in two major activities:
     • bringing money in through deposit-gathering activities, such as everyday banking and wealth management, and
     • sending money out through lending activities.

Banks compete for these two customer types and engage in these two major activities with the support of their marketing and service operations. These functions bring the traditional focus on the five "Ps" of marketing: product, place, price, promotion, and people.

From a risk-management perspective, technology is improving the tools available to manage risk by enhancing their speed, accuracy, and efficiency relative to existing legacy processes. In the competitive arena, technology has enabled fundamental change. It has created new channels for distribution, enabling new products and services. It has expanded data collection and utilization to identify customer needs and opportunities for cross-selling. Technology has also increased operational efficiency, leading to radical alterations in pricing structures. The impact of technology as a competitive force has been far greater than the impact of technology on risk management.

Let's investigate each of these two forces more deeply.

Risk Management

1. Banks Are Highly Leveraged Vehicles

The core business of banking can be broken down into operations on the assets side of the balance sheet and those on the liabilities side. With regard to assets, banks make loans, such as mortgages, and fund them through the liabilities side using customer deposits raised through various products such as savings accounts, checking accounts, or GICs. As regulated deposit takers, banks are very different from lenders, who primarily use their own capital to make loans. Lending processes are typically low-margin operations where the spread between what the lenders receive and what lenders pay is small. A firm simply involved in the lending of its own capital would not be able to achieve the high return on equity (ROE) of banks unless it lent to riskier borrowers at much higher rates.

Fortunately for banks, they are assisted by two special characteristics that enable them to earn large profits from otherwise low-margin activities: regulation and leverage.

386   Richard W. Nesbitt

Banks are significantly leveraged entities. Take the example of the mortgage portfolio. Each of the five largest Canadian banks has $150 to $200 billion in mortgages, so, collectively, more than $1 trillion of assets. If a bank has $200 billion of residential mortgages, how much equity does it have against that portfolio? Let's take a simple back-of-the-envelope approach to this question (with apologies to bank CFOs and treasurers who would shudder at the imprecision of this illustration):

- Around 50 percent of these mortgages are insured, either by the federal crown corporation Canada Mortgage and Housing Corporation (CMHC) or by an alternative private insurer (who is in turn guaranteed 90 percent by CMHC). In the case of these federally insured mortgages, there is zero capital required against this $100 billion.
- The remaining $100 billion of mortgages would have a loan-to-value (LTV) ratio below 80 percent, as that is the regulatory limit on uninsured mortgage lending in Canada. The average portfolio would have an LTV ratio of 50 percent. These mortgages would have less than a 20 percent risk weighting, so the bank's exposure from a regulatory perspective would be $20 billion (20 percent of $100 billion).
- The bank would hold approximately 10 percent regulatory capital against this risk-weighted exposure of $20 billion, or $2 billion of regulatory capital.
- Therefore $200 billion of assets are leveraged against $2 billion of capital, or 100-to-1 times.
- If the bank earns a return on assets (ROA) of 0.5 percent on these mortgages, the return on equity (ROE) is 50 percent, or $1 billion of net income divided by $2 billion of equity.

As this example illustrates, banks have 1 percent to 2 percent of regulatory capital backing these mortgage assets (subject to additional leverage capital requirements, generally managed at the total firm level. Basel III is also focused on leverage ratio, which becomes more of a binding constraint in low-risk assets like mortgages. In the real world, banks have a portfolio of low-risk [mortgage] and high-risk loans [e.g., credit cards and business loans], and the higher-risk loans drive a capital requirement well above their leverage ratio – hence the portfolio effect mitigating the overall impact). This example demonstrates that banks are highly leveraged, and it is this leverage that allows the banks to be so profitable. If you looked at the return earned by a bank on a mortgage without leverage, the returns would be very low. As soon as you apply leverage, the banks can generate a high ROE.

In summary, banks are highly leveraged vehicles that allow them to earn high ROEs on comparatively low margins. The banking industry is more leveraged than the economy in general. The average leverage ratio of the fifty-nine largest U.S. banks is 9.2, while the average leverage ratio of the S&P 500 varied between 1.3 and 4.3 in 2016.[2] Banks employ high amounts of leverage to turn low returns into respectable profits. It is critical to always remember, however, that leverage is a double-edged sword and amplifies risk as well.

2. Banks Are Highly Cyclical

If an organization is highly leveraged, it is usually not great to also be highly cyclical. What does it mean to say banks are highly cyclical? The first thing that comes to mind is volatility in credit-loss experience. As economies grow and contract, the bank's loan-loss experience is similarly affected. The second thing is variability in growth rates. Banks tend to find that these two variables are correlated. In an expanding economy, the loan book grows as more mortgages, corporate loans, and retail loans are added. Those loans are a response to increased demand from individuals and businesses operating in a growing economy, when credit conditions are typically improving and loan losses are declining. This is the virtuous part of the business cycle.

Some observers note that while banks' earnings have been historically cyclical, this may have moderated. We are currently in a long period of economic expansion in North America. Economies in countries like Australia have had an even longer period of sustained growth. In order for bank earnings to be cyclical you need the economy to be cyclical. Furthermore, improved activities such as credit scoring and stress testing are far more effective now than in the past. Reductions in exposure to high-risk products such as leveraged lending also have led to reduced volatility.

Time will tell whether the pattern of cyclicality has changed.

Near the end of the business cycle, when the economy turns down, banks get hit with the proverbial "double whammy." Credit losses start to rise, *and* growth starts to go down at the same time. This pattern is well known. This occurrence and the resultant expected impact on growth of earnings explains why bank stocks trade at multiples of ten to thirteen times earnings (P/E multiple), which is lower than the fifteen to twenty times earnings of stocks in many other industries. The low relative P/E ratio for banks is a signal that the marketplace understands this relationship. They may underestimate it, but they do understand it. Therefore, investors are not willing to pay as much for bank earnings, particularly at the peak of the economic cycle, as for earnings in some other industries.

3. Banks Are Highly Regulated

Banks exist in a highly regulated environment, and this allows them to operate differently from other lenders or companies in other industries. In exchange for existing in this highly regulated environment, banks are both lenders and deposit takers. In many countries, including Canada and the United States, special programs such as government-insured deposits and government-insured mortgages reduce the risk for qualified banks. The regulatory framework sets parameters for how much bank capital is required to safely backstop any losses that may occur in lending activities. Regulations require banks to assign risk levels to different asset types and then to allocate regulatory capital depending on this risk weighting. These same regulations allow the bank to use deposits from the liabilities side of their balance sheets to fund the asset side of the balance sheet. These regulations thereby require banks to hold only a fraction of the equity capital to fund this activity, leading to overall bank ROEs attractive to investors.

Regulatory requirements create a steep barrier to entry for other firms seeking to enter banking. This is a very important consideration for new, technology-based entrants into the financial-services industry. Reporting, legal, fraud, audit, anti-money laundering, and countless other regulatory requirements mean that potential firms must allocate significant resources just to get started. Large incumbents already possess the scale, expertise, and legacy systems to abide by these regulations. It is hard to overstate the importance of regulation to the profitability and even existence of modern banks. Their structure, business models, and operations have been shaped by regulation in one form or another. This is the primary special characteristic that separates modern banks from other lenders who extend credit using mostly their own capital.

In summary, the highly regulated nature of the banking system is a key feature of this industry. It allows banks to operate as they do and derive high profits from otherwise low-margin activities. The tightening or relaxation of future regulations is, therefore, a critical environmental factor that will influence banking profits. In the past decade, increased regulation has been associated with decreasing banking returns. Future trends in banking regulation are difficult to project, as there are many noneconomic factors, such as political sentiment, that can heavily influence lawmakers. In the past, bank regulators have leant heavily into the cycle to counter what they perceive as excesses in the economy. In recent years, we have seen regulators in Canada and around the world tightening credit availability, especially in the areas of mortgages.

Customer/Competition

1. Two Major Customer Types and Two Major Activities

While there are distinctions between the two major types of customers (business and retail) the reality is that the competitive forces brought to bear by technology are similar for both. For both segments, the type of activity is what dictates the degree to which technological forces can be brought to bear. These activities exist across a spectrum. In other words, at one end of the spectrum the customer entrusts its money to the bank, and at the other end of the spectrum the bank entrusts money to the customer.

The degree to which technological change can have an impact is determined far more by the type of activity than the type of customer. Customer sensitivity around where they deposit or where they have their money wealth managed can be high, whereas concern about where they borrow or transact can be low. The homogeneity of bank offerings and customers' price sensitivity have led to commoditization in these areas, increasing the impact of technological innovation. Wealth management, on the other hand, features high sensitivity because the customer is giving savings dedicated to a future purpose. The homogeneity of wealth products and the investment outcome are far less determined. The same is true for business customers where bespoke services exist, such as investment banking and structured lending. Historically these complex and/or bespoke services were not commoditized and were therefore resistant to technological replacement.

2. Marketing (Product, Place, Price, Promotion, People)

We now examine customer activities through the lens of marketing to see the impact of technological innovation, as well as some lessons learned about its limitations.

Innovation in Price

One of the greatest changes in pricing in financial services has been the decline in the commission charged for trading securities. It is a popular misconception that this reduction was driven by the advent of online trading and technological advances. The reality is that this decline was originally driven by regulatory changes and the opportunities they presented. Deregulation of commissions in Canada from fixed to negotiated commissions in the early 1980s meant price was now a factor in competing for a customer's business. Competitive forces ultimately led to the splitting of what had been one activity into two: (1) advice, and (2) transaction services. This split gave rise to the separation of discount brokerage services from full-service brokering.

Initially, there was no technological distinction between full-service and discount brokerage services. Both relied upon the 100-year-old technology of the telephone. Eventually, advances in technology led to innovations such as voice recognition for telephone-based services and online trading. However, the first and largest decline in commissions came about because of competitive forces unleashed initially by deregulation, not by technological innovation.

Prices varied between full-service brokerage firms, between brokers within the same firm, and between customers of the same broker. This process was not random and, in fact, proceeded in a logical fashion. Time was a scarce resource for brokerage-firm employees. Therefore, it was a natural path for them to gradually agree to lower commissions for simple transactions that did not require advice and were time-efficient. Although, this was a process of gradual retreat marked by low price transparency and the vested interests of legacy players, eventually market forces prevailed, resulting in the current world of dramatic volume expansion and fee compression. This process has led to $6.95 trades, and now free trades through robo-advisor fintechs. Deregulation, competition, and technology will continue to affect this distribution channel.

The vast changes in both price and service offerings in securities trading are a useful example of changes taking place in the framework surrounding a financial service that dictated technological adaptation.

Innovation in Place

We have often heard the claim that bank branches are going away. There have been multiple waves of predictions that branches were set to disappear from the retail banking landscape. The most important early wave was the introduction of the automatic teller machine (ATM). Customers could withdraw and deposit money from their account using a local machine that was available even when their branch was closed. Some predicted that the ATM was the harbinger of doom for the branch system. Some banks even bought into this idea, and started reducing branches and their network footprint while increasing the number of ATMs.

But it soon became clear that what customers really wanted was better customer service – a need that could not be solved solely by adding ATMs. One of the best examples was Canada Trust, later renamed TD Canada Trust after the merger with TD Bank.

Canada Trust realized that, in order for their trust company to compete with the larger banks, they needed a key point of differentiation in a system of larger banks that were mostly homogeneous. One element of Canada Trust's strategy was competing on the basis of customer service, particularly at the branch level, by expanding branch opening hours. This strategy led Canada Trust to introduce branches that were open fifty hours per week at a time when most banks were open only on weekdays for thirty-five hours per week. When TD Bank bought Canada Trust in 2000, they adopted this focus on enhanced customer service and introduced longer opening hours across their branches. TD Canada Trust soon dominated customer satisfaction and experience ratings, a development that fueled its rapid growth to become one of the dominant Canadian banks in the retail space.

While everybody was focused on a technological change (i.e., ATMs), TD had their eye on the customer and what the customer wanted. They understood that performing a homogeneous and commoditized activity using a new technology was not a replacement for a strategy to serve customers who viewed branch accessibility as important. Eventually the industry followed TD's lead and expanded branch hours to address this less homogeneous element of a customer's needs.

Innovation in Product

The common denominator for changes in product facilitated by technological innovation has been the implementation of straight-through processing wherever possible. Technology has enabled e-deposits and e-payments through the elimination of manual interfaces. These changes have resulted in improvements in speed, accuracy, efficiency, and cost.

The clear majority of product changes, however, is not related to the introduction of new products but rather to the commoditization of existing products. Once again, we find that technology is an enabler or tool but does not lead a change in business strategy. The banking system has been adapting legacy products and procedures to new capabilities, rather than engaging in shifts in strategy.

Consider a customer's perspective on how these changes have affected their banking experience. The ability to deposit a check by taking a photo is a major time saver. From the bank's perspective, the paper check has been converted into a digital form in their back offices for some time. Now the customer is doing it, eliminating this initial burden of physical check handling. The ability for customers to transfer money from one person to another has always been possible through either a bank wire transfer via telephone or through a check. Now e-transfers are a part of everyone's banking activities, reducing the need to write checks and wait for mail delivery. The bank experiences this as the customer inputting the data, with no need for bank personnel and a reduction in processing time when transferring funds. In both cases, technology has improved the customer's perceived level of service. And the bank has realized a major productivity enhancement by allowing the customer to do some of this work. However, in neither has technology actually led to real innovation in the product. Instead it has operated as a tool to facilitate higher volumes and efficiencies in the products.

While technological innovations in both promotion and people are also occurring, we leave it to the reader to think about examples and how they improve the customer experience but at the same time respond to the bank's need to compete using new technologies.

Technology Is a Tool, Not a Strategy

This chapter has argued that the essential nature of banks involves two major forces. Banks examine their strategies and activities through a risk lens, as they are highly leveraged, highly cyclical, and highly regulated. The second lens is customer/competition. Banks need to compete for customers, reduce the cost of their activities, and constantly improve customer service. Technology is a key enabler of strategy for addressing both risk and competitive forces.

Despite discussions of innovation and disruption, things are more the same now than they are different. Banks continue to be dominated by their risk-management needs and culture. They evaluate competitive forces across the spectrum of customer needs and their own productivity. They will deliver a bespoke, high-touch, relatively low-tech solution for the client where needs are highly individualized and margins are more favorable. For areas where customer needs are more commoditized, banks will develop more scalable, higher-productivity solutions. These behaviors have always existed. The check-clearing system of the past was a modern innovation at one time. The digital e-transfer system is a new version of that same system. The strategy that banks adopt – if truly strategic – should address both risk and competitive forces that allow them to move forward in the marketplace and provide them with a sustainable competitive advantage.

Benefiting the Customer – That's the Goal

Banks that use technology wisely will generally outperform their competitors. However, technology innovation also brings many uncertainties. Banks are chock full of an assortment of legacy systems and processes that are layered together as the firm grows and changes. As new layers are added, these systems can become inefficient and costly to maintain. Examples include multiple client databases, multiple sales platforms, and redundant forms and reports, to name a few. Through digital transformation, banks can consolidate resources and reduce process times for routine tasks such as account opening or loan approval. Yet this process cannot be taken lightly.

The recent failure of the United Kingdom's TSB Bank, formerly part of Lloyds Bank, to switch its systems from a legacy technology to a more modern one resulted in massive customer disruption that took months to remediate. The TSB story is one that makes bank executives proceed with technological change very carefully. BBC News reported the following headlines on 6 June 2018:

> When TSB split from the Lloyds Banking Group, it continued to use its computer system while a new one was developed. When it was ready, TSB moved customers' data from the Lloyds platform to its own. This was a long-planned disruption to the service. The bank said it informed customers of the change, and that it would lead to them being unable to use online banking or payment systems that weekend.
>
> That led to two problems. First, many customers said they were unaware of the changes and so were caught out. Second, customers experienced difficulties long after the deadline that TSB had promised things would be fixed.
>
> A TSB spokesperson said it was "doing whatever it takes to put things right for our customers and ensuring that no customer will be left out of pocket as a result of the recent IT issues."
>
> Many services have improved, but the situation remains unstable, with 40% of those trying to call the bank unable to speak to someone, while waiting times have run to more than 30 minutes.
>
> Fraud has become a problem, with confused customers being tricked into allowing access to their accounts. Yet the FCA said that TSB had failed to refund their money quickly enough.

As processes are automated using technology, cost reductions follow through reduced staffing requirements for rules-based tasks. However, banks need to proceed very slowly and cautiously on this journey so as not to jeopardize the trusted customer connection to their bank. The consequences of getting this wrong are severe for both customers and shareholders. It is also a topic of significant interest to regulators.

How clients interact with their bank will continue to change over the next few years. How banks react will have an impact on profitability. The number of in-branch interactions is falling, with roughly 65 percent of monthly banking interactions now occurring online, and with in-bank interactions declining by as much as 6 percent per year.[3] Customers are increasingly drawn to online and mobile platforms for their everyday banking. While it is common to predict the end of the bank branch, a more realistic outcome is the specialization of bank branches and the reduction of branch footprints. Customers continue to use branches to get advice on more complex and larger transactions, such as mortgages, or to seek in-person clarification of issues.[4] As simple financial tasks are increasingly serviced online or on mobile applications, branch staff will be freed to deal with more complex issues. This change in behavior will allow banks to reduce their footprint or modify existing locations to reduce costs.

Once a robust digital infrastructure is in place, the cost savings of servicing an account online versus at a branch are significant. The general impact of this shift in focus will be a reduction in cost to the banking industry for banks able to stay ahead of the trend. Those banks that do not adapt to changing customer needs are at risk of being left behind.

There has been a significant upward trend in the focus on technology developments by banks in the past three years. This has led to increasing spending and a variety of announcements that use technology to bring new functionality to the bank and to its customers. This change has been driven by several factors, including the following:

- increased availability of Capex funds for investment as other spending pressures from regulatory initiatives, anti-money laundering (AML), cyber threats, and sometimes fines have been a past focus;

- threats of bank competitors' partnering with techfins or fintechs in a way that outflanks the competition;
- the emergence of cloud technology that provides benefits to banks in capacity and speed to product introduction.

Banks will increasingly need to make the trade-off between speed to market and the risk of roll-out failure as they move forward using new technologies. Managing the speed and safety of the process of decommissioning legacy systems will be a significant issue in terms of risk management and customer satisfaction. The configuration of data repositories and networks going forward will also be a significant issue, especially since each geography has unique rules and requirements.

Conclusion

The technological innovation happening today is real, but there is very little happening that is new when it comes to how banking institutions react.

Technological developments and innovations are not core to a bank's strategy, although they are core to its successful competitive positioning. An individual bank's decision about how to utilize and react to such technological changes is an important foundational building block of its strategy.

For example, when the ability to pay a bill online was first adopted by the industry, this adoption could not be considered bank strategy, since the technology was widely available and became universally deployed. Where an individual bank's strategy becomes evident is in its idiosyncratic choices around the speed of implementation and the degree of innovation in its internal usage. As another example, historically we know that all major banks adopted online payments but that some banks also chose to develop unique, separately branded entities that offered fewer bespoke services (such as bank branch access) and instead limited the offering to online payments and ATM/online deposits. In these cases, strategy is built around customer segmentation, with technology only as an enabler.

Looking Forward

Technological innovation is an important part of a successful bank's product offerings for its clients. The banking industry takes relatively low-margin activities and, through leverage, turns those margins into much higher returns. Many external factors affect bank returns, including technological changes, customer preferences, and the state of the economy.

In the next five to ten years, technological changes are the most positively predicted of these external factors insofar as the banking industry is concerned. However, farther out on the horizon are two primary threats: the rise of disruptive technologies that allow nonfinancial firms to compete for financial products (such as payments), and changing customer needs where banks fail to adapt to new platforms and are left behind. The outlook on these two issues is less clear. However, conditions could arise that enable banks to prosper in this environment by incorporating emerging technologies and adapting to customer needs. They will achieve this as long as they build these objectives into their strategy of managing leverage, cyclicality, and regulation.

NOTES

1 The author gratefully acknowledges the contribution of senior executives from the banking industry and from my co-editor, Michael King. All views are those of the author.

2 S&P Capital IQ. (2017). Analyst data; CSIMarket, S&P 500 financial strength information.
3 Brunier, F., & Trombetta, S. (2015). Branching out: The case for the human touch in banking. Accenture.
4 Cognizant. (2016). Transforming the branch: What banks need to do.

Conclusion: Putting the Customer First

Michael R. King and Richard W. Nesbitt

In this final chapter, we summarize our key takeaways on the future of banking and financial services. We draw on the contributions from this edited volume, our discussions with industry thought leaders, and our own views on the strategic direction of this industry. Below we discuss our six key takeaways to guide both financial incumbents and new entrants over the coming decade.

1. Technology is transforming financial services, just not in the way you think.
2. Innovation is not a strategy. It is a tool to help achieve strategy.
3. Trust in banking is paramount, supported by data security and privacy.
4. Regulation and risk management remain pillars of financial services.
5. Not all fintechs will survive, but a few will have an over-sized impact.
6. Bank-fintech partnerships will deliver a superior customer experience.

1. Technology Is Transforming Financial Services, Just Not in the Way You Think.

Technology is clearly transforming financial services. But it is transforming all industries, the economy, and society at large. The Internet, smartphones, cloud computing, 4G and 5G networks, peer-to-peer (P2P) networks, distributed ledgers, big data, artificial intelligence, machine learning, biometric devices, the Internet of Things (IoT) ... these technologies and many others are being combined in different ways to disrupt, transform, and create industries. Technology and change have been constant forces pushing financial services, markets, and institutions for decades. Whether you view the most recent wave as a natural evolution or a revolution, change driven by technology will continue and likely accelerate in the coming years. But technology is not changing financial services in the way that you may think, or as fast as you may think.

Two myths about the technological transformation of financial services need to be debunked – the first around fintech disruption, and the second around the pace of change.

A first myth concerns the disruptive power of fintech start-ups. The typical media story five years ago portrayed these new entrants as disintermediating incumbents and radically transforming the financial sector. The accepted wisdom was that agile, innovative start-ups were identifying and draining the financial industry's profit pools. This narrative was supported by the billions of dollars of venture-capital (VC) investment that flowed into fintech start-ups globally post-2009. As a widely circulated Goldman Sachs report stated, "With millennials as important agents of change, new business models for crowdfunding, peer-to-peer lending, socialized payments, and automated investing are rising to take market share from existing banking channels."[1]

Five years on, the grim predictions of disruption have not materialized. While a handful of fintech companies have established themselves as leaders in their respective businesses – like PayPal, SoFi, and Square – the majority of start-ups are struggling to scale and achieve profitability. Entrepreneurs (and their VC backers) have recognized the high cost of acquiring customers and building consumer-facing brands. Meanwhile, regulatory scrutiny has increased. Many fintechs have pivoted from competing head-to-head with incumbents in the B2C space to licensing or partnering with them in the B2B space. Not surprisingly, global investment in fintech tracked by KPMG slowed in 2016 and 2017.[2] It more than doubled in 2018, but the rise was driven by a few mega deals in mature companies, including Ant Financial, Refinitiv, and WorldPay. Funding for early-stage start-ups has dried up.

A second myth is that technology will revolutionize financial services sooner rather than later. Take the hype around blockchain. This distributed ledger was trumpeted as the "truth protocol" that would revolutionize society by allowing consensus while avoiding centralized control and censorship.[3] One of the first experiments was a distributed autonomous organization (DAO), a form of digital corporation run by computer programs and electronic voting instead of human managers and paper processes. The German company Slock. It launched this DAO in early 2016 and the online crowdsale raised $150 million from more than 11,000 investors in less than a month. Unfortunately, on 17 June, the computer code managing this DAO was breached by hackers, who siphoned off $40 million. In a contentious debate about the so-called immutability principle of blockchains, the majority of investors voted to alter the ledger to undo the theft. The result may have been a success for democracy, but it was a high-profile failure for blockchain.

Many market participants have announced blockchain proofs of concept and prototypes, but there are still few production cases. The

Australian Stock Exchange (ASX), for example, announced plans in January 2016 to introduce a blockchain replacement for its core clearing and settlement system.[4] They partnered with Digital Asset Holdings, a leading blockchain start-up founded by Blyth Masters, and set an initial launch date of 2020. The first prototype was completed in mid-2016, after which the program stalled. According to media reports, the project is behind schedule because of disagreements between the partners. Masters resigned in late 2018, and the roll-out of a distributed ledger has been pushed back.[5] The key message? Replacing core systems is time consuming, expensive, and operationally very complicated, particularly for regulated financial entities like stock exchanges or banks.

Initial expectations for these technologies were simply too high. The reality has sunk in that the transformation will take longer than we think. But the words of Bill Gates remain true. As he wrote in his 1996 book *The Road Ahead*, "We always overestimate the change that will occur in the next two years and underestimate the change that will occur in the next ten. Don't let yourself be lulled into inaction."[6]

Just because a technology is over-hyped now, it doesn't mean that it won't be implemented sooner or later. As the father of disruption, Harvard professor Clayton Christensen, wrote, "Disruption is a process ... This process can take time, and incumbents can get quite creative in the defense of their established franchises."[7] Take the example of digital banking. In Canada, the first branchless, virtual bank was ING Direct Canada, launched in 1997 by the Dutch banking group. They imported this "challenger bank" model from Europe to disrupt the incumbent "Big Five" Canadian banks. The result followed Christensen's predictions. It was not until 2010 – more than a decade later – that one of the Big Five, CIBC, finally launched a competing online bank. Then in 2012, ING Direct was acquired by Scotiabank (and rebranded as Tangerine Bank). While their response was slow, ultimately all of the Big Five Canadian banks rolled out online banking, laying the foundation for mobile banking and other digital improvements. What's the key takeaway? Sometimes it is better not to be the first mover but to wait until the technology is proven and then be a fast follower who learns from the mistakes of others.

2. Innovation Is Not a Strategy. It Is a Tool to Help Achieve Strategy.

Technology is not a strategy but an important tool for the execution of strategy. Banks are primarily concerned with risk management and competition. Technology can provide improved tools to monitor and manage risks. And technology can be used to enhance operational efficiency and develop new products and services, increasing a bank's ability to compete. But technology is not an end in itself, despite what futurists would have us believe.

The flaw with some start-up business models is that they view technology itself as the ultimate value proposition for customers. But technology is not a source of sustainable competitive advantage, particularly when it is widely available and can be copied by competitors. Fintechs are learning that the biggest barriers to entry in banking are not technology or even regulation but access to customers. Using design thinking, start-ups may develop innovative products that provide a great customer experience, but that alone does not ensure success. You need to get customers to adopt it.

Banks and other financial incumbents are learning that innovation is not a strategy. Many have invested in "accelerators" or "innovation labs" filled with programmers and talent from outside the industry. But if these investments are not tied to the bank's business and integrated with the front line, they become showcases and theater without substance or results. Another mistake is to invest in research labs run by academics and divorced from the business. These facilities may sound forward-looking at first, but they risk raising expectations too high without delivering results. The bottom line is that, to be successful, an innovation lab needs to be run by a business person and integrated into the core business of the bank.

3. Trust in Banking Is Paramount, Supported by Data Security and Privacy.

In hindsight, the most enduring impact of the 2008–2009 global financial crisis (GFC) was the damage it caused to the public's trust in banks and other financial institutions. This loss of trust opened the door to new financial-services providers, including fintechs.

The damage to trust was greatest in countries where banks were nationalized or under substantial stress, such as Iceland, Ireland, the United Kingdom, and the United States. It was compounded in the European countries with high sovereign debt levels and exposure to domestic banks, such as Greece, Italy, Portugal, and Spain. Any remaining trust was further eroded in the years following the GFC when far too many banks were fined or charged for regulatory violations and criminal acts, including money laundering, price fixing, and the mis-selling of securities. Consumers have naturally turned to alternative financial-services providers, including fintechs. For their part, regulators have sought to increase competition and consumer choice while maintaining financial stability by reducing barriers to entry for digital-only challenger banks.

Trust in banks has remained high in countries like Canada and Australia where the banking systems were stable and the financial challenges were less onerous. Not surprisingly, these markets feature less penetration or adoption of fintech alternatives. Fintechs in these countries are either struggling to build customer-facing franchises or are choosing to partner with incumbents. Ultimately, we believe that banks and fintechs that form partnerships will be more successful in the long run.

Looking forward, trust in financial services is intertwined with cybersecurity and data privacy. These two issues are of paramount importance for consumers, businesses, and regulators.

Cybersecurity has become the biggest operational risk for financial institutions. Large financial institutions such as Equifax and JPMorgan Chase have been successfully hacked by cybercriminals who have stolen customers' identity and credit-card data. Leading consumer-facing brands such as Marriott and Uber have faced similar breaches. The approach going forward must shift from one of "if we are hacked" to being prepared for "when we are hacked." Developing strategies to reduce damage to customers and institutions from a cyber intrusion will be a continuing and growing challenge for all financial-services providers. Finding the intrusion fast, disclosing and dealing with it immediately, and minimizing the impact on customers will be critical. Unfortunately, technological progress with quantum computing and the use of artificial intelligence by illegal actors will make this an increasingly challenging arms race.

Data privacy is a second critical issue. Many consumers are concerned about the security and use of their personal data. In the age of e-commerce and social media, data are being collected through multiple channels: online portals, mobile banking and smartphone apps, point-of-sale devices, payment gateways, Internet-enabled devices, and many others. With the arrival of the Internet of Things and 5G communication networks, this data collection and transmission will increase exponentially. Consumers and privacy advocates are acutely aware of the mixed incentives created by the advertising-based business models of online platforms such as Facebook and

Google. Both companies have been fined for violations of privacy laws since passage of the European Union's General Data Protection Regulation (GDPR).

The debate on open banking sits at the nexus of these concerns. Open banking gives consumers the right to share their banking data with third parties, such as fintechs, other banks, credit unions, insurers, and asset managers. The legislation was first adopted in the European Union and the United Kingdom in 2018. Australia began rolling it out for its largest banks in 2019, while Canada, Hong Kong, and New Zealand are holding consultations. Contrary to the claims of some opponents, open banking may increase data security by creating a framework for the secure transmission of data using application programming interfaces (APIs). This security would be reinforced by ensuring that all open banking participants comply with the Payment Card Industry Data Security Standard (PCI DSS), a standard adopted by the major credit-card companies in 2004 to protect cardholder data.

4. Regulation and Risk Management Remain Pillars of Financial Services.

Regulation of financial services is not going away, nor should we want it to. Regulations exist to protect consumers and businesses, forcing banks to address risks and behaviors that are costly or detrimental to their customers and shareholders. Regulation creates a quid pro quo between banks and supervisors. Macroprudential regulations, such as Basel III, promote a level playing field and financial stability, while microprudential regulations guide individual bank behavior. The trade-off is that banks benefit from low borrowing costs and implicit or explicit government support, making possible their highly leveraged business models. The existence of good regulation also supports the trust relationship between the customer and the institution.

Banks and other financial intermediaries sometimes bemoan the costs of compliance, but they also realize that they must take responsibility for collective behavior that leads to credit and housing cycles, market corrections and crashes, and systemic crises such as the GFC. The leading banks actually support higher regulatory requirements to weed out bad actors, and want to see them extended to fintechs and the shadow banking system.

Maintaining a level playing field and avoiding regulatory arbitrage are important principles. Fintechs and other alternative financial providers need to be held to the same regulatory standards as incumbents. This is critical to ensuring that customers are treated fairly and transparently. It also strengthens the entire financial system. While start-ups may initially be allowed to meet a lower regulatory threshold to encourage their development of innovative customer offerings, at some point these fintechs will mature and need to get out of their "sandboxes."

An important consideration for banks and regulators is the trade-off between stability and efficiency. Some banks initially argued that the breadth and depth of regulations introduced post-GFC went too far, raising the costs of compliance to such an extent that profitability has fallen below the cost of capital. We hear less of these types of complaints today. But banks and shareholders should not expect a return to the 20- percent-plus returns on equity (ROEs) from pre-2008. These ROEs were not appropriately risk adjusted or sustainable, as revealed by the GFC. With higher capital requirements and lower leverage, ROEs closer to 10 percent will be the norm.

Is the financial system safer now that banks are more highly regulated? Are we safe enough? Is it worth the cost of billions for this peace of mind? There are no good answers to these questions.

The good news is that the pendulum swing of increased regulation may be reversing after a decade of increasing requirements. This easing will coincide with an end to central banks' quantitative easing (QE) and higher interest rates, increasing net interest margins. This reversal is also partly driven by political changes, such as the arrival of the Trump administration.

It remains true that effective risk management across the business cycle will continue to be a driver of bank success. Financial incumbents possess this expertise, providing a competitive advantage over new entrants. Fintechs and nonfinancial companies offering financial services will inevitably face the same need to invest in risk management and compliance to meet regulatory requirements, while at the same time serving their customers.

Facebook's recent proposal to launch a cryptocurrency may be a watershed moment for technology and financial services. The Libra coin will be backed by foreign-exchange reserves and operated by a consortium of twenty-eight nonbank partners, including credit-card networks (MasterCard, Visa), ride-sharing firms (Lyft, Uber), venture-capital firms (VCs), and nongovernmental organizations. By offering a digital means of payment and free money transfers over WhatsApp and Messenger to Facebook's 2.4 billion global users, Facebook will force policymakers and regulators to address some sticky issues. Should Facebook be regulated as a money service provider? Is the Libra coin a currency, a security, or a token? How will a universal digital means of payment affect the money supply and central bank policy? Who will own and control the data generated by the Libra network? And who will benefit from these data? Clearly, innovations like this one raise complex questions. But they signal a move towards a truly global form of digital cash that consumers clearly want. Many other competing forms will develop, including, perhaps, central-bank digital currencies.

5. Not All Fintechs Will Survive, but a Few Will Have an Over-Sized Impact.

With venture capitalists and other investors committing $410 billion to 13,000-plus fintechs since 2008, it is clear that these start-ups cannot all be successful. According to the VC rule of thumb, most of these businesses will fail, and only a few will deliver outsized returns. According to CB Insights, there were sixty-six fintech unicorns globally at the start of 2019.[8] Names like Ant Financial, Coinbase, Lu.com/Lufax, Paytm, and Robinhood may not yet be familiar, but if history is a guide they soon will be. The closest analogy is the 1999 dot-com bubble, which saw thousands of Internet-based businesses fail. The few that succeeded revolutionized their sectors, such as Amazon in e-commerce and PayPal in payments.

What is different this time is that the fintech bubble is global, with unicorns found in Europe, South America, and, most notably, China. Two Chinese companies are already revolutionizing financial services in their home market: Ant Financial and Tencent. Ant Financial is the payments giant spun out of Alibaba in 2011. While it focused initially on payments, Ant Financial now offers loans, banking, wealth management, and insurance products. Tencent is the social media and gaming company behind WeChat, which counts more than 1 billion users and offers the same array of financial services. These two companies are called techfins because they are using technology to democratize financial services. As multi-sided platforms, they have each built platform ecosystems that bundle financial products with nonfinancial services for the benefit of their customers.

Bigtech companies like Amazon, Apple, Facebook, and Google appear to be following the techfin playbook. They are also developing a platform ecosystem around a core service, and have built a beachhead in financial services around payments. With the data generated by their users and their expertise with technology, design, and customer experience, they will be fierce competitors in financial services.

Financial incumbents are being forced to adapt as these new entrants pose a realistic threat of disruption. Banks will struggle, however, held back by their legacy IT systems, their regulatory and compliance requirements, and their hierarchical, profit-driven cultures that do not support experimentation and failure, agility and innovation, and a willingness to acquire customers at a loss.

It is important to note that the impact of financial technology is quite different in developed versus developing economies. In developed countries, most (but not all) consumers have access to basic banking and financial services. But in many developing economies, consumers are underserved or unbanked because of low incomes and an undeveloped financial system. The physical infrastructure of bank branches and methods of payment (such as credit and debit cards) may not exist. In these cases, the increased penetration of the Internet and smartphones has allowed fintechs to offer digital financial services directly to unbanked consumers. In other words, fintech is democratizing finance by making it available at a low cost to unbanked consumers globally.

A widely cited example is Kenya's mobile-phone-based money M-Pesa.[9] M-Pesa was launched in March 2007 by Kenya's leading mobile network operator, Safaricom, in partnership with its parent company, Vodafone. M-Pesa allows customers to deposit money into an account stored on their cell phone using a network of local Safaricom agents. This money can then be used to make payments, to top-up airtime on their phone, to transfer money to other M-Pesa customers, or to shop and pay merchants using text messaging (SMS). Users can also withdraw money through a network of ATMs and receive money sent from abroad. The service is available twenty-four hours a day, 365 days a year, and is backed by security measures to protect customers' funds. In short, M-Pesa provides unbanked customers with a safe, secure, and low-cost means to send, receive, and store money using a mobile phone. It is now being used by 32 million users in multiple countries across East Africa, North Africa, and South Asia. Other fintech innovations are showing the same widespread adoption globally, illustrating the widely cited fact that one in every ten start-ups generates all of the returns in a venture capitalist's portfolio. The same will be true across fintech start-ups – a handful will succeed and have an outsized impact on the financial-services industry.

6. Bank-Fintech Partnerships Will Deliver a Superior Customer Experience.

In the years to come, it will be clear (if it is not already) that the biggest transformation brought about by fintech was not to leverage new technologies or to disrupt financial incumbents – it was to improve the customer experience in financial services. While incumbents have invested in new technologies for decades to please their corporate and institutional customers, small businesses and retail customers have been overlooked. Fintech companies are changing that.

Banks are product-centric. Far too many view customers as a means to an end, namely making money. Customers are segmented in groups that tally their revenue potential: retail, high net worth, institutional investor, small business, and business. Banks are organized in vertical silos: retail banking, commercial banking, wealth management, capital markets, and insurance. Within these segments, business units are identified by their main product: deposits, cards, loans, mutual funds, underwriting, auto insurance, etcetera. Staff are identified by functional roles: bank teller, loan officer, risk manager, treasurer, insurance salesperson, and IT. These product-centric organizations reflect the bank view of the world. They are not focused on customers, their needs, and their journey.

Fintech companies are customer-centric. They leverage technology to solve a single pain point, offering a value proposition that appeals to the customer. From this initial foothold, they are expanding beyond their initial use-case by adding complementary products to address customer needs. Payment providers such as Square have moved into merchant loans and alternative means of payment. Robo-advisors such as Wealthfront have added financial planning, lending, and real estate. P2P lenders such as SoFi have moved from student loans into personal and commercial lending, real estate, payments, P2P money transfers, and asset management. In each case, the goal is to grow revenues by diversifying to provide a better customer experience.

The banks of the future need to be customer-centric, like a fintech. They need to turn their organizational charts on their sides and follow the customer across their lifecycle. By mapping out the customer journey, they can understand and anticipate where financial services fit. No one wakes up each day excited to do their banking. They want to have a rewarding job, buy a home, pay for a child's education, travel, and save for retirement. If they could accomplish these goals without ever speaking to a bank again, many of them would. The way to serve this customer is to offer them the products they need, when they need them, and at a reasonable price. By focusing on the customer experience, banks can build and maintain customer relationships, making them loyal and sticky. This is the strategy employed by fintechs, techfins, and bigtech.

The bank of the future needs to combine its current comparative advantages with the strengths of fintechs. Banks need to be realistic about their own weaknesses and acknowledge how fintechs may help address any gaps. Banks have a number of clear advantages: a large customer base; access to stable, inexpensive funding; economies of scale and scope; and expertise in risk management and compliance. Fintechs have their own strengths: technological expertise, a culture of innovation, design thinking, new systems and applications, and a fresh perspective on the needs of the customer. Banks can teach fintechs about operating at scale, sound risk management, and regulatory compliance. Fintechs can teach banks about leveraging new technologies, promoting innovation, and being agile.

In the end, customers will be best served by banks that partner with fintechs to combine their strengths and provide customers with a superior experience at a lower cost. Ultimately, what is good for the customer is good for the bank and good for the fintech partner. By working together, banks, fintechs, and customers can win together.

NOTES

1 Terry, H.P., Schwartz, D., & Sun, T. (2015, 13 March). The future of finance part 3 – The socialization of finance, 1. Goldman Sachs Equity Research.
2 KPMG. (2019, 31 July). The pulse of fintech H1 2019. https://assets.kpmg/content/dam/kpmg/xx/pdf/2019/07/pulse-of-fintech-h1-2019.pdf.
3 Tapscott, D., & Tapscott, A. (2016). *Blockchain revolution*. New York: Penguin Random House.
4 Australian Stock Exchange. (nd). CHESS replacement. https://www.asx.com.au/services/chess-replacement.htm. Accessed 5 July 2019.
5 De, N. (2018, 19 December). ASX reaffirms 2021 DLT rollout after Blythe Masters steps down. https://www.coindesk.com/asx-reaffirms-2021-blockchain-rollout-date-after-blythe-masters-steps-down. Coindesk.
6 Gates, B. (1995). *The road ahead*. New York: Viking. Quoted in Brown, D. (2019, 4 December). This perfect Bill Gates quote will frame your next decade of success. Inc.com. https://www.inc.com/damon-brown/this-perfect-bill-gates-quote-will-frame-your-next-decade-of-success.html.
7 Christensen, C.M., Raynor, M., & McDonald, R. (2015, December). What is disruptive innovation? *Harvard Business Review*, 44–53, at 48.
8 CB Insights. (2019). The state of fintech: Investments and sector trends to watch. https://www.cbinsights.com/research/report/fintech-trends-q4-2019/.
9 Safaricom. (nd). M-Pesa. https://www.safaricom.co.ke/personal/m-pesa. Accessed 24 June 2019.

Contributors

ABOUT THE EDITORS

Professor Michael R. King, PhD, CFA, is the Lansdowne Chair in Finance at University of Victoria's Gustavson School of Business. He held the Tangerine Chair in Finance at Western University's Ivey Business School (2011–19), where he co-founded Canada's first fintech research center (the Scotiabank Digital Banking Lab). Before joining academia, he worked in investment banking in Zurich, New York, and London from 1990 to 1998 (Credit Suisse, RBC Dominion Securities) and in central banking in Ottawa and Basel from 2001 to 2011 (Bank of Canada, Bank for International Settlements).

Richard W. Nesbitt recently retired as CEO of Global Risk Institute (GRI), where he served from 2015 to 2018. He is an adjunct professor of the Rotman School of Management, University of Toronto. He is also a visiting professor at the London School of Economics. In June 2017, he published a book (with Barbara Annis) titled *Results at the Top: Using Gender Intelligence to Create Breakthrough Growth,* on the issue of men's responsibility for gender diversity to improve their organizations (Hoboken, NJ: Wiley). He was chief operating officer of Canadian Imperial Bank of Commerce (CIBC) until he retired in September

2014. He joined CIBC in 2008 following more than twenty years in the securities industry, including at CIBC Wood Gundy from 1987 to 1997. From 2004 to 2008, Richard was CEO of the Toronto Stock Exchange, having joined TSX as president of TSX Markets in 2001. Richard holds an MSc from the London School of Economics (1986), a Rotman School of Management MBA (1985), and an Ivey HBA (1978).

ABOUT THE CONTRIBUTORS

Jon Frost is a senior economist in the Innovation and the Digital Economy unit of the Bank for International Settlements (BIS). In this role, he conducts policy-oriented research on fintech and digital innovation. He has written on fintech credit, bigtech in finance, and technology and inequality. Previously, Jon worked at the Financial Stability Board (FSB), the Dutch central bank (DNB), VU University in Amsterdam, and in the private sector in Germany. Jon holds a PhD in economics from the University of Groningen. He is a policy fellow at the Centre for Science and Policy of the University of Cambridge.

Chuck Grace is a member of the finance faculty at Western University's Ivey School of Business, where he teaches courses on institutional investing, personal wealth management, and fintech. He also serves as a research engineer at the Centre for Quantitative Analysis and Modeling (CQAM). He previously chaired Ivey's advisory council for household finance research. Prior to pursuing his passions for teaching and consulting, Chuck held a progression of senior management positions with one of Canada's largest insurance and wealth-management companies.

Andrew Graham is co-founder and CEO of Borrowell, one of Canada's largest financial technology companies. Borrowell helps consumers make great decisions about credit and was the first company in Canada to offer credit scores for free; today, it has more than a million members. Borrowell has won numerous awards, including being named one of the top 100 fintech companies in the world by KPMG. Andrew holds an MBA from Harvard Business School and an MA in economics from the University of Edinburgh. He is a two-time Ontario finalist for EY's Entrepreneur of the Year award and has served on the boards of a number of Canadian nonprofits.

Peter Levitt has led CIBC's Treasury since August 2012. In this role, Mr Levitt is responsible for all aspects of CIBC's Treasury functions, including asset-liability management, structural balance-sheet risk hedging, liquidity risk management, capital management and optimization, funding, cash management, treasury analytics, funds-transfer pricing, and pension and treasury investment management. Mr Levitt was executive vice-president and treasurer at Manulife Financial (John Hancock in the United States) from 2007 to 2012. Prior to this, he led capital finance in TD Bank Treasury, was head of Treasury and global controller for TD Securities, and was chief financial officer of the wealth-management group at Canada Trust up to and including its integration with TD in 2000. Mr Levitt held a number of roles in technology, treasury, and finance at Canada Trust from 1982 to 2000.

Tiff Macklem is the dean of the University of Toronto's Rotman School of Management. Prior to his appointment as dean, he served as senior deputy governor of the Bank of Canada, as well as chief operating officer and a member of its board of directors. Dr Macklem has also served as associate deputy minister of the Department of Finance and Canada's finance deputy at the G7 and G20. In this role, he was the first chair of the Standing Committee on Standards Implementation of the Financial Stability Board. As chair, he worked to establish an international system of peer review to promote and assess the implementation of new financial standards across the twenty-four most financially important countries in the world. Since joining the Rotman School of Management, Dr Macklem has been appointed chair of the board of the Global Risk Institute, a director of Scotiabank, a member of the Advisory Board of Georgian Partners, and the chair of Canada's Expert Panel on Sustainable Finance.

Vicki Martin is a senior specialist in the Housing Finance Policy group of Canada Mortgage and Housing Corporation (CMHC). She is responsible for CMHC's surveillance of emerging mortgage technologies and researches fintech trends on the company's behalf.

Tom McGuire is executive vice-president and group treasurer at Scotiabank, where he is responsible for managing Scotiabank's global treasury and investment operations, including medium-term and capital funding, asset/liability management, liquidity, and public and private investment portfolios. Tom joined Scotiabank in 2018 as deputy treasurer, with responsibility for the bank's funding and liquidity. Prior to joining Scotiabank, Tom held leadership positions across the financial-services industry, most recently as treasurer for Barclays Americas and Barclays US LLC. Tom practiced law at a New York law firm, focusing on securities and international business transactions, and served as an infantry officer in the United States Marine Corps, achieving the rank of Major.

R. Jesse McWaters led the World Economic Forum's exploration of financial technology and innovation. His work focused on bringing together financial-services executives, fintech players, and global regulators to understand how emerging technologies and innovative new entrants are transforming the competitive dynamics of the global financial ecosystem. Jesse is a frequent media commentator on fintech, having been featured on CNBC's *Closing Bell* and quoted in the *Financial Times*, the *Wall Street Journal*, *Wired*, and *Bloomberg*. His work has also been cited by an array of global policymakers, including the Bank of England, the Financial Stability Board, and the World Bank.

Brian O'Donnell is currently chief data officer and strategic advisor at iisaac, a fintech company focused on providing personal data advocacy services to individuals in order to help them gather, own, and secure their personal data. Before joining iisaac, Brian spent two years as an executive-in-residence at the Global Risk Institute (GRI), where his research focused on big data, artificial intelligence, cybersecurity, and the evolving regulatory environment. Prior to joining the GRI, Brian was CIBC's executive vice-president and chief data officer, where he developed their data strategy and data-governance framework. Before becoming the chief data officer at CIBC, Brian led the Enterprise Risk Management group, including balance-sheet and capital management. Over the years he held a number of positions in the finance and risk-management groups, including chief financial officer of the Treasury Division. Brian is also a member of the Advisory Board at Fairom, a blockchain and smart contract company aimed at automating operations for complex financial derivative products in capital markets. Brian earned an MBA at McMaster's DeGroote School of Business and also holds a Certified Public Accountant designation.

Andrew Sarta is a PhD candidate in strategy at Ivey Business School and has more than a decade of experience in strategic change for a Fortune 500 organization. His research focuses on behavioral factors that influence the role of timing and speed in strategic decision making as organizations adapt to rapidly changing environments. More specifically, he examines the emergence of new financial technologies (fintechs) in financial services, including digital financial advice (e.g., robo-advisors) and the behavior of incumbents in response to fintech.

Satwik Sharma, CFA, works in investment banking at the TD Bank Group. He is a graduate of the Rotman School of Management and the Indian Institute of Management Calcutta. Satwik has worked internationally across a range of roles in financial services, including wealth and asset management, consumer banking, mergers and acquisitions, and investment banking for Standard Chartered Bank, Goldman Sachs, BMO Capital Markets, and now TD Bank. He was awarded the inaugural "Leader to Watch" award by the Rotman School of Management in 2018. Sharma and his wife currently live in Toronto, Canada.

Evan Siddall is president and CEO of Canada Mortgage and Housing Corporation (CMHC), a role he has held since 2014. Evan worked at some of the world's largest investment-banking firms in Canada and the United States from 1989 to 2008 (BMO Nesbitt Burns, Goldman Sachs, Lazard), then at Irving Oil from 2009 to 2011, before joining the Bank of Canada as special advisor to the governor from 2011 to 2013. He also helped launch a private entrepreneurial venture, Side Launch Brewing Company, where he serves on the Board of Directors.

Brenda Trenowden, CBE, CFA, CCMI, is global co-chair of the 30% Club and a partner with PricewaterhouseCoopers (PwC), United Kingdom, working with clients on workplace performance, culture, and communication. Prior to joining PwC, Brenda led the Financial Institutions Group in Europe for ANZ Bank, and was a member of their U.K. Management Board, and an executive director of ANZ's U.K. Bank subsidiary, ANZ Bank (Europe) Ltd, as well as ANZ's other U.K. subsidiaries. Brenda has more than twenty-five years of experience in capital markets, investment, and relationship banking, with sector expertise in financial institutions. She is also a strong advocate for women's economic empowerment and has been recognized with several awards for her global campaigning for greater gender balance across organizations as a voluntary, business-led imperative. Canadian by birth, Brenda was awarded a CBE in the Queen's Birthday Honours List in June 2018 for services to the financial sector and gender equality. She was also listed as the number one Champion of Women in Business 2018.

Greg Wilson is president of Greg Wilson Consulting, a niche consulting firm providing financial-services policy advice. Previously, he was a principal and senior advisor in the financial institutions group at McKinsey & Company, serving clients in the United States, Canada, and more than twenty other countries. Greg also served on the staff of the House Committee on Banking, Finance, and Urban Affairs and later as a political appointee at the U.S. Department of the Treasury. He is the author of *Managing to the New Regulatory Reality: Doing Business under the Dodd-Frank Act* (Hoboken, NJ: Wiley, 2011).

Jay D. Wilson, vice-president, is a senior member of Mercer Capital's Depository Institutions practice. Jay also leads Mercer Capital's financial technology industry team and publishes research related to the fintech industry. Jay is involved in the valuation of financial institutions and fintech companies for a variety of purposes, including employee stock ownership plans (ESOPs), mergers and acquisitions, profit-sharing plans, estate and gift-tax planning, compliance matters, and corporate planning. He has extensive experience in providing public and private clients with fair-value opinions and related assistance pertaining to goodwill and intangible assets, stock-based compensation, loan portfolios, and other financial assets and liabilities. Jay also directs special projects for financial institutions, including projects for strategic and capital-planning purposes such as stress testing, as well as projects in a litigated context, including tax disputes, dissenting-shareholder actions, and ESOP-related matters. Jay is the author of the book *Creating Strategic Value through Financial Technology* (Hoboken, NJ: Wiley, 2017).

Professor Markos Zachariadis holds the Greensill Chair in Financial Technology (fintech) and Information Systems at Alliance Manchester Business School at the University of Manchester. Previously he was associate professor of information systems management and innovation at Warwick Business School and the director of the Executive Education Diploma in Digital Leadership. He is also fintech research fellow at the Cambridge Centre for Digital Innovation (CDI), University of Cambridge. Markos's research sits at the cross-section of the economics of digital innovation, financial-technology studies, and network economics. He has studied extensively the economic impact of information and communications technology adoption on bank performance, the diffusion of payment networks, and the role of data and standards in payment infrastructures (SWIFT), financial markets (LEI), and digital banking (open banking), among other things. His research has been published in top academic journals such as *MIS Quarterly* and *Research Policy* and has been awarded the NET Institute Award (NYU Stern Business School) for his study on the economics of payment networks, and the SWIFT Institute, SMS, and GRI Awards for his research on open application programming interfaces (APIs) and digital transformation in banking.